Philosophy of
Education

Philosophy of Education

INTRODUCTORY READINGS

4th edition

William Hare and
John P. Portelli, editors

Brush
Education Inc.

Brush Education Inc.
www.brusheducation.ca
contact@brusheducation.ca

Copy editor: Meaghan Craven
Cover design: Dean Pickup
Cover photo: Front cover photo: ©Kitkana, Dreamstime.com; Back cover photo: ©Pedro Nogueira, Dreamstime.com

Printed and manufactured in Canada

Library and Archives Canada Cataloguing in Publication

Philosophy of education : introductory readings / William Hare and John P. Portelli, editors. – Revised 4th edition.

Includes bibliographical references.

Issued in print and electronic formats.

ISBN 978-1-55059-445-4 (pbk.). – ISBN 978-1-55059-446-1 (epub). – ISBN 978-1-55059-468-3 (pdf). – ISBN 978-1-55059-469-0 (mobi)

1. Education – Philosophy.   I. Hare, William, editor of compilation   II. Portelli, John P. (John Peter), editor of compilation

LB1025.3.P53 2013   370.1   C2013-902690-8   C2013-902691-6

Produced with the assistance of the Government of Alberta, Alberta Multimedia Development Fund. We also acknowledge the financial support of the Government of Canada through the Canada Book Fund for our publishing activities.

Contents

Acknowledgements

It is very gratifying to see the fourth edition of this collection of essays appear on the 25th anniversary of the publication of the first edition. We are very grateful to Detselig Enterprises for publishing the earlier editions, and we are delighted that Brush Education, successor to Detselig Enterprises, has invited us to prepare this new collection. The fourth edition represents an extensive revision and includes many recent essays. The now classic essay by Harold Entwistle on theory and practice is the only one that has appeared throughout.

We wish to thank the authors for giving us permission to include their work in this collection. At every stage they have responded in a timely and helpful manner. We acknowledge the support of OISE in providing us with the assistance of a graduate student, Danielle Sandhu, whose contribution is greatly appreciated. We also thank Meaghan Craven for her meticulous work as copy editor, and Niki Hare for her invaluable help at different stages of the project.

Our thanks to Fraser Seely and Lauri Seidlitz of Brush Education, who were very enthusiastic about this project from the beginning and have supported it in every respect.

And finally, as with our other editions, we would like to dedicate this book to our families.

William Hare
John P. Portelli
July 2013

Introduction

This fourth edition, like its predecessors, is designed first and foremost to make available a collection of essays in philosophy of education that will offer preservice teachers a stimulating and accessible introduction to some of the most important issues in the field. Classroom teachers, school administrators, teacher educators, educational policy makers, graduate students, and general readers alike will also find this collection a valuable resource in connection with problems that relate to educational theory and practice. As with the earlier editions, and given our intended readership, we have included contributions that connect philosophical reflection with current debates concerning approaches to teaching, methods of assessment, the content of the curriculum, and many other practical matters that relate to schools and student learning. This reflects our belief that philosophical understanding is a vital aspect of professional development. We have chosen essays that will challenge readers to formulate their own views on matters that are the subject of lively discussion among philosophers and educators, and that are intended to encourage a thoughtful engagement with theories and practices that shape contemporary education.

What kinds of philosophical problems are taken up in these selections? Reflective teachers will quickly find themselves involved with difficult and important questions that clearly have great relevance for educational policy and practice. Along with our contributors, readers will surely wonder whether a certain kind of testing is appropriate, what limits there might be on a teacher's conduct beyond the classroom, if and when it might be justifiable for a teacher to take a stand on a value issue, what would make a school or classroom democratic or socially just, how far we can rely on research findings about teaching, whether sensitive material should be discussed in class, what genuine dialogue involves, and so on. Such questions inevitably draw us into reflection on "common sense" views and assumptions about education and teaching that have been accepted without serious debate; they focus attention on the language we use to describe education, teaching, and schooling, and its influence on the way we understand and approach our work as educators; they require us to think more carefully about our educational aims and how they can be justified; moreover, they stimulate us to look for imaginative ways in which we might attempt to pursue our ideals or resolve dilemmas that we confront in our work.

In earlier editions, we put forward the view that philosophy of education involves a critical inquiry into educational concepts, values, and practices. Philosophy of education as critical inquiry means that philosophy itself is a practice that intrinsically raises critical awareness, encourages self-reflexivity, and contributes to the development of intellectual and moral virtues that are essential to good teaching. Our hope is that the selections included here will bear out these claims and show that critical reflection has an important bearing on practical educational decisions.

Student teachers and others encountering philosophy of education for the first time might wonder how best to approach these essays, knowing they will meet with controversial and provocative views and theories that may well conflict with their own ideas and values. Bertrand Russell remarks that if people "have a determination never to surrender certain philosophic beliefs, they are not in the frame of mind in which philosophy can be profitably pursued" (Russell, 1927, p. 299). This comment reminds us that we need to approach philosophical discussions with an open-minded outlook, ready to consider objections to our views and to revise them if we discover we are mistaken (Hare, 1979). Philosophy of education does not arrive at conclusions that all philosophers accept; philosophical ideas typically remain controversial and debatable. In the end, we must judge for ourselves, but this should come after we have given serious consideration to the best arguments we can find, and the conclusions we reach should be held in the same open-minded way. This attitude does not mean that we lack confidence in our beliefs or that we regard other beliefs as equally acceptable but that we see our ideas as open to revision in the light of further evidence and argument (Hare, 1993).

The topics, issues, and problems selected for inclusion in this volume are much discussed by philosophers of education today, and this has led to work of high quality that teachers and educators will find relevant and thought-provoking. Six major themes serve to organize the chapters into the various parts that comprise this collection. Each part has its own introduction providing an overview of the chapters in that group and drawing attention to important questions that arise from the discussion. In each part, readers will find there are arguments, insights, and examples that prove to be helpful in thinking about problems and issues that are discussed elsewhere in the book.

- Part I offers teachers provocative and informative perspectives on philosophy, theory, and practice. A central theme concerns the way in which philosophy and educational theory influence a teacher's outlook and independent views.

- Part II turns to certain issues that arise in classroom teaching. Attention is focused on pedagogical situations and controversial areas where teachers need to make difficult choices guided by educational principles.

- Part III takes up issues that concern democracy and social justice. These essays prompt reflection on the ideals and values embedded in these notions and what it would mean to see them reflected in education and schooling.

- Part IV deals with matters related to standards, efficiency, and measurement in education. The arguments here raise concerns about assumptions and practices prevalent in contemporary schooling that threaten to undermine our educational aims.

- Part V explores issues relating to rights, freedoms, and conflicts in education. The problem of balancing conflicting rights and freedoms is examined, and the possibility of understanding others with different values is explored.

- Part VI presents certain general conceptions of education and teaching. These discussions challenge teachers to look critically at the somewhat narrow ways in which their work is often defined and to develop a deeper understanding of their role.

There is a wealth of material for discussion and debate in these essays. Student teachers may find it useful to supplement these readings with case studies related to teaching and education (Hare & Portelli, 2003); those who wish to read further in philosophy of education can readily do so and references are provided below.

REFERENCES

Hare, W. (1979). *Open-mindedness and education.* Montreal: McGill-Queen's University Press.

Hare, W. (1993). *What makes a good teacher.* London, ON: Althouse Press.

Hare, W., & Portelli, J.P. (2003). *What to do? Case studies for educators.* Halifax: Edphil Books.

Russell, B. (1927). *Philosophy.* New York: W.W. Norton.

FURTHER READINGS

Bailey, R., Barrow, R., Carr, D., & McCarthy, C. (Eds.). (2010). *The Sage handbook of philosophy of education.* Los Angeles: Sage.

Cahn, S.M. (Ed.). (2011). *Classic and contemporary readings in the philosophy of education* (2nd ed.). New York: Oxford University Press.

Curren, R. (Ed.). (2006). *A companion to philosophy of education.* Malden, MA: Blackwell.

Hare, W., & Portelli, J.P. (Eds.). (2007). *Key questions for educators.* San Francisco, CA: Caddo Gap.

Johnson, T.W., & Reed, R.F. (Eds.). (2012). *Philosophical documents in education* (4th ed.). Boston: Prentice-Hall.

Kohli, W. (Ed.). (1995). *Critical conversations in philosophy of education.* New York: Routledge.

Siegel, H. (Ed.). (2009). *The Oxford handbook of philosophy of education.* Oxford: Oxford University Press. doi: 10.1093/oxfordhb/9780195312881.001.0001

Part I: Philosophy, Theory, and Practice

The essays in this section deal with the issue of the relationship between theory and practice in education, the value of empirical research in teaching, the role of philosophy in education, and the place of ideals in teaching. The issue of theory and practice is a classic one in debates about the nature of the preparation of those in professions such as teaching. Initial teacher-education students frequently doubt the value of theory, including philosophy of education, given the perceived importance of practical school-based experiences. What is the best or most appropriate way to prepare people to become competent teachers? Should the emphasis be on theoretical and philosophical concerns or practical concerns? Should and can the two be separated or should they always be seen in tandem? Do practical matters simply involve the application of skills? Can such issues be determined on empirical grounds? Is it not worthwhile to think critically about one's aims in teaching, and the values, principles, and ideals embedded in them? The replies to these questions will vary according to how one views the nature of theory and practice and the relationship between the two, the nature of empirical work, philosophy and ideals. And, in turn, such views will impact on how one constructs the nature of professions.

The first essay by Harold Entwistle tackles the issue of the possible causes for the split between theory and practice while developing a notion of theory from a critical stance. In this discussion Entwistle deals with several questions that have troubled educators: Is the role of theory to dictate specific actions to practitioners or to raise a critical awareness? Can and should the gap between theory and practice be lessened? What is the role of theory and practice in reflective practice? Entwistle refutes the rigid, traditional notion of theory that assumed neutrality and is expected to provide detailed, specific, secure, universal prescriptions or solutions. On the contrary, he believes that educational theory (including philosophy of education), of its nature, does not offer and is not meant to offer specific knowledge and skills "applicable to a given practical situation." For him the role of theory is to "evoke judgment rather than rote obedience," and to encourage professional autonomy, which entails developing new perspectives that help to analyze, question, and be aware of the complexities in the teaching context, and dealing with problems that arise from practice. Nonetheless, Entwistle concludes that although "learning the art of compromise" will help teachers to reduce the gulf between theory and practice, in the final analysis the gap is inevitable; struggling with this very fact will help us refine both theory and practice!

In the second essay Robin Barrow raises foundational questions about the nature and role of empirical research. To what extent can empirical research provide definitive answers to educational issues? Is it possible and meaningful for empirical research in education to mimic the nature of research in the natural sciences? Barrow argues that given the contested nature of education and educational concepts, as well as the fact that it is impossible to make meaningful educational claims without taking into account the unique nature of contexts that vary, it is not possible to expect exact and universal general rules that apply in a neutral manner. Expecting otherwise will limit, if not negate, the professional responsibility of teachers. For Barrow, philosophy has a crucial role in providing the clarity of educational concepts, which is needed in determining the nature of empirical research and its direction. Empirical research is inevitably based on philosophical premises and assumptions; sound empirical research needs to identify the philosophical underpinnings.

But how then should we view philosophy and its contribution to education? Is not philosophy of its very nature abstract and theoretical and hence not practical? In the third essay Heesoon Bai takes up such popular questions and articulates and argues for a conception of philosophy as practice that aims primarily to develop human agency and autonomy. Without the cultivation of human agency, which is a lifelong project, Bai contends, we would fall prey to fundamentalist dogmatism, whether it is of a religious or secular nature. Building on ideas from both Eastern and Western philosophy, she articulates a view of philosophy as "life-practice and self-making." While arguing against a utilitarian and positivist relationship between theory and practice, Bai offers world-making, dialogue, philosophical writing, and contemplative arts as ideal ways of cultivating human agency. Based on her experience as a university professor, Bai proposes a conception *and* practice of philosophy that are different from popular misconceptions of philosophy: philosophy is ultimately a way of being that symbiotically incorporates a certain kind of thinking and doing.

But is there room for ideals in education? Would not ideals hinder educators from fulfilling their publicly defined obligations, which are primarily practical and, to an extent, bureaucratic in nature? Consistent with the nature of theory and practice as envisioned by Entwistle and Barrow, as well as the dialectical tensions involved in developing human agency as identified by Bai, in the fourth essay, David Hansen argues for a balanced understanding of ideals—one that harmonizes the view that teachers should have ideals that go beyond societal expectations with the view that they have defined obligations. He reminds us that ideals are in fact human constructs that partly depend on contexts and, as such, deserve critical examination. Ideals are different than slogans, for while they are general and abstract they call for a critical and thoughtful *enacting* (rather than implementing) in the reality of life. As such, Hansen concludes that "idealism and respect for reality reinforce one another." Applying tenacious humility, according to Hansen, will greatly assist educators to navigate the productive tensions that arise between ideals and reality.

Although one may agree with the related positions developed in these essays, one may still ask, as many students have asked us: But is theory more important than practice? Are ideals more important than the actual living? The dictum of Chilean Nobel Prize winner Pablo Neruda helps: we need two hands to clap! Just as both hands are equally important for clapping, the same holds for theory (ideals) and practice (actual living). There is bound to be some division and even tension between the two. From this it doesn't follow that we should not be concerned with theory or that anything in the practice is acceptable. What matters, however, is the kind of theory and practice that we adhere to. Hence educators and teachers, as professionals, need to be careful what to expect or demand from theory, whether it is a theory developed by them or others. To avoid being unprofessional, we need to constantly remember the unending dialectic or tension between what we aim for and what ensues, what we believe in and what we are allowed to do, and the contingent and ambiguous versus the desire for certainty and stability.

From this perspective, while theory and practice are conceptually distinct, they are also inseparable, very much like the two sides of a coin. But as Paulo Freire (1998), one of the 20th century's most influential educators, advised, the balance or relationship between theory and practice requires critical reflection: "Critical reflection on practice is a requirement of the relationship between theory and practice. Otherwise theory becomes simply 'blah, blah, blah,' and practice, pure activism" (p. 30). Our challenge as educators at all levels is to maintain such a relationship by finding the theoretical in the practical and the practical in the theoretical—a relationship that today is once again threatened by neoliberalism based on excessive competition, rugged individualism, blind efficiency, and extreme utilitarianism.

REFERENCE

Freire, P. (1998). *Pedagogy of freedom: Ethics, democracy, and civic courage.* Lanham, MD: Rowman & Littlefield.

1

The Relationship between Educational Theory and Practice

A New Look

Harold Entwistle *

*This is a slightly modified version of a paper presented at Mount Saint Vincent University, Halifax, Nova Scotia, March 27, 1987.

Why a new look at educational theory and practice? I have been troubled by the problem of the relationship between the theory and practice of education for more than 40 years. As a student doing my teacher training in an English college of education (or training college as it was then called), I remember writing an article for the college newspaper denouncing the theoretical component of my course as being utterly irrelevant to conditions in the school as I found them on teaching practice. As a qualified teacher, I would experience similar frustration when inspectors, advisors, and other people who were no longer practitioners would come to my classroom and offer me unworkable advice. When I eventually went to do graduate work in education, I recall wanting to do my thesis on the relationship between theory and practice. My supervisor warned me off it—I think I now know why. Then I became a teacher trainer (or teacher educator) and found myself in the peculiar position of being accused by my own students of offering advice that was "all right in theory but no good in practice." I suspect that most of what I have to say is the result of my efforts to come to grips with the fact that I had now become just another starry-eyed theorist.

So, for me, this is a new look at an old problem (Entwistle, 1969, 1970, 1971). But I make this point about my own changing experience and changing perspective on the problem to suggest that whatever the solution is, it is far from simple. Indeed, I think that in terms of the way that the problem is usually posed, there probably is no solution. On the one hand, I believe practitioners have a perfect right to take theorists to task for what often is quite unrealistic advice about the practice of teaching. On the other hand, when you see it as a theorist from the other side of the fence, even when you have had practical experience of the problems of teaching yourself, the theory-practice problem has a new dimension and the discrepancy invites a different kind of explanation. And I think this fact, that when experienced and successful practitioners become theorists, even they become vulnerable to the charge of being unrealistic about practice, is salutary. It is sometimes suggested that the gap between theory and practice would be bridged if only we had the sense to fill colleges of education with practicing teachers. It may be a good thing, other things being equal, that teachers of educational theory should actually have taught in schools. But on the basis of my own experience, and the experience of colleagues and friends with whom I have discussed the problem, ex-practitioners can look as unrealistically theoretical to their students as anyone else.[1]

To come to my major points. I want to argue that there are two main reasons for the gap between theory and practice. On the one hand, from the side of the practitioner, I believe it often follows from a misunderstanding of what theory is. This is to say that practicing teachers are apt to demand of educational theory what it is not in the nature of theory to deliver. I am suggesting that, in part, the theory-practice gap is the "fault" of practitioners. I will come back to this point later.

On the other hand, I am also convinced that a gap between theory and practice frequently exists because theory is often quite inadequate. Practitioners who criticize theory are sometimes kind enough to say, "That's alright in theory but it won't work in practice," implying that there is really nothing wrong with the theory—that as theorists we have done our job well enough—but that practice is simply just a different world. I want to suggest, to the contrary, that the theory is often not alright; it is misleading and inadequate theory that practitioners have a perfect right to dismiss.

Let me give my reasons for saying this.

First, I believe that educational theory is often unacceptably utopian. An example of this would be in the conception of the child that dominates liberal educational theory. We assume the existence of a perfect learner—essentially innocent, insatiably curious, and intrinsically motivated. We rarely entertain the possible truth contained in Shakespeare's characterization of the second age of man as a period when the child inevitably goes "unwillingly to school." What follows from this Shakespearean assumption is that teachers will often be faced with an uncooperative learner and will need to have recourse to extrinsic motivational devices. Teachers, even good teachers, experience this problem daily in the classroom and I believe that they are right to distrust a sentimental model of the child that fails to take account of the reality of childhood.

This utopian assumption of original student perfection derives from one or the other of two sources. On the one hand, it is often a metaphysical fiction without any empirical basis; that is, it is a model of what we would like children to be, or, perhaps, a moral conclusion about what they ought to be. On the other hand, when it does have a basis in the real world, the perfectionist model is derived from child study that is conducted in privileged circumstances, indeed, in conditions that are near utopian from the standpoint of the typical classroom—in private schools, or with small groups of learners, or even, as with a good deal of Piagetian research, with individual children. In this connection, it is also worth noting that old-fashioned learning theory based on the study of animal behaviour was derived from the study of individual rats or pigeons.

This brings me to a second reason why educational theory is often inadequate. It is almost universally true that the institutional unit in which pedagogy has to be conducted is the class, a social group; occasionally, as in the graduate seminar, a group of half a dozen, but often in large lecture groups of several hundreds, or, if you are lucky, with a group of around 50. In elementary school, you may be lucky enough to have as few as 20 children, more likely to have around 30, but even there classes in excess of 40 are not unknown. Yet, despite this institutionalization of learning in the class grouping, liberal educational theory is overwhelmingly individualistic in orientation. Theory urges us to remember that each child brings a unique personal history to school that peculiarly affects his or her motivation and defines his or her idiosyncratic needs, interests, and preferences. We are even asked to entertain the view that each learner has a unique learning style and pace, such that the only adequate pedagogy would really be based on individualized instruction.[2] And logically, as is sometimes asserted, what this really adds up to is an individualized and personalized curriculum for every child. But the reality is that we do not, we cannot, teach children as individuals in schools, except occasionally and marginally. It is not even clear that it would be desirable to completely individualize instruction even if we could, for it is not only the existence of economic constraints that leads us to group students together in classes. The wealthy in society, who can well enough afford to buy individual tuition for their children, choose to send them to schools on the assumption that education is a social process requiring a social pedagogy. Yet teaching a group a common subject matter poses its own special problems to which few educational theorists address themselves, except for notable exceptions like John Dewey, whose embryonic project method was essentially a social pedagogy. What I am arguing here is that the educational individualism of liberal educational theory inevitably opens up a gap with practice because the context of institutional practice is inevitably a social one, the class.

Third, context of another kind is often ignored in a way that also serves to drive a wedge between theory and practice. It is a legitimate criticism by practitioners that educational theory often ignores the bureaucratic context of classrooms and schools. Here I am not using the word pejoratively; I take it that in the modern world bureaucracies are necessary to providing a public service like schooling or health care, and so on. But just as it individualizes the learner, educational theory often also implicitly individualizes the classroom and the school, in the sense that it assumes both to be autonomous associations in which the teacher is able to function independently, without bureaucratic constraints upon one's professional judgment and competence. But in classrooms, teaching and learning have to be accomplished subject to legal, economic, and other constraints, as well as with an eye on the competing (and often contradictory) claims of interest groups of various kinds and the expectations of parents that are not always in accord with academic realities or the norms of a liberal education. The result is that teachers often cannot avoid performing in a manner that their better judgment tells them is not exactly pedagogically sound. An obvious example of this would be the pressure to resort to rote teaching and learning to achieve success in external examinations.

One of the things that is implicit in the three points I have made about the responsibility which theorists have for the existence of the theory-practice gap is that practitioners know their work frequently involves compromise, but they believe that theorists refuse to recognize the inevitability that successful human action is full of compromise. We almost always use the word in a pejorative sense: "compromise" is associated with betrayal of principles, with untrustworthiness or want of integrity; it almost carries the implication of moral turpitude. In fact, compromise is part of the stuff of which successful and harmonious relationships are made. Husbands compromise with wives, parents with children, doctors with patients, law enforcement officers with offenders, politicians with other politicians and their constituents, even perhaps, clergymen with parishioners. And most teachers would hardly survive in the classroom without compromising with bureaucrats, with colleagues, with students, with parents, between the competing claims of individuals and of the individual student and the group, and between pedagogical and bureaucratic imperatives. Compromise is a fact of classroom life. The fact that compromise is necessary in applying theory to practice ought to be treated as an aspect of educational theory itself. That is, maybe the successful marriage of theory with practice is consummated, in part, by learning the art of compromise.

This brings me to my alternative explanation of the gap between theory and practice; the practitioner's misconception about the nature of theory. If part of the fault lies in inadequate theory, I believe it also follows from the unrealistic expectations that practitioners often have of theory and their failure to recognize that even the best of theories has to be applied with discrimination to the practical situation. It is in the nature of what a theory is that there can never be an exact, neat, one-to-one fit between theory and practice. Theories are generalizations about practice, while practical situations are particular, peculiar, and widely varied. A theory draws its relevance and cogency to every conceivable situation it seeks to explain only by being an exact description of none of them. There never can be a one-to-one correspondence between theory and practice, if by this we mean theory that predicts accurately every contingency in a practical situation. As Donald Schön (1983) puts it in *The Reflective Practitioner*: "An overarching theory does not give a rule that can be applied to predict or control a particular event, but it supplies language from which to construct particular descriptions and themes from which to develop particular interpretations" (p. 273).

This means that educational theories have to be applied by practitioners in an active, thoughtful, creative sense, not passively as though applying predigested instructions or advice. The application of theory to practice, instead of being an exercise in carrying out good advice, is rather a matter of learning to ask a variety of questions about practical situations with the guidance of relevant axioms or generalizations. The philosopher Immanuel Kant put it this way: "A set of rules, presented in a certain generality and with disregard of particular circumstances is called a *Theory* ... The practitioner must exercise his *judgement* to decide whether a case falls under a certain rule" (as cited in Rabel, 1963, p. 253). That is, the job of a theory is to evoke judgment rather than rote obedience. The application of theory to practice means bringing critical intelligence to bear on practical tasks rather than merely implementing good advice. We have to learn not only rules, theories, and principles but also how to interpret and apply them appropriately. That is, some initiative is required from the practitioner in discovering the pertinence of theory to his or her own peculiar practical situation. But if practitioners do not do this, or do not know how to do it, this may also be a fault that we have to lay at the door of teachers of theory. Too often, educational theories are taught not as analytical tools but as ideologies or dogmas that brook no argument. I suggest that just as teacher educators should confront teachers with the fact that compromise is a fact of life in classrooms, they should also accept the fact that part of the teaching of educational theory must consist of teaching exactly what a theory is, what it can and cannot be expected to do for practice, and the various ways in which theories have to be applied.

What I have just said about the practitioner's responsibility for actively applying theories, exercising judgment or critical intelligence, can be summed up in Schön's (1983) notion of the reflective practitioner in his book of that name.[3]

With reference to schooling, the notion of the reflective practitioner is the idea of a professional in a practical situation confronting the problems and the opportunities it poses, asking intelligent well-informed questions about the situation, acting in a manner suggested by the answers to these questions, evaluating the results, reflecting again on the implications of these, and so on. The result of this inter-penetration of theory and practice is to develop what is sometimes referred to as *praxis*. Out of this continuous reflection on practice, one develops one's own practice-relevant theory, one's own charac-terizations of what one is trying to do in the classroom, why one suc-ceeds or sometimes fails, and what has to be done to accommodate the failure, either by improving one's practice or, perhaps, by redefin-ing the situation. This raises the question of what it is that causes the practitioner to reflect critically on his or her practice and, especially, what it is, if anything, that academic educational theory contributes to intelligent reflection on practice.

One answer to this last question about the relevance of educa-tional theory for reflective practice is that it contributes nothing, or very little. This is a point of view that might be expected from the cynical or disillusioned practitioner who feels that he or she has been left to work it all out alone. But the view that educational theory does little to inform educational practice, that it has no impact upon the teacher's reflection on practice, is one that one hears occasionally from educational theorists themselves.

I have in mind here the view that when it gets down to the bare boards of the classroom floor, the only relevant guides to prac-tice are common sense and worldly wise axioms or aphorisms like "Praise is better than blame," "Don't expect them to sit and listen for too long," "When they get restive give them something to do," "Test them at fairly regular intervals," "Give them feedback as soon as pos-sible," "Spare the rod spoil the child," "Open the windows," "Never turn your back on them," "Start tough and then you can afford to relax," and so on. I remember spending some time several years ago with an American educationalist on sabbatical leave at the university's department of education where I worked. He spent most days sitting at the back of a classroom at the local primary school. A good deal of his time at recess, lunch break, and at the end of the school day was spent discussing with the class teacher how she had seen the les-son or the day. Inevitably, he argued, her account of how things had gone consisted of observations on individual children, wondering if a particular child had been unwell, or feeling the strain of family breakdown, or was watching too much television for too long, or how much the class had been distracted by interruptions from outside, perhaps a change in the weather, or how some of them did math last year with Miss Smith who really drills them in the fundamentals, and some of them with Mr. Jones who is a super teacher when it comes to language arts but who is bored to distraction by math and does not do much more than go through the motions.

These kinds of reflective comments on the successes and failures of the teacher's day may be more or less subtle and insightful, but, according to my American friend, they seem to depend hardly at all on a knowledge of academic educational theory. Evidently, what the teacher reflecting on his or her day does not do is to wonder what Piaget would have said about these things, or whether Plato or R.S. Peters might throw some light on his or her problems, or whether, like so many other things, they do it better in Sweden, or whether, according to Bernstein, it is all a matter of direct and elaborated language codes, or whether it all really comes down to the correspondence principle and, like Bowles and Gintis claim, the point is that we will never get schooling right until we get rid of capitalism. I do not know which discipline from educational theory I have omitted from that list, but if there is one, the reflective practitioner does not draw on that either to explain his or her day and to plan for a better tomorrow.

Now it may be that in reflecting on practice, the teacher rarely makes explicit or conscious reference to academic educational theory. But the fact is that not all homespun reflection on the practical situation in the classroom is equally relevant, equally cogent, or equally sensitive to moral standards and interpersonal relationships. And mere reflection from out of a teacher's own untutored cognitive resources may fail to come to grips with the complexity of a practical situation, or to explore the wide range of alternative explanations of classroom phenomena or alternative solutions to educational problems. Nor is all folk wisdom equally sensitive to the moral issues arising in the classroom. After all, Jim Keegstra was presumably a reflective practitioner, according to his own lights.[4] And he may be unique, but on my own experience of staffroom reflection, rednecks, racists, sexists, and chauvinists are not unknown, nor are practitioners who expect nothing of children and whose conception of what it means to be an educated person would make a Dickensian schoolmaster look like a liberal do-gooder.

I want to suggest that intelligent, well-informed, critical reflection on practice can be the outcome of familiarity with academic educational theory, however tacitly this theory may enter into thinking about practice. In fact, I would make much the same claim for the practical outcomes of a knowledge of academic educational theory that Peters does for the influence of the academic disciplines of the school upon the education of the person. As Peters suggests, the point of a liberal education is not that one arrives at a destination but that one travels with a different point of view (1965). One of the things I take this to mean is that the educated person is not merely satisfied to acquire a repertoire of relevant skills and knowledge that satisfies one's needs, ministers to one's interests, and assists one in solving problems in the here and now. In Peters's sense, a liberal education transforms one's perception of what the problems are, what opportunities are offered by life, and what new interests might enrich one's daily experiences. Being educated, one is aware of new needs and interests, and the relevance of knowledge has to be tested with reference to the possibility of a changing and developing, not a given static, way of life. It seems to me that theory of education—psychology, comparative studies, philosophy, history, and sociology of education—does not provide knowledge and skills that are applicable to a given practical situation: it provides new perspectives, such that one confronts educational problems and opportunities from a different point of view. Educational theory can provide a liberal education, such that the teacher's reflection on practice becomes intelligent, morally sensitive, capable of making finer conceptual distinctions and more subtle analyses of educational problems, and well-informed about the various relevant contexts of educational practice. The justification for educational theory is the same as the justification for liberal education itself. The teacher reflecting upon teaching equipped with more subtle educational theory is much like the liberally educated citizen reflecting intelligently upon public affairs.

To look for an educational theory that eliminates the gap between theory and practice is to chase a will-o'-the-wisp. Indeed, it is arguable that good educational theory that sensitizes the teacher's capacity for reflection will inevitably widen the gap. To elaborate this point, I want to give a brief account of what Schön (1983) says about the reflective teacher.

First, it is interesting that Schön assumes that the teacher will carry on his or her reflective activity in terms of the individual model of education to which I referred earlier. The teacher's reflection is never about problems of teaching the class or the group but always in terms of the individual learner, his or her needs, interests, strengths, and weaknesses. What will inevitably emerge from this reflection is a curriculum and teaching strategies defined entirely by reference to individual need.

Second, the teacher's reflection (which, among other things, will give rise to a completely new conception of the nature of curriculum) will inevitably bring him or her into conflict with bureaucratic norms and requirements. Things like timetabling, required syllabuses, objective testing, uniform student records, and many of the disciplinary and control mechanisms of the school will all seem to stand in the way of ministering to the individual student's educational needs.

Third, the teacher will conclude that reflective practice is hardly compatible with the kind of student-teacher ratio that is common in the public schools.

Notwithstanding these pessimistic conclusions that the reflective practitioner will inevitably discover a widening gap between one's increasingly sensitive theory and the given objective conditions of classroom life, the teacher must choose between two options that offer themselves at this point. He or she may choose to abandon the role of reflective practitioner, concluding that reflective practice is just another example of those things that look good in theory but, because of the bureaucratic and economic contexts of teaching, do not work in practice. One can reject the notion of the reflective practitioner as one of those utopian fantasies that do not fit the real world: something that looks good in theory but will not work in practice.

Or we can settle for half a loaf and see reflective practice as one of those things about which we have to learn to compromise. Indeed, one of the things that reflective practice would entail is thinking about the compromises that are necessary and possible and justifiable in the classroom. This amounts to repeating what I concluded earlier—that part of teacher education in both its theoretical and practical aspects is learning the art of compromise.

My conclusion is that the gap between theory and practice is probably inevitable, and that attempts to bridge the gap may even make it wider. Perhaps this conclusion is all that has come out of my new look at the problem. But far from this conclusion being regrettable or a source of disillusionment with theory, it seems to me to constitute rather an opportunity. I have argued that one of the things that educational theory has to do is to give an account of why the discrepancy between theory and practice is there, and how one might learn to live with it, not as a blemish or something that disfigures the educational enterprise but as something that nurtures both theory and practice. The continuous process of interrogating our practice with theory and refining our theory in the crucible of practice is the condition of our growth as both theorists and practitioners.

REFERENCES

Entwistle, H. (1969). Practical and theoretical learning. *British Journal of Educational Studies, 17*(2), 117–128. Retrieved from http://dx.doi.org/10.1080/00071005.1969.9973245

Entwistle, H. (1970). *Child-centred education.* London, UK: Methuen.

Entwistle, H. (1971). The relationship between theory and practice. In J.W. Tibble (Ed.), *An introduction to the study of education* (pp. 95–113). London, UK: Routledge and Kegan Paul.

Peters, R.S. (1965). Education as initiation. In R.D. Archambault (Ed.), *Philosophical analysis and education* (pp. 87–111). London: Routledge & Kegan Paul.

Rabel, G. (1963). *Kant.* Oxford: Clarendon Press.

Schön, D.A. (1983). *The reflective practitioner.* New York: Basic Books.

Simon, B. (1985). Why no pedagogy in England. In B. Simon (Ed.), *Does education matter?* (pp. 77–105) London, UK: Lawrence & Wishart.

NOTES

1 In speculating on the reasons for this, I recall a comment made by my own education lecturer in response to the critical article in the college newspaper to which I earlier referred. This was along the lines of: "What you are pointing out is not a gap between theory and practice but a gap between my theory and practice and your practice." Implicitly, it was not only the theory he taught that differed from my practice; his practice (which he believed to be quite consistent with his theory, since he had hammered out his theory from reflection on his practice) also differed from mine: he had been an experienced practitioner. I was merely a tentative, vulnerable, inexperienced novice. Reflecting on his wise observation over the years, I have concluded that one reason why experienced practitioners appear to give unrealistic advice to novices is that their theory is a reflective account of their long, experienced, and successful practice. When experienced practitioners become theorists, they probably give an honest account of their own reflections on practice, practice refined by familiarity with educational theory and tested through trial and error over the years. It is this description, explanation, and analysis of their own work as experienced teachers that students are apt to reject as unrealistic when applied to their own practice. In fact, it is unrealistic only in their own circumstances, inexperienced and differently contexted in time and place. But, in turn, the reflective practitioner will fashion his or her own theory from his or her own experienced practice; as such, it may well seem unrealistic to an inexperienced colleague.

2 For the argument that personal learning styles probably differ much less than our individually oriented educational theory suggests, see Simon (1985, pp. 94–95).

3 Although Schön (1983) makes passing reference to teaching, he does not analyze the notion of the reflective practitioner in relation to teaching anywhere near the length to which he does for some other professions. So, what I want to say about the teacher as a reflective practitioner does not necessarily closely correspond with the brief observations he makes on the subject.

4 Keegstra was a history teacher in Alberta who was found guilty of fomenting racial hatred through teaching, amongst other things, that the Holocaust never happened. See further, Chapter 23 in this collection.

2

Empirical Research in Education

Why Philosophy Matters

Robin Barrow

Introduction

Governments in many jurisdictions are currently obsessed with "evidence-based" research. It is worth stressing at the outset that "evidence-based" does not have to mean "empirically tested." A legal judgment, for example, may be "evidence-based" without being empirically established in the sense understood by educational researchers and policy makers. However, we are in practice talking about *empirically researched claims.*

In what follows, I am going to focus on empirical research into teaching methods. But I want to stress that in so far as my argument about teaching is sound, it applies equally to research into other things, such as leadership, classroom management, and several other psychological and social factors affecting student learning. Indeed, it applies to research in the social sciences generally and has implications for our attempts to answer a much wider range of questions, including "What difference do orchestral conductors make?" "How important are football managers or coaches?" and "Do politicians actually make any difference?"

The question I wish to explore is this: are we to presume that there is a given set of "best" practices or methods in education that transcends cultural differences, such that the most effective way to teach in the Yukon is also the most effective way in Delhi, regardless of what or whom one is teaching?

It will be noted that the question as I have posed it is about allegedly generic qualities of teaching, or methods and techniques that are supposed to represent good practice regardless of a particular context. Clearly, in any specific situation there may be better and worse ways to proceed, and one might be able to establish in particular cases which ways were most effective. But research, particularly so-called "scientific" research, is primarily concerned with establishing general laws. So, my concern is not with suggestions about good and bad ways to proceed in fairly well-defined particular circumstances, but rather with general prescriptions for teaching, of the type "small group discussion is more effective than lecturing" or "students prefer written instructions to oral instructions."

The suggestion that we should answer the question "Is there a given set of best practices?" in the affirmative seems to me absurd. Such are the manifest differences between the situations in, say, central Paris and a small rural settlement in Siberia, that one would surely expect very different approaches to teaching might be desirable. And if that is so, why should one assume or expect there to be a significant set of practices that are consistently "best" within a particular culture, given that within a given culture there are almost invariably further distinct subcultures? Why presume that methods that will prove effective with children from poor disadvantaged and dysfunctional families in downtown Vancouver, British Columbia, will also be the most effective methods to use with the children of wealthy educated parents in a private boarding school in rural British Columbia?

Consider, for example, the use of overheads when lecturing. There is a wide consensus that the use of overheads when making a presentation is desirable. I question this consensus; but even if one were to accept that overheads always enhance a lecture for any audience, it is surely obvious that the specific form, nature, and use of overheads might have to differ considerably to be effective with audiences of different, ages, cultures, and backgrounds. But to admit that is to render the advice "use overheads" more or less useless. To make it useful, I would need information about what would please particular members of my specific audience, even assuming that individually they would all welcome overheads.

But what suits a particular audience or individual members of that audience, which is precisely what should be of concern to individual teachers as they face their class, is not what empirical researchers are generally interested in, because they see themselves as playing a role in developing a science of teaching. To establish what would ideally suit a particular audience is quite different from establishing general principles or rules of good lecturing.

The more one thinks about it, the more the idea that using overheads must be a good or a bad thing across the board seems implausible. We are never going to establish the value of using overheads as a mode of teaching in itself: the value will vary depending on context, circumstance, and situation, as well as the particular form of use.

Here I must warn against a very basic but prevalent error: to say that we will never establish best practice empirically is not to deny that the question of whether a given practice is or is not efficacious is an empirical one. (Some would accuse philosophers of claiming that whether or not, for example, the use of overheads is desirable is ultimately a philosophical question. But that is not so.) The misunderstanding arises because philosophers rightly say that much empirical work is vitiated by a failure to deal with certain necessary conceptual and logical issues. But it does not follow that there are *only* philosophical issues to deal with. For example, most research on happiness is seriously deficient because it proceeds without explicitly providing a clear and adequate conceptualization of happiness; as a direct consequence of not having done the conceptual work before constructing the research model, researchers effectively define happiness purely in terms of the instruments and tests they use. But, given that this is empirical research, the instruments and tests used are exclusively focused on what is directly observable or can in some other way be monitored. Thus, the research is not actually into the elusive phenomenon of happiness. It is not directly focused on the inner state of mind of a happy person but on signs that are taken to be indicative of a person experiencing happiness. In fact, most research on happiness is into some perceived index or indices of happiness. Frequently it is into people's own perception of their happiness, which, in the absence of any shared and convincing conception of happiness, is quite a different thing. Or the factors monitored will be things such as smiling, being in good health, being successfully employed, having a secure income, being in a loving relationship—all of which may be related to happiness in some way for some people but none of which are necessarily aspects or features of the state of happiness.

It is thus fair to conclude that, generally speaking, empirical research into happiness is not in fact focused on happiness. Although such research might be of use in establishing what things different people think might make them happy, it is of little value in respect of happiness itself; it has no direct bearing on what actually will make people happy or on the logically prior question of what happiness is: in what the state of being happy consists.

The position for which I am arguing, then, is that while questions of best practice in teaching are undoubtedly empirical, for the most part we will not be able to answer them usefully or satisfactorily, still less definitively, by conducting empirical research. Of course, there are working generalizations or rules of thumb that we can, do, and probably must make use of. For example, generally speaking, the teacher should make him/herself audible, clear, sympathetic, and encouraging. But these terms have to be interpreted in each differing context—what is clear to one person is not clear to another—and the particularity of every teaching situation should never be forgotten.

It is also important to note that some of the putative characteristics of the good teacher are demanded for ethical reasons rather than reasons of efficiency or competence. Thus, we may ask for sympathy in our teachers not necessarily because it is productive in some way, though it well may be, but because we think it morally desirable that teachers should be sympathetic persons. In so far as that is the case, empirical research into the efficacy of sympathy is neither here nor there.

Furthermore, to subsume the question of how a teacher should proceed under a set of general rules is a denial of responsibility. In the end, what one should actually do in a given situation—as a teacher, administrator, or a leader—is context bound. Although we may reasonably generalize at times, every situation is, strictly speaking, unique. There is no escaping the personal responsibility one has for making judgments and decisions. To base one's practice on allegedly empirically proven strategies and techniques is to ignore the uniqueness of every situation and to run away from the need to assess every situation personally; it is to avoid the responsibility of assessing the needs of particular students in particular situations.

Research into Physical Health

Few would deny that over the centuries, particularly in the last two centuries, we have made enormous advances in our understanding and control of physical health. We have left the world of phrenology—reading people's character and proclivities from the bumps on their head—behind, although little more than a century ago it was still taken seriously. We no longer have to extract teeth with the help only of a bottle of whisky and rope to tie the patient down. Cholera and TB are no longer the killers they were in many parts of the world, and where they remain a threat it is not because we do not know what in principle needs to be done to combat them. We are far better at prognosis and prevention than we once were, and far better at treatment and cure, whether by drugs, surgery, or lifestyle change.

I do not, by the way, dispute the dangerous and immoral behaviour that pharmaceutical companies are capable of, the ignorance that individual doctors may still be prone to, the facts of corruption and self-interest, or indeed the making of genuine mistakes. But these are contingent difficulties. In principle they can be eradicated. In terms of our medical understanding, we have made quite startling progress. And the progress has been essentially empirical: that is to say, while it is wrong to see science as simply a matter of measurement, observation, and experiment, since obviously conjectures and insights, hypotheses, and theories are also crucially involved—nonetheless, ultimately conclusions have been empirically established.

Why have we made such progress in this field? Why have we been able to empirically establish a large and convincing set of "best practices" in medicine, best practices that are truly transcultural? Practices that are bound to be as effective in Turkey as in Scotland; practices that do not vary in their efficacy with different sexes, different age groups, differences in wealth, different values, or different belief systems. The answer is fourfold:

1. First, generally speaking, the elements under consideration are clearly defined. We know the precise nature of drug X; we know what we mean by a malignant tumour; there is no lack of clarity about what constitutes a broken bone or pancreatic cancer.

2. Second, not only are most of the concepts involved clearly defined, they can also, this being physical medicine, to a large

extent be physically monitored. We can in some fairly direct sense "see" whether or not a tumour is malign; we perceive the effects of a drug; we feel the broken bones; we smell decay.

3. Third, other variables that might affect the issue are relatively few and, again, can be monitored and controlled for. Why is this so? It is partly a direct by-product of working with relatively clear concepts and concepts that can be monitored without unnatural distortion. But it is also partly that over time we have built up a body of scientific knowledge, such that we can now rule out thousands of what might once have been considered possible variables. We no longer need to consider, for instance, whether some new form of cancer is the consequence of the patient committing some crime, of their impious thoughts, of the size of their brain, of their being rejected as a child, or of the failure of the corn crop. Various factors besides, for example, high blood pressure may be involved in causing a stroke, but we don't have to spend time checking out the phases of the moon. To be sure, even in a physical example such as a stroke, various psychological and sociological factors may partially be involved, although the direct causes are likely to be physical or biological. But the fact remains that researchers have been able to back their hunch and, by controlling for a manageable set of variables, establish conclusions. Diagnosis and treatment relating to strokes and their prevention *work*.

4. But above all, and what to some extent makes the first three conditions operable, is the fact that we do not have any real disagreements, doubts, or conceptual confusion or inadequacy over what counts as physical health. Self-evidently, if we did not know anything about what constituted health, we would have no way of recognizing it and hence no way of testing whether something did or did not contribute to it. It is because we agree on what counts as health that we can engage in meaningful research into what contributes to it and what militates against it. Furthermore, physical health or lack of it is once again something that is ultimately observable.

So, there seem to be at least four requirements of successful empirical inquiry: clear concepts, more or less directly monitorable concepts, a reasonable hope of anticipating and controlling for possible variables, and a clear conception of what constitutes success and failure in the field in question—physical health and sickness in my example.

Research into Mental Health

Why, when we turn to the field of mental health, is there considerably more disagreement and unease, as well as sometimes quite extreme, even violent, altercation between experts in the field? Why does the public at large have a quite different, much more skeptical or worried attitude to issues of mental health? The answer is surely quite obvious. The four conditions noted in relation to physical health are not met in anything like the same degree in respect of mental health.

First, the definitions, the concepts pertaining to mental states, are generally extremely opaque, often confused, and sometimes downright disputed. *The Diagnostic and Statistical Manual of Mental Disorders* (DSM) of the American Psychiatric Association, for example, routinely annually redefines, removes, and creates new concepts, often seemingly widening the definition of particular mental ailments simply to extend the field. What used to be referred to as "manic/depressive" tendencies, for instance, which phrase was simply descriptive of a behaviour pattern, is now relabelled "bipolarity," a change that, by giving a name to this set of tendencies, immediately both suggests that we are dealing with a known medical condition, understanding of which is within the scope of the expert, and also, by substituting the technical and arcane language of the professional for everyday terminology, further distances this condition from the understanding of the lay person. The fact of the matter is, of course, that we do not know any more about "bi-polarity" than we knew about "manic/depressive" tendencies. Similarly, what counts as "autistic" has proved a moveable feast in recent years. The definition is constantly changing, generally speaking to become more embracing—wider and, to some extent consequently, more vague. But labelling or putting a name to it goes a long way toward suggesting, misleadingly, that we are dealing with some specific and unequivocal state of mind, and one of which we have full understanding.

Many mental health concepts are socially constructed rather than given in nature. That is to say, unlike a broken leg or cancer (which are what they are regardless of one's culture, time, or preferences), what counts as eccentricity, madness, depression, despair, misery, and so forth, is highly debatable and is without question to some extent culturally variable. For example, what used to be perceived, and still is in some cultures, as simply a tendency not to pay attention for one or more of a long list of possible but familiar reasons, is now exalted to the level of "Attention Deficit Disorder" in North American culture.

But the notion that there is in some sense a "condition" that necessitates an inability to attend—as distinct from a failure to attend on different occasions for various different reasons—is no more than conjecture. Once again, providing a label unwarrantably reinforces the idea of an identifiable condition.

Second, unlike most physical conditions, mental conditions cannot obviously be directly observed or monitored. In physical medicine we can observe the cancer itself; in medicine relating to mental health we cannot directly observe the depression.

Third, the potential variables that may affect mental health are far less well-mapped and accounted for than is the case in the field of physical medicine. Partly as a consequence of the two previous points (in sum, that a broken leg, a common cold, and a headache are clear and observable phenomena in a way that depression and compassion are not), we do not have a significant prior body of knowledge to work from, in the way that we do with physical medicine. We can rule out the time of the year as a cause of cancer, but can we rule it out in the case of depression? We can rule out what was eaten for lunch as a cause of a broken leg, but can we rule it out as a cause of a sense of well-being? Who knows what might improve a particular person's self-esteem or help another cease to despair? A relationship with a grandmother, a failure at school math, a success at college baseball, a marriage, a relationship with children, diet, conditions at work, may all, for all we know, in some way have a bearing on a person's "self-esteem," whatever that may mean. But they certainly don't have anything to do with a broken leg or malaria.

The point here is that the list of possible variables that conceivably might have a strong bearing on mental states is enormously, perhaps unmanageably, longer than it is in the realm of physical health.

Fourth, and above all, the problem is that the concept of mental health is itself dramatically contested. Different cultures certainly have different ideas about what is mentally healthy and what isn't, and there is in fact considerable variation relative to these ideas even within given cultures. Nor should we presume that because a group of professionals agrees on some broad set of indices of healthy or unhealthy behaviour, in for example the DSM, it follows that they have a *clear* conception. It does not follow, and it is generally not the case, that they have a clear concept of mental health, let alone that it is a plausible one.

The fact is, you cannot pursue empirical inquiry, you cannot set up an empirical research project, into a contested concept, unless you offer a clear account of your view of the concept. In that case it becomes research not into, say, happiness per se, but into your particular view of happiness. That would be fine if we, the audience for your research, are aware of and accept your conception, but this virtually never happens. If one studies research on happiness (see Barrow, 2012) one finds, first, that for the most part the researchers do not explicitly provide a full account of what they understand by the term "happiness." Second, not surprisingly, as a consequence it turns out that different studies are in fact about different things (different conceptions of happiness). Third, if, in the absence of a clear definition, one attempts to deduce or reconstruct a particular researcher's understanding of the concept from the measures, indices, and other items involved in the research, which is all that one can do, nine times out of ten it will be found to be inadequate.

The main reason for this inadequacy is that, being constrained by the nature of empirical research to focus on the observable or otherwise monitorable, it will inevitably miss an essential aspect of happiness, which is, on anyone's view, that it is more than a set of behaviours. That I say that I am happy, that I am wealthy, healthy, and married, and that I smile a lot, may or may not be good reasons to conclude that I am happy, but whatever such facts suggest they do not *mean* that I am happy (i.e., they do not define the term), and they do not amount to demonstration or proof that I am happy. To know whether or not a person is happy, it is necessary to have a clear conception, but it is also necessary to have an adequate, plausible, or convincing conception, and to get that we need to get inside people's minds, which not even self-reporting (indeed perhaps self-reporting least of all) can reliably do. It is a vicious circle. For how can I report accurately on my state of happiness if I have no clear idea of what happiness is? How can I have a clear idea without reflection on the experience of happiness? How can I reflect on the experience if I am not clear what the parameters of the experience in question are? How can I know those parameters if I have no clear idea of what happiness is?

(But there is a way out of this vicious circle: it begins with philosophical reflection on the concept of happiness.)

Research into Teaching

The situation with education is comparable to that of mental health but worse. First, if we are to proceed empirically, the various things we want to consider and therefore need to monitor include such things as "progressive teaching style," "caring," "inspiring," and "motivating" on the part of the teacher; "paying attention," "enthusiasm," and "understanding" on the part of the student. All such concepts are, on the face of it, very unclear.

Second, one thing we can say is that to a marked degree such qualities, characteristics, and styles are not directly observable or monitorable.

We could of course insist that, since we want to conduct empirical research, we will ignore complex and not directly observable concepts such as "interest," "passion," "understanding," and "appreciation," and focus instead on "talk time," "eye contact," and "attendance" rates. But to proceed in that way is both to distort the particular concepts in question and to dramatically limit, not to say emasculate, our overall picture of the enterprise of schooling and education.

How does one conduct research into progressive teachers without a clear definition of "progressive teaching"? How does one distinguish progressive teachers from others without a definition; how does one pick them out to study in the first place? And can one reasonably define progressive teaching simply in terms of observable behaviours? How exactly are we to monitor the nature, extent, and degree of a child's understanding or appreciation of a novel or poem, of a historical event or even a scientific theorem?

Whether or not a person is paying attention cannot be deduced from observation alone—unless one does what in fact researchers are driven to doing: defining the concept in observable terms, such as "eyes on teacher" or "nods head," which clearly distorts the concept; a list of observable behaviours, such as "keeps eyes on teacher," does not constitute an adequate definition, and as likely as not it gives an incorrect reading: the student who has eye contact and nods her head is not necessarily paying any more or better attention than the one staring out of the window.

In addition to ignoring and distorting various important concepts, empirical research for the most part focuses on short-term results. This is a result of the practical needs of the business of research: it is extremely costly and in other ways impractical to seek to follow through to see what effect their particular educational experiences had on pupils in later life. Also it becomes immeasurably difficult to attempt to distinguish between "effects" that are truly the product of education and those that are the product of various other factors in life. But successful education should surely ideally be judged from a long-term point of view. Whether one is thinking in terms of times tables or response to poetry, one would expect educators to be more concerned about what schooling means to individuals over the course of their lives than what it "shows" students to have achieved at the end of a given year or on leaving school.

Third, the variables that potentially need to be considered as possibly affecting what is going on are, as in most cases of human interaction, effectively numberless. In the physical or natural sciences we can, generally speaking, confine ourselves to physical phenomena: the mood of the observer and the temperament of the observed do not come into it. But in the teaching situation any number of psychological and sociological, biological and physical, emotional and intellectual factors may play a part: what a particular student gets out of a particular lesson may owe as much to his hunger, his resentment, his prior learning, his headache, his general ability to concentrate, and so forth, as to anything specifically to do with teaching or learning.

Why is there a problem with controlling for such variables? In the first place, there is a problem in thinking out what they might be. This is partly because of the absence of a developed body of knowledge akin to that in the natural sciences—which has already narrowed the field by eliminating various factors as irrelevant—and partly because the lack of clear concepts makes it hard to rule anything out: if we are dealing with something as open yet opaque as "enthusiasm," how do we begin to imagine what might or might not affect it? If we are not sure what counts as being well educated, how can we begin to short list factors that might affect it? But it also just seems to be the case that there is an enormous number of things that may affect a child's progress through school, in a way that there is not an enormous number of things that might conceivably be thought to cause physical sickness of one kind or another or that might help or hinder the growth of a plant.

We are told, for example, that students have an optimum attention span. Twenty minutes, as I recall from my teacher training days, being the maximum length of time that an audience can concentrate with full attention on a lecture. First, I doubt that this claim is or ever was true even as a generalization. Wouldn't optimum attention span depend on such things as the age of students, on the activity in question, on the conditions in the lecture theatre, on the lecturer? But even if it were true to the extent that in a given culture students tend to pay attention for a certain period of time only, it would obviously not necessarily be true for all cultures. That is because the extent of our ability to concentrate is very obviously partly governed by practice, expectation, and experience. Greek rhapsodes could recall and recite the entire Homeric poems; most of us cannot recite a short poem by Tennyson. Why? Because these things are not given in nature but are primarily the product of need, training, practice, and acclimatization. The reason that people cannot pay attention for long in contemporary Canadian culture is that their way of life—including their obsession with technological gadgets and rapid short-hand communication in particular, and the fewer demands made on them in respect of paying attention and of related achievement—*cultivates* or *creates* such inability.

Fourth, most important and most obvious, the end is not clear. What counts as success is neither spelled out nor agreed on. Education is a prime example of what W.B. Gallie (1955) famously called an essentially contested concept. It is not only a complex concept but also one that people inevitably argue about. That is to say, it is not given that being "educated" involves such and such, as it is given that triangularity involves a three-sided figure, the internal angles of which add up to 180°.

As it happens, I share the view, most fully expounded by Richard Peters (1966), that to be educated is to have a developed understanding that is both broad and worthwhile, and that involves cognitive perspective and commitment. I think that one may reasonably assert that historically and cross-culturally it is evident that all people share this view. But any more detailed specification of being educated is going to depend upon a host of culturally variable factors, including, but by no means only, differences in values. Classical Spartans and Athenians, as well as contemporary peoples of India, Canada, and Britain, would all, I think, confirm Peters' view: each of them tries to pursue what they regard as a necessary breadth of worthwhile knowledge. But, of course, they do not necessarily share a view on what is worth knowing or in what that breadth should consist, often very reasonably so: it made sense for the Spartans, for example, who did not have a developed discipline of science or a significant literary culture but who did have to keep control of a numerically vastly superior slave class, to regard military skill, martial courage, and loyalty as things pre-eminently worth understanding. It made less sense to the Athenians, and makes very little sense indeed to contemporary Canadians.

Bearing in mind, then, that for some a well-educated person is a Renaissance scholar, for others a good citizen, for some a moral being, and for others still one who has a more limited set of marketable skills (and bearing in mind that "many" though not "any" such competing views may be equally acceptable, given differences in situation, knowledge base and values), what on earth is one to make of the claim that research shows that such and such a teaching method is effective? Or, worse, is "best practice" or *the* appropriate method? Effective to what end? "Best" in the light of what view of success? *The* appropriate method in respect of what cultural ideal?

In practice, as we have seen, success is always defined as a short-term end or set of ends, and an end that is observable and can be monitored. Even in the university context we see it happening, as we are increasingly confronted with assessment exercises. These exercises are allegedly concerned with the quality of teaching and scholarship but are in fact nothing more than quantitative estimates of publications, of perceivable activities such as conference attendance, of grant dollars, and of student perceptions of teaching competence (often confused with popularity). The focus on quantitative factors is, of course, the direct consequence of the widespread and misplaced faith in empirical or scientific research as the only legitimate source of knowledge. It really shouldn't need spelling out, however, that publishing a lot of books doesn't necessarily prove an individual to be particularly wise or scholarly; the lecturers whom most students like most are not necessarily the best; and the contemporary emphasis on attracting research funding is hopelessly confused: failing to bring in research funding, if, for example, it is for the simple and excellent reason that one does not require it, is surely to be praised rather than penalized. (It would probably be unwise for me to comment further on the conspicuous waste all too often involved in academic conferences.)

Just as it is true, in the words of the eminent IQ researcher E.G. Boring (1957) that "I.Q is what I.Q tests test," so it is also true that what empirical researchers mean by educational success is simply success relative to their instruments and tests. The crucial question is thus whether or not their view of success is sufficiently compelling: whether or not short-term success on their tests of observable skills is satisfactory as a definition of educational success. In my view, it never is and it never can be.

I cannot think of any findings from over 100 years of research into teaching that may plausibly be said to be both significant and unexpected, and to have required systematic or formal empirical research to uncover them. What we often get from such research are necessary truths along the lines of: good teachers interest their students, are "with it," and get students to spend time on task. These are "necessary" truths inasmuch as the claim that "X is a good teacher who does not interest his students" would seem to be a contradiction in terms. They are banal and unhelpful since what interests is variable, what counts as being "with it" is negotiable, and the question is how much time—and presumably that will vary from student to student and task to task.

I have been criticized in the past on the grounds that, even if I am right in saying that research has not produced many if any significant laws of teaching, it is nonetheless, for example, "unreasonable" "to fail to take notice of a body of research that found that a high percentage of a large number of [autistic] children found it easier to follow instructions that were written down" rather than communicated orally. But how unreasonable is it? The specific numbers in question are not given, but if we generously assume that both the "large number" and the "high percentage" referred to in that quotation from Barrow and Foreman-Peck (2005) are 75% of their totals, then we are being told that 75% of 75% of a group of autistic children respond better to written instructions. That is in fact to say that 56 out of 100 autistic children in one study responded better. This does not seem to me to constitute particularly helpful information for a teacher faced with her own class of autistic children. She would be far better advised to study the particular students in her own class and draw her own conclusions about what they, being the individuals they are, need, than to proceed unthinkingly in line with a very broad generalization based on inappropriate and hence inadequate research methodology.

It has also been suggested that I fail to appreciate the extent to which researchers have produced strikingly counterintuitive claims, which illustrates both the value of such research and the fact that there are significant rules to be found. An example that has been cited in this connection is some recent research conducted at Stanford University. In this research, the seemingly obvious assumption that teachers should make themselves clear to their students is shown to be not necessarily true. The research indeed claims to show that some students actually benefitted from their teachers being unclear.[1]

That I can well believe. So, I don't question the integrity of the research. But such a finding is both easily explained and in fact confirms my point that research is not producing meaningful findings. It is explainable in several ways: perhaps the students were preparing for exams and, frustrated by their teachers, they went off to the library and studied on their own; perhaps they were just generally highly motivated students; perhaps they were irritated and determined to show their teachers a thing or two; perhaps in this case certain peers were more influential than the teacher. Whatever the explanation, it is clear that the conclusion from this research is that, far from there being rules of good teaching and far from this being a useful research finding, even seemingly self-evidently good methods do not always work, are not in every case appropriate. Surely the researchers are not going to claim to have established the counterintuitive proposition that teachers should generally be *unclear.* What they have established is that sometimes a lack of clarity may be productive, from which I would draw the obvious conclusion that even when it comes to something like being clear there are no hard and fast rules in teaching.

Are There Any Significant Laws of Teaching?

The argument so far has been largely about the plausibility of the idea of our being able to discover generic rules or laws of good teaching by a process of systematic empirical inquiry. But perhaps the reason the research is getting us nowhere is that there are no rules.

In the natural sciences we look for laws that transcend cultural difference. It was the growing realization that there were rules and the subsequent discovery of many of them that gave rise to the very idea of science. Because we can locate laws in nature we have the natural sciences. In the domain of the social sciences, we proceed as scientists without having any prior assurance that there are any laws.

As I have already said, the notion of laws that govern teaching is highly suspect. Even being clear, it transpires, is not always desirable. The "findings" of empirical researchers are not only generally speaking unhelpful and questionable, they are also potentially highly dangerous: less thoughtful teachers, teacher educators, and administrators—assuming that since academic research is highly funded, based on "science," and carried out by "experts," it must be significant—may simply accept the conclusion that what matters is to attempt being "with it," for example, in a way that "interests" students, and to spend "time on task." The notion that there are rules naturally tends to promote the idea that good teachers are those who know them and follow them, which in turn tends to lead to practitioners who accept various prescriptions rather than those who take responsibility for analyzing each situation for themselves. The view that we can establish the laws of teaching thus gets in the way of something supremely important: namely our understanding of the fact that human actions and interactions are by their nature particular. Every human encounter is unique. It is our individuality that is being ignored. And in turn our recognition that we are responsible for our actions. We are not victims of circumstance. We cannot live our lives fully and successfully by prescript.

There are, of course, things we don't know in education that a degree of empirical research would usefully throw light on. What are the effects of boarding? What are the pros and cons of same-sex or mixed-sex schools? What are the advantages and disadvantages of mixed-ability grouping as opposed to setting by readiness and aptitude? Although such research would need to be conducted with clear conceptions, and focused on long-term results in relation to a full, clear, and persuasive account of what counts as educational success, it could be appropriately carried out and it could be informative. But this does not apply to research into teaching for all the reasons I have given: we can in principle observe one group of children in a single-sex setting and another in a mixed setting, and note specific differences in achievements and development, and we can in principle see whether or not students taught math at a certain level in a mixed-ability class do better or worse than those in a group determined by aptitude and readiness. We can, with less certainty, even conclude that certain methods tend, on balance, to lead to certain, specifiable, short-term consequences, such as that repetition of times tables enhances memory of them in the short term. What we cannot do is establish that certain specific methods or teaching techniques should be generally advocated and adopted by all teachers because they necessarily lead to a better education for our students.

The Practical Value of Philosophy

Empirical research has become quite an industry. Huge sums of money are spent (not to say "wasted") on empirical research projects in the social sciences. By contrast, philosophy, along with the humanities generally, tends to be dismissed by government and policy makers as being of no economic utility and no practical value. (Ironically, this is partly because it doesn't cost much to engage in it: we unfortunately tend to value things in relation to their cost, being, like Oscar Wilde's cynic, people who "know the price of everything and the value of nothing.") It seems to me that this is all upside down. Because social scientists call themselves scientists and proceed by aping the ways of the natural sciences, it is assumed that they are productive of knowledge, scientific information being regarded as the only true knowledge. But the reality is that scientific knowledge or understanding is not the only kind of knowledge there is, and social science, when it is genuinely scientific, covers only a limited field of human endeavour, and much of the time, not least in the field of education, actually has very little of importance to tell us. By contrast, philosophy has enormous practical value.

First, as should by now be clear, philosophy is vitally important in clearing the ground, in sweeping away the confusion and false assumptions that get in the way of sound thinking and sane practice. It is essential, too, and as such of inestimable practical value, in carrying out the necessary constructive work of analyzing and clarifying our key concepts. And when it comes to this positive role, we should not be put off by the admission that many key concepts are essentially contested. We may not all finally agree on the finer points of what constitutes being well educated, but we can each one of us at least come to a clear, coherent, and fully developed conception, such that we collectively know what we are variously talking and arguing about.

One very important positive point to be made is that teaching is a polymorphous term. That is to say, teaching cannot be defined in terms of a specific activity, such as instruction, facilitating, or monitoring; nor in practice can it be defined in terms of a definitive set of activities, for the truth is that in teaching one may and should engage in countless different kinds of activity at various times. This is a point that needs to be emphasized, given the widespread tendency of educators to dismiss activities they don't approve of as "not really teaching," as in "Oh, she's not really teaching, she's just lecturing," or "You call that teaching? I call it a love-in."

Philosophy may further help us to realize that we are perhaps completely wrongly orientated. I have been talking about empirical research into teaching methods, albeit very critically, because the world we live in has emphasized and dignified such work. But perhaps, when it comes to producing teachers, it is not discussion of methods or techniques that we need at all, so much as consideration of the type of character we require in teachers.

There are good schools where success in producing people of a certain character and attainment is certainly not the result of the teachers concerned being fitted out with any particular teaching skills, because the schools I have in mind are famous, or notorious, for not requiring formal teaching certification or training for their teachers. Their teachers are not better trained or trained at all in any formal sense. What largely characterizes such schools is that they employ teachers of a certain type or character. Teachers in such schools are almost invariably appointed because they are themselves well educated and primarily motivated by love of their subject, enthusiasm for imparting that love, and a wider desire to see a world of cultured civilized people. There is no necessary either/or here, but contrast that with the tendency for the professional bodies, including teachers' unions and teacher-training establishments, at least in my part of the world, to stress caring for kids, techniques of teaching, protocols for lesson plans and report cards, and commitment to some kind of social agenda.

How to get there is another matter. But we certainly won't get it by pursuing the "best practice" approach or by assuming that one can get far by teaching would-be teachers how to teach in terms of a set of techniques, behaviours, and exercises. Those precepts we do pass on should be subject and age specific rather than generic, which is to say they should be of the form "how to teach math to eight-year-olds with a certain background in the subject" rather than "how to teach anything to anybody." Most of all hope for the future depends upon commitment to a shared vision. Teacher education should therefore focus not on how to teach but on why we are teaching in the first place. What is it all for? What is our concept of educational success? And that is a job for philosophy.

What I have tried to suggest is that most empirical educational research, given the fact that it is empirical—which is to say by definition focused on the observable and measurable—proceeds as if, and reinforces the idea that, humans are essentially no more than automata who respond to stimuli. Philosophy helps to remind us that humans are not simply sophisticated machines or relatively complex animals. Our possibly unique kind of linguistic capacity has led to the development of our minds, which in turn gives us autonomy. We do not simply *behave*; we for the most part *act intentionally* and in the light of our reasoning, regardless of how adequate that reasoning may be. To understand humans and their interaction, one needs to understand their reasoning, enter their minds, know their intentions. To understand situations one needs to understand their particularity.

The ideal teacher seeks to develop in the student understanding and appreciation of, engagement with and commitment to, worthwhile subject matter. To do that successfully requires primarily a clear idea of what that subject matter is and why one is studying it, and an openness to how one should proceed, coupled with the realization that how best to proceed has to be determined by combining insight into the particular situation and a firm eye on what one is ultimately trying to achieve.

This is why philosophy matters in education. In any business or activity, without an understanding of what you are trying to achieve, what constitutes a successful outcome, what you are aiming at, you cannot coherently plan your campaign, evaluate the steps along the way, or judge your success or lack of it.[2]

REFERENCES

Barrow, R. (2012). *Happiness.* Oxon & New York: Routledge.

Boring, E.G. (1957). *History of experimental psychology* (2nd ed.). New York: Appleton-Century-Crofts.

Barrow, R., and Foreman-Peck, L. (2005). What use is educational research? A debate. *Impact* No. 12. London: Philosophy of Education Society of Great Britain.

Gallie, W.B. (1955). Essentially contested concepts. *Proceedings of the Aristotelian Society.* 1955–56: 167–198.

Peters, R.S. (1966). *Ethics and education.* London: Allen & Unwin.

NOTES

1 My information relating to the research on clarity comes from a public lecture given by Denis Phillips. I may have misunderstood or misremembered exactly what was said, but even if my account is inaccurate as to fact, the example as given nonetheless makes my point.

2 An abridged version of this paper was delivered at the International Seminar on Philosophy of Education, organized by Azim Premji University, Bangalore, India, on January 25, 2013.

3

Philosophy for Education

Toward Human Agency

Heesoon Bai*

*This chapter was first published as Bai, H. (2006).
Philosophy for education: Towards human agency.
Paideusis, 15(1), 7–19. Reproduced with permission.

● ● ● ● ● ● ● ● ● ● ● ● ● ● ● ● ●

[The philosophical act] raises the individual from an
inauthentic condition of life, darkened by unconsciousness
and harassed by worry, to an authentic state of life, in which
he attains self-consciousness, an exact vision of the world,
inner peace, and freedom.

—Pierre Hadot (1995, p. 83)

Prospectus

There is a contribution that I think philosophy is well equipped to make in education. If there is an end to which education is fundamentally committed, and philosophy is superbly equipped to further this end, then philosophy's contribution to education is indisputable. Modern education is dedicated to the cultivation of autonomy as human agency. (As we shall see, this quest for autonomy is not just modern fare.) Through education, we want our fellow individuals to think for themselves and to make reasoned ethical decisions. This capacity to enact one's freedom grounded in personal knowledge and ethics is what I mean by autonomy.[1] I believe that the call for autonomy as the *sine qua non* of human agency is urgent today in a world besieged by the global forces of corporatization, fundamentalism, consumerism, and other ideological and structural malaises and inertia that render human beings increasingly powerless to *act* and reduce them to only *behave* (Arendt, 1998).[2]

Lately there has been much promotion in Canadian education for cultivating students' social and moral responsibility—a salutary cause, for sure.[3] School mandates and mission statements have been revised to reflect this. As well, various social skills and moral education programs have been adopted. However, the prerequisite to any responsibility is autonomy founded in personal knowledge and ethics. Only a person capable of autonomy is fit to take up the call to exercise responsibility. Without the cultivation of autonomy, teaching social and moral responsibility may well turn out to be no better than yet another measure of social conformity.[4]

I intend to make a plea for a conception of philosophy as a *practice* devoted to the cultivation of fundamental human agency, namely autonomy. My arguments will be accompanied by a synoptic exploration of several exemplary philosophic arts pertaining to this cultivation, such as world-making, dialogue, philosophical writing, and contemplative arts. My selection is certainly not exhaustive, nor its interpretation orthodox, and leaves room for adding other examples and interpretations. In my exploration, I draw from both the Western and Eastern philosophical traditions, the latter being an area that is largely left out of our current scholarship and practice of philosophy of education.

In the Beginning Was Philosophy

The long history of philosophy in both the East and the West shows an incredible diversity of worldviews and perspectives. Still there seems to be a foundational quest underlying them all. The quest,

I would surmise, has to do with human agency: how shall human beings apprehend the world and their place within it so as to lead more responsible lives? This question, asked 2,500 years ago and still today, explains why we still read the works of thinkers like Plato and Confucius and draw insights and inspirations from these ancients. The same cannot be said about alchemy in the study of chemistry, for instance. Chemistry superseded alchemy; we consider alchemy a superstition, not another plausible competing conception of life.

What is remarkable about the above question regarding human agency is that it was asked at all. If human beings did not see their being in the world as problematic, as needing a fresh reconceptualization, then such a question would never have been asked. That the problematization of life and the universe rather suddenly emerged 25 centuries ago seems to suggest that, before this time, human beings lived rather unquestioningly, therefore unself-consciously, within the prescribed inherited worldviews of their ancestral cultures, be they Olympic mythologies, the Hindu cosmology, the tales of the Chinese Yellow Emperor, or the story of Ravens. The world and human life were a determinate given, set forth and by and large managed by forces outside humanity; the most that human beings could do was to follow obediently heaven's will (or however it was known to different groups). We might characterize this mode of being in the world as *heteronomy*. Heteronomous human beings would not conceive of themselves as having an individual inner core of freedom to will their own action in accordance with independent thoughts and interpretations about the world. All this changed, however, somewhere between the sixth and fourth centuries BCE. Many refer to this remarkable period as the "Axial Age" and mark it as the advent of philosophy in both East and West.[5] This seems to be the beginning of humanity's quest for autonomy: the self-conscious realization that human beings are to think for themselves and that how we live has all to do with how we conceptualize and apprehend the universe and human life therein. It was as though the childhood of humanity came to an end and a sense of self-responsibility and the possibility of self-making seized *Homo sapiens*.

These axial folks did not banish the gods or God: the world they envisioned was by and large still theistic or animistic. The real change had to do with the burgeoning autonomy: the sense that, notwithstanding the gods' or God's existence, human beings had to do their part in figuring out with their own intelligence such vitally important issues as what kind of place is our universe, what is human nature, what is the purpose of human life, and what is the form of government that best supports human flourishing. In Solomon and Higgins's (1996) words, these axial thinkers were "sages, wise men, confident of their own intelligence, critical of popular opinion, persuasive to those who followed them" (p. 1). These seekers and lovers of wisdom—among them, Confucius (551–479 BCE) and Lao-tzu (sixth century) in China, Siddhartha Gautama (563–483 BCE) in India, Zarathustra (ca. 628–551 BCE) in Persia, and Socrates (470–399 BCE) in Greece—attracted students and disciples and formed schools and learning communities. Different schools mean different cosmologies and speculations about human nature and about the best ways to conduct human life. Lively debate and rivalry raged. Incited by these exemplary teachers, humanity entered, perhaps reluctantly, the young adulthood of self-responsibility and self-care. Such was, it seems, the beginning of philosophy and its quest for self-responsible human agency or autonomy.

The Axial Age Continues

The so-called Axial Period is by no means over, for the quest for autonomy goes on—and *must* go on. The world awaits another turn of human evolution on the plane of consciousness in the direction of taking better responsibility for how we think and conduct ourselves. We need to become far more responsible than we have been and there is urgency to this demand now. By all accounts, we are irrevocably damaging the Earth Community and all its biotic members and also are incurring a scale of human suffering that boggles any sane mind. How can we be so blind, heedless, greedy, and violent?

Many are tempted (or committed) to abandon the axial quest. They would say that the quest was a mistake. Human beings should have never left the secure ground of the theistic teleological worldview. We should have stuck to the notions of the divine plan and heaven's mandate. We can still go back, they are trying to persuade us. Religious fundamentalism is currently sweeping over the world. Ironically, some secular versions of fundamentalism are perhaps even more powerful. Take economic determinism, for instance. The market economy has become the current God of the secular, and transnational corporations, its new priests.

Fundamentalism and determinism demand heteronomy from us. We recognize fundamentalism and determinism by the telltale sign of ideologies. I like John Ralston Saul's (1995) definition of ideology: "Tendentious arguments which advance a worldview as absolute truth in order to win and hold political power" (p. 168). If something is an absolute truth, it is useless, if not stupid, to argue about it, let alone against it. The only reasonable thing to do is to accept it and live in accordance with it. In this way, absolute truth breeds heteronomy. We get to live in a deterministic universe wherein there is no need for individuals to think critically and creatively and envision different possibilities of reality. Thus, we let the Other (whatever form it might take) govern us, and we are thus relieved from self-responsibility and self-making. We become defectors of the axial quest. Philosophy, the original impetus behind the axial quest, urges us to get back to it. Childhood cannot be prolonged indefinitely. Time is running out. We need to grow up and embrace autonomy.

The Discovery of *Worlds*

Autonomy is the original philosophical project. My historical telling of this notion above left out an account of how autonomy came to be conceived and desired. In one such account, the ancient Greek "discovery" of autonomy with Plato as the key discoverer, we rediscover our ground of autonomy and thereby reaffirm philosophy's axial project.

Plato was gripped by the idea of Ideas. For him, the real world was the world of *Ideas*, the sphere of *nous* or Understanding, not the physical phenomenal world of matter and flux. What made Plato consider the world of Ideas, the suprasensible world, as more real than the sensible world of physical reality? Here is my conjecture.[6] "Real" is a value term: what is real is what really matters and has the power to affect us most deeply. In my revisionist interpretation, Plato was one of the original "discoverers" of the power of the human mind; that is, the capacity to conceptualize and interpret reality. Physics may be a given to us, but metaphysics is the way we take the given and generate a new order of meaning and power.

We do not "directly" perceive reality: perception is mediated by our conceptualizing minds. The conceptualizing mind superimposes the order of meaning upon the raw materials of sensuous perception. For example, one whose conceptualizing mind is normally functioning does not just see a rose, a certain physical entity, but rather sees the rose through the filter of a particular constellation of meanings, a personal history of experience and knowledge. This particularity renders meaning-making *subjective*: no one else would have exactly the same meaning-constellation. When 10 people gather in a room, although they share one room and may physically see the same things, they inhabit 10 separate and subtly or grossly different *worlds*. Though the physical reality may be the same for everyone insofar as it physically impinges on everybody equally, the reality of understanding and experience—which we shall now call the *world*—emerges as separate particulars on the plane of meaning. It is in this sense that we speak of the plurality of worlds and also the idea of *world-making* (Goodman, 1978). We should also speak of world-travelling, since, as individuals, we do not dwell in one fixed world that we have created but continually generate new worlds; as well, through various modalities of communication, we intersect each other's created worlds. What we are speaking of here is *ontology*: an inquiry into the metaphysical reality of worlds and how our minds participate in their creation and enactment. This may explain why traditionally ontology was considered the first philosophy.

The key to our world-making and world-travelling is the vigorous activation of the conceptual mind—the mind that articulates reality through images, symbols, concepts, words, and other symbolic expressions. Such articulation of reality is what language makes possible. Of the different languages (images, symbols, and so on), philosophy's particular fluency lies with concepts. Deleuze and Guattari (1991) said it well: "[P]hilosophy is the art of forming, inventing, and fabricating concepts" (p. 2). And what a time-honoured, superabundant, exuberant tradition and discipline philosophy is! Joining philosophy is like entering the world's oldest and biggest museum, but a teaching museum, where one can find all the concepts that humanity has ever created. But the museum analogy breaks down here because, unlike philosophy, museums do not manufacture the items to be displayed. The analogy of the workshop or studio may work better. Philosophers are conceptual artists who specialize in concept invention and revision. In being apprenticed to them, we learn in their studio the craft of reinterpreting experience, seeing what was subvisible or invisible before, articulating what was only half thought and felt, reconfiguring the subtle body of reality, re-evaluating the values assigned to things, and hundreds of other creative acts of *ontological shifts*.

Discursive language is a superb carrier of concepts. As such, in philosophers' deft hands, language manipulates concepts, thereby enacting ontological shifts. In this way, language is an ontological "lever" for shifting worlds. This sort of appreciation of the supreme importance of language to our apperception of reality has been the hallmark of philosophy. Recall the oft-quoted line from Wittgenstein (1961): "The *limits of my language* means the limits of my world" (p. 115). The inseparable intimate connection between word and world has been the subject of sustained contemplation from Plato to Rorty. Philosophy does not just *use* words to refer to and describe how the pregiven world *is*. Its relationship to language goes beyond representation, hence, instrumentality. Rather, philosophy is the tectonic activity of shifting and turning the very foundation of reality, continually bringing forth a new world through a new awareness afforded by language.

How do we enact for education the above understanding of philosophy as world-making, or, as I would put it, ontological "shape-shifting"? One time-honoured philosophic practice stands out: dialogue.[7] "Dialogue" is composed of *dia* (through) and *logos* (word), and their combination connotes the peculiar human ability of apprehending reality through the power of words, as well as the ability to communicate this apperception with fellow human beings. Worlds are created and shared through words. This wondrous phenomenon is what we have been highlighting in this section. But there is another reason why dialogue is so important to world-making. Through dialogue, we turn information into personal knowledge.

Only personal knowledge is useful to world-making: information, however correct and erudite, does little to contribute to world-making. This is because world-making is a subjective affair taking place on the metaphysical plane of personal understanding and interpretation. Mere *information*, that is, received knowledge not yet appropriated by the subjective core of the individual, fails to contribute to the building of personal knowledge. The form of discourse called dialogue vitally aids this process of appropriation. Let us see how. Here we follow the example of Socrates, our Western exemplar *par excellence* of dialogic interlocutor.

Dialogue is not simply an informative exchange of thoughts between conversation partners. As Pierre Hadot (1995) points out, dialogue has the form of a "combat," albeit amicable as between friends, in which interlocutors compel each other to examine critically, with utmost rigour, their thoughts, perceptions, and impressions for self-contradiction and superficiality, confusion, and deception. No part of one's interiority is spared this critical challenge. We cannot have a genuine dialogue if we cannot rise to the challenge of such rigorous examination. For this reason, Hadot (1995) reminds us, "[d]ialogue is only possible if the interlocutor has a real desire to dialogue: that is, if he truly wants to discover truth, desires the Good from the depths of his soul, and agrees to submit to the rational demands of the Logos" (p. 93). To emphasize, the aim of such challenge is not to see who wins (the purpose of debate); rather, the aim is personal knowledge and authenticity. Personal knowledge consists of visions and views that are intensely personal and yet equally intensely comprehensive and viable because they have been tested in the interpersonal crucible of dialogue; authenticity is the condition of the self who has withstood these challenges, resulting in a sense of integrity and conviction. Thus, personal knowledge need not be *merely* subjective, that is, idiosyncratic. From the intersection of the private and the public emerges personal knowledge.

I offer philosophical dialogue as a tool of resistance against the increasing emphasis in today's schooling on the acquisition of more and better information and skills. Nowadays, we are not even subtle about what kind of information and skills our students need: those that will render them successful in the global market economy. Here it is well to recall the ancient animosity between Socrates and the Sophists. The latter specialized in equipping students with useful knowledge and skills so they could be successful in acquiring wealth and status. Socrates revolted against this popular wisdom of the day and placed before his fellow citizens a rival picture of an educated person: authentic personality realized in personal knowledge and ethics. Socrates upbraided his fellow Athenians for concerning themselves with a life of material and social acquisition and not with cultivation and care of the self. His mission was to "persuade each of you to concern himself less with what he *has* than with what he *is*, so as to render himself as excellent and as rational as possible [emphasis added]" (Plato, 1961, 36b4–c6). These words, spoken 2,500 years ago, are as timely now as then.

Autobiographical Experiment

I now take a big temporal leap from Plato's legacy, to Descartes, Montaigne, and Nietzsche to talk about another gift that philosophy has for education. Talking appreciatively about Descartes's legacy goes against the current grain of anti-Cartesian sentiment. But we must not forget Descartes's championing of intellectual autonomy. True, we can find lots of faults with his worldviews and methods of thinking, such as his boundless faith in deductive thinking, his conception of the human self as the disembodied monological centre of consciousness, or the wholesale devaluing of all that does not possess the mind as dead matter (and these are serious faults). Notwithstanding these, "Descartes' emphasis on what has since been called 'subjectivity'—one's own thought and experience are as authoritative as the established teaching and authority of others, including the Bible—was a truly revolutionary move in philosophy" (Solomon & Higgins, 1996, p. 184).[8]

Three hundred and some years have passed since Descartes. Shuffling between modernity and postmodernity, we may not find the idea of self-authority and intellectual autonomy as revolutionary as the Enlightenment folks did in Descartes's own time. In fact, in our current individualist rights-based age, there is much appearance of having accepted the norm of self-authority. What individuals say and do is to be morally respected and protected by law. Yet in an insidious way, self-authority is a most undermined practice in this age of expert knowledge. Although we may *say* otherwise, from the way we practice schooling as primarily a business of stuffing students with useful knowledge and skills to the way we fail to function as active citizens in a truly participatory democracy, intellectual autonomy is hardly a societal norm in our highly conformist culture of professionalization and institutionalization of all human functions, as well as of mass media and advertisement-driven consumption. Hence, intellectual autonomy needs more than ever vigorous promotion and nurturance, and I think we are justified in looking to schooling for a major share of this work.

I do not think it a stretch of the imagination to pose a parallel between the intellectual scene that backgrounds Descartes's philosophizing and that of our own. Scholasticism is the theme for these scenic variations. In Descartes's time, scholasticism took the form of church doctrines. In our own time, it takes the form of ideologies, whether secular or religious. The most powerful of these ideologies currently is the doctrine of progress through economic means. Descartes revolted against the massively monolithic authority of the Catholic Church by insisting that true authority lay in the individual's subjectivity and with the capacity to think for oneself. This was an astonishingly bold claim in his time. Since what disables the capacity to think for oneself is the insistent imposition of ready-made ideas and channelling of mental activities only to rearrange acquired ideas, reclaiming of self-authority has to begin with a self-critical examination of received ideas. Descartes's gift to us was a demonstration of this process of self-examination that is the basis of philosophical thinking. To drive home a cardinal point, philosophical thinking is not just having and manipulating ideas. The latter is a necessary but not a sufficient condition for philosophical thinking. What turns working with ideas into philosophical thinking is the crucial presence and activity of the self that refuses to accept any idea without putting it to the "laboratory" test of one's own interiority. We see this laboratory test demonstrated in Descartes's *Meditations* (1962).

Descartes begins his series of meditations with a personal confession that he has waited for a long time for this moment to undertake a radical examination, and if necessary a general overthrow, of his acquired beliefs and opinions. The significance of this proposal lies in the implied shift in the position of authority, from what is external to the self to what is internal to the self. The self is a legitimate source of *authority* insofar as it is an author of its own experience, aided by the power of analysis and interpretation. Now, power is something that can be potential as well as actual. To bring it from the former to the latter takes development and augmentation. What is Descartes's method of developing such power? Essay writing.

In employing the essay style, Descartes was following the example of Michel de Montaigne (1533–1592), who, deeply influenced by the Stoics' textual practice of self-reflective writing in Hellenistic times, started the modern genre of essay writing. Essays (from the French, *essayer*, meaning, "to try") could be trials of self-interrogation and interpretation upon one's perceptions, feelings, thoughts, and action. The point of such trials is to *intensify* and *widen*, to use Foucault's words (1988, p. 28), and in general to transform experience. Or, to express it in another way, essay writing aims at *autopoiesis*—self-making. Through clarifying and articulating, reinterpreting and re-evaluating, our experiences, we recompose the latter and, hence, if appropriately guided, the self. For when we can see, understand, and evaluate our experiences in a better (deeper, wider, clearer, more intense, charged, comprehensive, coherent, meaningful) light, we can come to have a different sense of what we and the world are like, and we can entertain different possibilities of being. Philosophical writing, then, has this potential to transform the self through, shall we say, the *alchemical* process of transmuting experience, as from lead to gold.

To discuss philosophical writing as a pursuit of autopoiesis would be incomplete without mentioning Nietzsche, our first depth psychologist, although it may seem most inchoate to juxtapose Descartes with Nietzsche. But they stand on one common ground: the philosophical textual practice of transforming the subject. (That Descartes and Nietzsche turned out to represent two diametrically opposed mentalities does not invalidate my claim.) Nietzsche, too, was indebted to Michel de Montaigne for the "experimental" method of writing whereby the self tests its responses to the various topics and situations. As Graham Parkes (1994) puts it, it is an experiment in the "laboratory of one's own psyche" (p. 5). In this laboratory, alchemical transmutation of experience into insight and insight into new experience takes place. Nietzsche's writings are the autobiographical records of his constant effort to transform and renew his experience and his life as a whole. Parkes (1994) states:

> [Nietzsche's] texts are intended not as expositions of the truth or accounts of the way the world really is, but rather as invitations to entertain a variety of perspectives and consider what changes this effects on one's experience. His psychological insights are presented in the same spirit: not as ultimate truths about the human condition but as hypotheses to be tested in one's experience, as experiments to be conducted in the "laboratory" of the psyche. (p. 5)

What contribution can the above understanding of philosophical essay writing make to education? Again, our appreciation of a contribution is relative to the context. The general context of today's schooling is that we do not sufficiently encourage and enable students to do their own "experiment" in the laboratory of their psyche. We are still by and large fixated on knowledge transmission and acquisition based on external authority. This is not merely harmless: it deprives human beings of their vitality and agency and wastes their precious time. Alfred North Whitehead (1957), that gentle sage-like philosopher, even said that he experienced rage when he thought of the young lives thus wasted. He insists on what he calls the "utilization of ideas": "relating [an idea] to that stream, compounded of sense perceptions, feelings, hopes, desires, and of mental activities adjusting thought to thought, which forms our life" (Whitehead, 1957, p. 3). No one hopes to satisfy hunger just by carrying around a bag of groceries or a pocketful of menus: actual food has to be ingested, taken into one's digestive system, and the whole mechanical and chemical process of breaking down, digesting, and metabolizing has to occur. Philosophical thinking is foremost an equivalent process at the level of the mental-conceptual. Ideas are brought into one's interiority and ruminated by means of questioning: What do I think of this idea? How does it relate to certain views I hold in life? What feelings does this idea provoke and why? If I take this idea seriously, can I continue to live my life the way I have? If others adopted these ideas, how might it change the world? and so on. We mix the ingested ideas with our own perceptions and feelings, hopes, and desires as we mix food with our digestive juices. Ideas that have not been subjected to this digestive process, that is, "ideas that are merely received into the mind without being utilised, or tested, or thrown into fresh combinations" remain "inert" (Whitehead, 1957, p. 1). Inert ideas do not contribute to building the person and fueling his or her agentic vitality. The result is an impoverished mind-heart-soul, even if glutted with "scraps of information," as Whitehead (1957, p. 1) contemptuously called it. Philosophical essay writing, à la Montaigne, Descartes, and Nietzsche, is the strong digestive process on the mental plane.

To many undergraduate students long trained almost exclusively to compile and compare expert views and impersonal information under the rubric of a "research paper," the opportunity to write philosophical essays in the voice of "I" can be a paralyzing and disheartening experience. (I am tempted to carry on the digestion analogy and say "dyspeptic experience.") Unable to articulate their own views and insights, or only coming up with trivial flaccid opinions, lacking depth of analysis and critical understanding, many confess they feel stupid. Such sight of suffering makes me, their teacher, experience Whitehead's rage. What sort of nonsense enterprise is our formal education that after 12 or more long years we end up producing people unable to entertain and articulate their own views that reflect a measure of critical intelligence, imagination, and insight? Are we, in worshipping scientific impersonality and objectivity, training students out of their agentic development that is to render them increasingly articulate, thoughtful, and insightful about their views? In this lamentable situation, philosophical writing must serve as a basic tool of agentic empowerment.

Philosophy as Life Practice

I now would like to turn to a couple of Eastern philosophical traditions to see what insights and inspirations we can garner. Confucian philosophy has been the mainstay of many Far Eastern cultures for over two millennia. The key aspect of the Confucian philosophy that I wish to explore here is its fundamental commitment to the cultivation of humane sensibility, 仁 (ren), through the communal effort of person-making. In the face of today's world crises, typically precipitated by violent confrontation of conflicting ideologies and religions, the cultivation of humane sensibility or benevolence is an urgent task in which philosophy can play a vital and crucial role. We see this possibility superbly instantiated in a philosophy like Confucianism. For Confucians, philosophy is not mainly an intellectual exercise but, as Li Zehou (2000) puts it, "pragmatic rationality" that works out the "mutual penetration and merging of sensuality and rationality, individuality and sociality, physiology and sociology, from consciousness to unconsciousness" (para. 14). The ultimate goal of Confucian philosophy is the cultivation of the whole person who is fully integrated and harmonized intrapsychically, body-heart-mind, and interpsychically with all social and natural orders of the world. It is a philosophy *par excellence* for holistic education.

In Chinese, the homophonous words, 仁 and 人, both pronounced as "*ren*," designate two distinct but intimately related meanings. First, as a zoological designator, 人 means "human being" (technically, *Homo sapiens*, the species of bipedal primates to which modern humans belong). Its ideogram character indeed shows two spread-out legs joined at the trunk of the body, emphasizing humans' bipedality. But the other word, 仁, meaning "humanity, humaneness, benevolence, or kindness," has an additional stroke signifying the number two to the right of the ideogram for the zoological human being. In other words, this word is composed of two characters: "two" and "humans." What has this etymology to do with the way Chinese and Far Easterners influenced by classical Chinese letters and culture think about the world and human beings? Specifically, how does Confucian thought appropriate this linguistic peculiarity?

In Far Eastern countries such as China, Korea, and Japan, the common notion is that we *become* human beings, as opposed to being born human beings. For instance, in Korea, one would hear constant references to *making* and *becoming* human beings. One of the most frequent expressions of moral criticism, especially with respect to young ones, is that so-and-so has failed to become (literally, has not been made into) a human being. A more severe criticism is that someone is born with a human mask, meaning that for this person, being human is *only* a biological endowment. This indeed is the most serious condemnation one can make of another human being. Being human as a biological endowment is a given that a person does not have to earn, but being human as a personal entitlement is a supreme educational achievement demanding lifelong commitment and self-effort. Moreover, recalling the Chinese ideogram for humanity being composed of "humans" and "two," this process of becoming human properly pertains to the communicative interactive realm of social-cultural-political interrelationships that define the progressively expanding order of family, community, country, world, nature, and beyond. The Confucian philosophy is this life practice of establishing and integrating the self in ever-expanding concentric circles of communities, all the way from household to cosmos.

For Confucius, philosophy is not a field of theoretical knowledge. This does not mean that in Confucian philosophy there is no theoretical inquiry, such as debates about human nature, limits of knowledge, moral conduct, and best forms of government. But such inquiry is never divorced from, but grows out of, the enquirer's own ceaseless life practice of becoming human. For Confucius, the supreme goal of philosophy is becoming human. The self-cultivation therein encompasses all the aspects of the person: the body, psyche, temperament, mind, sentiment, passions, morals, will, speech, conduct, and so on, down to manners and gestures. Thus, for Confucians, philosophy is understood as a comprehensive art of lifelong self-making. Confucius sums up his own pursuit of this art thus: "At fifteen my heart-and-mind were set upon learning; at thirty I took my stance; at forty I was no longer of two minds; at fifty I realized the *ming* of *t'ien*; at sixty my ear was attuned; and at seventy I could give my mind-and-heart free rein without overstepping the mark" (as cited in Hall & Ames, 1987, VII).[9]

The Confucian conception of philosophy as life practice and self-making would strike a sympathetic cord with pragmatists, past and present. Indeed, among contemporary pragmatists, there is a vigorous revival and promotion of philosophy as life practice. Shusterman (1997) maintains that "[pragmatism] is no 'evasion of philosophy', but the revival of a tradition that saw theory as a useful instrument to a higher philosophical practice: the art of living wisely and well" (p. 5). "Philosophy," he says, "began not with a paradigm text, but with an exemplary life, a dramatic model of living—and dying" (Shusterman, 1997, p. 17). He goes on to call upon a whole line of illustrious philosophers in the West, from Socrates to Wittgenstein, including John Dewey and, not surprisingly, Michel Foucault, to illustrate his argument about the main business of philosophy being the practice of self-transformation. Referring to Wittgenstein, Dewey, and Foucault, Shusterman (1997) further comments, "philosophy had a much more crucial, existential task: to help us lead better lives by bettering ourselves through self-knowledge, self-criticism, and self-mastery" (p. 21). It is very refreshing and heartening to hear an appraisal like this about philosophy. Philosophy has become all too academic and technical in modern times, neglecting its original mission as "a way of life."[10]

To encapsulate, in the face of increasing technicization of teaching and learning, the Confucian philosophy holds up the primary aim of education as the cultivation of humanity. Without negating other aims, especially the aim of subject mastery, the Confucian philosophy insists that still the primary and universal aim is nurturing the humanity (*ren*) in all. Not only is this a most basic aim but also a most urgent one in these times of violent conflicts among nations and ethnic groups. Second, in response to the increasing fragmentation and incoherence of postmodernity, the Confucian philosopher of education would say it is the proper task of education to enlarge progressively our capacity to integrate the self into the ever-expanding circles of interrelationship in both human and more-than-human realms. The key to this integration is the cultivation of humane feelings, especially sympathy. "By privileging sympathy as the defining characteristic of true humanity, Confucians underscore feeling as the basis for knowing, willing, and judging. Human beings are therefore defined primarily by their sensitivity and only second-arily by their rationality, volition, or intelligence" (Wei-Ming, 1994, p. 180).

Third, the Confucian philosopher educator is dedicated to fostering relationships and establishing a learning community. The cultivation of sympathy can only be carried out through actu-ally living humane and responsible interpersonal relationships, which necessitates creating and fostering a learning community in the first place. It is in this vein that for Confucius, nurturing is before teaching and both are before governing (Kupperman, 1999). Thus, the primary role of the Confucian teacher is nurtur-ing leadership, and the primary method is modelling exemplary personality.

Every aspect of the teacher's being and life becomes an illustration and demonstration to students. Textbooks and curricula are second-ary to the teacher's own body-mind-heart and her life as a whole. A concept in classical Chinese thought, *teaching by the body*, recognizes the fundamental importance of embodied teaching and learning wherein the whole personality and life of the teacher and learner are involved.[11] Such teaching practice is, of course, impossible if the teacher has not seriously engaged in some kind of life practice of his or her own, being able to demonstrate, as a result, a measure of achievement as an authoritative (not authoritarian) human being. An assumption here, which is characteristic of Confucian thought, is that the mastery of a particular subject matter is a way of becoming an accomplished human being. Hence, in traditional China, a per-son who has mastered a subject but remains unexemplary as a human being (say, childish, greedy, or insensitive) represents a failure of education (Kupperman, 1999).

There has been a growing tendency to regard, implicitly or overtly, teachers as purveyors of information and technicians of teaching. The Confucian pragmatist call for life practice and education as the cultivation of the whole person offers a much needed antidote to this tendency.

Contemplative Arts

I now wish to address something that does not figure centrally in the traditional fare of the Western philosophy of education: the art of contemplation.[12] Although there are different notions of contemplation, the one I have in mind concerns the practice of freeing ourselves from the incessant automatic (because conditioned) conceptualization, thereby allowing ourselves to experience what is called *nondiscursiveness*—the state of consciousness that is free from conceptual constructs, including words. At the beginning of this chapter, I was vigorously arguing for the primacy of world-making through conceptualization. I am now arguing for freedom from conceptualization. But I am not contradicting myself or undoing what I claimed. In all pursuits, there can be imbalance and blindness symptomatic of doing something obsessively, with no conscious control, let alone reflective innovation. Such, I suggest, is the case with our ordinary linguistic conceptualization: we are so caged up in our thought constructs that we have difficulty realizing that these are *just* our thoughts, *just* constructs of reality. This is not to be dismissive of thought constructs. They are the very substance of our world-making, and world-making is human beings' particular and proper way to inhabit and work with reality. But when we are caged up in concepts and are driven by them, we do not have the freedom to make worlds as we see fit. Such freedom requires that we can disengage ourselves, temporarily putting down our building tools to take a break from the construction to reassess and revision our project.

That we are normally caged up in thought constructs is more serious than not having the scope for virtuoso construction. Being entrenched in thought construction, we are prone to identifying our notions (pictures of reality) with the reality itself, thereby easily falling into dogmatism. Mistaking the map for the road, we forget that it is made to help us navigate a journey. Map-makers consider their maps the true description of reality, leading to ideological battles that are not harmless diversions but produce suffering and carnage. September 11 gave us a terrifying example of an ideological battle fought at multiple levels: East vs. West; modernism vs. premodernism; haves vs. have-nots; Islamic fundamentalism vs. market fundamentalism, and so on. Each party thinks the other irrational and evil and that the way to peace is to wipe out the other side.

What do we do about mistaking the map for the road? It does no good to *tell* the deluded that they are deluded. They must step outside their present framework. Is experiencing without maps, that is, without thought constructs, like asking fish to come out of the water and breathe air? The suggestion is not as radical as it sounds. There are well-established traditions of contemplative practice that we can tap into. One example is the Buddhist practice of introspection known as the mindfulness practice (*satipatthana*). The key to this practice is experiencing the gaps between thoughts (Rinpoche, 1993, p. 75).[13] Being between thoughts, these gaps are thought-less, that is, nondiscursive, free of representation and interpretation. Such gaps can be experienced with knowledge and discipline, which may take time. The key is calming and slowing down the usual frenzy of thoughts and simultaneously increasing attentiveness. The time-tested method is anchoring the attention to one's breathing: trying to keep one's focus on the rhythm of deep breathing and bringing the wavering and wandering attention back to it (Gunaratana, 1991).[14] This is the basic practice of Buddhist mindfulness (Brown, 1986).[15] It is enough that we talk about the basic practice of witnessing the gap, for we are interested in disengaging the mind from compulsive thought construction and giving it an opportunity to experience nondiscursive states of awareness in the gap between thoughts.

There is no autonomy when we are conditioned to do something and constantly driven by it. This is addiction. Contemplative arts help us to overcome our addiction to conceptualization, not to stop our practice of thought construction but to achieve virtuosity in our world-making without dogmatism. The most stubborn dogmatism that plagues us is naive realism: the view that what we perceive is what is "out there," objectively. The experience of nondiscursive (object-less, thought-less) awareness can help dispel naive realism and its categorical separation of the subject and object. Virtuoso world-making is possible only when we break out of naive realism and its subject-object dichotomy. Thus, world-making and contemplative practice must go together for mutual support and balance.

Closure

The common notion that philosophy is impractical should be relegated to the list of outdated myths and popular misconceptions. There is the valid distinction between academic technical philosophy and philosophy as art of living (which can be technical!), and in modern times the former has been privileged over the latter to the poverty of public life. But in philosophy of education it is not difficult to appreciate and tap into the conception of philosophy as an art of living. The particular claim to the art of living that philosophy makes is the promotion of autonomy, and it is on this ground that philosophy intersects education.

REFERENCES

Arendt, H. (1998). *The human condition.* Chicago: University of Chicago Press.

Brown, D.P. (1986). The states of meditation in cross-cultural perspective. In K. Wilber, J. Engler, & D.P. Brown (Eds.), *Transformations of consciousness* (pp. 219–283). Boston: Shambhala Publications, Inc.

Deleuze, G., & Guattari, F. (1991). *What is philosophy?* (H. Tomlinson & G. Burchell, Trans.). New York: Columbia University Press.

Descartes, R. (1962). *Meditations and selections from the principles of philosophy* (J. Veitch, Trans.). LaSalle, IL: The Open Court Publishing Company.

Foucault, M. (1988). Technologies of the self. In L. H. Martin, H. Gutman & P. H. Hutton (Eds.), *Technologies of the self: A seminar with Michel Foucault* (pp. 16–49). Amherst: University of Massachusetts Press.

Goodman, N. (1978). *Ways of worldmaking.* Brighton, UK: The Harvester Press Limited.

Gunaratana, H. (1991). *Mindfulness in plain English.* Boston: Wisdom Publications.

Hadot, P. (1995). *Philosophy as a way of life* (A. Davidson, Ed.; M. Chase, Trans.). Malden, MA: Blackwell Publishers.

Hall, D.L., & Ames, R.T. (1987). *Thinking through Confucius.* New York: State University of New York Press.

Kupperman, J.J. (1999). *Learning from Asian philosophy.* New York: Oxford University Press.

Parkes, G. (1994). *Composing the soul: Reaches of Nietzsche's psychology.* Chicago: University of Chicago Press.

Plato. (1961). *The collected dialogues of Plato* (2nd ed.) (E. Hamilton & H. Cairns, Eds.). Princeton, NJ: Bollingen Series.

Rinpoche, S. (1993). *The Tibetan book of living and dying* (P. Giffney & A. Harvey, Eds.). New York: Harper Collins Publishers.

Saul, J.R. (1995). *The doubter's companion: A dictionary of aggressive common sense.* Toronto: Penguin Books.

Shusterman, R. (1997). *Practicing philosophy: Pragmatism and the philosophical life.* London, UK: Routledge.

Solomon, R.C., & Higgins, K.M. (1996). *A short history of philosophy.* Oxford, UK: Oxford University Press.

Usher, R., & Edwards, R. (1994). *Postmodernism and education.* New York: Routledge. doi:10.4324/9780203425206

Walsh, R. (1992). Can Western philosophers understand Asian philosophies? In J. Ogilvy (Ed.), *Revisioning philosophy* (pp. 281–302). New York: University of New York.

Wei-Ming, T. (1994). Embodying the universe. In R.T. Ames, W. Dissanayake, & T.P. Kasulis (Eds.), *Self as person in Asian theory and practice* (pp. 177–186). New York: State University of New York.

Whitehead, A.N. (1957). *The aims of education.* New York: Macmillan Co.

Wittgenstein, L. (1961). *Tractatus logico-philosophicus* (D.F. Pears & B.F. Guinness, Trans.). London, UK: Routledge & Kegan Paul.

Zehou, L. (2000). *Modernization and the Confucian world.* Presented at Symposium on Cultures in the 21st Century: Conflicts and Convergences. Colorado Springs: Colorado College. Retrieved from http://coloradocollege.edu/Academics/Anniversary/Transcripts/Welcome.htm

NOTES

1 Autonomy has come under serious attack in these postmodern times. See, for example, Robin Usher and Richard Edwards's (1994) *Postmodernism and Education.*

While sympathetic to these postmodern criticisms of autonomy, I maintain that a conception of autonomy that celebrates and promotes the individual capacity to think for oneself and to enact such freedom is an indisputable human good. Thus, I distinguish this modest conception of autonomy from the problematic ontological conception that posits an atomistic view of the individual and privileges the self over the other.

2 I am indebted to James Conroy for sharing his unpublished paper on a study of Hannah Arendt's (1998) distinction between action and behaviour.

3 An acknowledgment is due to Sheila Rawnsley, who, as part of her coursework, surveyed some of the popular programs in use in Lower Mainland schools in British Columbia. She lists programs like Second Step (1992); Focus on Bullying (1999); Positive Echoes (1995); and the Virtues Project (2000).

4 It troubles many educators interested in moral education, including myself, that a number of the moral education programs in use today (some of which fall under the rubric of life skills or social skills education) achieve no better than programming students' behaviour, and even that, with dubious results like students being able to correctly identify moral behaviour on paper and "performing" such behaviour within the instructional setting but not achieving an authentic moral agency that is constant, solid, and ever self-improving.

5 Many have written about this transitional period. Amongst these are Karl Jaspers, Eric Havelock, Morris Berman, and Robert C. Solomon. By *axial*, a major paradigm shift, a turning point, is indicated, and in this case, it is a shift in the modality of human consciousness, in our self-perception of what we are about.

6 If I may dare to say so, the trouble with Plato is that he, being utterly impressed with the mind's capacity to form ideas, reifies ideas and creates an independent and privileged reality just for idea-objects. We should be impressed with the mind but reification should be dispensed with. Thus, I reject Plato's ontology but accept his epistemology. Through the mind that conceptualizes and forms ideas, we have intelligible access to reality, and the result of such access is what we call world-making.

7 Of course, dialogue is not the only practice that facilitates world-making. Other philosophic arts I mention later in this essay—for example, philosophical essay writing and contemplative practices—can be equally useful for this purpose. But in acknowledgment of Socrates and Plato, to whom I attributed the first honour of world-making, I chose dialogue as the exemplary practice.

8 I must note a parallel revolution (of shifting the ground of authority from the external to the internal position) that took place outside Europe and close to two millennia earlier. The personality behind this earlier revolution was Siddhartha Gautama, the historical Buddha, who taught his disciples to put everything that one hears and learns, including religious texts, to the test of one's own experience.

9 This verse is found in Confucius's Analects, 2/4. The words *ming* of *t'ien* translate as "the Mandate of Heaven." In more modern parlance, it means something like knowing one's vocation or calling.

10 Shusterman (1997) is not the only figure in this recent renaissance of philosophy as life practice. Some other authors I am familiar with are Richard Rorty, Stanley Cavell, Pierre Hadot, and Alexander Nehamas. All these authors, in their respective research specialties, address the theme of philosophy as art of living.

11 To this day, the custom of the student going into the teacher's household to live with him and his family is kept for the study of traditional arts. This custom stems from the classical Chinese thought, of which Confucianism is part, that all learning of nontrivial subjects is at the foundation tacit, embodied, and involves the whole personality.

12 Roger Walsh (1992) has a fascinating article in which he argues persuasively that Western philosophers trained exclusively in analytic thinking cannot really understand traditional Eastern philosophies (e.g., Vendanta, Buddhism) because what is involved in the latter is a shift in the paradigm of consciousness for which

a different kind of training is required, such as contemplative arts (e.g., yoga, meditation).

13 Soygal Rinpoche (1993, p. 75) quotes his own teacher Jamyang Khyentze, who explains what Buddhist meditation essentially is: "When the past thought has ceased, and the future thought has not yet risen, isn't there a gap?" Jamyang Khyentze goes on to say that meditation consists of prolonging the gap.

14 Nowadays there is no lack of reputable instructional books on mindfulness practice. One such book I could recommend to the interested reader with no previous knowledge and experience in the practice is by Venerable Gunaratana (1991). For a scholarly scientific account of Buddhist meditation, see Daniel P. Brown (1986).

15 Beyond the basic stage that we are talking about in this essay, the Buddhist mindfulness practice (insight or vipassana meditation) in higher stages is an analytic tool for examining the consciousness and arriving at certain psychological "truths" about consciousness (for example, different forms of consciousness, the process of mental construction), as well as certain "truths" about phenomenal existence (impermanence, suffering, egolessness).

4

The Place of Ideals in Teaching

David T. Hansen *

*This chapter has been reprinted from Hansen, David T. (2001)
The place of ideals in teaching. In Lynda Stone (Ed.), *Philosophy of Education*
(pp. 42–50). Urbana, IL: Philosophy of Education Society. Reprinted by
permission of the Philosophy of Education Society.

Do ideals and idealism have a role to play in teaching? Two quick
answers come to mind. The first is that they have no place, or at
most a very limited place. According to this line of thinking, teaching
is a well-defined occupation with well-defined goals. Our Romantic
impulses may tell us otherwise. They may lead us to envision teachers
as artists and as transformers of the human spirit. However, a critic
might argue, teaching is not an artistic endeavour because teachers
are not artists, save from the point of view of method and even then
only in a metaphorical sense. Unlike painters at their easels, teachers
cannot create whatever they wish in the classroom. They are public

servants beholden to the public to get a particular job done. Idealism is warranted as a source of motivation, but teachers' ideals had better not take them away from the job itself. According to this point of view, the only ideal teachers should hold is, ideally, that of fulfilling their publicly defined obligations in a responsible and effective manner.

The second answer advances the opposite position. Teachers must have ideals, and their ideals must reach beyond societal expectations. According to this argument, teachers are not bureaucratic functionaries whose only charge is to pass on to the young whatever knowledge and skills the powers-that-be have sanctioned. Teachers do play an important role in socializing students into expected custom and practice. But as teachers, rather than as mere socializers, they also help equip students to think for themselves, to conceive their own ideals and hopes, and to prepare themselves for the task of making tomorrow's world into something other than a tired copy of today's.

Both answers contain truth. Taken as they are, however, the responses polarize conservative and progressive aspects of teaching that could, in my view, be brought into a working (if not always harmonious) accord. I propose to make a start toward picturing such an accord by identifying some ambiguities and problems associated with ideals. I will argue that ideals figure importantly in teaching, but they are ideals of character or personhood as much as they are ideals of educational purpose.

The Promise and Perils of Ideals

Ideals point to territory beyond the familiar, the known, the previously attainable. They embody possibilities the human spirit generates. Even though they may be out of reach, ideals can provide a source of guidance and courage. A teacher whose ideal it is for all students to learn, and to enjoy learning, may not need a tap on her shoulder to remind her of how challenging, or perhaps impossible, the ideal is to realize. Nonetheless, the teacher relies upon the ideal to strengthen and to broaden her pedagogical efforts. The ideal helps the teacher identify short-term goals and aims. It provides a wellspring, or source of inspiration, for choosing specific instructional activities and curricular materials—those that will help her, in her view, move closer toward realizing the ideal of universal student learning in her classroom.

However, some critics would still argue that ideals should have only a limited place in the practice of teaching (if not in other practices, as well). They emphasize two concerns: the power of ideals to develop a momentum of their own, and their propensity to lead people to substitute hypothetical goals for real possibilities.

For critics in this camp, the fact that ideals can propel people to action is the very reason to be cautious in how we handle and respond to them. Ideals can inspire people on the basis of passion rather than of careful foresight. The emotion and energy ideals trigger can substitute for a prudent but determined desire to improve conditions. According to this argument, people do not need to be inspired to act beneficently, as if they were bulls in need of a red flag. Instead, human beings need and deserve an education in thoughtfulness. Ideals grow abundantly and easily—it is not difficult to latch onto one, critics might point out—but thought requires nurturance, care, patience, and commitment. Thought helps us differentiate worthy ideals that enhance the human condition from those that lead to harm. History shows what can happen if an ideal embodies injustice in its very form and content. People have been "idealistic" or have cited ideals to excuse harmful treatment of others. Consequently, critics argue, ideals should not be uncaged without prior thought. Otherwise, they might operate uncritically upon the human mind and imagination.

This concern gives rise to a second worry about ideals. People can end up treating ideals as more important than actual human beings. In other words, people might come to prefer the ideal to the real. The ideal is pure, distinct, unadulterated, uncompromised, and untainted. The real is complex, frustrating, unpredictable, opaque, overwhelming in its human variety. As a response, people may privilege the ideal rather than keeping their vision clear to appreciate the needs, the circumstances, and the hopes of others. Eventually, they come to see only the ideal, with potentially harmful results. In a discussion of the virtues and vices of various political ideals and systems, Maurice Merleau-Ponty (1969) shows how people can end up defending the ideal of freedom more than they do actual free men and women. They uphold an ideology—a term closely related to an ideal—and sing its praises rather than seek harmonious, just relations with their fellow human beings. George Eliot (1874/1985) reminds us that "[t]here is no general doctrine which is not capable of eating out our morality if unchecked by the deep-seated habit of direct fellow-feeling with individual fellow-men" (p. 668). She implies that ideals can isolate and alienate people from others without their even being aware of the cause.

Critics could argue that the history of education provides abundant examples to bear out their worries. They might spotlight reformist ideals that have generated new programs, plans, and structures for teaching. The reformers tout the new programs as breakthroughs. Many regard the ideals behind them as marvellous, inspiring, even universally applicable. However, argue the critics, the fact that the programs are based in ideals, and in the closely related reformist zeal to change things, produces harmful consequences. In the absence of sober, careful analysis, the ideals and associated programs may be too narrowly conceived and not reflect an adequate study of the many factors at play in any specific attempt to improve education.

Lisa Delpit (1995), for example, suggests that a liberal or democratic education centred on student decision making, initiative, and freedom of expression is splendid—as an ideal. She contends, however, that the ideal has problematic results for some urban black children. She argues that many such children are already imaginative and adept at self-expression. However, many lack skills of reading, writing, numerating, and more, which in Delpit's view should be given sustained attention since these skills are required for access to sources of opportunity and power, access that some proponents of the ideal perhaps inadvertently take for granted. Delpit does not commend a minimalist back-to-the-basics curriculum, which has at times been the staple educational fare for children of the poor. Rather, I read her as calling for careful consideration of local contexts, circumstances, and communities, which she implies can temper otherwise admirable ideals.

Delpit's claims have generated controversy and debate. As she acknowledges, there is evidence that minority youth in the American inner city can learn foundational skills while also being challenged with the most liberal, project- or discussion-oriented instructional approaches.[1] But the issue of concern here is not the virtue of one pedagogical orientation as compared with another. Critics of ideals would draw from Delpit's work, and from that of others who have called for a second look at various reforms, the lesson that ideals may sometimes lead people to overlook vital human concerns.

Michael Oakeshott (1991) writes that ideals can have a valuable place in individual lives, spurring people to act better or to strive harder in developing themselves than they otherwise might. However, he argues, ideals can lead to harm when carried uncritically to a social and political level. In some cases, people may wield ideals as if they were weapons, using them to combat the opposition and to mask the exercise of their power and ambition. In other contexts, people may use them to legitimate any number of social and political reforms, in which those who are to be reformed often have little say. "Every moral ideal," Oakeshott cautions,[2] "is potentially an obsession" (p. 476). He suggests that the tragedy of such ideals is that those who act upon them often mean well; they are not operating on the basis of malevolent impulse. But ideals become like the proverbial log in their eye, blinding them to the human realities that their ideals simply pass over.

Inhabitable Ideals in Teaching

Our discussion seems to have reached an impasse. From one point of view, ideals are problematic. To judge from the historical record, they appear to have caused as much harm as good in human affairs. From another point of view, individuals and societies alike seem to need ideals to motivate and guide their actions. They cannot live without ideals, without images of a better world.

Christine Korsgaard (1996) suggests that such images are built into our human fabric. She speaks of "ideas" we develop about what could be different, with that term rooted (as I interpret it) in a Kantian use of the German word *Idee*, meaning a picture or image that is generated by reason infused with hope. "It is the most striking fact about human life," she writes,

> that we have values. We think of ways that things could be better, more perfect, and so of course different, than they are; and of ways that we ourselves could be better, more perfect, and so of course different, than we are. Why should this be so? Where do we get these ideas that outstrip the world we experience and seem to call it into question, to render judgment on it, to say that it does not measure up, that it is not what it ought to be? Clearly we do not get them from experience, at least not by any simple route. And it is puzzling too that these ideas of a world different from our own call out to us, telling us that things should be like them rather than the way they are, and that we should make them so. (p. 1)

According to this perspective, ideals or, if you will, images of goodness, seem to spring upon us. They emerge from our very nature as social beings dwelling in more or less imperfect association with others. Nobody can fail to observe societal and individual shortcomings. But nobody can deny, Korsgaard argues, that human beings, time and again, have conceived ideals of a better world and have acted upon them to bring us closer to, rather than farther from, such a world.

Recent research on teaching suggests that many teachers have ideals and take them seriously as sources of moral and intellectual guidance.[3] Many teachers talk and act as if it would be impossible to teach without them. Their ideals appear to vary. For some, the ideal boils down to keeping in mind an image of a growing, educated person. For others, the ideal pinpoints the personal relationship between teacher and student, a relationship perceived as crucial to establishing an environment in which the student can learn and flourish. Some teachers' ideals centre on notions of human dignity and social justice. Others are animated by the desire to produce caring, compassionate people. For still others, the ideal pivots around a conception of their discipline and of instructional method, and of implementing that conception as best as possible in the school and classroom. According to the research literature, these ideals motivate, guide, strengthen, and encourage teachers to perform their best, in both the short and the long run.

Teachers' testimony suggests that ideals do not automatically blind persons to the real. On the contrary, the perspectives revealed in the literature indicate that, at least for some teachers, their ideals derive *from* paying attention to the real. Their ideals are securely moored to their understanding and knowledge of students and of the promise of education. Posed differently, their ideals take form as they teach, as they come to grips with the terms of the practice and with what it means to be responsible for educating the young. In such cases idealism and respect for reality reinforce one another. The teachers' respect for reality disciplines their idealism by preventing it from flattening out the complexity of teaching and learning and from overlooking real constraints and real needs. Their ideals prevent their sense of reality from unilaterally dampening their hope and vision.

Harriet Cuffaro (1995) describes ideals not as end points but as sources of insight. She writes,

> The reality of society—the reality of exclusion, inequity, repression, violence, and despair—is far from the ideal. Yet, the ideal is there not as unattainable perfection but to inform the present, to underline what we must attend to, and to help in locating what obstructs the realization of the ideal. An ideal locates the territory of interest and concern, points to desired characteristics and qualities of the landscape, and indicates those features that obstruct the growth of the person and of society. The informing of the real by the ideal focuses the work to be done to lessen the distance between the two. (p. 100)

We might say that in the very best educational practice, the real and the ideal mutually inform one another. The teacher strives to establish an environment in which students can learn while also keeping in view, or letting herself be guided by, images of the kind of flourishing adults students can become. She assists a student struggling with reading while holding onto an image of the student as a successful reader; that image strengthens her resolve and fuels her energy. Over the course of a school year, her idealism propels her to undertake steps to lessen the distance between the student's current and future status as a reader. In the long run, the teacher's ideal-in-practice boosts and enriches the student's life chances, and, in turn, those of the other people whom the student might one day be in a position to help and to serve. The student might attain such a position only because, long ago and with the help of a teacher, he or she learned how to become a reader.

Teacher educators might interject, perhaps reluctantly and unhappily, that the argument thus far has posed things backwards. In so doing, they would return us to some of the concerns about ideals that I elaborated previously. Teacher educators might point out that for many persons new to teaching, it is not, metaphorically speaking, reality first and ideals second. Rather, many new candidates enter their professional development programs fired by ideals, in many cases well before they have obtained a sense of the reality of teaching in today's schools and classrooms. To be sure, some candidates take to the work quickly and successfully. They may have worked with young people before, or they may simply be people who embody idealism wedded to respect for reality. However, teacher educators emphasize that, for many candidates, ideals constitute a mixed blessing. They fuel candidates' enthusiasm, but they also blind them to pedagogical realities. As a result, when candidates encounter the messiness of working in schools, some feel they have run into a brick wall. In spiritual as much as in practical terms, they do not know how to respond to a mentor teacher who does not share their ideals, to students who do not love learning like they do, to school schedules that make them feel like Charlie Chaplin on the assembly line, and more. In some cases, teacher candidates succumb to the inevitable disappointment that follows in the wake of punctured ideals. Some leave their programs or abandon teaching after a brief stint. Others narrow and harden their sensibilities and just try to get through. They may remain in teaching, but they do so with a cynical or even callous state of mind.

Teacher educators familiar with this portrait might also add another twist to the concerns I discussed previously about the power of ideals to develop their own momentum and to swamp respect for reality. Teacher educators could tell us about the problems and the pain that ensue from their own ideals as teacher educators. They would have in mind not the sometimes innocent ideals of new candidates referred to above, which might, in fact, be focused and matured through a good preparation program and thoughtful classroom experience. Rather, they would caution their fellow teacher educators about rooting out candidates' own ideals and putting in their place ideals those educators themselves prefer. Unless teacher educators undertake a profoundly sensitive and responsible job of instilling such ideals, they may compromise their graduates' subsequent teaching. Graduates might enter the field well versed in a particular ideology but inadequately prepared for the difficult moral and intellectual task of letting ideals and human realities mutually inform one another.

Tenacious Humility: An Ideal of Personhood

The place of ideals in teaching remains ambiguous and uncertain. However, the analysis undertaken thus far does not rule out the possibility that good teaching can be based on ideals of *some* kind. Without ideals of human flourishing, the work is reduced to mere socialization, or to a functionalist fulfillment of externally dictated ends. I believe we can say that, at least in many cases, good teaching reflects an appreciation, on the part of the teacher, for both large and indefinable human possibilities, and for ever-present constraints. This posture does not imply being either stoic or zealous. It need not generate resignation to current pressures to teach in a particular way nor an arrogant claim that one occupies the moral high ground to go it alone.

Tenacious humility serves as an apt descriptor for this standpoint. Tenacity implies staying the course, not giving up on students or on oneself. Tenacity involves fostering and extending one's sense of agency as teacher. It means expanding and deepening one's person, one's conduct, and one's moral and intellectual sensibility. Humility is also an active rather than passive quality. For many people, or so it seems, humility does not come naturally. It has to be worked at, developed, and refined. For a teacher, humility entails a refusal to treat students as less worthy of being heard than the teacher him- or herself. It means retaining a sense of students' as well as one's own humanity. Humility attests to a grasp on the reality of human differences, institutional constraints, and personal limitations. Tenacity, on the other hand, compels the teacher not to treat those differences, constraints, and limitations as hardened and unchanging.

Tenacious humility helps teachers hold at bay the tempting lure of ideals, theories, and ideologies that purport to "explain" schools and students. Those standpoints can release them from having to deal with complexity and from having to think about, rather than to label, whatever does not fit their outlook. Posed differently, tenacious humility suggests that there are ideals that reach beyond the vise of any particular hard-and-fast cluster of beliefs. These are ideals of character or personhood. As such an ideal, tenacious humility can motivate a person not to rest on the oars of unexamined belief and expectation. It can fuel a person's willingness to be self-critical. That disposition becomes crucial if an ideology is understood to be a system of ideals and views that is closed to further questioning (Brann, 1979). As John Wilson (1998) cautions, I may be dedicated to an ideal or ideology, but "I may not seriously monitor it in the light of reason. The ideology is something I *have*, a kind of personal possession or insurance policy; whereas the monitoring is something that I *do*, not which I *own*" (p. 145). Part of being tenaciously humble is not falling back upon an idealized or ideological "possession" when pressed to listen, think, question, reconsider, re-examine.

The project of becoming tenaciously humble does not render a person into a hardened or fixed character. Rather, it illuminates how character or personhood can genuinely emerge and grow, even in the face of any number of societal, cultural, familial, or psychological constraints and forces. Like all ideals, tenacious humility is not attainable in any final or penultimate sense. In metaphorical terms, it is always receding, always just over the horizon no matter how much one strives to realize it in practice. Nonetheless, as an ideal it can, as Cuffaro puts it, "inform" the present. It can position a teacher to think, feel, and work in imaginative ways he or she might otherwise not even realize are possible.

Tenacious humility operates as what Dorothy Emmet (1994) calls a "regulative ideal," a concept she borrows from Kant but which she extends. According to Emmet, a regulative ideal helps set a direction for conduct or for a given practice. It steers persons away from settling for half-measures or surrogates. While a regulative ideal is not realizable "in particular instances," Emmet writes, "it can help set a standard for thought and action" (p. 2). She clarifies the two central terms: the "ideal aspect" gives an orientation to an endeavour or mode of conduct, while the "regulative aspect" guides the actual approach (p. 9). In other words, a regulative ideal describes both a destination and how to conduct oneself in striving to reach it. A regulative ideal is a guide-in-practice. Moreover, it is dynamic. "The ideal is not sufficiently specific to define the final objective," Emmet claims, "but we can know enough about it in general to indicate a progression" (p. 9). This is accomplished, she points out, by learning more and more about the nature of the ideal as one moves toward it.

For teachers the ideal aspect of tenacious humility gives an orientation to their thought and imagination, while the regulative aspect helps guide their concrete approach in the classroom. The ideal aspect, captured in the root terms tenacity and humility, helps them ponder the persons and teachers they are becoming. That same aspect merges with a regulative dimension, as the ideal helps them to plan for and to participate in classroom life in attentive, responsive ways that support students' and their own growth. Teachers do not need a fixed image of tenacious humility, or a preset plan of action for realizing it in practice. How could they, one might ask, when understanding the nature and meaning of the ideal takes time and experience (and seems always to leave many questions unanswered)? How could teachers spell out an airtight protocol for self-development when they do not know how each group of new students will respond to their curriculum and to each other? Tenacious humility emerges through everyday conduct in teaching. Teachers can learn more and more about the nature of the ideal, and how to bring it into being, as they engage the terms of the practice.[4]

Conclusion: Ideals and the Practice of Teaching

Many serious-minded teachers appear to guide their work by ideals such as fuelling societal betterment, producing caring persons, and equipping students for a good life. These are big, broad ideals, familiar and, one could argue, compelling. But the critics who worry about "big" ideals help us appreciate the dangers of heeding them unchecked by a sense of reality and responsibility. Ideals can become ideological or doctrinaire and can lead teachers away from their educational obligations and cause them to treat their students, and perhaps themselves, as a means to an end. Moreover, a purely personal ideal may mirror all the dangers of a purely impersonal ideology. An ideal that is subjectively sufficient may be wanting in terms of the objective or nondiscretionary demands of the practice of teaching, such as the need to teach rather than to intimidate, indoctrinate, or coerce students.[5]

Tenacious humility describes an ideal disposition, a moral ideal of character or personhood. Its pursuit constitutes a quest to become a better person and teacher. This project of self-improvement differs from self-absorption. Eliot reminds us of the dangers of the latter: "Will not a tiny speck very close to our vision blot out the glory of the world, and leave only a margin by which we see the blot? I know no speck so troublesome as self" (p. 456). Striving to be tenaciously humble positions teachers to be outward rather than merely inward looking. The quest can motivate them to see students for who they are, to listen and question and think with them rather than see them solely through the lens or the terms of a big ideal. This orientation will not prevent teachers from making mistakes and misjudgments, but it will enable them to learn and to stay the course. Tenacious humility becomes a durable humanizing ideal that can guide both big ideals and inner reflection, keeping them in the service of teaching and learning.

REFERENCES

Ben-Peretz, M. (1995). *Learning from experience: Memory and the teacher's account of teaching.* Albany, NY: State University of New York Press.

Berlin, I. (1992). *The crooked timber of humanity: Chapters in the history of ideas.* New York: Vintage Books.

Brann, E.T.H. (1979). *Paradoxes of education in a republic.* Chicago: University of Chicago Press.

Cuffaro, H.K. (1995). *Experimenting with the world: John Dewey and the early childhood classroom.* New York: Teachers College Press.

Delpit, L. (1995). *Other people's children: Cultural conflict in the classroom.* New York: The New Press.

Eliot, G. (1985). *Middlemarch.* Harmondsworth, UK: Penguin Books. (Original work published 1874)

Emmet, D. (1994). *The role of the unrealisable: A study in regulative ideals.* New York: St. Martin's Press.

Foster, M. (1997). *Black teachers on teaching.* New York: The New Press.

Hansen, D.T. (1995). *The call to teach.* New York: Teachers College Press.

Hansen, D.T. (1998). The moral is in the practice. *Teaching and Teacher Education, 14*(6), 643–655. doi:10.1016/S0742-051X(98)00014-6

Hansen, D.T. (2001). *Exploring the moral heart of teaching: Toward a teacher's creed.* New York: Teachers College Press.

Haroutunian-Gordon, S. (1991). *Turning the soul: Teaching through conversation in the high school.* Chicago: University of Chicago Press.

Henry, A. (1998). *Taking back control: African Canadian women teachers' lives and practices.* Albany, NY: State University of New York Press.

Hostetler, K. (1997). *Ethical judgment in teaching.* Boston: Allyn and Bacon.

Johnson, S.M. (1990). *Teachers at work: Achieving success in our schools.* New York: Basic Books.

Korsgaard, C. (1996). *The sources of normativity.* Cambridge, UK: Cambridge University Press. doi:10.1017/CBO9780511554476

Ladson-Billings, G. (1994). *The dreamkeepers: Successful teachers of African American children.* San Francisco: Jossey-Bass.

Merleau-Ponty, M. (1969). *Humanism and terror: An essay on the communist problem* (J. O'Neill, Trans.). Boston: Beacon Press.

Oakeshott, M. (1991). *Rationalism in politics and other essays.* Indianapolis: Liberty Press.

Wilson, J. (1998). Seriousness and the foundations of education. *Educational Theory, 48*(2), 143–153. doi:10.1111/j.1741-5446.1998.00143.x

NOTES

1 See Sophie Haroutunian-Gordon (1991), Annette Henry (1998), and Gloria Ladson-Billings (1994).

2 For a comparable analysis, see Isaiah Berlin (1992).

3 See, for example, Miriam Ben-Peretz (1995), Michele Foster (1997), David T. Hansen (1995), and Susan M. Johnson (1990).

4 I have tried to characterize the terms of the practice in Hansen (1998) and Hansen (2001).

5 Karl Hostetler (1997) provides a useful example of the problems that can arise when a teacher's personal ideals seem to interfere with carrying out the tasks that accompany the role.

Part II: Classroom Discussions and Controversial Issues

This section of the volume focuses on several issues in classroom teaching that create uncertainty for the teacher about what course of action is most appropriate, and a thoughtful response involves recognizing the nature and significance of the problem and how it relates to one's goals in teaching. Every teacher will encounter such situations, and how they are to be addressed will depend very much on the particular circumstances of one's own teaching context. Philosophical reflection can be of great value in helping us to gain insight into the central concepts in question and to achieve a better understanding of the principles and ideals that we draw on to guide our decisions.

Andrea English focuses attention on the manner in which teachers listen, especially at those moments when it becomes clear that the students are confused in a way that John Dewey considers essential to their learning. Dewey, as English reminds us, proposed an educational ideal of learning as active inquiry, an ideal that remains influential today, where students confront and work on genuine problems. This approach to learning inevitably means that students will experience puzzlement and uncertainty at certain points, prompting unexpected comments and questions that call on the teacher to listen and respond in such a way that the process of inquiry can continue. English identifies and develops a conception of *educative listening* that she believes should characterize the work of any genuinely reflective teacher in such circumstances. Her essay explores several important questions: What does it mean in practice for teachers to engage in educative listening? What attitudes characterize the teacher who listens in this way? How does such listening help to foster student learning? How does educative listening differ from other ways in which teachers listen? English concludes by outlining certain practical ways in which philosophy of education classes can help cultivate educative listening in student teachers.

How is it that classroom discussions of ethical issues so often come to a halt before they have had an opportunity to develop into a useful exchange of ideas? Douglas Simpson and William Hull highlight various kinds of remarks that serve to close down such discussions, and they remind us that closure sometimes results from apparently innocent questions that actually have very negative consequences. Their detailed account of such attempts to inhibit discussion will be extremely helpful to classroom teachers who will be better prepared to recognize them when they occur and to look for ways in which they can be turned to advantage. The many examples offered show how comments and questions can seek to minimize personal responsibility, imply that a certain point of view is unassailable, or take the form of an attack on the speaker rather than a critique of his or her argument. Are teachers aware that they can slip into using such tactics themselves and thereby make it less likely that their educational aims will be realized? In view of the difficulties involved, is there a temptation for teachers and students alike to simply avoid discussing ethical issues? Simpson and Hull urge teacher educators to take these problems seriously and seek to develop in student teachers the skills and attitudes that will serve them well in facing ethical issues in the classroom.

Claudia Ruitenberg focuses on the problem of relativism concerning moral beliefs that reflects, she argues, a failure to distinguish between preferences and judgments and a lack of clarity about ethical pluralism. Disagreement about ethical issues, she believes, should lead to a careful consideration of the reasons that we and other people have for our different views, but relativism rules this out by insisting that "we are all entitled to our own opinion" and there the matter ends. If this attitude dominates classroom discussions, Ruitenberg fears that schools will not play their part in preparing students for a more public world of ideas where a wide range of moral views can be found; students will miss out on an opportunity to explore moral views that conflict with their own and to appreciate the importance of justifying moral judgments. Since moral education inevitably suffers when relativism disrupts attempts at open-minded inquiry about values, several issues merit close attention: What can teachers do to encourage students to examine their own moral views and to engage in a serious conversation with others about ethical issues? How should teachers respond in situations where a comment made in class is such that it would not be appropriate to simply "agree to disagree"? Are teachers themselves adequately prepared to help students distinguish between pluralism and relativism?

Michelle Forrest explores the challenging case of controversial issues that are *sensitive* in that the classroom discussion itself may prove hurtful to some students whose own personal experiences are closely, or even directly, connected to the issue in question. Given the sensitive nature of the issue, the teacher is faced with a difficult choice where careful and responsible judgment is called for. As Forrest makes clear, to discuss the issue at all is to risk causing distress to those students whose lives have been affected by it; to avoid the discussion is to leave important matters unexamined with potentially harmful consequences, such as students thinking that the issue does not warrant consideration. Forrest draws the reader into an examination of several complex questions that have a close bearing on our teaching practices. How are we to teach in a genuinely caring manner? What is it to be ethically attentive in our teaching? What does it mean to teach in a truly critical spirit? Are there certain qualities or virtues that would serve teachers well when they discuss controversial issues that involve sensitive matters with their students? How are we to achieve a critical perspective on our own attempts as teachers to engage in, and foster, critical discussion of sensitive issues?

Teachers sometimes face pressure from the community to include (or exclude) certain topics. Eugenie Scott examines the ongoing attempts by various groups to show that the theory of evolution is fundamentally flawed, and she focuses on the "Teach the Controversy" slogan that is associated with the Discovery Institute and the idea of "intelligent design." Educational slogans, as Israel Scheffler (1960) notes, "provide rallying symbols of the key ideas and attitudes of educational movements" (p. 36), and as such they deserve careful attention and analysis. At first glance, the "Teach the Controversy" slogan might seem to reflect the important educational aim of students at school approaching controversial material in an open-minded way and coming to their own conclusions as a result of critical reflection. There are, as Scott makes clear, many controversial issues within the theory of evolution, as there are in every scientific field, but the intent of the slogan, she contends, is to insinuate the mistaken view that scientists regard the theory itself as controversial. This, Scott concludes, can only be miseducative. Several questions arise for teachers to ponder: How do we teach students to recognize what counts as a controversial issue in science? Should creationism and related topics be included in the science curriculum? How do we exclude what we view as pseudoscience without inviting the accusation that our own position is dogmatic?

Philosophy of education brings to light difficulties and problems in the context of teaching that we might never think about or notice as we go about our everyday tasks. As a result, where once we might have proceeded without any qualms, we find ourselves puzzled about what we should say or do in a certain situation. Although we may have more doubts and questions as a result of philosophical reflection, it is important to remember that philosophy still has much to offer and leaves us in a stronger position than we were before. How is this possible? Bertrand Russell (1973) helps to make this clear: "Philosophy, though unable to tell us with certainty what is the true answer to the doubts which it raises, is able to suggest many possibilities which enlarge our thoughts and free them from the tyranny of custom" (p. 91). In our professional capacity as teachers, we have the responsibility to decide from the many possibilities that result from our inquiries and analysis of the context in which we work, rather than expect philosophy to provide answers that are suitable for every situation.

REFERENCES

Russell, B. (1973). *The problems of philosophy.* Oxford: Oxford University Press.
Scheffler, I. (1960). *The language of education.* Springfield, IL: Charles C. Thomas.

5

Listening as a Teacher

Educative Listening, Interruptions, and Reflective Practice

*Andrea R. English**

If we make the "draft character" of good preparation clear enough to ourselves—for any planning of instruction can be only provisionally valid—then it is quite consistent to rate the instructional planning process highly, while at the same time recognizing that, in the end, each and every lesson holds in store a myriad of unforeseeable possibilities and that the

> openness of teachers' minds to new situations, impulses, and
> the difficulties arising from the moment is a criterion of their
> pedagogical competence.
> —Wolfgang Klafki (1958, p. 143)

The author Grace Paley (1994) remarks that it is useful for writers to have two ears, "one for literature, and one for home" (p. x). A similar remark can be made about teachers. Teachers need two ears, one for teaching, and one for—well, everything else. The ear of the teacher presents itself when it is focused on cultivating learning. To say that listening is part of teaching is neither a surprising nor controversial statement. Most practicing teachers might say they do not have much of a choice but to listen in the varied situations that comprise their job. I will not attempt to discuss all the situations that arise in teaching practice. Rather, I would like to define the concept of educative listening as distinct from listening in nonteaching situations and to make clear the difference between the listening of the teacher and the listening of the student.

Listening as a topic of educational philosophy has been largely overlooked until recently.[1] In teaching, listening plays a vital role in helping the teacher gauge and understand the learning process of students. However, the educative aspect of listening can be taken for granted, not only by educational theorists but by practicing teachers themselves. This is partly because experienced teachers tend to forget the learning process that went into figuring out how to skillfully and tactfully deal with the students' unexpected questions or unforeseeable responses. While the novice teacher may still consider unexpected responses as interruptions in their instruction, experienced teachers come to see these as part of the normal course of teaching, taking a (perhaps resigned) view of "expect the unexpected."

But such a view disguises the educative meaning of interruptions for all teachers. Interruptions in a teacher's listening, which I define as any unexpected verbal response from a student to the material presented—for example, a challenging viewpoint, a difficult question, or a confusing reply—open up unforeseeable possibilities for cultivating learning. Through listening, teachers can become open to difference and otherness that arises in the teacher-learner relation.

In this inquiry, I develop the meaning of educative listening as a mode of listening to interruptions in a way that promotes students' thinking and learning. To begin, I draw upon Dewey (1900/2008) to examine the connections between listening and learning in teacher-student interaction. In the second section, I explicate the implications of Dewey's theory of learning for a theory of listening in reflective teaching. Here I contend that reflective teaching entails educative listening. In the final section, I inquire into how teacher education can productively address the connections between learning to listen and learning to teach reflectively.

Dewey on Listening in the Teacher-Learner Relation

On the topic of teacher-student interaction, in *Democracy and Education*, Dewey (1916/2008) writes, "the teacher is a learner and, without knowing it, the learner a teacher" (p. 167). While agreeing with Dewey's statement, I argue this view of the teacher presupposes a certain understanding of teaching as a reflective practice, a notion that itself presupposes a certain understanding of how teachers listen. In other words, teachers who allow themselves to learn from their students are ones who listen to their students in a specific way.

To draw out the connections between listening and reflective teaching, we can first examine the role of listening in Dewey's (1900/2008) early critique of the traditional model of instruction in *The School and Society*. Dewey's (1900/2008) critique centres on defining the problems with the kind of teachers who view their job as imparting information for students to take in passively and recite back accurately when called upon (p. 21f.; see also Dewey, 1916/2008). For Dewey, there is a direct connection between listening and learning that is assumed on this model of teaching: the student is expected to listen such that listening is nearly equated with learning. The traditional classroom setting with rows of desks and chairs facing forward is for Dewey symbolic of the type of learning that is based in passive listening to what one hears or reads and absorbing a series of prepackaged truths determined to be important and worthwhile by the school board and teacher (Dewey, 1900/2008, p. 21f.). "Listening" on this model means obeying and passively accepting the judgments of others, judgments concerning both the worthwhile content of instruction and also concerning what is deemed right and wrong in both epistemological and moral terms.

In the discussion that follows, I will refer to this type of teacher as the normative teacher in order to demonstrate how such teachers can be distinguished from reflective teachers. The *normative teacher* views learning as a standardized process leading to standardized forms of knowledge and skills. Dewey's assault on this traditional method of teaching, though political and moral in its implications, is grounded in a theory of learning. Dewey points out that what results from this type of normative teaching via the uniformity of curriculum and teaching methods is not the student's learning but the "dependency of [his] mind upon another" (Dewey, 1900/2008, p. 47f; see also Dewey, 1916/2008, p. 166f). In this way, the individual may be trained to repeat what he is told, but he will not truly learn in the sense of knowing how to evaluate the truth of what he is told, under what conditions it may be true, or why it is necessary or important.

On Dewey's notion of learning, learning is an individual process. People do not learn in a standardized way, and teaching processes that seek to mould learners so they conform to oversimplified standards fail to see what is necessarily individual about every learning process. Since Dewey's writings, developments in understanding difference in education surrounding questions of race, gender, or religion and policies of inclusion make it seem that teachers and other educators have made progress in recognizing the individuality and uniqueness of each learner. While recognition of these differences is important and vital in a democratic learning community, if we start from these categorizations to address difference in education, then there can be a tendency for teachers to categorize an individual before or independent of his or her learning process. The very prejudices sought to be redressed instead can be reinforced, an inversion of the initial intention. Rather than starting from external factors that characterize the individual, in his learning theory, Dewey is interested in the individualization of the learner that arises from within the personal learning process itself.[2]

To address the difference and otherness of learners that arise in their individual processes of transformation, Dewey (1916/2008) develops the notion of learning as discovery. *Learning as discovery* seems to place emphasis on the active side of learning, in contrast to the passive model of learning he opposes. However, it would be a misconception only to understand his view as promoting the child's self-activity, or simply "learning by doing," and thereby to overlook the passive component to his idea of learning. "Discovery" implies not only finding something that is new and different but also the "undergoing" and "suffering" that accompanies any encounter with the unfamiliar and unexpected (compare Dewey, 1916/2008, p. 147f.) Individuals do not learn when they are given predigested problems, or as Dewey calls them "ready-made problems" (see e.g. Dewey 1916/2008); rather, they learn when they find out what is difficult, confusing, or strange for them and inquire into what exactly is obstructing thought or action. Dewey (1916/2008) seeks to point out that by recognizing that learning processes have the quality of a search to understand new and unfamiliar ideas or subject matter, we can recognize that learning processes necessarily involve a struggle: "Only by wrestling with the conditions of the problem at first hand, seeking and finding his own way out, does [the child] think. ... If he cannot devise his own solution ... and devise his own way out, he will not learn, not even if he can recite some correct answer with one hundred percent accuracy" (p. 167). For Dewey, all learning processes are coupled with this type of struggle, be it that of a child learning to read, a scientist making a new discovery in a lab, an artist working with new materials, or a teacher gaining new insight into his or her practice. This struggle, in which learners seek their own way out of perplexing situations, points to the discontinuity of learning. (Learning does not occur as a smooth transition from ignorance to knowledge but rather entails breaks, gaps, and disruptions that occur when we encounter something unexpected and new; these interruptions in our experience are constitutive of learning.)

Dewey's idea that learning is necessarily accompanied by a struggle is not a new idea. Rather, this idea of learning can be traced back through the traditions of educational philosophy. For example, in Plato's *Meno*, Plato describes the learning slave boy who attempts to answer Socrates's questions as disillusioned and perplexed about his own knowledge (Plato, 380 BCE/1997). Through this process, the boy eventually is led to proclaim that he does not know. This initial admission of ignorance is a precondition for the boy's search for knowledge. Modern educational theory has also emphasized various forms of negative experience[3] in aesthetic, cognitive, and moral learning and experience. In *Émile*, Jean-Jacques Rousseau emphasizes that children necessarily experience perplexity and disillusionment in developing sense perception (Rousseau, 1762/1979). German philosopher Johann Friedrich Herbart (1806/1902) placed particular significance on the indispensability of the learner's struggle in the realm of moral learning.

For Dewey, the experience of struggle as an experience of perplexity, frustration, or confusion is central to all realms of learning. Experiences such as frustration and doubt arise when our seemingly continuous stream of experience is *interrupted* due to our encounter with something new, unfamiliar, and thereby unexpected. Since learning necessarily involves movement toward the unfamiliar, all learning involves interruption when we experience something unanticipated that throws us off course. This experience of interruption is itself prereflective, but it can be transformed into a reflective aspect of experience if it is consciously and thoughtfully addressed and not ignored. In order for this transformation to take place, we first must recognize the interruption as pointing to a negativity of experience that is something beyond the limits of our present knowledge and ability. Only then can we begin to ask ourselves, what happened? What went wrong? What might I need to change?

Dewey pulls apart this moment of perplexity in learning, demonstrating it as a productive and educative space of experience in which individuals are held in suspense; they find themselves in the in-between of learning and can begin to inquire into and reflect upon themselves and the situation in which they are stuck. Reflection is a specific aspect of this process of inquiry that is important for both teachers and learners. It must be noted, however, that not all forms of thought qualify as reflection. In this context, *reflection* should be understood as the inquiring form of thinking that kicks in when we find ourselves in a state of doubt or difficulty, when we begin to understand that something went wrong even if we do not know exactly what it was. Finding a way out of this difficulty does not mean ignoring it; rather, it means directly addressing the discontinuity in our experience and searching for what is needed to "resolve the doubt, settle and dispose of the perplexity" (Dewey 1933/2008, p. 121). Dewey views reflection as a means of dealing with the perplexities, difficulties, and frustrations that are constitutive of all learning processes. When reflection sets out to explain interruptions in our experience, it seeks to transform our modes of simply directly experiencing the world into processes of learning about the world and ourselves.

The moment of interruption in a learner's experience has educative meaning for the teacher. When a learner's experience is interrupted by stumbling upon something he does not understand, such as a word in a story he is reading, or something he is unable to do, such as drawing a horse in an art class, the teacher's experience is also interrupted. The learner's difficulty presents the teacher with a challenge as to how to address that learner's individual learning process. The reflective teacher addresses the learner's difficulty, seeing it as an opportunity for reflection on how to expand the learner's understanding and knowledge to deal with the given situation.[4] In these moments, the reflective teacher asks, how can and should I proceed with teaching?

Dewey provides some insight into how the learner's listening changes on this model of reflective teacher-learner interaction. Instead of listening to obey, learners listen with a desire to learn, to seek the answer to questions that arise when their experiences do not meet their anticipations and they do not see a way out of their difficulties (Dewey, 1900/2008).[5] As Dewey points out, it is only through participation in the world and communication with others that learners find out what is difficult or challenging for them personally.[6] Teacher-learner interaction involves facilitating and cultivating moments for learners to find out for themselves wherein their difficulties lie, where their blind spots are, where their abilities and knowledge need expansion. But how can we describe the teacher's listening in this type of teacher-learner interaction? Although Dewey addresses to a certain extent how the learner's listening changes in the transition from a traditional method of learning to his model of reflectively learning by discovery, he says little about the implications of his model for the teacher's listening. In the next section, I seek to draw out these implications to develop a notion of how the reflective teacher listens and how this relates to understanding the teacher as a learner.

Listening to Learn—Listening as a Reflective Teacher

The reflective teacher, first and foremost, is open to the idea of learning from the teacher-student interaction. This openness is characterized by the teacher's openness to new and unexpected situations; that is, to considering the interruptions in the learner's experiences as points of departure for innovative thinking about improving teaching practice. When these interruptions are mediated by listening, they come forth for the teacher in classroom discussion as unexpected responses, contradictory viewpoints, confusing replies, or difficult questions the teacher is not prepared to answer. When listening to the learner is aimed at initiating and engaging interruptions in the learner's experience, it becomes educative. The teacher's listening is educative when the teacher is engaged in listening for signs that a productive struggle is taking place in the learners' experiences, and simultaneously, for ways to support learners' transformation of this struggle into aspects of reflective learning processes. On this account, when teachers are engaged in educative listening, they are particularly attuned to interruptions in their own experience that can be indications of interruptions in the learner's experiences.

There are various ways a teacher might be listening to interruptions without the educative quality of listening. I would like to look at three such problematic modes of listening in teaching that lack the educative aspect of listening and may be considered *uneducative.* Following this, I will examine how educative listening manifests itself in reflective teaching. The examples of listening below do not cover all possible ways of listening in teaching, but they are common to many teachers and can occur in teaching any subject matter to any age group. Here, I illustrate the dynamics of listening using a teacher-student interaction that might occur in arithmetic instruction.

To begin, we can look at the type of listening that occurs when a teacher asks such general questions that we can scarcely determine what qualifies as an interruption in the teacher's listening. If a teacher, for example, wants to teach the relation between multiplication and addition, she might write an example on the board such as $5 \times 5 = 5 + 5 + 5 + 5 + 5$ and then ask the class, "Are there any questions?" The teacher's question is too general, such that it invites either no response at all from students or invites questions unrelated to the material, such as "Can we play a game?" In this case, a teacher is open to all kinds of responses from the students but is not able to listen in such a way that connects the students' inquiries to what she is trying to teach. The teacher's questioning and listening are not of a sort that initiates learning in others. For this teacher, all responses from students are equally expected and unexpected and therefore can be hardly classified as interruptions. The teacher lacks an ability to listen within a certain horizon of expectations and thus lacks the ability to anticipate how the students might respond to the lesson at hand.

A second problematic mode of listening in teaching is listening as a means of mechanically filtering right and wrong answers. This type of listening can be attributed to normative teaching. As discussed above, teaching for the normative teacher is largely characterized by the motto "the teacher teaches, the student learns," which in practice generally amounts to "the teacher speaks, the student listens." Dewey (1916/2008) identifies this shortcoming in traditional models of instruction, in which the teacher provides "ready-made subject matter and listens to the accuracy with which it is reproduced" (p. 167). For example, the teacher may didactically present the "fives" of the multiplication tables on the board and then ask the class, "What is five times five?" If a student's answer is "10," it is deemed wrong and the teacher may listen on but only to wait for a student to arrive at the right answer. This framework for a teacher's questions is reserved for confirming the acquisition of specific knowledge, so that interruptions, such as differences of opinion or unexpected responses in the classroom, are classified as a lack of understanding, nothing more than "wrong answers." In this context, interruptions inform the teacher only in a limited sense about the learning student, only in terms of how the student compares to the predefined outcomes of learning set by the teacher or the book. Learning is conceived of here as a linear model of moving from point A to point B, or, more broadly speaking, from ignorance to knowledge. This "teacher-centred" model of teaching, and the corresponding normative mode of listening, does not further the student's learning process in a transformative way.

Whereas in normative teaching all interruptions are heard as wrong answers, a teacher might also listen to hear interruptions as "right answers." In this third problematic mode of listening, the teacher's listening is focused on finding ways to reconfigure students' unexpected responses into continuities with the planned lesson. For example, if a student responds with "10" to the question "who knows what 5 times 5 equals?" then the teacher may reply by saying, "Yes, that's true, if we're asking what 5 *plus* 5 equals," and then repeat the original question. While this teacher has a clear direction for her lesson and seeks to guide students in that direction, her listening is reserved for changing what she actually hears to conform to what she wants to hear. The potentially educative discontinuity of the interruption is subsumed into an overarching continuity with the lesson. In the end, while teachers who listen in this way may value encouraging students' thought, they ultimately shade over the differences between what they want to teach and what the students know or want to learn. In the process, the interruption is not a guide to transforming the teacher's practice because the uniqueness of the student's contribution is overlooked. The learners may feel encouraged by this teacher, but they are ultimately not learning the similarities and differences in forms of knowledge because the teacher is not pointing them out.[7] Since everything students say is woven into a continuity of the planned lecture, the teacher is only truly interrupted when students' questions and responses are so unexpected that they do not fit into the lesson at all, leaving the teacher at a complete loss for how to proceed.

What is different about how the reflective teacher listens to interruptions? For the reflective teacher, interruptions in listening are the heart of the educational matter. Interruptions point out the differences in the ways of thinking between the teacher and students and between the different students in the classroom. The reflective teacher does not listen normatively as a mechanical filter for right and wrong answers nor seek to transform all answers into right ones. The reflective teacher aims to ask questions to interrupt the learner's flow of experience, cultivating the learner's struggle with understanding the material and listening to see if this struggle is taking place. Although this may seem like an abstract approach, we can take the earlier arithmetic example and imagine a plausible dialogue between a teacher and students that shows how the pedagogically tactful teacher might guide a class through the material in this way. Such a dialogue might look something like this:

> Teacher: "Who can tell me what 5 times 5 equals?"
> Student 1: "10."
> Teacher: "OK, how do we get to 10? How many 5s are there in 10?"
> Student 2: "Two."
> Teacher: "OK, so if we take two 5s and add them together, 5 + 5 = 10, right?"
>
> The students understand addition and have no objections.
>
> Teacher: "So, how many 5s do we need to add together in 5 times 5?"
> Student: "Five."
>
> The teacher asks the student to write it out on the board and add them together: 5 + 5 + 5 + 5 + 5 = 25.
>
> Teacher: "Good. So, 5 times 5 = 25. Now let's go back to look at the number 10. We said 5 + 5 is 10; that's 5 times what number equals 10? Can anyone tell me what number is missing?"

The significance of this example is that the teacher expected that the students would be able to answer the first question about multiplication, but when an unexpected (and, in this case, incorrect) answer is heard, it is drawn on to explore differences and connections between what the students already have learned and what the teacher is now trying to teach them. The teacher thereby shows the students ways of understanding the connections between addition and multiplication. Of course, there are many possible questions and answers that could lead to a different dialogue, depending on what level of knowledge the students already have and depending on whether there are specific right or wrong answers to the questions at hand.

Independent of the subject matter, reflective teaching involves working out the student's frustration and difficulties dialogically. Accordingly, teaching entails helping the students discover the similarities and differences between what they know and what they still can learn. This is a process that involves both questioning and listening. This notion of teaching entails what Gert Biesta (2006) calls the educational responsibility, a responsibility that lies in asking "difficult questions," those with "the potential to interrupt" learners in their being (p. 150). It also entails listening to see if students are thinking beyond what they already know—that is, thinking about what they do not know or do not understand—and thus trying to grasp something new. By listening to the students, the tactful reflective teacher is implicitly asking herself, "What do I need to hear so that I know that thinking and learning are taking place?" The answer to this question is never straightforward, regardless of the subject matter. It is a difficult task in teaching to decipher whether or not a student is really thinking about the material. The teacher might wonder if the student gave a right answer only as a repetition of what was read in the book or if the right answer truly demonstrates understanding. A similar dilemma may arise in considering if a student's wrong answer is just an arbitrary guess or if it represents a genuine attempt to grasp the material.

The reflective teacher seeks to listen between right and wrong answers, in the "gray zones" of students' thinking and learning that are revealed in the interruption.[8] While the reflective teacher can anticipate certain potential answers due to her knowledge of the level of her students, at the same time she understands that she can never know exactly what to expect from learners' responses. She allows the unexpected responses to interrupt in an educative way that causes her to hesitate, suspend judgment, and become perplexed by what she hears. Philosopher of education Sophie Haroutunian-Gordon (2003) has examined interruptions in listening and importantly emphasizes that they are central to the process of changing one's beliefs. This manifests itself in dialogue with others who have differing beliefs such that "the nature of the interruption determines the direction of the shift in subsequent listening" (Haroutunian-Gordon, 2003, p. 13).[9] Genuine interruptions signal blind spots in a teacher's own thought and knowledge that make her consider a perspective she has never considered before.[10] When the teacher becomes aware of her own blind spot through a student's question or response in classroom interaction, then the teacher learns and the student is, as Dewey (1916/2008) put it, "without knowing it, a teacher" (p. 167).

When a teacher is attuned to interruptions arising within teacher-learner interaction, she is listening to the otherness and difference of the learner, with the risk and even the desire to break with her ideas about teaching and learning, and about human beings. As philosopher Maxine Greene (1995) relates, "[I]f I and other teachers truly want to provoke our students to break through the limits of the conventional and the taken for granted, we ourselves have to experience breaks with what has been established in our own lives; we have to keep arousing ourselves to begin again" (p. 109). The process of teacher-student dialogue is transformative insofar as both teacher and learner begin to hear how they are being heard by each other; on this basis, they can seek out ways of learning from one another. Nicholas Burbules and Suzanne Rice (1991) make an illuminating point about all dialogue across difference, one that proves essential for understanding educative teacher-student dialogue: "as a process, dialogue requires us to re-examine our own presuppositions and to compare them against quite different ones; to make us less dogmatic about the belief that the way the world appears to us is necessarily the way the world is" (p. 405; see also Laverty, 2007). By listening to oneself as a teacher, teachers can become aware of their process of teaching and, in turn, aware of the fact that this process can be changed by their decisions.

Learning to Listen and Teacher Education

Teacher educators generally accept that dialogue and discussion are to be part of any future teacher's classroom. Teacher education programs that want to move away from understanding teaching as transmission expect preservice teachers to learn to teach in such a way that initiates dialogue and discussion in young learners. This implies that if learners are to engage in discussion in classroom learning and not become passive listeners, then teachers must learn how to differentiate what they hear and understand how a student's response relates to how that particular student is thinking about the subject matter.

In his early essay on listening, philosopher of education William Hare (1975) cautions educational theorists to resist the temptation to believe that listening is something people do naturally and thus to assume that it does not require special attention. When listening is educative, teachers learn how to guide learners—not simply toward predefined answers but toward figuring out what questions to ask, or, more generally, how to productively engage with the struggle of learning. This idea of educative listening in teaching thus relates to what William Hare (1975) calls "being a good listener." Hare (1975) points out that being a good listener involves judgment of what is heard and knowledge of "how to take things and what to listen for" (p. 9). This type of knowledge and judgment must itself be learned. Hare's discussion of the good listener makes clear that a certain interrelationship must exist between the listener and the speaker in order for listening to be generative for both. According to Hare (1975, 1983), a good listener is one who is open-minded and willing to listen to the ideas and thoughts of the other person in such a way that allows those heard ideas to potentially change the way the listener thinks.

For teachers to begin to understand themselves as critical, reflective, educative listeners, they must first understand how to become open to learning within the teacher-learner relation. For prospective teachers and in-service teachers to learn to listen in such a way that, through their listening, they are figuring out the limits of the student's knowledge and ability as well as their own, they have to learn to understand that listening involves becoming open to another person and to new ideas. As Jim Garrison (1996) points out, the openness required by listening to the other involves taking a risk and becoming vulnerable: "Remaining open is awkward. We must be willing to live with confusion and uncertainty about both ourselves and the other person we are attempting to understand" (p. 433). An essential part of what it means to be a teacher is learning how to take this risk and, in the process, begin to define yourself in terms of the other, the learner.

Teacher education must guide preservice teachers to transform their notion of "teaching as telling" to one of "teaching as questioning, listening, and pointing out." Philosophy of education can contribute to this process significantly, not only by helping prospective teachers come to a theoretical understanding of educative listening but also by helping them connect theories of listening to their own teaching practice. This process could begin by first having prospective teachers prepare a lesson plan on a philosophical text to teach in a class discussion. This preparatory phase serves to help the particular student create expectations about how the class discussion might unfold.

Prospective teachers often have difficulty with creating open questions. Their lesson planning will often amount to didactically listing a series of important points to cover with few questions. To address this, in a second phase, the student could discuss her plans with the teacher educator, who can help her transform her lesson plan into open questions that can guide classroom dialogue. The transformed lesson plan can serve as a guide for creating expectations about what she will hear in the context of classroom discussion about a particular subject matter. Teacher educators can facilitate this transformation because they listen differently than the student and have developed different expectations about what might be heard in the discussion.

In a third phase, the student can then be given the opportunity to test the transformed lesson plan by teaching the text to classmates while remaining open to the fact that expectations may be defied by unanticipated responses. In a concluding phase, the student can take account of the interruptions that occurred in the practice of listening and use these again to transform her questions and expectations anew. Through this process, prospective teachers not only can become aware of the fact that lesson-planning is a dynamic process—one that involves taking account of the learning individuals in the classroom—but they can also learn of their own expectations and how these are not static but rather flexible and transformable.

As teachers become more experienced in teaching their subject, they begin to expand their expectations by gauging the types of responses or confusions students typically have. Of course, no teacher can ever fully know what to expect from students, and when expectations become fixed they can serve as a hindrance rather than a help to education. An example of this is found when school policy makers and teachers make generalizations such as correlating genders with the potential to excel or fail in a particular subject. Such generalizations diminish the possibilities of reflective teaching that seeks ways in which students defy expectations and continue to make unique and innovative contributions to their own learning processes.[11]

By listening to learners, teachers make possible this shift in learners' experiences: the shift from being passive recipients of knowledge to being active participants in their educational process. Philosopher of education Paolo Freire (2005) highlights the paradox of listening in teaching with his point that only "by listening to learners" can "teachers learn to talk with learners," and, in turn, "teach the learners to listen to them as well" (p. 115). Freire's point makes clear that when teachers acknowledge the difference and otherness brought by learners to the educational situation, then learners, in turn, desire to listen—not because an authority compels them, but because they begin to view listening as a path to their own learning and growth. To take this idea seriously, we must consider that if we value cultivating transformative educational experiences for learners, then we must create opportunities for listening that stem from their desire to learn rather than from a dutiful or forced obedience.

Conclusion

One might ask, are there times in teaching when correction of error takes precedence over listening, such that a return to normative teaching is justified? The fact remains that the normative teacher fails to see that the method of correcting error does not necessarily achieve the desired result, namely the student's changed belief. The reflective teacher recognizes that correction of error is vital but also that the method by which a teacher corrects the student is directly related to how, and whether or not, the student learns.

Reflective teaching entails listening to students in a way that is open to interruptions; it deals with these productively by incorporating them into the students' learning processes such that the students begin to understand and question why they believe what they believe.

Teacher education must find ways to open up, pull apart, and make explicit the space of interruptions in teaching that typically do not affect experienced teachers in the same way they can affect novice teachers. By making this process explicit, teacher education programs can come to recognize the specific difficulties involved in learning to listen and question, and learning to teach. Thereby, preservice teachers can begin to understand, as Wolfgang Klafki (1958/2000) puts it, the "draft character" of planning and preparation for classroom situations (p. 143).

The "blind spots" of practice and experience are not something we can ever fully avoid. Certainly, it would not be Dewey's intention to say that mastery of reflective thinking can lead to mastery over the unexpected and unknown. Rather, these blind spots are to be cherished; they remind us that we cannot fully foresee the future. They are what keep us humble and reveal to us that we are only human and cannot know everything. It would be a dire situation if we could know everything and foresee the future such that there were no surprises and no interruptions—which, in turn, would mean no innovation, no need for exploration, no learning from difference. A society that claims to have all the answers, such that we could all stop looking, would be a society that has fallen into the clutches of dogmatism. In the words of Hannah Arendt (1958/1997), "Our hope always hangs on the new which every generation brings; and because our hope is based on this alone, we destroy everything if we try to control the new such that we, the old, can dictate how it will look" (p. 192). Teacher education can and must help prospective teachers understand how to reflectively deal with the difficulty inherent in their practice, a difficulty intimately tied to the fact that teachers have to acquaint the next generation with the world as it is, while preparing them for a future yet to be discovered.[12]

REFERENCES

Arendt, H. (1997). The crisis in education. In *Between past and future: Eight exercises in political thought* (pp. 173–196). Harmondsworth, UK: Penguin. (Original work published 1958)

Benner, D. (2003). Kritik und Negativität. Ein Versuch zur Pluralisierung von Kritik in Erziehung, Pädagogik und Erziehungswissenschaft. *Zeitschrift für Pädagogik, 46,* 96–110.

Benner, D., & English, A. (2004). Critique and negativity: Toward the pluralisation of critique in educational practice, theory and research. *Journal of Philosophy of Education, 38*(3), 409–428. doi:10.1111/j.0309-8249.2004.00394.x

Biesta, G.J.J. (2006). *Beyond learning: Democratic education for a human future.* Boulder, CO: Paradigm.

Buck, G. (1981). Negativität, Diskontinuität, und die Stetigkeit des Bios. In G. Buck (Ed.), *Hermeneutik und Bildung* (pp. 71–94). München, Germany: Fink.

Burbules, N., & Rice, S. (1991). Dialogue across difference: Continuing the conversation. *Harvard Educational Review, 61*(4), 393–416.

✗ Dewey, J. (2008). *Democracy and education: The middle works* (Vol. 9) (J.A. Boydston, Ed.). Carbondale: Southern Illinois University Press. (Original work published 1916)

Dewey, J. (2008). *How we think: The later works* (Vol. 8, pp. 105–352) (J.A. Boydston, Ed.). Carbondale: Southern Illinois University Press. (Original work published 1933)

✗ Dewey, J. (2008). *The school and society: The middle works* (Vol. 1, pp. 1–112). (J.A. Boydston, Ed.) Carbondale: Southern Illinois University Press. (Original work published 1900)

English, A. (2007). Interrupted experiences: Reflection, listening and negativity in the practice of teaching. Special Issue on Reflection and Listening. *Learning Inquiry, 1*(2), 133–142.

English, A. (2009). Listening as a teacher: Educative listening, interruptions and reflective practice. Special Issue on Open-mindedness and the Virtues of Education. *Paideusis, 18*(1), 69–79.

English, A. (2013). *Discontinuity in learning: Dewey, Herbart, and education as transformation.* New York: Cambridge University Press. doi:10.1017/CBO9781139177825

Freire, P. (2005). *Teachers as cultural workers: Letters to those who dare teach.* Boulder, CO: Westview Press.

Garrison, J. (1996). A Deweyan theory of democratic listening. *Educational Theory, 46*(4), 429–451. doi:10.1111/j.1741-5446.1996.00429.x

Greene, M. (1995). *Releasing the imagination: Essays on education, the arts, and social change.* New York: Jossey-Bass Publishers.

Hare, W. (1975). Has listening had a fair hearing? *Agora, 3*(1–2), 5–13.

Hare, W. (1983). *Open-mindedness and education.* Kingston, ON: McGill-Queen's University Press.

Haroutunian-Gordon, S. (2003). Listening—in a democratic society. In Kal Alston (Ed.), *Philosophy of Education 2003* (pp. 1–18). Urbana, IL: Philosophy of Education Society.

Haroutunian-Gordon, S. (2007). Listening and questioning. Special Issue on Reflection and Learning. *Learning Inquiry, 1*(2), 143–152.

Haroutunian-Gordon, S. (2009). *Learning to teach through discussion: The art of turning the soul.* New Haven, CT: Yale University Press.

Herbart, J.F. (1902). The science of education. In H.M. Felkin & E. Felkin (Trans.), *The science of education, its general principles deduced from its aim, and the aesthetic revelation of the world.* Boston: D.C. Heath & Co. (Original work published 1806)

Klafki, W. (2000). Didaktik analysis as the core of preparation of instruction. In I. Westbury, S. Hopmann, & K. Riquarts (Eds.), *Teaching as a reflective practice: The German Didaktik Tradition* (pp. 139–160). Mahwah, NJ: Lawrence Erlbaum Associates. (Original work published 1958)

Laverty, M. (2007). Dialogue as philosophical inquiry in the teaching of sympathy and tolerance: Special Issue on Reflection and Listening. *Learning Inquiry, 1*(2), 125–132.

Meyer-Drawe, K. (1984). Lernen als Umlernen—Zur Negativität des Lernprozesses. In W. Lippitz & and K. Meyer-Drawe (Eds.), *Lernen und seine Horizonte: Phänomenologische Konzeptionen menschlichen Lernens—didaktische Konsequenzen* (pp. 19–45). Frankfurt am Main: Scriptor.

Meyer-Drawe, K. (1987). Die Belehrbarkeit des Lehrenden durch den Lerneden—Fragen an den Primat des Pädagogischen Bezugs. In W. Lippitz & K. Meyer-Drawe (Eds.), *Kind und Welt: Phänomenologische Studien zur Pädagogik* (pp. 63–73). Frankfurt am Main: Athenaeum Verlag.

Paley, G. (1994). *The collected stories.* New York: Farrar, Straus and Giroux.

Plato. (1997). Meno. In J.M. Cooper & D.S. Hutchinson (Eds.), *Plato: The complete works* (pp. 870–897). Cambridge, MA: Hackett Publishing Company.(Original work published 380 BCE)

Prange, K. (2005). *Die Zeigestruktur der Erziehung. Grundriss der operativen Pädagogik.* Paderborn, Germany: Ferdinand Schöningh.

Rousseau, J.J. (1979). *Emile or On education* (A. Bloom, Trans.). New York: Basic Books. (Original work published 1762)

Schultz, K. (2003). *Listening: A framework for teaching across difference.* New York: Teachers College Press.

Waks, L.J. (2007). Listening and questioning: The apophatic/cataphatic distinction revisited. *Learning Inquiry, 1*(2), 153–161. doi:10.1007/s11519-007-0019-8

Waks, L.J. (2008). Listening from silence: Inner composure and engagement. *Paideusis, 17*(2), 65–74.

NOTES

1 See, for example, recent studies on dialogue and listening in educational contexts, Burbules and Rice (1991), Garrison (1996), Schultz (2003), Haroutunian-Gordon (2003, 2009), Waks (2008), and the special issue of *Learning Inquiry*, entitled "Listening and Reflection," edited by Leonard Waks (2007) for contributions from many of these and other authors, including my own contribution, "Interrupted Experiences: Reflection, Listening and Negativity in the Practice of Teaching" (English, 2007), and also English (2013).

2 The democratic import of Dewey's learning theory lies in its implications toward being open and tolerant toward difference (on these issues, see Burbules & Rice, 1991; Garrison, 1996; Haroutunian-Gordon, 2003).

3 In this context, the term "negative" is not meant in a pejorative sense, nor does it necessarily refer to something unpleasant. On the concept of negativity in the traditions of educational philosophy, see Benner (2003) and Benner and English (2004). On the notions of interruption and negativity of experience in reflective teaching with particular reference to Dewey, see English (2013). See also Buck (1981) and Meyer-Drawe (1984).

4 We can say that in the experience of teaching, teachers are interrupted in a twofold manner: the learner's interruption, her doubt or difficulty with particular subject matter, can initiate a teacher's doubt or difficulty about how to help the learner deal with that difficulty. On this point, see English (2013).

5 See also Haroutunian-Gordon (2003) on listening and questioning in dialogue across difference.

6 On this point, see also Garrison (1996).

7 On the idea of teaching as "pointing out," see Prange (2005).

8 This concept of reflective teaching connects to a notion I have developed called pedagogical tact. *Pedagogical tact* relates to Aristotle's concept of *phronesis*, or making wise decisions in the moment (English, 2013).

9 See also Haroutunian-Gordon (2007) and Waks (2007). See also Schultz's (2003) study on listening and how teachers can create listening communities in classrooms in which teachers listen to students and students begin to listen and learn from each other.

10 On this point, see Meyer-Drawe (1987).

11 In my research on listening, I incorporated these phases into an advanced philosophy of education seminar, co-taught with Dietrich Benner, on "Childhood, Youth, and Adulthood," designed for preservice teachers and educators in the philosophy of education section of the teacher education program at Humboldt University Berlin. I interviewed five participating students individually before and after the process to understand their expectations and how these changed. Two questions were particularly informative in the interview conducted after the final stage of this process. I asked the student to reflect first on what changed from her initial instructional planning for the class discussion and her transformed lesson plan, and, secondly, to reflect on the difference between what answers to her questions she expected to hear from her classmates and what answers they actually gave. This reflective phase in journalling or discussion could be used as a closing phase to the process to help students become aware of their own learning process and begin to see connections between learning to listen and learning to teach. The interview questions were informed by Wolfgang Klafki's (1958/2000) notion of instructional planning. Special thanks to Dietrich Benner and the participating students.

12 This article is a revised and extended version of an earlier article of mine with the same title. Content for this revised version is reprinted with permission from my book *Discontinuity in Learning: Dewey, Herbart, and Education as Transformation* (English, 2013). The original article was published as "Listening as a Teacher: Educative Listening, Interruptions and Reflective Practice" (English, 2009).

6

Discussing Ethical Issues in the Classroom

Leveraging Pedagogical Moments That May Otherwise Undermine Important Discussions

Douglas J. Simpson and
William J. Hull, Jr. *

*This chapter was first published as Simpson, Douglas J. and Hull, William J. Jr. (2011). Discussing ethical issues in the classroom: Leveraging pedagogical moments that may otherwise undermine important discussions. *The International Journal of Progressive Education* 7(3), 6–26. Reproduced with permission.

Introduction

Conflict is the gadfly of thought. It stirs us to observation and memory.

It instigates to invention. It shocks us out of sheep-like passivity.

–John Dewey (1922, p. 300)

Most of us have probably been silenced in various situations—more than once—as children, students, colleagues, and teachers.[1] Women, people of colour, recent immigrants, individuals with alternative lifestyles, gays and lesbians, and people with non-traditional religious affiliations in particular settings may have their voices silenced more routinely. Indeed, it is difficult for many people, regardless of their backgrounds, to develop their voices, to question established mores, or to express their ideas in paternalistic, patrician, or oppressive situations. In addition, many teachers may find it disappointing to encounter pedagogical situations where students consciously or unconsciously make comments that silence or intimidate their classmates and, thus, thwart learning opportunities. Perhaps even more distressing are accounts of how a colleague[2] responded to students in ways that silenced them, invalidated their ideas, or inhibited discussions.[3]

Discussing Ethical Issues

Discussions involving ethical issues are especially vulnerable to silencing because they are filled with controversial assumptions, delicate nuances, personal sensitivities, problematic arguments, cultural issues, and religious controversies. Thus, encouraging students to express their reflective opinions about ethical issues may be as risky for both students and teachers as it is desirable for everyone. Even when dialogical parameters are identified and agreed upon (e.g., Freire, 2003, pp. 88–92), some discussions (e.g., racism) are "excruciatingly difficult" for many if not most of us (Nieto, 2000, p. 5). Holder (as cited in Weiss, 2009) clarifies that part of the difficulty of discussing racism is that many people are afraid to express their views. However, fear-filled issues are often the ones that are most in need of guided, insightful, open, informed, and sensitive analyses (Forrest, 2009; Oakeshott, 1991). Yet, preparing for these difficult conversations can help reduce the fear and anxiety of individuals and, thereby, encourage silenced voices to engage in dialogues that are essential in democratic institutions and societies (Center for Faculty Excellence, 2004; West, 1993).

Teachers' Perspectives

In view of the personal discomforts, conceptual ambiguities, knowledge-claim controversies, social tensions, and pedagogical challenges, a teacher can understandably decide not to discuss important ethical issues rather than raise educative questions and encourage students to think and learn together. Indeed, an ethically sensitive teacher may not even want to initiate a discussion that could lead to misunderstanding, class disunity, or distrust. Ethical issues are frequently, however, too important to ignore. Plus, merely condemning unethical attitudes and affirming ethical ones are insufficient responses if we want to nurture democratic citizens, expand democracy, and help students discover their voices and identities. So, it appears that teachers need to help students understand why some behaviours are proscribed, others are prescribed, still others are tolerated, and yet others are ignored.

Notwithstanding some teachers' personal discomfort with ethical controversies, a democratic society depends in significant ways on teachers recognizing and promoting democratic ethical values, and these include the free exchange of controversial ideas (Dewey, 1916). To advance the development of democracy, Holder (as cited in Weiss, 2009) adds that society must overcome its fear of conflict and develop the courage to discuss its most pressing issues. How is such possible if many teachers avoid cultivating both courage and communication? Fortunately, many other teachers (Bernstein, 1990; Claire & Holden, 2007; Williams, 1994) want to do a better job of creating classroom environments and atmospheres where democratic values—respect for persons, arguments, evidence, academic freedom, and so forth— are genuinely practiced and not simply professed.

Given the interest of many in becoming more effective as teachers and the need for such, this study identifies several hindrances to classroom discussions of ethical matters and offers suggestions on how to facilitate discussions of ethical controversies in more knowledgeable, approachable, reflective, and respectful ways. In particular, the study focuses on three types of comments that inhibit rather than invite student and teacher discussions: *dismissive/evasive tactics*, *logical stoppers*, and *ad hominem arguments*. For the purpose of this study, a statement is *dismissive* or *evasive* when a person uses it to extricate her- or himself from some form of ethical responsibility or moral accountability; a statement or action is a *logical stopper* when it specifies or implies that a conversation will or should not continue; and a statement is an *ad hominem argument* when it explicitly or implicitly attacks a person for some real or assumed personal characteristic rather than addressing the individual's arguments. In discussing these realms, we draw upon relevant research, experiential knowledge, and literature—including fictional and nonfictional—to clarify and illustrate ideas.

Two Qualifications

Two qualifications regarding our focus are important. First, our examination is restricted to three types of comments that often have a silencing effect on dialogue. Many of the ideas discussed, however, apply to other settings, including informal learning situations. Further, we focus on questions rather than declarative statements, because they can appear more innocent and disarming yet be more pedagogically deadly. Our classification system, of course, would be misleading if it influenced us to think in discrete, trichotomous categories. A comment by a person may simultaneously fall into all three categories.

Second, questions themselves may be pedagogically and ethically neutral, positive, or negative depending on a host of factors, e.g., a person's intentions, body language, prior comments, verbal inflection, tone, pitch, and emphases. Moreover, as Habermas (1984) notes, different cultural gestalts are embedded in our linguistic creations and usages and should be recognized if not appreciated and critiqued. Our specific concern is with those questions that are frequently "burning statements"; the kind that may or may not be accompanied by the "killing tools" of laughter (Hurston, 1978, p. 10). Instead of employing burning and killing actions in classrooms, we encourage a dialogical model that is partially Hurstonian, one where at least part of the time people sit and pass "around the pictures of their thoughts for the others to look at and see" (Hurston, 1978, p. 81). Or, as Camus (1995, p. 70) observes, there are times when argumentative comments need to be set aside so people can simply talk and seek mutual understanding. The other part of our dialogical model[4] is the evaluation of ideas, arguments, and data that should be encouraged when the goals and grounds of discussion have been clarified and accepted at least provisionally and the diversity of epistemological orientations is acknowledged and, perhaps, encouraged (Brookfield & Preskill, 1999; Dewey, 1916; Freire, 2003; Habermas, 1984). Eryaman (2007, p. 18) identifies another fundamental presupposition of our model when he raises the question: what does it mean "to be an agent in the world"? Indeed, what might it mean for teacher educators, teachers, and students when they are intellectually, emotionally, and existentially recognized as agents?[5]

Evasive/Dismissive Tactics

The Tactics Themselves

Evasive and/or dismissive tactics take many forms. Central to identifying them is that the person raising a question attempts to evade or dismiss personal responsibility. A high-school student, for example, described his former dismissive attitude toward others' problems: "If it doesn't affect me, why bother?" (Freedom Writers with Gruwell, 1999, p. 170). But what, we inquire, happened to change his mind? A variety of experiences, no doubt, but visiting the United States Holocaust Memorial Museum was so upsetting for him that he demanded,

"How could this have happened? Why didn't someone stand up for these people?" (Freedom Writers with Gruwell, 1999, p. 169). At a minimum, this student's case illustrates how dismissive tactics can be partially overcome by informal educational experiences and underlines the importance of learning outside of the school and classroom.

Examples of Evasiveness

Among a plethora of examples of evasiveness are some that may be seen as relevant to personal responsibility, fairness, and practicality: Why should my parents pay higher taxes to provide safety nets for the lazy? Why should we allow undocumented immigrants to stay here when they pay no taxes, deprive us of jobs, and disrespect our values? How can she be held accountable when her principal told her to do it? As we recognize implicit and explicit evasive and dismissive—not to mention stereotypically loaded—questions, we can become better prepared to use these same statements as valuable educative opportunities. Indeed, we can even have students analyze these questions before they are raised and, thereby, avoid the discomfort of preventable awkward situations for a student who might raise them.

Sometimes an evasive or dismissive comment can be, on some level, at least partially correct. However, such comments often need contextual positioning to ascertain their significance. For example, few, if any, 21st-century students could possibly have participated in the legal exploitation, torture, rape, and murder of Indigenous peoples or people of African descent in North America. Consequently, we might not be surprised to hear, "Since I didn't have anything to do with slavery or oppressing Lumbees and black people, why do people keep trying to make me feel guilty for what others have done in the past?" While the speaker may be partially correct, that does not mean she or he is adequately informed about the multilayered dimensions of racism. In reality, the questioner can still be largely incorrect in his analysis of a larger racial issue and, if not reflective, develop an attitude that is offensive. Thus, the previous student's question—like the earlier ones—opens the door to potentially fruitful discussions. For instance, consider an illustration about discussions of racism in its personal, institutional, and systemic forms. First, as Nieto (2000) observes, it is important that students understand that even today, hundreds of years after racist atrocities were introduced to North America:

> Racism as an institutional system implies that some people and groups benefit and others lose. Whites, whether they want to or not, benefit in a racist society; males benefit in a sexist society. Discrimination always helps somebody—those with the

most power—which explains why racism, sexism, and other forms of discrimination continue. (p. 37)

If Nieto's ideas are correct, a person who is not a racist and was not involved in the establishment of a systemically racist society can still profit from it. An individual can still be an heir and beneficiary of racism—inherit privilege, status, resources, property, stocks, bonds, and power—even when he or she is not personally racist. So, if we are interested in mutual respect, equal opportunity, equity, justice, reparation, and freedom, we need to speak openly to the question, "Why do people keep trying to make me feel guilty for what others have done in the past?" *and* proceed further to other queries, such as, "What can we do in the present to identify and diminish current forms of racism and their effects?" When we pursue these kinds of questions, our hope is that the critically self-conscious student comes to understand that "right thinking belongs intimately to right doing" (Freire, 1998, p. 42). To effectively advance our antiracist education, even to understand what is at issue, we need to retain the ability to dialogue about the persistent malignant power of systemic racism and distinguish between the pernicious racist beliefs and practices of individuals and systemic racisms wherever they appear in the world (Bales, 2004; Bhattacharyya, Gabriel, & Small, 2002).

Evasive and dismissive tactics seem most common when complexity surrounds a controversy, and, as Campbell and Huxman (2009) state, topics are complex when they are experientially remote, embedded in other issues, or require technical expertise. Dialogues on ethical matters are regularly complex because many of them are experientially remote and require expertise in several realms of inquiry, e.g., ethics, history, law, culture, and epistemology (Wagner & Simpson, 2009).

Logical Stoppers

Paul Hirst (as cited in Gribble, 1969, p. 35) is credited with using the phrase *logical stopper* to indicate when a person implies, claims, or acts as if there is a point at which no one can question a particular claim. Inquiry may be accepted up to a point or in certain spheres, but then several other beliefs fall into a "No Inquiry Zone," where no one who has any doubts may enter. Importantly, the "No Inquiry Zone" may be implicit or explicit and often includes prohibitions that are connected to ideas about truth, virtue, and reality. In this realm, Holder's (as cited in Weiss, 2009) call for courage is a reminder of the obligation to ask unwanted questions and to be aware that unwelcomed inquiries are usually related to people's highly cherished beliefs (Campbell & Huxman, 2009).

Truth Claims

Hirst's idea is beautifully—and appallingly—illustrated in life and literature. Jun-ling, in Mah's *Falling Leaves* (1997), encounters an interrogative statement that may be intended as a logical stopper. When she asks her brother Zi-jun if he wants to read letters that have a bearing on her truth claim, he responds, "'Is there such a thing as absolute truth?'" and quickly adds, "'It all depends on a person's viewpoint.'" As if to emphasize that Jun-ling has entered a "No Inquiry Zone," Zi-jun dismisses her question: "In any case, it's all water under the bridge" (Mah, 1997, p. 269). Consequently, Jun-ling did not continue her inquiry.

Truth, Zi-jun argues, is entirely determined by—"it all depends on"—one's perspective. The popular assumption that truth depends utterly on one's perspective can easily derail discussions and immediately discredit anyone who questions another person's truth: "You may believe that, but I don't. Each of us is entitled to her opinion." This kind of logical stopper can have educationally deadening implications and may have hidden in it a questionable ethical assumption: I have a right to silence a person anytime I disagree with her. Similarly, the stereotypical implication that everyone who pursues understanding also wants to find, make, and impose claims about "absolute truth" can end inquiries. This inquiry-ending capacity is what makes a statement or question a logical stopper. If these logical stoppers concerning perspective and truth are unchallengeable absolute claims, discussion of nearly every ethical issue may be nullified, even a discussion of ethical principles that are promoted by national charters and constitutions and international organizations and courts, such as the Declaration of Human Rights of the United Nations and the International Criminal Court.

In reality, we can accommodate the notion that our perspectives influence what we see, think, and value, while validating the idea that truth or knowledge claims are not absolute, without coming to the conclusion that one opinion is as good as another. Like Dewey (1929), we can conclude that, if possible, all perspectives and data need to be examined as we seek to identify secure but not certain knowledge. But whatever our conclusions about truth claims and perspectivalism, neither we nor our students are well served by allowing logical stoppers to keep us from examining important claims.

Value Claims

A second common logical stopper regards explicit values—especially virtues—and so nearly any kind of ethical claim. Alexey, in Dostoyevsky's (1982) *The Brothers Karamazov*, tells us that virtue is a relative matter, presumably governed exclusively by one's culture. He asks "[W]hat is virtue?" and answers his own question by claiming, "It's one thing to me and another thing to a Chinaman—it's a relative thing" but then seems to vacillate: "Or is it?" (Dostoyevsky, 1982, p. 696). Are virtues completely a matter of what one's culture teaches, and are the teachings of different cultures hopelessly antithetical? At a minimum, recent empirical research raises serious questions about these as absolutist empirical assertions (Alexander, 2007; Axelrod, 1984; Coles, 2000; Peterson & Seligman, 2004), and philosophical inquiry has long indicated multiple conceptual, logical, and evidentiary problems for unsophisticated ethical relativism (Barrow, 1991; Dewey, 1948; Ennis, 1969; Holmes, 2003; Peters, 1970; Wagner & Simpson, 2009; Wong, 2006). Again, whatever our conclusions are in this realm, neither we nor our students are well served by allowing logical stoppers to block our inquiry into beliefs that some want to remain unexamined.

Reality Claims

Corrine, in McInerney's (2006) *The Good Life*, provides another example of a possible logical stopper. She notices a man, named Luke, who staggers toward her a day after 9/11. She stares at him: "His knees showed through the ripped legs of what until recently had been a pair of dress slacks. The hard hat looked anomalous, and indeed, as he tilted his head back, it fell to the curb, exposing a dark tangle of hair, streaked with ubiquitous talcy ash" (McInerney, 2006, p. 70). As Corrine talks with Luke, she discovers that he had had an appointment postponed approximately 24 hours earlier, an occurrence that had probably saved his life. As he pauses to get his bearings, he volunteers to Corrine that she is the first person he has seen and adds, "Unless I'm imagining you" (p. 70). Corrine takes time to assure him that he is not imagining her but then pauses to qualify her declaration: "It's hard to tell, though. What's real, I mean" (p. 70). No doubt, such a response was understandable considering the circumstances surrounding the story. Used as a logical stopper, however, a question—e.g., "We can't really tell what happened in the Jewish holocaust, can we?"—may seek to reduce historical inquiry to ideological propaganda and dogma. Ethically, thinking that denies the possibility of any knowledge of reality may trivialize some of the greatest past and current issues, relegate them to private impressions, and not allow public research and debate. Hence, we then have no way of determining when Muslims, atheists, and other groups are excluded from the opportunities and resources that are legitimately theirs in a democracy.

Cumulatively, these three queries and related ones can easily stymie classroom discussions and silence, if not slay, would-be gad-flies. Consequently, we could have students, including future teachers, who conclude that every detail of reality is always hopelessly fuzzy, virtue is completely relative, and truth claims are entirely subjective perceptions. These conclusions frequently seem to be reached, not as a result of sustained study, but as a consequence of accepting cultural clichés. But logical stoppers predicated on clichés are educationally important because of their potentially dialogue-closing effects on discussions. While these conclusions may be arrived at via persistent and reflective inquiry, passing them on without an open examination appears to be educationally counterproductive.

The silencing of critical deliberations may become more serious if someone intimidates others with extensions of these three logical stoppers. Namely, a student may ask, "Who are we to decide what is right or wrong for a student or school?" Further, someone may personalize the question, implying that each class member should ask her- or himself, "Who am I to say that a certain act is ethical or unethical?" Or, a person may inquire, "Who are *you* to decide what is right or wrong for your students and colleagues?" Happily, these questions and similar ones can be raised with praiseworthy intentions in mind and should not be avoided by teachers (Dewey & Tufts, 1932).

These questions can also open the door to educative dialogues and may not even be designed as logical stoppers. The questioner may merely want some suggestions about how to answer these questions. Regardless of the reasons for the questions, like Dewey (1922), we can appreciate the provocative nature of these questions and the stimuli they provide for reflection. Future and current teachers do, indeed, need to be able to discuss how these and many other questions might be examined and addressed. One way of addressing these questions is to examine them, first, in university teacher-education programs by well-prepared professors (Center for Faculty Excellence, 2004) and, later, by well-prepared classroom teachers (Hess, 2009). A re-articulation technique—rephrasing questions—can be employed so that the ideas more easily stimulate classroom discussions, e.g.,

"Does a teacher ever have the responsibility to determine if a particular act may be wrong and, if it is, forbid it?"

Ad Hominem Arguments

Attacking people rather than evaluating their ideas is a perennial challenge in institutions and society. The seeming proliferation of personal attacks in political circles and on the World Wide Web is regrettable and probably has residual effects in classrooms. Even if this is not the case, the need to work toward open inquiring climates in classrooms is a largely but not totally uncontested suggestion and nowhere more evident than in discussions of values. An ideal that is difficult to abandon, particularly if we are teachers, is expressed in Jones's *The Known World* (2003) by the character Barnum: "A body should be able to stand under some ... kinda light and declare what he knows without retribution" (p. 303). For socially and academically vulnerable students or teachers, retribution for doing just that can come in many forms. A student's fear of being silenced during a discussion and being emotionally slain by others can make him or her feel particularly exposed to retaliation. Here Holder's (as cited in Weiss, 2009) exhortation to be courageous is sobering, especially if institutional and classroom safeguards are not in place. When safeguards have not already been institutionalized, a priority for educators should be to help encourage and establish policies, regulations, and laws regarding the study and teaching of controversial issues. With the backing of professional associations and unions and legislative leaders, educators need to work toward the passage of laws, policies, and procedures that enhance teaching controversial ideas in all kinds of educational institutions (Fisher, Schimmel, & Kelly, 1999; Stadler, 2007; Wagner & Simpson, 2009).

Psychological Effects

Problems with classroom attacks go beyond their logical irrelevance and pedagogical destructiveness to their psychological effect. While some questioners might be just seeking to expand an issue or place it in a context, genuine attacks can be so insidious that they gnaw on our psyches for days, weeks, and months. The inner anguish experienced is sometimes nearly overwhelming. We, much like Jadine in Morrison's *Tar Baby* (1982), might be tempted to declare, "I want to get out of my skin and be only the person inside—not American—not black—just me" (p. 48). Accepting externally imposed stereotypes and definitions that others foist on us—and maybe rejecting our identities in the process—shows the destructiveness of some ad hominem comments. Why would we willingly reject our own identities except for the exhausting attacks some of us endure? As teachers, we have an obligation to collaborate with our students and one another to help create healthy classroom and school spaces for inquiry and for developing the strength to reject the cutting definitions of definers (Morrison, 1987, p. 190).

Illustrative Situations

Illustrations of ad hominem arguments abound, but we use just one that shares a person's experiences with both school and university classmates and teachers. We begin with Walls's (2005) scenario about her informal conversation with another university student and continue with her formal discussion with a professor. During both, Walls was attempting to keep her past, nomadic, dysfunctional, and impoverished family life and her parents' current, semi-stable, but homeless lifestyle, secret. The context is her description of her family's sometimes self-inflicted, occasionally compelled, but recurrently painful struggles and treks from California to Arizona to West Virginia to New York.

In back-to-back examples, Walls's stories illustrate how ad hominem ideas and arguments can bring public embarrassment, personal stress, and self-hatred. The first describes part of a conversation she had with a fellow student as they walked down Broadway. In keeping with her habit of giving homeless people spare change, she offered a young fellow some money and was interrupted by Carol, her companion, who said: "You shouldn't do that." "It only encourages them. They're all scam artists" (Walls, 2005, p. 256). Hearing this stereotype of homeless people, Walls wanted to exclaim, "*What do you know?*" (p. 256). Her legitimate anger almost led her to orally attack her acquaintance rather than respond to her typecasting. Instead, her fear of revealing part of her history and her parents' circumstances caused her to say nothing. She silenced herself, going her "way without saying a thing" (p. 256).

Walls's (pp. 256–257) second scenario is more detailed, multilayered, complicated, and may have caused her to recall a fifth-grade experience. Her professor may have begun her assault after Walls stated in class that some homeless people did not fit into the either/or (i.e., conservative or liberal) explanations that were mentioned. No doubt thinking of her university-educated parents (depicted as an eccentric want-to-be-artist-despite-the-traumatic-consequences mother and an alcoholic want-to-do-things-my-own-way-regardless-of-the-outcomes father), she said, "I think that maybe sometimes people get the lives they want" (p. 256). After making her statement, the ensuing professor-student interactions occurred:

"Can you explain yourself?"
"I think that maybe sometimes people get the lives they want."
"Are you saying homeless people want to live on the street?"
"Are you saying they don't want warm beds and roofs over their heads?"
"Not exactly."
"They do. But if some of them were willing to work hard and make compromises, they might not have ideal lives, but they could make ends meet." (pp. 256–257)

The three professorial questions might have been an innocent attempt to get Walls to examine, explain, or justify her thoughts. The professor may have been using sound pedagogy. Maybe her probing was well intentioned even if her use of personal pronouns was ill timed. But when the professor walked from behind the lectern to ask two additional questions, her intentions seemed either to change or become more manifest. Walls heard her own previously unarticulated question— What do you know?"—echo in her mind:

"What do you know about the lives of the underprivileged?"
"What do you know about the hardships and obstacles that the underclass faces?" (p. 257)

Seeing a student who appeared to be a white, middle-class, privileged female, the professor may have assumed that Walls knew nothing about the topic at hand and was merely voicing her unrecognized ignorance, unexamined ideology, or, worse, her own deep-seated prejudices. Like Hurston's (1978) Janie when speaking to Jody, Walls may have wanted to whisper to her professor, "Mah own mind ha tuh be squeezed and crowded out tuh make room for yours in me" (p. 133). Surveying the stares of her fellow students, she may have recalled her fifth-grade teacher's question ("Perhaps you'd like to explain yourself?") and her classmates as they "swiveled their heads around to stare" (Walls, 2005, p. 138). In the end, she acquiesced: "You have a point" (p. 257). She, like Simone, concluded, "Who am I to argue?" (Belenky, Clinchy, Goldberger, & Tarule, 1986, p. 216).

Like Walls's professor, we can make faulty assumptions about students and combine them with defective reasoning and poisonous pedagogy and use an ad hominem argument. In the process, we can not only silence the voices of those who are more knowledgeable, better experienced, and more reflective than we are, but we may also quell opportunities for genuine class inquiry. But even if Walls were an ill-informed, privileged, white female, her ideas needed to be analyzed, not her personhood attacked. Even if Walls had misconstrued her experience and her parents' choices and preferences, her professor's response was toxic. Forgotten were some pertinent clichés that a student is "entitled to her opinion" and that "[r]easonable people can disagree about this" (McInerney, 2006, p. 226). As teachers, we may be well advised to reflect on Nafisi's (2004) declaration about "the most unsympathetic characters" who appear, lecture, and scold in novels: their "incapacity for true dialogue implies an incapacity for tolerance, self-reflection and empathy" (p. 268).

Conclusion

Several ideas deserve attention at this time. First, though we have been critical of several kinds of questions, it is clear that sound pedagogy makes generous use of numerous queries. Raising questions is a vital part of many—perhaps most—classrooms. Asking questions, in our opinion, should be encouraged not discouraged. Indeed, we want to encourage students and teachers to become reflective, questioning gadflies and work toward school environments that nurture settings to facilitate the intellectual, social, and emotional development of everyone involved. To help students think clearly, evidentially, cogently, critically, and comprehensively about ethical issues in our fields of expertise is no insignificant part of their educations. We are only discouraging the use of questions that are actually "burning statements" that are sometimes combined with other anti-educational behaviours that are "killing tools" (Hurston, 1978, p. 10).

Second, even though many questions are inappropriate because they stymie discussions, they may be invaluable indicators of related matters that we need to discuss. The questions—and statements—may be more important than the planned curriculum. So in a way, no matter how unfortunate the thought behind a question may be, we may thank students for providing educational opportunities when they express their dismissive/evasive tactics, logical stoppers, and ad hominem arguments. They help us, or at least create opportunities for us, to become better teachers.

Teachers also have to grapple with legal mandates (e.g., curriculum specifications and standardized tests) and administrative obstacles (e.g., leadership fear of community mores) that can silence or inhibit classroom learning. These and related obstructions can disrupt the work of many teachers, especially new ones who are often the most defenceless. Certainly, legal threats and administrative impediments that inhibit reflective teaching and student engagement may contribute to teacher attrition (Kozol, 2005, 2007). Of course, when teachers and schools focus on which instructional approach is effective in a certain situation and neglect social environments, teachers may end up implementing a technological, manufacturing, predetermined approach to education (McLaren, 2010; Schwandt, 2002). While these emphases may help some students perform successfully on standardized tests and in market-driven classrooms, they may limit the flexibility that teachers have to adapt the curriculum to students' personal and local backgrounds (Eryaman, 2006, 2007). Encouraging teachers to develop and exercise good judgment or wisdom, however, can broaden classroom perspectives and provide students with opportunities to discuss sensitive issues while providing a counterbalance to the narrow view of the teacher as classroom manager (Kozol, 2005). In all of these situations, it is important that teachers understand and remind one another that "the world is not as dangerous as many in the older generation want to believe" (Kozol, 2007, p. 193). So, teachers and their allies need to work wisely toward their ideals, lest they "choke on their beliefs [and] … never know the taste of struggle in a decent cause and never know the thrill of even partial victories" (p. 193).

Third, we seem to be well advised to anticipate patterns of student comments so as to be able to use their ideas in non-inflammatory but stimulating ways. So, if students appreciably control our classes by comments that tend to obstruct educative conversations, we need to reconsider our instructional practices (Schön, 1983). Staying abreast of contemporary student cultures and beliefs can be a very useful means of professional development and enable teachers to better anticipate students' expressions of their beliefs. Staying abreast of our legal rights as educators is also important. Hence, as teachers we need to attend to recent developments in the field of school law, support local workshops on educational law, and attend professional conferences that address our rights and freedoms as educators. Moreover, we need to study dialogical practices as a profession so that we better understand and utilize the limits of our freedoms and rights as professionals (Cambron-McCabe, McCarthy, & Thomas, 2009; Essex, 2006; Fisher, Schimmel, & Kelly, 1999; Siegel, 2007; Stadler, 2007).

Fourth, as teachers we are not only responsible for nurturing healthy classroom environments but also for examining our own passions and prejudices and ensuring that they do not prompt us to mistreat students or unfairly present ideas. If we ignore our ethical responsibility to treat students with respect (regardless of how ill-founded we may deem their views), we run the risk of creating an ethical chasm between what we say our interests are and what we do in class (Gay, 2000). As Freire (2003) observes, when we act contrary to what we profess, we enlarge the gap between our ethical profession and our ethical practice and lose our credibility.

Fifth, if as teachers we are also teacher educators, it is at least arguable that we have a responsibility to better prepare aspiring teachers to address ethical questions in their classrooms. That is to say, we appear to have a professional duty to help our university students understand ethically significant questions and to handle delicate issues in pedagogically sound and intellectually honest ways. Preparing students who intend to be teachers and contributors to the development of democratic citizens demands such, for democracy itself is loaded with ethical questions and concerns (Dewey, 1916; Freire, 1998; West, 2004). Moreover, we may need to challenge our university students to critique their and our assumptions, reasoning habits, and linguistic patterns that tend to inhibit rather than facilitate discussions and that have a tendency to close rather than open minds to important realms of inquiry. Extrapolating from Hess's (2009) remarks about preparing to teach high school students, we can say that preparing future teachers for these activities takes a great deal of preparation and study of positive examples of how to discuss controversies in the classroom. Together with the previous thoughts, it seems that we should assist aspiring and practicing teachers as they seek to understand how they may maintain open minds about the credibility of longstanding and emerging knowledge claims (Hare, 1979, 1993), dig into their ideological assumptions and presuppositions for clarity (Shermer, 1997), interrogate their privileged beliefs and practices (Kincheloe, 2005; McLaren & Farahmandpur, 2006), think critically about their everyday and professional beliefs and values (Paul & Elder, 2005; Stone, Patton, & Heen, 1999), identify their fallacious ways of thinking (Ennis, 1969; Norris, 1992) and scrutinize their beliefs to determine which are intelligent beliefs and disbeliefs (Noddings, 1993). The reflective spirit, as is widely known, is a two-edged sword and calls for an examination of our own beliefs— whether we are teacher educators, teachers, or students—and not just those of others. Similarly, Paz (1985) tells us that we must begin to identify and evaluate our own ideologies before we can expect others to do the same. Even so, these preparations alone may not be sufficient: a teacher education program that seeks to foster reflective practitioners who acquire practical wisdom is also demanded (Eryaman, 2007).

Finally, in a Siegelian (Siegel, 2007) spirit, we conclude that we think we have offered ideas which appear credible and worthy of further consideration. We hope that multiple kinds of gadflies will critique, if not apply, our ideas. Rather than automatically condemning gadflies as being on the side of devils and designating ourselves as being on the side of angels, we hope they—with all of their idiosyncratic, irritable, questionable, and irreverent tendencies—will be encouraged to inquire into "indiscussible" questions, the protected dogmas of contemporary societies (Pinker, 2008). Of course, we need not be as optimistic as Mill (2004) to encourage gadflies to join more discussions. Likewise, we need to remember that in encouraging warranted discussions of sensitive and controversial topics we are not interested merely in open discourse but in dialogues that enable us to grow in our understanding of and acting with one another for the common good of our schools, communities, societies, nations, and world (Freire, 2003).

Perhaps it is almost superfluous to say that we are not encouraging a false open-mindedness where teachers feel obligated to provide a so-called fair study of everyone's proposed issue, such as, say, the views of those who claim that the peak of African slave trade was limited to a few thousand people (Hare, 2009). Nevertheless, teachers need to be prepared to address when and why a question is ever closed and what needs to occur if a closed topic is to be reopened in a classroom setting (Hess, 2009). Likewise, toxic speech practices have no room in educative settings. Instead, classrooms need dialogue that avoids both "overly controlled" and "undisciplined" interactions (Freire, 2005, p. 81). Unfortunately, many of us seem to lack the courage that Holder (Weiss, 2009) supports so that we can discuss important topics in appropriate ways. Likewise, dialogical cultures that facilitate considered or educative discussions are often lacking in schools and communities, and that lack probably accounts for part of the fear Holder noted (Hess, 2009; Wagner & Simpson, 2009). In view of these circumstances, much culture-and-courage building is needed in schools and classrooms. Leveraging pedagogical moments that may otherwise undermine important dialogue provides opportunities for culture-and-courage building by teachers and students and, thereby, opportunities for ethical and democratic growth, not to mention the intellectual and emotional development that occurs in fields of inquiry and creativity.

REFERENCES

Alexander, J. (2007). *The structural evolution of morality*. Cambridge, UK: Cambridge University Press. doi:10.1017/CBO9780511550997

Axelrod, R. (1984). *The evolution of cooperation*. New York: Basic Books.

Bales, K. (2004). *Disposable people: New slavery in the global economy* (Revised ed.). Berkeley: University of California Press.

Barrow, R. (1991). *Utilitarianism: A contemporary statement*. Brookfield, VT: Edward Elgar Publishing Company.

Belenky, M., Clinchy, B., Goldberger, N., & Tarule, J. (1986). *Women's ways of knowing: The development of self, voice, and mind*. New York: Basic Books, Inc.

Bernstein, B. (1990). *Class, codes and control: The structuring of pedagogic discourse*. London: Routledge and Kegan Paul. doi:10.4324/9780203011263

Bhattacharyya, J., Gabriel, J., & Small, S. (2002). *Race and power: Global racism in the twenty-first century*. New York: Routledge.

Brookfield, S., & Preskill, S. (1999). *Discussion as a way of teaching: Tools and techniques for democratic classrooms*. Hoboken: John Wiley & Sons.

Cambron-McCabe, N., McCarthy, M., & Thomas, S. (2009). *Legal rights of teachers and students* (2nd ed.). Boston: Allyn & Bacon.

Campbell, K., & Huxman, S. (2009). *The rhetorical act: thinking, speaking, and writing critically* (4th ed.). Belmont, CA: Wadsworth.

Camus, A. (1995). *Resistance, rebellion, and death* (J. O'Brien, Trans.). New York: Vintage Books.

Center for Faculty Excellence (2004). Teaching Controversial Issues. *For your consideration … suggestions and reflections on teaching and learning* (CFC, No.21). Retrieved March, 6, 2010, from http://cfe.unc.edu/pdfs/FYC21.pdf

Claire, H., & Holden, C. (Eds.). (2007). *The challenge of teaching controversial issues*. Stoke-on-Trent: Trentham Books.

Coles, R. (2000). *The moral life of children*. New York: Grove/Atlantic.

Dewey, J. (1916). *Democracy and education: An introduction to the philosophy of education*. New York: The Free Press.

Dewey, J. (1922). *Human nature and conduct: An introduction to social psychology*. New York: Modern Library.

Dewey, J. (1929). *The quest for certainty*. New York: Minton, Balch and Co.

Dewey, J. (1948). *Reconstruction in philosophy* (Enlarged ed.). Boston: Beacon Press.

Dewey, J., & Tufts, J. (1932). *Ethics* (Revised ed.). New York: Holt.

Dostoyevsky, D. (1982). *The brothers Karamazov* (D. Magarshack, Trans.). Harmondsworth, UK: Penguin Books Ltd.

Ennis, R. (1969). *Logic in teaching*. Englewood Cliffs, NJ: Prentice-Hall.

Eryaman, M. (2006). A hermeneutic approach towards integrating technology into schools: Policy and practice. In S. Tettegah & R. Hunter (Eds.), *Technology: Issues in administration, policy, and applications in K–12 schools* (pp. 143–167). Philadelphia: Elsevier Science Publications. doi:10.1016/S1479-3660(05)08011-X

Eryaman, M. (2007). From reflective practice to practical wisdom: Towards a post-foundational teacher education. *International Journal of Progressive Education, 3*(1), 1–23.

Essex, N. (2006). *A teacher's pocket guide to school law*. Boston: Pearson.

Fisher, L., Schimmel, D., & Kelly, C. (1999). *Teachers and the law*. New York: Longman.

Forrest, M. (2009). Sensitive controversy in teaching to be critical. *Paideusis, 18*(1), 80–93. [See also page 116 of this volume.]

The Freedom Writers, with Gruwell, E. (1999). *The freedom writers diary: How a teacher and 150 teens used writing to change themselves and the world around them.* New York: Broadway Books.

Freire, P. (1998). *Pedagogy of freedom: Ethics, democracy, and civic courage* (P. Clarke, Trans.). New York: Rowman & Littlefield Publishers, Inc.

Freire, P. (2003). *Pedagogy of the oppressed* (30th anniversary ed.). (M. Ramos, Trans.). New York: Continuum.

Freire, P. (2005). *Teachers as cultural workers* (Expanded ed.). (D. Macedo, D. Koike, & A. Oliveria, Trans.). Boulder, CO: Westview Press.

Gay, G. (2000). *Culturally responsive teaching: Theory, research, & practice.* New York: Teachers College Press.

Green, J. (1999). *Deep democracy: Community, diversity, and transformation.* Lanham, MD: Rowman & Littlefield Publishers, Inc.

Gribble, J. (1969). *Introduction to philosophy of education.* Boston: Allyn and Bacon, Inc.

Habermas, J. (1984). *The theory of communicative action.* Boston: Beacon Press.

Hare, W. (1979). *Open-mindedness and education.* Montreal: McGill-Queen's University Press.

Hare, W. (1993). *Attitudes in teaching and education.* Calgary, AB: Detselig Enterprises, Ltd.

Hare, W. (2009). What open-mindedness requires. *Skeptical Inquirer, 33*(1), 36–39.

Hess, D. (2009). *Controversy in the classroom: The democratic power of discussion.* New York: Routledge.

Holmes, R. (2003). *Basic moral philosophy* (3rd ed.). Belmont, CA: Thomson/Wadsworth.

Hurston, Z. (1978). *Their eyes were watching God.* Urbana: University of Illinois Press.

Jones, E. (2003). *The known world.* New York: Amistad.

Kincheloe, J. (2005). *Critical constructivism primer.* New York: Peter Lang.

Kozol, J. (2005). *The shame of the nation.* New York: Crown Publishers.

Kozol, J. (2007). *Letters to a young teacher.* New York: Crown Publishers.

Mah, A. (1997). *Falling leaves: The memoir of an unwanted Chinese daughter.* New York: Broadway Books.

McInerney J. (2006). *The good life.* New York: Alfred A. Knopf.

McLaren, P. (2010). Afterwords. *Educational Theory, 60*(3), 391–393. doi:10.1111/j.1741-5446.2010.00365.x

McLaren, P., & Farahmandpur, R. (2006). The pedagogy of oppression: A brief look at *No Child Left Behind. Monthly Review (New York, N.Y.), 58*(3), 94–99.

Mill, J. (2004). *On liberty.* New York: Barnes & Noble.

Morrison, T. (1982). *Tar baby.* New York: A Plume Book.

Morrison, T. (1987). *Beloved.* New York: A Plume Book.

Nafisi, N. (2004). *Reading Lolita in Tehran: A memoir in books.* New York: Random House.

Nieto, S. (2000). *Affirming diversity: The sociopolitical context of multicultural education* (3rd ed.). New York: Longman.

Noddings, N. (1991). Stories in dialogue: Caring and interpersonal reasoning. In C. Witherell & N. Noddings (Eds.), *Stories lives tell: Narrative and dialogue in education* (pp. 157–170). New York: Teachers College Press.

Noddings, N. (1992). *The challenge to care in schools.* New York: Teachers College Press.

Noddings, N. (1993). *Educating for intelligent belief or unbelief.* New York: Teachers College Press.

Norris, S. (1992). *The generalizability of critical thinking.* New York: Teachers College Press.

Oakeshott, M. (1991). *Moral consciousness and communicative action.* Cambridge, MA: MIT Press.

Paul, R., & Elder, L. (2005). *Critical thinking: Tools for taking charge of your learning and your life* (2nd ed.). New York: Prentice Hall.

Paz, O. (1985). *The labyrinth of solitude* (L. Kemp, Y. Milos, & R. Belash, Trans.). New York: Grove Press.

Peters, R. (1970). *Ethics and education.* London: George Allen and Unwin.

Peterson, C., & Seligman, M. (2004). *Character strengths and virtues.* Washington, DC: Oxford University Press.

Pinker, S. (2008, January 13). The moral instinct. *The New York Times.* Retrieved January 29, 2008, from http://www.nytimes.com/2008/01/13/magazine/13Psychology-t.html

Schön, D. (1983). *How professionals think in action.* New York: Basic Books.

Schwandt, T. (2002). Evaluation as practical hermeneutics. In T.A. Schwandt (Ed.), *Evaluation practices revisited* (pp. 59–74). New York: Peter Lang Publishing.

Shermer, M. (1997). *Why people believe weird things: Pseudoscience, superstition, and other confusions of our time.* New York: Henry Holt & Company.

Siegel, H. (2007). What is freedom of speech in teaching? In W. Hare & J. Portelli (Eds.), *Key questions for educators* (pp. 64–67). San Francisco, CA: Caddo Gap Press.

Simpson, D., & Hull, W., Jr. (2011). Discussing ethical issues in the classroom: Leveraging pedagogical moments that may otherwise undermine important discussions. *International Journal of Progressive Education, 7*(3), 6–26.

Stadler, D. (2007). *Law and ethics in educational leadership.* Upper Saddle River, NJ: Pearson/Merrill/Prentice Hall.

Stone, D., Patton, B., & Heen, S. (1999). *Difficult conversations: How to discuss what matters most.* New York: Viking.

Vogt, W. (1997). *Tolerance & education: Learning to live with diversity and difference.* Thousand Oaks, CA: Sage.

Wagner, P., & Simpson, D. (2009). *Ethical decision making in school administration: Leadership as moral architecture.* Thousand Oaks, CA: Sage.

Walls, J. (2005). *The glass castle: A memoir.* New York: Scribner.

Weiss, D. (2009). Holder says US is "Nation of Cowards" in racial discussions. Retrieved February 21, 2009, from http://abajournal.com/news/holder_says_us_is_nation_of_cowards_in_racial_discussions

West, C. (1993). *Race matters.* Boston: Beacon Press.

West, C. (2004). *Democracy matters: Winning the fight against imperialism.* New York: Penguin Books.

Williams, J. (1994). *Classroom in conflict: Teaching controversial subjects in a diverse society.* Albany: State University of New York Press.

Wong, D. (2006). *Natural moralities: A defense of pluralistic relativism.* New York: Cambridge University Press. doi:10.1093/0195305396.001.0001

NOTES

1 The terms *teachers* and *teacher* are used throughout this work to include anyone who teaches in a university teacher-education program or a P–12 school. Similarly, the terms *students* and *student* are employed to include anyone who is studying to become a teacher in a university preparation program or studying in a P–12 school.

2 The word *colleagues* is an inclusive term that includes anyone who meets the previously stated definition of a teacher.

3 The focus of this paper is on those occasions when inappropriate silencing of students occurs, not on those instances when a student or teacher violates legal or institutional free speech laws or policies. This focus, however, does not assume that all legal and/or institutional free speech laws and policies are ipso facto flawless.

4 Our general model is implied, in part, by references to Zora Neale Hurston (1978), Cornell West (2004), Paulo Freire (2003), Albert Camus (1995), John Dewey (1916), and Jurgen Habermas (1984). In short, our theoretical orientation is rooted in a liberal and humane view of a deep democracy (Green, 1999), one that is concerned with learning from the diversity of thought and values that exist in society, and one that is founded at a minimum on a tolerance of ideas that are repugnant but also a critique of ideas that are both disagreeable and agreeable (Vogt, 1997). Of course, there are numerous other thinkers who have helped shape our dialogical model and democratic ideals, such as Wong (2006), Siegel (2007), Peters (1970), Mill (2004), Noddings (1991, 1992), Hare (2009), and Campbell and Huxman (2009).

5 The authors employ a form of classroom dialogue that is designed to be democratically situated, epistemologically inclusive, and educationally oriented. Although there are problems and challenges that are intrinsic to this approach, we think our approach can be substantially justified by considering our conception of dialogue itself when undertaken in public institutions in a liberal democracy. In general, our approach to dialogue is to be as inclusive as is educationally appropriate, so that it may include as much diversity of thought as possible. The approach is dynamic and multi-theoretical, so that it may be enhanced as contexts and discussions suggest modifications are needed. For more details regarding our thinking, see footnote 5 in D. Simpson and W. Hull, Jr. (2011).

7

"That's Just Your Opinion!"

American Idol and the Confusion between Pluralism and Relativism

*Claudia W. Ruitenberg**

*This chapter was first published as Ruitenberg, C.W. (2007). "That's just your opinion!"—"American Idol" and the confusion between pluralism and relativism. *Paideusis, 16*(1), 55–59. Reproduced with permission.

Those of you who, like me, watch too much junk TV may have come across a phenomenon called *American Idol.* In this "reality" television series thousands of people between the ages of 16 and 28 audition in a singing contest, in the hopes of becoming "the next American idol" and winning a music contract.[1] The opening episodes of each series feature many contestants who believe they sing wonderfully well but who are tone deaf, randomly jumping from key to key in the short song fragment they perform, or who produce sounds not associated with "singing" even in the broad sense of the word. Some of these contestants receive the feedback of the judges graciously; many others, however, show indignation at a negative evaluation. A commonly heard response to such an evaluation is, "That's just your opinion!"

Whatever the psychological explanations for this defensive response may be, in a philosophical sense, "That's just your opinion!" expresses confusion between a preference and a judgment. Unfortunately, this confusion extends far beyond *American Idol.* One of the factors contributing to this confusion is that in our everyday language, the word "opinion" can refer both to a preference and to a judgment. If someone asks me, "What is your opinion about the new leader of the Liberal Party?" I assume I am expected to provide a judgment for which I have reasons. When contestants on *American Idol* say, "That's just your opinion!" they typically mean, "That is merely a personal preference, for which you have no reasons!"

From the teacher education courses I have taught, including, most recently, ones on critical thinking, I have the impression that many student teachers (as well as many of the students they teach) share the confusion about preferences and judgments. A major contributing factor to this confusion, I surmise, is the popular idea that "everyone is entitled to her or his opinion." When it comes to mere preferences, such as my preference for dark over white chocolate or someone else's preference for writing at night rather than during the daytime, I share the idea that everyone is entitled to her or his preferences and that, as is implied by this idea, people should not be required to justify these preferences. When it comes to judgments, however, it is a different story.

If our students believe that everyone is entitled to her or his judgments, i.e., that people have a right to form whatever judgments they wish and that others have no right to question those judgments, they have moved into the territory of relativism. In the case of *American Idol,* we are confronted with *aesthetic relativism,* the belief that there are no objective or intersubjective criteria for aesthetic quality and that what counts as aesthetic quality is entirely dependent on one's framework or perspective. Aesthetic relativism conflates aesthetic judgments with aesthetic preferences: "My singing is good because my mother likes it."

In our classrooms, we may encounter aesthetic relativism, but also other relativisms, such as moral relativism. *Moral relativism* is the belief that there are no objective or even intersubjective criteria for morality and that what counts as "moral" is entirely dependent on one's framework or perspective. For some of you, alarm bells may be ringing at this point. "What is she getting at? She is not seriously going to argue in our 'postmodern condition' (Lyotard, 1979/1984) that there are universal moral truths, is she?!" No, I am not going to argue that there are universal moral truths. What I am going to argue, however, is that many of our students fail to understand the difference between pluralism and relativism, and that their fear of moral absolutism leads them to espouse relativism when they should be promoting pluralism.

Pluralism is the view that there is more than one set of values that is legitimate and worth pursuing, but not an infinite number. We might say that most of us show ourselves to be pluralists in our individual lives as we espouse a range of values, some of which are at odds with each other, such as justice and mercy. The question of pluralism is raised most often, however, about societies in which individuals and groups with different sets of values seek to cohabit. Isaiah Berlin (1998), a well-known champion of pluralism, writes,

> *If pluralism is a valid view, and respect between systems of values which are not necessarily hostile to each other is possible, then toleration and liberal consequences follow, as they do not either from monism (only one set of values is true, all the others are false) or from relativism (my values are mine, yours are yours, and if we clash, too bad, neither of us can claim to be right). ("Pluralism," para. 4)*

Berlin is aware of the impossibility of fixing once and for all how many sets of values ought to be respected, and who should be the arbiters of this selection. In fact, it is likely that there will always be disagreement about the range of values. What matters in pluralism, however, is that an ongoing conversation about the boundaries of the moral is maintained, and that this conversation meets certain criteria. Perhaps most important among these criteria are that the interlocutors understand the difference between preferences and judgments, that they provide reasons for their judgments, and that all judgments and reasons are open to interrogation by others.

Blake, Smeyers, Smith, and Standish (1998) explain moral relativism as "the view that there are no objective moral or ethical standards, that each must live according to her own lights and, most fundamentally, each is immune to moral critique by others" (p. 9). The kind of relativism I have described above, which rejects not only objective but even intersubjective criteria, is a particularly pernicious and popular variety of relativism that Blake et al. call "subjectivism" (p. 12).

Subjective relativism fails to distinguish between *contingent* and *arbitrary* moral standards; it treats all historically or culturally contingent moral standards as arbitrary and hence rejects them as any standard at all. Judging a particular act—say, sexual intercourse with a woman against her will—to be immoral is based on a moral standard, in this case one of individual bodily integrity. I may well recognize this moral standard to be based on cultural conventions in which women and men are considered worthy of equal moral concern, and in which an individual woman has the right to protect her body from unwanted bodily invasions by any person, regardless of her relation or kinship to that person, and so on and so forth. Recognizing this moral standard to be *contingent* on those cultural conventions—for which good reasons can be and have been provided—is not at all the same as recognizing this moral standard as *arbitrary*, based solely on personal preferences or wishes. An arbitrary moral standard would say, for example, that one cannot have sexual intercourse with a woman against her will if she is wearing a green skirt (but it's okay if she's wearing a red skirt). Considering such an arbitrary standard to be of equal value as the moral standard of bodily integrity is a serious mistake.

The mistake may spring from what Eamonn Callan (1997) calls "a tendency to attend only to what are usually the more tractable aspects of diversity—the outward trappings of ethnicity, say, or divergent lifestyles" (p. 207). Discussions about the contingency of "opinions" often revolve around questions of food and fashion, debating, for example, the consumption of shrimp versus crickets. "This is misleading," Callan points out, "because ethnic differences or variety of lifestyle can thrive alongside an amicable moral unanimity, and ethnic commonality and convergent life-styles may coincide with profound and divisive moral conflict" (p. 207). *De gustibus non est disputandum*—there is no arguing about taste—but the point is precisely that moral judgments are not matters of taste, and that we do not treat disagreements about moral judgments "with the friendly indulgence" that Callan, for instance, extends "to those who foolishly prefer scotch to Irish whiskey" (p. 207).

Some people use the term "relativism" when they mean what I have described as pluralism. Blake et al. (1998) distinguish pluralism from relativism in the following way:

> There is a moral view, arguably a coherent one, which some call relativist, that
> we should cherish and respect genuine moral diversity while fearing moral dogma
> and pressures toward moral conformity. We are hesitant, though, to use the word

relativism here (preferring pluralism), because such a view clearly pulls certain non-negotiable commitments back in by the back door: commitments to, for instance, a certain moral humility and respect for the judgments of others. (p. 9)

The justifiable fear of moral absolutism leads some educators to fear even such minimal standards as moral humility and respect for (which is not the same as agreement with) the judgments of others. Such standards, however, are necessary if we wish to prevent our students from falling into the solipsistic traps of subjective relativism.

Student teachers in my class have given me some examples from their practica that illustrate the relevance of understanding the difference between preferences and judgments, and between pluralism and relativism. In one elementary classroom, a student declared that "married people cannot get AIDS, because AIDS is a punishment from God." This is not only a dangerous misunderstanding of the nature of the virus involved but also a serious moral judgment about people with HIV/AIDS. When expressed in a classroom, this judgment requires a response from a teacher who understands the difference between a judgment and a preference and who can distinguish stronger from weaker reasons. The response, "You are entitled to your opinion," would be entirely inappropriate and miseducative.

The obviously defensive stance, "That's just your opinion!" sometimes comes disguised in other forms that can make it harder to recognize. Two such forms are "I respect your view," and "Let's agree to disagree." Both phrases have appropriate uses, even when judgments rather than preferences are involved. In the political arena, for example, a social democrat might find herself disagreeing with a political opponent about the relative role of personal responsibility. "I respect your view" here might mean "I respect your legitimacy as political adversary and I recognize the reasons you have provided for your judgments, but at the end of the day, I will still disagree with your view that greater income inequality is justifiable as an incentive." Likewise, "let's agree to disagree" can usefully exclude a divisive topic that threatens to derail a discussion about another topic. Someone might suggest, "Let's agree to disagree for the moment about the possibility of nondogmatic religious faith so that we can focus on our discussion about the legitimacy of antiabortion protests outside abortion clinics."

Both phrases, "I respect your view" and "Let's agree to disagree," are also used in the classroom, however, and sometimes in inappropriate ways. If a child remarks that "Indians are poor because they're lazy," then that is not a view to be "respected," nor is it an appropriate moment for an educator to "agree to disagree," no matter how much he or she wishes to stay away from this discussion or get on with a lesson. Such a judgment, when entered into the classroom conversation, must be examined, and to do so the educator needs to understand the difference between a judgment and a preference and be able to distinguish stronger from weaker reasons. In the classroom, we should be happy to agree to disagree about whether chocolate ice cream is preferable to vanilla, or the other way around, but when it comes to judgments about issues of "more than slight moral consequence" (Callan, 1997, p. 204), educators have an educative responsibility to help students examine these judgments and the reasons provided for them.

Let me close with a brief consideration of the specific nature of the space that provides the context for this discussion: the classroom. The classroom is not a truly public space in the way a public square or park are public spaces. There are restrictions as to who can be in the classroom, and there are differences in authority between students and teachers that distinguish their interactions from those of citizens in a public square or park. The classroom is also not a truly private space, however, in the way someone's home is a private space. Neither teacher nor students have control over the particular students who are assigned to the classroom and many students are strangers before meeting each other in the classroom. If we conceive of education as a social practice that straddles the public and private sphere, and that "mediates [the] passage between the specificity of intimate relations and the generalities of the public world" (Grumet, 1988, p. 14), the classroom fulfills a particular role in students' transition from the private to the public.

The public world provides encounters with those who hold opinions (both in the sense of preferences and in the sense of judgments) different from one's own. In the classroom, students need to be prepared for such encounters both by learning to justify their own judgments and by learning to examine the judgments and justifications that others provide. If the classroom becomes a space in which a discussion can be shut down by declaring someone's judgment "just their opinion," it does not fulfill its role as a transitional space between the private and the public. Pluralism can only be sustained by an ongoing public conversation about the sets of values that should or should not guide the lives of members of the diverse polity. The refusal to expose one's own opinions to the scrutiny and potential disagreement of others is a refusal to engage in the public qua public. When "that's just my opinion" is used to shield one's views from public scrutiny, or "that's just your opinion" is used to disavow one's responsibility to engage another's views, these phrases do not belong in the classroom. And that is not just my opinion.

REFERENCES

Berlin, I. (1998, May 14). My intellectual path. *New York Review of Books.* Retrieved from http://www.nybooks.com.

Blake, N., Smeyers, P., Smith, R., & Standish, P. (1998). *Thinking again: Education after postmodernism.* Westport, CT: Bergin & Garvey.

Callan, E. (1997). *Creating citizens: Political education and liberal democracy.* New York: Oxford University Press.

Grumet, M.R. (1988). *Bitter milk: Women and teaching.* Amherst: The University of Massachusetts Press.

Lyotard, J.-F. (1984). *The postmodern condition: A report on knowledge* (G. Bennington & B. Massumi, Trans.). Minneapolis: University of Minnesota Press. (Original work published 1979)

NOTE

1 *American Idol* is based on the British televised singing competition, *Pop Idol,* and first appeared on American television in 2002. It has become one of the most watched shows in American television history and is broadcast to over 100 countries. Canada had its own *Canadian Idol* series from 2003 to 2008.

8

Sensitive Controversy in Teaching to be Critical

Michelle Forrest*

*This chapter was first published as Forrest, Michelle E. (2009). Sensitive controversy in teaching to be critical. *Paideusis 18*(1), 80–93. Reproduced with permission.

Introduction

One of the difficult balances to achieve in teaching philosophy of education to preservice teachers is that of discussing a controversial issue the substance of which has had a direct negative impact upon one or more students in the class. The problem concerning sensitive controversies in the classroom is one I first encountered when, as a novice teacher, I taught *The Merchant of Venice* in high-school language arts. Shylock, the Jewish moneylender, is the villain of the piece, and Shakespeare evokes all the stereotypes of his day to heap invective upon him. Though I did not and still do not believe the play should be avoided in secondary-school language arts, I did feel uncomfortable even as I taught the context of anti-Semitism from which Shakespeare's characterization sprang. I had a pervasive sense of empathy for any Jewish student in the class and couldn't help but wonder how he or she might be feeling. And yet, the history of anti-Semitism, racism, sexism, and other systemic bigotry needs to be examined, especially by those most at risk of adopting the quick and easy stereotypes that propel intolerant attitudes.

Different controversies are sensitive to greater or lesser degrees depending upon numerous variables, such as the current climate of public debate around a given controversy and the way in which it comes to light. As William Hare (1985) points out, "[i]t is important to notice that value questions can reach the public forum ... in a different way. This difference hinges upon the way in which we are disturbed" (p. 112). Take, for example, the claim of Digby, Nova Scotia, residents that the local Royal Canadian Mounted Police (RCMP) detachment is guilty of racist behaviour and attitudes. Following an incident involving an off-duty Mountie and a member of Digby's African Nova Scotian community, black citizens affirmed that RCMP harassment and intimidation had been long-standing, while Mounties blamed a previous detachment commander, a few specific officers, and exaggerated reports by the media (Medel, 2008a, 2008b). What if, while the community is in the midst of heated debate over this incident, a teacher in the predominantly white local high school decides to raise the news incident in her class for debate? How might we consider this decision? On the one hand, while community feelings remain raw, this could be a risky or even irresponsible move on the part of the teacher. The way in which the community has been disturbed by the issue of racism is such that a class discussion could generate more heat than light and even escalate tempers in the wider community. Though a teacher may be keen to teach students to be critical in light of community issues pertinent to their immediate experience, there are safety and other considerations that impinge upon this educational aim. On the other hand, what would this fictitious Digby teacher be implying by not taking up this troubling incident involving racism and the questions it raises? In addition to the inevitable focus on the incident within the community where it occurred, there was ongoing province-wide attention by news media, unlikely to have escaped students' notice. To remain silent within the school could be an equally risky strategy since tension and fear fester and ripen when mistaken assumptions and half-baked ideas are left unaired. To say nothing could imply a range of untenable notions, not least of which are that sensitive issues do not belong in the school curriculum, high-school students are too immature to discuss with seriousness matters of grave concern to adults, and racism is not an important problem in this community. The ways in which this incident disturbed small-town Nova Scotia, the province with the largest percentage of African Canadian citizens, can hardly be hived off from the formal school curriculum without raising charges of systemic racism, which lie at the heart of the incident itself.

Hare (1985) reminds us that since education is an interdisciplinary affair, there are times when philosophical analysis is not sufficient to provide the necessary evidence for determining whether one should include within one's curriculum a specific controversy at a specific time. Hare provides a thorough and convincing logical argument for the place of controversy in the curriculum but adds that a practical recommendation regarding the inclusion of a particular issue in its context requires further evidence, such as psychological evidence that a certain group could not understand the controversy, or sociological evidence that any presentation of the issue would lead to a "distorted grasp" (p. 115). While the community of Digby struggles with the situation and race relations are particularly strained, it is possible that an in-class discussion on racism could lead to a distorted grasp. A teacher faced with such a situation, and believing this is the moment to raise the issue precisely *because* it is hotly debated in the community, may reason that as it is her responsibility not to shrink from controversy this is her best chance to engage students in one. Hare's point is instructive here since she must weigh her belief in the importance of including controversy against other educationally relevant considerations. Though controversy has a vital role to play in the formal curriculum, *not* to take up a sensitive issue under circumstances of imminent volatility could demonstrate wiser judgment. Certainly the teacher would be wise not to wade in without serious reflection on the range of possible responses from students, how she might react appropriately and have the necessary resources to do so, and the potential consequences of her decision and reactions upon the wider community in light of students' best interests.

When faced with a sensitive controversy, how is the teacher to weigh her pedagogical choices along a continuum between taking up the issue at the risk of exacerbating a volatile situation and avoiding it, thereby reneging on her responsibility to teach students to be critical? Is there guidance to be found within the conceptualization of critical thinking as an educational ideal? These questions shall be taken up as follows: I will examine what makes a controversy sensitive, and how caring and empathy are involved in its treatment, and then move to that component of the concept of critical thinking referred to as the critical spirit, suggesting how the teacher might respond in discussions of sensitive controversy such that she acts in the spirit of criticism. I will then look at strong reflexivity in terms of its importance to the critical spirit and conclude with some thoughts on working across social difference as taking a "doubled view," as suggested by Todd (2003).

Sensitive Controversy, Empathy, and Caring

What is at issue, then, is a subset of controversies, here referred to as "sensitive," the very discussion of which can exacerbate the hurt and indignity already experienced by discussion participants as a result of the realities the controversy represents. George Dei (1996) points out that, in respect to the concepts of race and racism, "educators cannot overlook the fact that the theoretical exercise of debating the intellectual validity of these concepts can be painful for individuals who live the experiences being conceptualized" (p. 28). To focus then on the teacher-education classroom, here are two questions, variations on which frequently emerge in my philosophy of education course as we discuss case studies from schooling:[1]

1. In the interests of promoting anti-racism education, should we drop from the curriculum even those books in which racist language and behaviour are depicted as deplorable?
2. In light of the statistics on teen pregnancy among young adolescents, should the facts about abortion be included in the middle-school health education curriculum?

An important part of teacher education involves the realization that because of her or his influential position as authority figure, the teacher must consider when, how, or if it is appropriate to express a personal view on a topic under discussion. As the example of race relations in the town of Digby suggests, these considerations are of particular importance in discussing controversies of a sensitive nature.

Before examining what it is that makes a controversy sensitive, let us consider what makes a disagreement controversial. Though there can be various reasons for and conditions under which people disagree, Dearden (1984) reserves the term *controversy* for a disagreement on which "contrary views can be held ... without those views being contrary to reason" (p. 86). As McLaughlin (2003) points out, it is Dearden's isolation of this epistemic criterion of controversy that helps us identify which type of disagreement is appropriate for attention in the classroom (p. 150).[2] Part of Dearden's purpose in providing an epistemic criterion of the controversial is to further refine a mere behavioural criterion, which, by naming as "controversial" any disagreement by numbers of people, fails to distinguish disputes over matters trivial from those of a deeper kind. If teachers are to include controversy in their curricula, Dearden's distinction is useful in making judicious choices. Although it is never possible to predict or control fully when a controversial matter might arise in classroom discussion, the teacher can design lessons so as to raise issues strategically, thereby attempting to develop students' logical and analytical skills in discussions of simple matters of disagreement before moving to full-blown controversies. It may be prudent to begin with those controversies already resolved by theoretical developments (e.g., Ptolemaic vs. Copernican systems, divine right of kings vs. democratic theory). This allows for skill development without the complications that unresolved controversy might entail, while demonstrating to students how what is controversial at one point in time can change with empirical and theoretical developments. The teacher could then introduce discussion of topical controversies (e.g., competing definitions of "black hole," direct vs. representative democracy), and these may usefully precede those of a sensitive nature, such as the questions above regarding race and abortion.[3] What is it, then, that further distinguishes a controversy as one of a sensitive kind?

In fact, it is not the controversy that is sensitive but rather the person responding to it who is very open to or acutely affected by the matter under discussion. The phrase "a sensitive controversy" is a transferred epithet. In the noun plus modifying clause "a controversy to which people are sensitive," the epithet after the noun is condensed into the word "sensitive," which is then transferred to the adjective position. More correctly, then, to examine what makes a controversy sensitive is to consider why people are sensitive to certain topics. Certainly there are countless reasons why an individual might be acutely affected by the discussion of a controversy; however, for our purposes, we shall set aside reasons of accidental association (e.g., the topic reminds one of something upsetting but not substantively related to the matter at hand), and those of personal affect incidental to the controversy in question (e.g., an individual is upset by the emotional impact of people disagreeing). Although it is possible and even probable that both of the foregoing reasons may also impinge upon the person sensitive to a controversy in the sense

I shall next distinguish, I am suggesting these reasons for sensitivity be set aside when they exist devoid of the special distinction deemed "sensitive controversy." The reason for sensitivity that I suggest be used to distinguish that which we deem a "sensitive controversy" is the following: a person is acutely affected as a result of having been directly involved and/or having experienced the reality to which the controversy substantively refers. For example, question 1 raises a sensitive controversy in my philosophy of education class because in the predominantly white culture of Canadian universities, any student of colour will have been subject to the racism under discussion. Question 2 is sensitive because in a Canadian teacher-education class, students are predominantly female. Odds are more than one of the women in the class will have had an abortion, have had to contemplate having an abortion, or acted in a support role for a friend or relative facing such a decision.[4]

The dilemma for the teacher is this. At one extreme, in discussing a sensitive controversy the very discussion of it by anyone unsympathetic to those sensitive to it can inflict upon them further pain and indignity, as the quote from Dei (1996) above indicates. On the other hand, fear of offending those sensitive to the realities of the controversy can manifest itself in the silence of political correctness, thereby stifling honest dialogue and leaving prospective teachers unprepared for critical discussion of controversy in their own classrooms. In my experience in the teacher-education classroom, the newcomer to a discussion of a given sensitive issue is, in most instances, not intending to be hurtful with his or her comments; but what is hypothetical for one person can be a bitter reality for another. A common tack of the teacher is to attempt to develop empathy in those who, by virtue of not being directly implicated in the realities of the issue under discussion, are unable to understand how views offered on it, as if from a distance, can be hurtful to those sensitive to it. The very tone of voice used to stand back and generalize can evoke painful memories of rationalizations used to justify past injustices.

Typically, the pedagogical project of developing empathy in one's students has taken the form of appealing to their imaginations by describing how life might be for a victim of the circumstances entailed in an issue under discussion. It has been one of the roles of literature to recreate the imaginary world with which the reader may engage. Storytelling and drawing from historical evidence serve to help students understand what it might be like to be in the place of the Other. If, for example, I imagine myself a person of colour in a white society, constantly bound by assumptions and points of view not my own, I can imagine being infuriated listening to members of the dominant race debate the pros and cons of censoring all depictions of racism from the classroom. If I put myself in the place of the woman who has had an abortion or had to contemplate having one, I can imagine how difficult it would be to listen to others, particularly men, cavalierly offer definitive views on the subject. Being able to put oneself in the position of someone gravely affected by the issue suggests that one possesses what Passmore (1985) terms "sympathetic imagination": "a capacity to understand how other people are feeling. Such imagination," says Passmore, "is inherent in the capacity to cooperate. Always difficult, it becomes even more difficult when the people in question are culturally and socially remote" (p. 16). Passmore (1983) emphasizes that imagination is an essential part of what he terms the critical spirit: "Imaginatively to think through alternatives is at the same time to consider them critically" (p. 474).

A common fallacy that sympathetic imagination can lead to, however, is the assumption that to imagine another's circumstances is necessarily to understand them and to, therefore, understand that person. Noddings (1984) takes issue with what she refers to as the "particularly rational, western, masculinist way" (p. 29–30) of looking at *empathy* as manifest in the *Oxford English Dictionary* definition: "The power of projecting one's personality into, and so fully understanding, the object of contemplation." The notion of "feeling with" that she explicates in her ethic of care involves reception rather than projection. She avoids the temptation to analyze and plan; rather, she receives the Other into the self and becomes a duality. As she puts it, "[t]he seeing and feeling are mine, but only partly and temporarily mine, as on loan to me" (p. 30). In a similar reaction against the common understanding of empathy as putting oneself in another's place, Sharon Todd (2003) cites Anna Freud's comment that the process actually works the other way round: "empathizing involves, rather, putting another in *yourself*, becoming another person's habitat as it were, but without dissolving the person, without digesting the person" (p. 57). Though, as Todd points out, imagining another's feelings is significant in how we think of ourselves in relation to others (p. 56), we must take into serious consideration the fact that, in effect, this amounts to defining the other in terms of "the limits or expansiveness of one's imagination" (p. 57). How then do we dwell with the Other in the discussion of sensitive controversy without dissolving or digesting that person? As Todd contends, "engaging across differences through empathy may provide us with the raw material for *self* reflection after the fact, but it cannot offer the ethical attentiveness to difference *qua* difference so necessary to projects of social justice" (p. 63).[5]

In his conceptualization of empathy as a quality possessed by the kind of person we want to teach our children, Hare (1993) warns against those who "encourage us to believe that we cannot enter imaginatively into the lives of those whose cultural experiences we have not shared" because they "endanger values such as respect for persons and other cultures. For how," he asks, "can we respect that which we do not understand?" (p. 159). He calls Noddings's distinction between caring as projection and caring as reception "a distinction without a difference" since, whether we step into the Other's shoes or have them placed on us, "the central truth is that we have to understand how the other person sees the situation and feel how it feels to him or her" (p. 107). "We cannot care for someone," Hare says, "without trying to understand their situation and their reactions" (p. 108). I would suggest that the operative phrase here is "trying to understand." Noddings's distinction may well offer no significant difference if one assumes that understanding is the inevitable result of applying one's sympathetic imagination to the Other's situation. If, however, one recognizes, as Hare appears to, that understanding is something one tries to achieve with no guarantee of success, the metaphor of reception rather than the usual one of projection could act as a reminder of the fallibility of one's efforts, regardless how well-intentioned. Though empathy is necessary to understanding the Other, it is not, as Todd suggests, sufficient. To this I doubt Hare would object, since he contends, following Weiss, that no one quality is sufficient to make a person virtuous (Hare, 1993, p. 15).

In my experience, preservice teachers are quick to accept and attempt to incorporate caring into their teaching; however, they are confused by and resist Noddings's insistence that the ethic of care goes beyond caring feelings and good intentions. The question arises: "If I feel that I care, how can you say that I don't?" As Noddings (1984) says, "[c]aring involves two parties: the one-caring and the cared-for. It is complete when it is fulfilled in both" (p. 68). She cites Aristotle's point that one process may be actualized in another, and compares her concept of care to a concept of teaching that is dependent upon learning having taken place (p. 69). The idea that the teacher's good intentions and caring feelings are insufficient is a hard pill to swallow, but it is one Noddings believes we must accept, and, I would suggest, its recognition can figure significantly in the development of teachers' ethical attentiveness. It is incumbent on the teacher educator, therefore, to help students distinguish between caring as a feeling and caring as a relationship, the first being necessary but not sufficient for the relational ethic in teaching. In discussing a sensitive controversy, caring about the Other as an unactualized relation is not only not enough, it may even interfere with the confidence and calm a teacher needs in the face of such discussions. As Noddings points out, reciprocity on the part of the cared-for is what maintains the relation and "serves to prevent the caring from turning back on the one-caring in the form of anguish and concern for self" (p. 74).

Returning to the example in which I found myself caring for a student whose cultural context may have made him or her sensitive to our in-class discussion of anti-Semitism in *The Merchant of Venice*, I now see the effects of unreciprocated caring. My caring became, in effect, a concern over my own concern—i.e., a concern for self—and as such was tied up in a series of what-ifs. What if there is a student here with Jewish parentage? What might he or she be thinking (of me)? What if he or she describes our discussion at home? What if I am seen as insensitive or even racist? Hare (1993) reminds us that the good teacher cares not only "because what happens to the other person will reflect somehow on our own performance, or on our own self-assessment, so that prudence, pride or personal gain become the determining factors" (p. 101). The tack I took in that situation was to offer the standard explanation that Shakespeare's characterization of Shylock demonstrated the virulent anti-Semitism of his age and that, therefore, the play alerts us to the dangers of similar attitudes in our own time.[6] I felt then that my justification was necessary and sufficient for my teaching to be critical. I no longer consider it sufficient. It served me at the time, insofar as I felt prepared to respond to my own what-ifs should I be called to account. What I failed to do, which is likely why this anecdote has recurred in my thinking about teaching to be critical, was receive the Other instead of merely projecting what I imagined to be his or her reality, to use Noddings's language. Or, in Todd's terms, I was not ethically attentive to difference *qua* difference. One might ask if it is even reasonable to expect a beginning teacher to be capable of such attentiveness. Possibly not—however, by including in teacher education opportunities for preservice teachers to consider the pedagogical role of ethical attentiveness, the chances of its development are more likely to increase.

Beyond being attentive for signs that reciprocity has been achieved in one's caring acts and attitudes, how might the teacher attend to what Todd (2003) refers to as "difference *qua* difference" (p. 63)? What conditions are necessary for the teacher to be prepared to attend to others' sensitivities, spoken or not? We shall now consider whether the concept of critical thinking offers the teacher guidance in teaching sensitive controversy.

Teaching (in) the Spirit of Criticism

In his influential article, "Teaching to be Critical," Passmore (1972) takes the reader through various possibilities of what it is to teach a student to be critical. Neither imparting facts nor training habits and skills are sufficient conditions for teaching to be critical. Possessing facts *about* criticism is insufficient for being critical. Being drilled into the habit of uttering stock criticisms is also insufficient. In fact, as Passmore emphasizes, drilling students "in doctrines and in stock replies to stock objections to doctrine" is the very definition of indoctrination (p. 26). One could develop complete mastery over a text on critical thinking, demonstrating perfect recall when questioned, without learning to be critical.

Passmore (1972) quotes Plato on skills being "capabilities for opposites" (p. 28); the skillful thinker can detect as well as conceal fallacies in reasoning. An abuse of critical skills was precisely the criticism Socrates launched against the Sophists and their teachings. What Passmore calls the "forensic" skills of criticism (p. 30), which, incidentally, he claims are likely to be developed through the practice of formal debating, are devoid of the critical spirit. It is critical thinking in this forensic sense of using skills to relentlessly scrutinize that is the version of critical thinking critiqued by constructivists such as Barbara Thayer-Bacon (2000). Such critiques are in effect only debunking a skills-only concept of critical thinking. This is not the version of teaching to be critical that Passmore or Siegel (1988 and 1997) advocate.

According to Passmore (1972), the disinterested attempt to arrive at the truth requires what he calls the "critical spirit," and he stresses that the educator is interested in encouraging it in a sense by which it cannot be misused (p. 28).[7] He implies that a coldly analytical, uncaring application of critical skills is not consistent with possessing the critical spirit. He compares the spirit of criticism to that of justice: "The skills of a judge, or the skills of a critic, can be used or misused; justice or the critical spirit can be neither used nor misused. And this is because neither being just nor being critical is a skill" (p. 28). Todd (2003) raises a related point from Levinas, that ethical responsibility cannot be reduced to adherence to the laws of institutions even though justice is exercised through them. As Levinas puts it, "justice … must always be held in check by the initial interpersonal relation" (as cited in Todd, 2003, p. 144). I suggest that possessing the spirit of criticism entails a similar regard for the encounter with the Other. It is this that guards against its misuse.

For Passmore (1972), possessing a critical spirit is a character trait and, as such, relies strongly upon the examples that are set for the student and upon "the atmosphere of the school" (p. 28). He illustrates how the teacher falls short of exercising the spirit of criticism by merely drawing attention to the defects before her. Authoritarian systems of education commonly "produce pupils who are extremely critical, but only of those who do not fully adhere to the accepted beliefs, the accepted rules, the accepted modes of action" (p. 29). Here we have an example of the skills of criticism being misused. In common usage, to call a person "highly critical" is not a compliment; rather, it implies that such a person only finds fault. Passmore suggests that being highly critical is not acting in the spirit of criticism (p. 27).

Possessing the spirit of criticism gives one the capacity to perceive when the very grounds upon which one stands need to be reassessed. As Passmore (1972) says:

> [T]o exhibit a critical spirit one must be alert to the possibility that the established norms themselves ought to be rejected, that the rules ought to be changed, the criteria used in judging performances modified. Or perhaps even that the mode of performance ought not to take place at all. (p. 30)

In teaching sensitive issues, the teacher possessing a critical spirit may feel that the very mode of critical performance ought to be suspended. Take, for example, a scenario during an in-class discussion in which student A takes up an example offered by student B. The teacher suspects that student B is drawing from her own experience, even though the example is couched in general terms, and that it was difficult for her to articulate this example in the public space of the classroom. Perhaps her willingness to disclose a personal, emotionally charged example is a testament to the atmosphere the teacher has worked to achieve with his students. Let us imagine further that the other student, student A, is adept at critical analysis and begins picking apart the example from student B, not suspecting, as the teacher has, student B's personal connection to it and not recognizing her resulting discomfort at being under scrutiny. What should the teacher do?

Assuming he does not want to draw further attention to student B, thereby exacerbating her discomfort, the teacher could take up student A's analysis himself, engaging in furthering it with the hope of achieving a conclusion that might make student B more comfortable. I have found myself in such a situation numerous times, hearing a student A dissecting with obvious enjoyment the example of a student B sorely prepared for or inclined to engage in critical scrutiny, and I have taken on the argument myself, but not with satisfactory results because the point, insofar as the critical spirit is concerned, is not about winning an argument. The point is to encourage the critical spirit that, as Passmore (1972) says, cannot be abused. The spirit of criticism entails the dispositions, habits of mind, and capacities that safeguard against the thoughtless application of critical skills. One option for the teacher under these circumstances may well be to tactfully and quickly shift attention away from the example in question and go on to other things. This action under these circumstances could exhibit a spirit of criticism on the part of the teacher.

As Passmore (1972) points out, unlike other qualities of character such as courtesy, justice and consideration, the critical spirit is a more difficult example to set for one's students (p. 29). The foregoing scenario demonstrates how true this can be. It is likely that students would not recognize the example of the critical spirit the teacher has set. He may have used an evasive strategy, such as moving on to another topic, to cut short student A's forensic critique and, although the evasion may have been noticed, it is not likely to be recognized as part of the conception of critical thinking itself.[8] For the teacher to draw attention to the example of the critical spirit he has set would undermine the very strategy he used in the spirit of criticism to save student B further discomfort. His recognizing the appropriateness of suspending the specific critical activity of the moment to better serve the more pressing needs of student B suggests he is able to weigh competing goods in the broader context within which critical thinking is taking place. One strategy for bringing out the practical considerations adhering to the spirit of criticism for preservice teachers would be to offer for consideration and discussion the above scenario, or one similar to it, which suggests the importance of knowing when it is more fully critical to suspend a given critical act.

Are there traits or qualities specific to the larger purpose of judging the context and consequences of our critical thinking that ought to be considered relevant, particularly in discussing sensitive controversies? What might these be and how might they be nurtured in the process of teaching to be critical? Lundquist (1999) argues that "fundamental to learning is reflection and the ability to draw conclusions from more or less successful attempts to come to an understanding of the issues at hand" (p. 524). In the spirit of criticism, one needs to be able to reflect upon a sensitive controversy under discussion within its emotional and socio-political context, accept that trying to understand the reality of another is contingent upon multiple factors, and hold one's conclusions tentatively. Benhabib (2006) says that "[t]he narrative view of culture permits one to identify cultures without falling into a correspondence theory of truth" (p. 384) and adds that the observer of a culture "seeks for more unity and coherence in identifying a culture than does the participant" (p. 385). In identifying a culture, therefore, the observer and, by extension, the teacher needs to be aware of "alternative stories and competing points of view" (p. 385) and not jump to judgment, regardless of how apparently supportive of the other she may believe her judgment to be.

If we add context to the fictional scenario above, moving it into a predominantly white Digby high-school class who are discussing the appropriateness of requiring students to read vivid depictions of racism, and imagine student B to be the only student of colour while student A belongs to the dominant culture, how might a teacher prepare for the tension likely to arise? Instead of evading it by moving on to other things or being drawn into student A's argument, a teacher prepared for the sensitivity of this controversy might offer alternative narratives, knowing, as she does, that the issue cannot be discussed without evoking thoughts of the current racial tensions in the community. She could raise competing points of view from the news reports themselves: the story of long-term harassment and intimidation versus the story of media exaggeration and fault on the part of a previous commander. Depending upon her subject-area expertise, the teacher could offer additional competing viewpoints in the form of historical or literary accounts. Were this discussion taking place in the context of studying *The Merchant of Venice*, the story of intolerance in Shakespeare's England problematizes traditional interpretations of Shylock the Jew.[9] The examination of different interpretations of his characterization within the Elizabethan and modern-day contexts could be extended to an analysis of different points of view in news reporting on race-relations in Nova Scotia. In short then, as Todd (2003) points out, "the specifically *ethical* possibility of education, this possibility for nonviolent relation with the Other, can only surface when knowledge is not our aim" (pp. 15–16). This seems antithetical to the common understanding of what teaching is; yet making sense of it is a vital step to teaching in the spirit of criticism. The role of one teaching to be critical in this strong sense is not to seek for "more unity and coherence in identifying a culture than does the participant" (Benhabib, 2006, p. 385).

Hare (1985) points out as significant the fact that among social studies educators it is common to use the term "handling" in reference to dealing with sensitive issues in the classroom. The term, says Hare, "suggests that the teacher needs to be wary, cautious and discreet" (p. 116). The term "handling" is appropriate, in Hare's view, because "in the case of empirical disputes the teacher must take care to avoid suggesting that we are closer to the truth than we are, and in the area of value disputes he must avoid the very real danger of indoctrination" (p. 118). The term "handling" suggests that one is taking great care, as in handling something fragile or even toxic. As with any metaphor, however, it can cut both ways. "Handling" can also connote that the handler is seeking control or mastery.[10] George Dei (1996) recalls being reminded by one of his graduate students that "when academics engage in such theoretical exercises, they would do well to remember that they are talking about people's actual lived experiences of being violated, constrained and dominated" (p. 28). Our wariness, caution, and discretion in discussing sensitive controversy in the classroom must certainly focus on avoiding bias: in selecting materials and topics, in the tone of delivery, and in the overall frames of reference in which we position the topics we plan for discussion. Of immediate importance, however, is to be wary, cautious, and discreet as regards the pain of others.[11,12] This must entail more than the novice teacher's litany of self-protective what-ifs when caught off guard in discussing a sensitive issue. Reflecting on the teacher's task involves a reflexivity necessary to the spirit of criticism. With reflexivity in mind, we will now turn to the theorizing of feminist standpoint epistemology (FSE).

What has Feminist Theory to Offer the Concept of Critical Thinking?

An obvious question is why, having considered critical thinking as conceptualized by traditional rationalists, one would turn to FSE? No claim is being made here for the adoption of any version of feminist standpoint epistemology. I find the arguments for FSE unconvincing; however, I sympathize with the reasons for which an alternative theory of knowledge has been theorized, and I will suggest that critical thinking theorists can benefit from some of the constitutive claims for FSE without agreeing that traditional epistemology is masculinist, misguided, and/or in need of revision. To begin, it is useful to revisit the central confusion that has resulted in so much sparring between these traditions.

In an interview with Israel Scheffler, Harvey Siegel (2005) presses Scheffler for his views on the justification of rationality *vis à vis* feminist claims. He asks: "Would you say that there could be some sort of gender bias in the valorisation of rationality or reason?" (p. 650). Scheffler responds that "the notion that rationality is less suitable for women or that they are less able to reflect rationally on anything is just insulting to them" (as cited in Siegel, 2005, p. 650). He goes on to explain that there are social constraints that call into question the rationality of women, and it is these social inequities that need to be challenged, not the high value placed on rationality (p. 651). Siegel recounts what he takes to be the common feminist criticism: namely, that the conception of rationality in the West values "rational disputation and cold calculation" while undervaluing the private domestic sphere traditionally consigned to women (p. 651). Scheffler then makes the pertinent point: "to what exactly is this argument an objection? Certainly not to rationality as such but rather to the way it is presumed to have been conceived" (as cited in Siegel, 2005, p. 651). It is this presumption regarding how rationality has been conceived to which we will now turn.

Sandra Harding's (1993) account of how rationality has been conceived traditionally has been one of the most influential within the feminist literature. She uses the phrase "the view from nowhere" to describe the common belief that it is possible to achieve an absolute view of reality, a view which might then be presented as if from no particular point of view and that such a view defines objectivity (p. 49). Harding claims that, unlike "the view from nowhere," feminist standpoint epistemology offers a stronger form of objectivity. Rather than reject the concept of objectivity completely, Harding chooses to redefine it. To reject the concept of objectivity by means of expository argument would be a performative contradiction, i.e., contradicting one's claims through one's actions since, presumably, Harding wants the reader to accept her claims as having some purchase on reality. Harding avoids the contradiction. She defines her version of objectivity as follows: "[s]trong objectivity requires that the subject of knowledge be placed on the same critical, causal plane as the objects of knowledge. Thus, strong objectivity requires what we can think of as 'strong reflexivity'" (p. 69). She further claims that FSE accepts individual difference without sinking into a nihilistic form of relativism, i.e., one that assumes that since nothing can be known absolutely, knowledge is worthless or, conversely, that all knowledge is of equal value. Harding claims that it is because of its strong reflexivity that standpoint epistemology offers a stronger form of objectivity.

Siegel (1997) offers what I believe to be a convincing refutation of FSE. To conceive of traditional versions of rationality as dependent upon a "view from nowhere," as Harding and other feminists do, is, according to Siegel, a misconstruction. As he says, "[w]e always judge from the perspective of our own conceptual scheme; there is no way to escape from all schemes and judge from a God's-eye point of view" (Siegel, 1997, p. 175). On this, traditional rationalists are in agreement with feminists. The divergence of views hinges upon what is drawn from this. Siegel rejects feminists' claim that universality—i.e., the view unencumbered by particular points of view—is impossible. In denying the universal, one embraces it: "one can't escape the universal by denying it" (p. 174) since the denial is itself a universal claim. In refuting certain claims made by postmodernists, Siegel makes a useful distinction between *moral* and *epistemological* failings, which reflects the point from Scheffler above and helps counter the claim that universality is impossible. He says: "To silence or marginalize is unjustifiably to deprive people from full participation in social life. It is unjustifiably to presume that their perspectives are inferior or without value. It is to sin against them *procedurally*" (p. 133). He points out that this moral failing of exclusion does not necessarily mean that the product of the resulting dialogue will not be rationally substantive; and, conversely, inclusion does not necessarily guarantee rationality. In his words, "procedural justice is neither a necessary nor a sufficient condition for substantive rationality (or epistemic worthiness more generally)" (p. 133). In regards to the exclusion effected by patriarchy, Siegel says: "[t]here is no Enlightenment *principle* which forces Patriarchy. It is rather the manifestation of deficient *practice*" (p. 136).[13] Though traditional rationalists would agree with feminists that specific universal claims have been misused to marginalize and oppress, they would agree with Siegel that to stand up against victimization we need the conceptual tools to establish principles for rejecting it in all instances, i.e., the ability and agreed upon procedures to generalize from particular instances and extend resulting principles universally, which is not to say that this proceeds infallibly. Feminist standpoint theorists would agree with Siegel that deficient practice has been rampant, but they lay the blame on a deficient theory of knowledge. It is an empirical question whether or not individual interpretations of traditional epistemology, whether from a feminist or rationalist point of view, have been illogical and/or deficient in practice. But, if one portrays traditional epistemology in the best light, it is reconcilable with feminist premises regarding the role of situated knowledge *vis à vis* a theory of knowledge. How then have feminists construed strong reflexivity, and how is it implicated in the critical spirit needed for teaching sensitive controversy in the classroom?

Harding's (1993) concept of strong reflexivity can be read as useful in the traditional rationalist's as well as the feminist's project. It is just such a capacity that is needed in the fictional scenarios of teaching to be critical considered earlier. Strong reflexivity consists of placing the subject of knowledge on the same critical, causal plane as the objects of knowledge. A controversy is sensitive because living in and through its direct effects causes one to react emotionally to the discussion of it. If she considers the initial interpersonal relation with the Other secondary or tangential, a teacher can get carried away by the seeming importance of her plans and designs, and unwittingly harm the very people she intends to help. The metaphors of stepping back and gaining distance to see things in perspective can lead to the mistaken assumption that a God's-eye view is achievable. Haraway (1988) says that feminist objectivity "allows us to become answerable for what we learn how to see" (p. 583). For a teacher to come to the realization that a sensitive issue should be taught entails a serious responsibility, and to be continually answerable for it is a condition requiring reflexive consideration of one's critical dispositions, habits of mind, and affective capacities, and their pedagogical effects on self and Other.

One may ask if the feminist account of strong reflexivity differs substantively from traditional rationalism's requirement for impartiality and open-mindedness in minimizing bias. By my reading, it does not differ. Hare (1993) points out that "close proximity is no guarantee of awareness and can militate against it" (p. 3), an observation that seems to fly in the face of the feminist argument that objectivity is positioned rationality (Haraway, 1988, p. 590). Pohlhaus (2002) is helpful here. She suggests that standpoint theory is not social enough (p. 292) and that we abandon metaphors of place and perspective and place the emphasis on our abilities to forge relations with one another. By conceptualizing knowing as an activity within communities, struggle is struggle-with not struggle-against (pp. 290–291). I would suggest that the traditional rationalist's requirement that the critical thinker strive for the ideals of impartiality and open-mindedness can be viewed as the feminist "achievement of reflexivity to form the following question: What is the relationship between my actual social position and the ability to forge a critical standpoint?" (Pohlhaus, 2002, p. 288).

Hare (1985) contends that it is not part of the role of a teacher as teacher to make a contribution to knowledge. This may occur, but it is secondary to the teacher's responsibility of "bringing others to knowledge, and bringing others to the point where they can make a contribution to knowledge" (p. 116). I see no substantive difference in Hare's point and Todd's (2003) that the possibility for nonviolent relation with the Other must take precedence over aiming for knowledge in our teaching. Their views can be reconciled if, assuming I am correct, Hare takes *knowledge* to include knowing how and Todd does not. Surely nonviolent relation with the Other requires degrees and subtleties of procedural knowledge. A student teacher or an experienced teacher may falsely assume that her contribution to knowledge should take precedence over students' needs. To practice in such a way is to fail to understand what strong reflexivity entails in teaching to be critical. Discussing sensitive controversy in the classroom brings the teacher face-to-face with difference *qua* difference, indissoluble in ready-mixed plans and procedures. "The critical thinker," says Siegel (1988), "must care about reason and its use and point" (p. 40). The "reasons conception" of critical thinking rejects a distinction between cognition and affect, accepting Peters's belief that reasoning is passionate business (Siegel, 1988, p. 41). Reasoning and teaching reflexively (in) the spirit of criticism is a demonstration of character as well as an act of thinking.

Conclusion

Todd (2003) describes her project as building on tensions: two views are held in tension without collapsing the significant differences of either.[14] Her strategy is one the teacher could adopt in working within and through encounters with difference in the classroom. Todd calls her approach that of taking a "doubled view," which entails letting go any need to incorporate both views (p. 13). She says of the doubled view that it "paints a more complex picture of what occurs in classrooms in the here and now, one that might inform an ethical time of nonviolence, a time that is infinitely momentary" (p. 13). I have tried to trace a path here that connects the complex nature of teaching across difference to the equally complex project of reconciling difference across theoretical traditions. In our difficult moments as teachers, attempting to discuss issues that have already stripped some students bare, it may help to remember their doubled view as they struggle to join in and block out the pain such remembrance evokes. Using Haraway's (1988) words, "I am arguing for the view from the body, always a complex, contradictory, structuring, and structured body" (p. 589). Strong reflexivity entails this view from the body, and, as I have argued and attempted to demonstrate through example, it can and does help us teach in the spirit of criticism, an attitude crucial to discussion of sensitive controversy. I have offered my own missteps and indecisions in classrooms as part of the examples here considered. Fear of recognizing and admitting my own complicity in silencing those I was trying to teach impeded my adoption of what Boler (1999) calls "the pedagogy of discomfort," which is a call to action, not by enforcing a political agenda (p. 179), but as a way of inhabiting ambiguous selves (p. 196). "The best antiracist and anti-sexist work" she says, "is not about confrontation but rather a mutual exploration" (p. 199). In teaching sensitive controversy this would mean "to 'share' the suffering and vulnerability, to explicitly discuss the pedagogies and one's own emotional challenges" (p. 199). As Hare (1993) reminds us, "there is no denying that some ethical issues resist universal agreement, indeed provoke violent and profound animosity. It is not wise or accurate, however, to judge the whole field of morality by the most controversial elements in it" (p. 3). For readers dissatisfied with this inquiry, drawing from insights across traditions and discovering no clearly defined procedures for practice, I can only say that, though I share the feeling, I am learning to dwell in the ethical challenge discomfort affords.

ACKNOWLEDGEMENTS

A version of this paper was presented at the conference on Open-mindedness and the Virtues in Education in honour of William Hare at Mount Saint Vincent University, Halifax, October 4, 2008. Considerable further development to that draft is due in large part to the extensive and extremely helpful suggestions from anonymous reviewers who suggested useful readings in social justice education and critical social theory and prompted me to extend my examples to reflect insights gained from that work.

REFERENCES

Benhabib, S. (2006). The "claims" of culture properly interpreted: response to Nikolas Kompridis. *Political Theory, 34*(3), 383–388. doi:10.1177/0090591706286779

Boler, M. (1999). *Feeling power: Emotions and education.* New York: Routledge.

Dearden, R.F. (1984). *Theory and practice in education.* London: Routledge and Kegan Paul.

Dei, G.J.S. (1996). *Anti-racism education: Theory and practice*. Halifax: Fernwood Publishing.

Haraway, D. (1988). Situated knowledges: The science question in feminism and the privilege of partial perspective. *Feminist Studies, 14*(3), 575–599. doi:0.2307/3178066

Harding, S. (1993). Rethinking standpoint epistemology: What is "strong objectivity"? In Linda Alcoff and Elizabeth Potter (Eds.), *Feminist Epistemologies* (pp. 49–82). New York: Routledge.

Hare, W. (1985). *Controversies in teaching*. London, ON: Althouse.

Hare, W. (1993). *What makes a good teacher: Reflections on some characteristics central to the educational enterprise*. London, ON: Althouse.

Hare, W., & Portelli, J.P. (2003). *What to do? Case studies for educators*. Halifax: Edphil.

Lundquist, R. (1999). Critical thinking and the art of making good mistakes. *Teaching in Higher Learning, 4*(4), 523–530. doi:10.1080/1356251990040408

McLaughlin, T. (2003). Teaching controversial issues in citizenship education. In Andrew Lockyer, Bernard Crick, & John Annette (Eds.), *Education for democratic citizenship* (pp. 149–60). Hants, UK: Ashgate Publishing.

Medel, B. (2008a). Expert: Black history lesson for Digby Mounties would help ease tensions. *The Chronicle Herald*. Halifax, 26 Sept., p. B1 & 7.

Medel, B. (2008b). Mounties tailed me, racism expert says. *The Chronicle Herald*. Halifax, 27 Sept., p. A1 & 2.

Murphy, R. (2009). When art becomes agitprop. *The Globe and Mail*. Toronto, 16 May.

Nasrallah, D. (2009). Rex Murphy's column last week about Caryl Churchill's play was skewed by anger and oversimplification of the play and its intentions. *The Globe and Mail*. Toronto, 23 May.

Noddings, N. (1984). *Caring: A feminine approach to ethics and moral education*. Berkeley: University of California.

Passmore, J. (1972). On teaching to be critical. In R.F. Dearden, P.H. Hirst, & R.S. Peters (Eds.), *Education and reason* (pp. 25–43). London: Routledge.

Passmore, J. (1983). Education and adaptation for the future. In D.J. Ortner (Ed.), *How humans adapt* (pp. 457–476). Washington: Smithsonian Institution Press.

Passmore, J. (1985). Educating for the 21st century. *The fourth Wallace Wurth Memorial Lecture*. University of New South Wales, 22 April.

Pohlhaus, G. (2002). Knowing communities: An investigation of Harding's standpoint epistemology. *Social Epistemology, 16*(3), 283–293. doi:10.1080/0269172022000025633

Siegel, H. (1988). *Educating reason*. New York: Routledge.

Siegel, H. (1997). *Rationality redeemed? Further dialogues on an educational ideal*. New York: Routledge.

Siegel, H. (2005). Israel Scheffler interviewed by Harvey Siegel. *Journal of Philosophy of Education, 37*(4), 647–659.

Sontag, S. (2003). *Regarding the pain of others*. New York: Farrar, Straus and Giroux.

Statistics Canada (2008, May 21). Induced abortions. *The Daily*. Retrieved November 29, 2008, from www.statcan.gc.ca

Thayer-Bacon, B. (2000). Constructive thinking versus critical thinking. *Paideusis: Journal of the Canadian Philosophy of Education Society, 13*(1), 21–39.

Todd, S. (2003). *Learning from the Other: Levinas, psychoanalysis, and ethical possibilities in education*. Albany, NY: SUNY.

White, P. (2009). What kind of mother would send her child to second grade with a swastika on her arm—and help her redraw it after a horrified teacher washed it off? *The Globe and Mail*. Ottawa/Quebec Edition, 26 May.

NOTES

1 The book of case studies I use is *What to do? Case studies for educators* by Hare and Portelli (2003).

2 McLaughlin (2003) does not adhere to Dearden's strict use of the term "controversy"; rather, he uses the term more broadly as is the case in everyday speech and he distinguishes "grounded" controversies as the deeper disagreements about matters epistemological or ethical.

3 The foregoing account of the introduction of discussion issues along a continuum from simple disagreement to sensitive controversy could apply to the planning of instruction for schools as well as for teacher education.

4 According to Statistics Canada, in 2005 there were 96,815 induced abortions on Canadian women. For every 100 live births there were 28.3 induced abortions. Among women under age 20 there were 13 induced abortions for every 1000 women (Statistics Canada, 2008).

5 Todd (2003) describes her ethics as "implied" as opposed to the traditional approach, which she considers "applied" in that one theorizes and applies regulations, rules and guidelines to educational issues. The latter "inevitably renders education as instrumental to its purpose" (p. 5); whereas, implied ethics thinks about ethics *through* education (p. 29). Although Todd acknowledges Noddings's ethic of care as allied to hers in that Noddings privileges the situational aspects of ethics, Todd still considers it part of applied ethics in that "appropriate" forms of interaction are deduced from quite specific definitions of the concept of care (p. 5). It is not that Todd dismisses the role of concepts, but rather that she warns "against the assumption that education can be a panacea ... as though it can innocently reconstruct the world with better curricula, for this underestimates the powers and hazards of education itself as a practice" (p. 6). What is not clear, however, is how her use of theoretical material from Anna Freud, Levinas, and others escapes the charge of being "applied" to educational situations. She says that exploring the idea of implied ethics "necessitates reading teaching-learning encounters for the way they promote conditions for ethicality as they promote conditions for being, both of which involve relationships between self and Other" (p. 29). Also unclear is how this differs from what Noddings (1984) does in distinguishing her project of practical ethics from the feminine view from that of utilitarian practical ethics (p. 3). Does Noddings's positioning of ethical behaviour in human affective response differ significantly from Todd's emphasis on relationality? Hare (1993) questions the "alleged opposition between caring and principles," seeing it as another of the dualisms against which Dewey warned (p. 106). He suggests that this either/or is "made superficially plausible just because having principles is portrayed in the worst possible light" (p. 106).

6 As I write I am chilled to recall a recent front-page headline in *The Globe and Mail*: "What kind of mother would send her child to second grade with a swastika on her arm—and then help her redraw it after a horrified teacher washed it off?" (White 2009, A1).

7 Siegel (1988) uses the phrase "critical spirit" interchangeably with "critical attitude," which includes the attitudes, dispositions, habits of mind, and traits of character necessary for one to actually engage in critical thinking (pp. 39–40). He offers a useful distinction between the account of critical thinking and the account of the critical thinker—a distinction between acts of thinking and traits of persons. His reasons conception of critical thinking includes both accounts (p. 41).

8 Unless, that is, the teacher has already introduced the reasons conception of critical thinking with its critical spirit component.

9 For a debate over whether a play concerning the Arab–Israeli conflict is art or anti-Semitic propaganda, see Murphy (2009, May 16 & 23) and Nasrallah (2009).

10 My thanks to an anonymous reviewer for pointing out how the term "handling" is also implicated in the rhetoric of mastery and control.

11 An anonymous reviewer suggests that this point is so commonsensical as to not be worth making. Part of my impetus for writing this chapter is a noticeable shift in the last 15 years in the attitudes of the preservice teachers in my philosophy of education classes toward raising controversy in their classrooms. The majority has gone from fear and unwillingness to touch the controversial to an almost foolhardy impulse to include it. As I have no empirical evidence upon which to assume that this shift extends beyond the Nova Scotian context in which I teach, I am grateful to the reviewer for helping me better contextualize my concern. I would speculate, however, that popular mass-media culture has been and is affecting people's tolerance for aggressive debate, which suggests that a renewed emphasis on caution may be needed. As an addendum to this point, there is new reason for caution in Alberta with the adoption of Bill 44. It enshrined gay rights in provincial human rights legislation at a cost of giving parents the right to pull their children out of classes dealing with sex, religion, or sexual orientation, which requires school boards to notify parents in writing anytime controversial topics will be explicitly covered in class (Retrieved June 3, 2009, from http://www.ctv.ca/servlet/ArticleNews/story/CTVNews/20090602/alta_law_090602/20090602?hub=CTVNewsAt11).

12 In considering how photographic images of others' pain are being sapped of their efficacy through overuse and vulgarity, Susan Sontag (2003) argues that our sense of reality is being eroded: "There is still a reality that exists independent of the attempts to weaken its authority. The argument [that the ethical pertinence of photographs is being sapped] is in fact a defense of reality and the imperiled standards for responding more fully to it" (p. 109).

13 It is interesting to note that Siegel (1997) mentions a helpful suggestion from Barbara LeClerc, namely, that certain inconsistencies in Harding's position suggest she may in fact be opposing a false universality rather than universality wholesale (fn. 4, p. 213). He also compares Harding's attempt to reconcile objectivity and situatedness with his attempt to reconcile universality and particularity (fn. 23, p. 215).

14 The two views she refers to are the discourses of psychoanalysis and Levinasian ethics, which she takes to be incommensurable.

9

What's Wrong with the "Teach the Controversy" Slogan?

Eugenie C. Scott*

*This chapter was first published as Scott, E.C. (2007). What's wrong with the "teach the controversy" slogan? *McGill Journal of Education, 42*(2), 307–315. Reproduced with permission.

"Teach the controversy" is a phrase that teachers may encounter in many venues: in newspaper and magazine articles, in letters to the editor, in conversations with neighbours, or even in the supermarket checkout line. Where teachers are unlikely to encounter "Teach the controversy" is in science education journals or the journals of professional scientists. So what does this phrase mean in the context of science curriculum and instruction? "Teach the controversy" might mean that teachers should teach controversies taking place in science. And, of course, science is full of controversies. In a recent issue of *Science*, biologists debated dangers associated with the chemical dioxin, while astronomers discussed competing theories about a long-standing problem concerning the shape of the moon, its orbit, and its motion. Also in this issue, there was a debate over the risks of human and avian flu organisms swapping genes: how dangerous would this be? Yet proponents of "teach the controversy" have a very selective—even myopic—focus: they are only interested in teaching what they describe as the controversies concerning biological evolution.

Real Scientific Controversies, Not Creationist Pseudoscience

Finding genuine controversies within the evolutionary sciences is not difficult; evolution is a very rich and active scientific field, and like all such fields, is full of contending ideas. There are numerous controversies concerning how evolution happens, having to do with both the patterns and processes of evolution. Controversies concerning the patterns of evolution revolve around questions such as how closely related are Neanderthals to modern humans? Which group of mammals is most closely related to whales? What is the relationship between birds and dinosaurs? Controversies about the processes of evolution involve such issues as the relative importance of natural selection to genetic drift and other mechanisms of evolution, the evidence for and against allopatric speciation, and the adaptive value of sex compared to asexual reproduction. Yet the slogan "teach the controversy" does not concern teaching students about the fascinating controversies about pattern and process within the rich field of evolutionary biology.

Rather, what's concealed behind the slogan "teach the controversy" is the idea that teachers should teach students that there is a controversy among scientists over whether *evolution*, descent with modification from common ancestors, takes place. Scientists find this claim baffling. To scientists, evolution, the most important organizing principle in the biological sciences, is not a "theory in crisis." Statements from scientific societies from across the globe reflect the view of the Royal Society of London (2006):

> *Since being proposed by Charles Darwin nearly 150 years ago, the theory of evolution has been supported by a mounting body of scientific evidence. Today it is recognized as the best explanation for the development of life on Earth from its beginnings and for the diversity of species. Evolution is rightly taught as an essential part of biology and science courses in schools, colleges and universities across the world.*

Issues of *Science, Nature,* and other well-respected scientific journals contain numerous articles about evolution, and whole journals, and even academic departments, are devoted to research in the evolutionary sciences. Arguably the most exciting new area in biological research is developmental evolutionary biology—"Evo-Devo"—which brings together developmental biology, based upon cellular and molecular processes, and traditional evolutionary concerns of phylogeny (Carroll, 2005). Biology, long fragmented into hyphenated subspecialties, is reuniting because of the power of evolution to bring together different areas of study within the discipline.

In fact, it appears that more scientists are involved in evolutionary studies than ever before. Contrary to what "teach the controversy" proponents assert, there is no long line of scientists questioning whether living things had common ancestors. There are many scientists arguing about pattern and process, but that is quite different from questioning the big idea of evolution. To teach students that there is a controversy where none exists would seriously miseducate them.

The History of "Teach the Controversy" and "Intelligent Design"

"Teach the controversy" is a phrase promoted by members of the Discovery Institute and other supporters of the neocreationist movement called intelligent design (ID), a relatively recent movement that began in the mid-1980s. It did not become generally known to the public, however, until the late 1980s and early 1990s. In 1989 a high-school supplemental textbook, *Of Pandas and People* (Davis & Kenyon, 1989), was published by a small Christian ministry called the Foundation for Thought and Ethics (FTE). Although FTE had published some earlier works expressing most of the same general ideas (Thaxton, Bradley, & Olsen, 1984), *Of Pandas and People,* sometimes referred to as simply *Pandas*, was the first book to use the phrase "intelligent design" in its current sense.

Pandas was intended to supplement standard high-school biology textbooks to provide "the other view." Traditionally in creationist publications, evolution is one view, with the other view being "special creation," the belief of some Christians that God directly created things (from stars and galaxies to living beings) in their present form. This belief is incompatible with evolution since evolution describes the universe as having had a history rather than springing forth full-blown in its present form. Biological evolution is the inference that living things have descended with modification from common ancestors. In the 1960s, *creation science* was developed as a means of promoting the teaching of special creationism in the public schools. Creation *science* contends that biblically related claims—such as a young Earth, an historical Noah's flood, and the sudden appearance of all plants and animals at one time—can be supported by scientific evidence. Needless to say, such views are roundly rejected by most scientists (Sager, 2008).

By the late 1980s, creationists in the United States had learned to be very careful about using the term "creationism" in the public schools because of the defeats creation science received at the hands of the courts. In the United States, the First Amendment of the Constitution requires that public institutions be religiously neutral: a governmental body, such as a public school, may neither promote nor denigrate religion. In the late 1970s and early 1980s, creationists tried to pass laws requiring equal time for evolution and creation science. Citing the First Amendment, courts repeatedly struck down such laws. Creation science adapted by evolving into ID, which is much less explicit about its religious underpinnings. *Of Pandas and People* was published shortly after the release of a Supreme Court decision, *Edwards v. Aguillard* (1987), declaring that laws requiring equal time for creation science are unconstitutional.

Pandas, then, was very careful to avoid identifying the "other view" as creationism. It did not include traditional, young-Earth creationist arguments about a 10,000-year-old Earth, or of the coexistence of humans and dinosaurs, or the ubiquity of catastrophic geological processes. The *Pandas* authors were unable to avoid at least veiled references to the Creator, however: a reference is made to a "master intellect" (Davis & Kenyon, 1989, pp. 58, 85) that in context must be transcendent, and there is even a nod to the bible's version of the creation of the "kinds" in a reference to "the role of intelligence in shaping clay into living form" (Davis & Kenyon, 1989, p. 77). But there are no references to creation science; instead, *Of Pandas and People* attempted to strike hard at the validity of the theory of evolution itself. And in truth, previous creation science publications similarly had argued that evolution was a weak theory; the bulk of creation science content consists of "proving" creationism by "disproving" evolution.

The authors of *Pandas*—two university-level biology professors with creation science affiliations—tried to make the case that the evidence was stacked high against evolution. The fossil record, they contended, has too many gaps, and the Cambrian explosion causes difficulties for evolution by natural selection. Furthermore, the biochemical similarities and differences among organisms, ordinarily considered to be solid evidence for common ancestry, were presented as refuting evolution. Rather than directly asking students to choose between creationism and evolution, as is typical in creation science publications, *Pandas* presented a choice between "natural causes" (evolution) and "intelligent causes" (Davis & Kenyon, 1989, p. viii). If evolution supposedly could not explain something like the Cambrian explosion, students were encouraged to conclude that therefore "intelligence" explained it. In this dichotomy, if "natural" evolution didn't cause something, then the only other choice was that it was caused by an intelligent agent.

But there is no true distinction between "natural" and "intelligent" because natural agents such as humans and higher mammals are intelligent. If intelligent extraterrestrials exist, they also would be natural agents. So the natural/intelligent dichotomy is spurious. The true distinction is between natural causes and supernatural causes, not natural causes and intelligent causes. Of course, the authors of *Pandas* wanted students to infer that the intelligent agent was God, a supernatural, rather than a natural, agent. However, too much explicitness here would doom ID to the same unsuccessful legal fate as creation science; God had to be concealed under the inadequate disguise of "intelligent cause."

The chapter on biochemistry in the second edition of *Pandas* was written by biochemist Michael Behe (Davis & Kenyon, 1993, pp. 135–148), the author of the later ID book, *Darwin's Black Box* (Behe, 1996). Behe proposes that certain cellular structures are *irreducibly complex*—a type of complexity that by definition cannot be explained through natural processes. They therefore have to be explained by the actions of an intelligent agent. A structure like the bacterial flagellum cannot have evolved, he claims; it had to have been assembled as a "purposeful arrangement of parts" by an intelligent agent (Behe, 1996, p. 112). The intelligent agent is not named, but despite token references to the possibility of extraterrestrials or time-travelling designers, it was clear that a supernatural agent—God— was intended. The basic argument of ID, here and elsewhere, is that natural causes are insufficient to explain a biological phenomenon, and hence it is necessary to posit an intelligent designer. The content of ID, then, is a list of "problems" or "weaknesses" of evolution.

Another seminal book promoting intelligent design was published in 1991 by Phillip Johnson, a University of California, Berkeley, law school professor. In content not much different from previous creationist screeds, *Darwin on Trial* received wide attention, primarily owing to the novelty of creationism being promoted by a well-credentialed professor at an elite university—in famously ultraliberal

Berkeley, at that! *Darwin on Trial* took the same approach as *Pandas*: criticize evolution, present it as weak or inadequate science, attack the restriction of science to natural causes, and imply, without stating directly, that God created things in their present form. Subsequent ID books and articles have not veered far from this approach. ID's mission is to discredit evolution.

During the mid-1990s, a Seattle-based think tank known as the Discovery Institute took the place of the Foundation for Thought and Ethics as the leading proponent of ID. During the late 1990s, fellows of the Discovery Institute promoted teaching ID in public schools: they claimed it was pedagogically, scientifically, and legally proper to do so (DeWolf, Meyer, & DeForrest, 1999; 2000). In the early 2000s, the Discovery Institute began to alter its strategy of encouraging districts or states to require that ID be taught. The main reason for this change of tactics, in my opinion, was the unlikelihood of ID surviving a legal challenge. Presented with the standard ID argument that evolution cannot provide adequate answers, and thus an intelligent designer must be postulated, one can well imagine a judge asking "who is the designer"? It becomes quite clear that the designer is God, and therefore ID cannot lawfully be taught in American public school science classes, which, because of the First Amendment, must remain religiously neutral. God is too large to be hidden behind the vague "intelligent agent." And, in fact, in December 2005, in *Kitzmiller v. Dover* (2005), a federal district court in Pennsylvania declared that ID was not science but a form of creationism and therefore to advocate it in the public schools is unconstitutional.

During the early 2000s, the Discovery Institute refocused its efforts from promoting ID to concentrating on the "weaknesses of evolution." This required little change in content: ID reflects a dichotomous belief that demonstrating the inadequacies of evolution suffices to prove ID correct. *Of Pandas and People, Darwin on Trial*, and *Darwin's Black Box* all consist of lists of "evidence against evolution." ID proponents (correctly) feared that teaching ID would result in legal problems; they believed they could avoid such challenges by merely denigrating evolution. Since the dichotomy that underlies creationism in all its forms is widely shared, their expectation is that students who are told that evolution is flawed will conclude that God created— without the school or teacher becoming entangled with the First Amendment.

This was the origin of the "teach the controversy" slogan, which implies that evolution is a controversial—and weak and unsupported— scientific theory that students should reject. Proponents of creation science broached a similar "evidence against evolution" strategy in the wake of the *Edwards* decision (Institute for Creation Research, 1987), but failed to pursue it in any systematic and effective way. Since the emergence of intelligent design, however, "teach the controversy" is an approach that has been promoted widely.

Ohio ID proponents supported by the Discovery Institute succeeded in 2002 in persuading the Ohio state Board of Education to include in its state science education standards a benchmark requiring teachers to have students discuss how scientists "investigate and critically analyze" evolution. A series of model curricula was to accompany the state science education standards, and the lesson plan developed for the "critical analysis" benchmark reflected "teach the controversy" topics originally developed by Discovery Institute fellow, Jonathan Wells (2000), in his book, *Icons of Evolution.* These topics included the familiar ID complaints about homology, the Cambrian explosion, embryology and evolution, and the fossil record—a regular laundry list of "arguments against evolution."

Icons of Evolution was excoriated by the scientific community in a series of reviews (Scott, 2001; Coyne, 2001; Padian & Gishlick, 2002; Gishlick, 2003). Scientists criticized Wells's presentation of science as misleading or wrong. To present the *Icons*-based content of the Ohio lesson plan as accurate science would truly have been a disservice to the students of Ohio. Fortunately, in the spring of 2006, a more moderate Board of Education, apparently prompted by the *Kitzmiller* decision and an incriminating paper trail of public documents, rescinded the "critical analysis" benchmark and the lesson plan.

"Teach the controversy" has had other successes in the last few years. In the state of Kansas, creationist state Board of Education members in 2005 infused the science education standards with *Icons of Evolution*-inspired wording. However, in the August 2006 primary election, the seats of four creationist members of the school board were challenged by moderates. A 6–4 moderate majority took office in January 2007. They promptly overturned the "teach the controversy"-inspired standards.

Unfortunately, the situation is not as positive in the state of South Carolina, where in 2005 a conservative state legislator pressured the Department of Education to insert Ohio-type "critically analyze" language into the science standards. As other state science education standards come up for revision in the next few years, it is certain there will be many challenges to the inclusion of evolution. "Teach the controversy" has also emerged as a problem in local school districts, where local creationists use it to encourage school boards to disclaim evolution, teach the "evidence against" it, or even to teach ID.

In Canada provinces vary regarding how religion is reflected in the curriculum, but as many religious schools in Canada receive at least some governmental funding, there is more religion taught in Canadian publicly supported schools than in the United States. There is no strict Canadian equivalent to the First Amendment of the US Constitution. Thus far, provincial education ministers have not promoted the teaching of ID or the "teach the controversy" approach. Canada is rather more "top-down" in its educational policy than the US, which means that local school boards do not have as much authority to determine curricula. It also means that should a provincial minister become convinced of the validity of ID or its recent manifestation, "teach the controversy," there could be substantial changes in educational policy. The growth of intelligent design in Canada, as in the United States, needs to be monitored.

"Critical Analysis" and Conclusion

An argument that has been persuasive in both the United States and Canada is the claim that having students decide between ID and evolution, or to have students "critically analyze" evolution, is pedagogically sound critical-thinking instruction from which students would benefit. Of course, all teachers want students to be critical thinkers! It might be a useful critical-thinking exercise for students to debate actual scientific disputes about patterns and processes of evolution, as long as they have a solid grounding in the basic science required. (For further discussion, see Alters & Alters, 2001; Scott & Branch, 2003; Dawkins & Coyne, 2005.) It would, however, not be a good critical-thinking exercise to teach students that scientists are debating whether evolution takes place: on the contrary, it would be gross miseducation to instruct students that the validity of one of the strongest scientific theories is being questioned. It would, therefore, be gross miseducation to teach students the inaccurate science presented in *Icons of Evolution*, and other intelligent design literature.

Teachers, therefore, need to be on guard against "teach the controversy" policies and proposals that may appear in the district or province, because some exhortations to improve students' critical-thinking abilities are actually anti-evolution proposals. "Teach the controversy" is not a pedagogically sound, critical thinking-promoting teaching strategy in which legitimate scientific controversies are discussed and evaluated by students. On the contrary, "teach the controversy" is a pedagogically unsound approach that promotes ignorance about the true nature of evolution and its importance in biology. It is also a cleverly worded attempt to smuggle creationism into science. It does not belong in any classroom.

REFERENCES

Alters, B.J., & Alters, S.M. (2001). *Defending evolution: A guide to the evolution/creation controversy.* Sudbury, MA: Jones & Bartlett.

Behe, M. (1996). *Darwin's black box: The biochemical challenge to evolution.* New York: The Free Press.

Carroll, S.B. (2005). *Endless forms most beautiful: The new science of evo devo and the making of the animal kingdom.* New York: W.W. Norton.

Coyne, J.A. (2001, April 12). Creationism by stealth. *Nature, 410*(6830), 745–746. doi:10.1038/35071144

Davis, P.W., & Kenyon, D.H. (1989). *Of pandas and people.* Dallas, TX: Haughton.

Davis, P.W., & Kenyon, D.H. (1993). *Of pandas and people* (2nd ed.). Dallas, TX: Haughton.

Dawkins, R., & Coyne, J. (2005, September 1). One side can be wrong. *The Guardian.* Retrieved from http://www.guardian.co.uk/science/2005/sep/01/schools.research

DeWolf, D.K., Meyer, S.C., & DeForrest, M.E. (1999). *Intelligent design in public school science curricula: A legal guidebook.* Richardson, TX: The Foundation for Thought and Ethics.

DeWolf, D.K., Meyer, S.C., & DeForrest, M.E. (2000). Teaching the origins controversy: Science, or religion, or free speech? *Utah Law Review, 39,* 40–110.

Edwards v. Aguillard, 482 U.S. 578 (1987).

Gishlick, A.D. (2003). *Icons of evolution? Why much of what Jonathan Wells writes is wrong.* Retrieved August 30, 2013, from http://ncse.com/creationism/analysis/icons-evolution

Institute for Creation Research (1987). *The Supreme Court decision and its meaning.* Retrieved January 29, 2007, from http://www.icr.org/articles/printI274/

Johnson, P.E. (1991). *Darwin on trial.* Washington, DC: Regnery Gateway.

Kitzmiller v. Dover Area School District, 400 F. Supp. 2d 707 (M.D.Pa. 2005).

Padian, K., & Gishlick, A.D. (2002). The talented Mr. Wells. *Quarterly Review of Biology, 77*(1), 33–37. doi:10.1086/339201

Royal Society. (2006). A statement by the Royal Society on evolution, creationism and intelligent design. Retrieved February 5, 2013, from http://ncse.com/media/voices/royal-society

Sager, C.E. (Ed.). (2008). *Voices for Evolution* (3rd ed.). Oakland, CA: National Center for Science Education.

Scott, E.C. (2001, June 22). Fatally flawed iconoclasm. *Science, 292*(5525), 2257–2258. doi:10.1126/science.1060716

Scott, E.C., & Branch, G. (2003). Evolution: What's wrong with "teaching the controversy?" *Trends in Ecology & Evolution, 18*(10), 499–502. doi:10.1016/S0169-5347(03)00218-0

Thaxton, C.B., Bradley, W.L., & Olsen, R.L. (1984). *The mystery of life's origin: Reassessing current theories.* New York: Philosophical Library.

Wells, J. (2000). *Icons of evolution: Science or myth? Why much of what we teach about evolution is wrong.* Washington, DC: Regnery.

Part III: Democratic Education and Social Justice

The terms "democratic education" and "social justice" have become popular slogans in education. Almost invariably, education policy documents make reference to democracy and social justice. Teacher education programs promote themselves by referring to their work on democracy and social justice in education, and many have developed cohorts that focus exclusively on social justice education. Broadly stated, democratic education is the kind of education that is consistent with democratic values and practices. However the matter is much more complex: What does it mean to follow democracy as a way of life? Which and whose way of life? Do the neoliberal values of individualism, competition, a free market, and reductionism contradict the spirit of democratic learning and hence reproduce an inequitable education? Why is it that genuine social justice education requires us to go beyond tolerance and endorse hospitality? The chapters in this section focus on the meanings and justification of democratic education and social justice in education, the challenges that one encounters in enacting such an education, the possibilities that exist, and the values that underlie democratic and social justice education.

But why is a democratic way of life crucial in education? Why is it important to consider democratic values in education? What are the practical implications of a democratic education perspective? The first essay by Laura Pinto highlights important distinctions between democracy as a form of governance and democracy as a way of life; democracy *in* education and education *for* democracy; procedural matters and substantive matters in democracy; equality and equity; thin and thick (robust or critical democracy). Pinto contrasts critical democracy with liberal democracy, market democracy, deliberative democracy, and agonistic democracy, and makes a case for critical democracy, which in her view, deals with the major criticisms that have been raised against other forms of democracy. Ultimately, critical democracy is a way of life that substantively deals with controversial issues by creatively involving participation of community. It honours equity and social justice that address systemic issues of power and oppressive conditions, builds on the organic and intersubjective notion of the individual which cannot exist outside of a community. Moreover, while it relies on deliberation and reasonableness it also highlights the importance of activism. In the final section of the chapter Pinto offers several examples of what critical democracy means in education.

There is no doubt that democratic education entails a form of social justice education. In the next article, Kathy Hytten argues that democratic education cannot fulfill its promise without a robust notion of social justice. Are competition, individualism, and a free market contrary to social justice? Are the notions of the common good and rationality sufficient in achieving social justice? What notion of critical thinking is compatible with social justice? While addressing these kinds of questions, Hytten highlights the role of philosophers of education in the ongoing struggle to actualize social justice in the continuous reconstruction of the democratic project. Traditionally philosophers have relied on the importance of developing critical-thinking abilities as a means of achieving social justice education. While not eliminating the importance of this tradition, Hytten urges us to deal with more substantive issues (such as white privilege, Eurocentricism, and capitalism) as well as the need to question "abstract and decontextualized ways of questioning, reasoning, and behaving in the face of diversity." At the same time she is concerned that we can get paralyzed with critique. Hence she suggests and argues for two alternatives as possibilities for pedagogical engagement: "experiential accounts and narratives" and "performance activities."

In the *Politics* Aristotle noted that the nature of education needs to be consistent with the agreed political government of a group of people. In our case, if we are indeed living in a genuine democracy, we need to ask: What form of schooling is consistent with the educational ideals that emerge from democracy? What are the principles of learning that underlie democratic learning? Should we have alternatives available in educational institutions? The next two essays, one by Emery Hyslop-Margison and Samuel LeBlanc, and the other by Nel Noddings, deal with these questions.

Hyslop-Margison and LeBlanc argue that the neoliberal and post-neoliberal conditions have exacerbated the impact of a free-market economy on education, which has led to a narrow form of instrumentalism that has privileged skills over other dispositions, attitudes, and qualities that are needed to develop a truly democratic citizenry. The social and economic reality created by neoliberalism and its aftermath gave the impression that such realities are fixed and cannot be otherwise. As a result, the importance of human agency, critical education beyond skills, and multiple knowledges and understandings have suffered. Instead, the emphasis has been on standardization and the reduction of everything to "brute facts." According to Hyslop-Margison and LeBlanc the attacks on basic democratic rights and freedoms of both teachers and students, the restriction of academic freedom, and the reduction of dissent have substantively diminished democratic learning in educational institutions. In opposition to the post-neoliberal policies, they remind us of the importance of the principles of democratic learning that for them rest on: the ability and the freedom of students to critique current practices; the importance of introducing students to alternative perspectives on social and economic matters so students can indeed make informed decisions; and the belief in and possibility of social transformation based on "informed political participation."

For Noddings, education for a truly democratic citizenry cannot and should not be based on one form of education for all. She argues that of its very nature democracy does not rest on forcing a one-size-fits-all mentality; democracy needs to respect and offer different ways of educating people, and all should be considered of equal value. Ultimately her argument for diverse offerings rests on the notion of social justice that honours different talents, needs, and interests. While not eliminating the route that prepares students for a college education, she insists that vocational/industrial and commercial routes that are also based on intellectual abilities need to be available, and students need to be well informed so they can make appropriate choices. She is also concerned that the intellectual realm has been traditionally too narrowly defined—a definition that does not allow us to see the intellectual other than what has been considered to be a normal intellectual subject. She contends that cooking and motorcycle repair, for example, do not contain less intellectual thinking than algebra. For Noddings, the intellectual, the moral, and the aesthetic realms are intricately related. As such, she concludes that vocational and commercial education is not intellectually inferior to traditional academic subjects. At the same time, she warns that it is crucial not to interpret vocational education in narrow ways that could lead to a dangerous form of tracking for "minority and low SES students." Such an interpretation would be equally antidemocratic and unjust.

Having considered the different meanings of democratic education and social justice education, as well as the forms of education and learning that are consistent with these concepts, we return in the next chapter by Trudy Conway to the concern with the virtues and dispositions associated with democracy and social justice. How should we deal with different views and people? Is tolerance appropriate and sufficient? How do we relate with "strangers"? Conway argues that tolerance is insufficient and needs to be supplemented by hospitality. Besides compassion, dialogue, open conversations, open-mindedness, courage, and imaginative empathy, she argues that we need to take hospitality seriously if we are truly interested in actively engaging differences. The traditional liberal principle of "live and let live" is based on a notion of individualism that focuses exclusively on autonomy and not interfering with others. Hospitality contrasts with the indifference of tolerance. Hospitality troubles excessive individualism and morally pushes us to enter into a genuine humble encounter with "the Other." Hospitality brings us back to the core of democracy that honours and respects different views. Hospitality encourages us to reconsider what amounts to a humane manner, and reminds us that what we may have by habit considered to be humane may be less so. Of course, hospitality requires openness from all and not just some. Moreover, the encounters of hospitality can also entail different asymmetrical relations. The challenge is how to deal with differences that are considered to be creating violent and oppressive conditions. But as Tahar Ben Jelloun (2011), the noted Moroccan novelist, stated: "Democracy is not like an aspirin that you dissolve in water." Democracy and social justice demand a constant struggle.

REFERENCES

Ben Jelloun, T. (2011, October 17). Interview with Tahar Ben Jelloun by Ruth Schneider. *Exberliner.*

10

The Case for Critical Democracy

Laura Elizabeth Pinto*

*This chapter draws on information and research originally published in
Laura Elizabeth Pinto, *Curriculum Reform in Ontario: "Common-sense" Policy
Processes and Democratic Possibilities*, © University of Toronto Press, 2012.
Material reused with permission of the publisher.

Through education, we learn to do and to be—and this includes our
role in a democracy. Benjamin Levin (1998) reminds us that "the ideals underlying education are similar to those underlying democracy,
suggesting that schools should embody the principles of democracy
for students as part of a sound education" (p. 57). Now, there is no
shortage of discussion among philosophers, theorists, and educators
about the relationship between education and democracy. In fact,
just about every educational theory since John Dewey (1916/1966)

conveys the widespread view that education ought to foster democracy and equip those being educated to participate successfully in a democratic society. Education, the argument goes, is essential to the cultivation of deep understanding of democratic principles, enabling involvement through a curriculum for democracy and nurturing the democratic mind (Dewey, 1916/1966; Darling-Hammond, 1996; Gutmann, 1999; Boler, 2004; Olssen, Codd, & O'Neill, 2004).

This intimate connection between education and democracy has two components. First, democracy *in* education requires an educational structure that is democratic to all involved, including students, teachers, administrators, and the community. Second, education *for* democracy means that schooling should prepare learners to participate as citizens. John Dewey (1916/1966) argues that both society and education ought to be democratic in content and style: "A society which makes provision for participation in its good of all its members on equal terms and which secures flexible readjustment of its institutions through interaction of the different forms of associated life is in so far democratic. Such a society must have a type of education which gives individuals a personal interest in social relationships and control, and the habits of mind which secure social changes without introducing disorder" (p. 99).

Achieving Dewey's vision requires us to (re)consider the aims of schooling in a democratic context. The relationship between education and democracy, however, is not without tensions. Our collective "educational traditions" are, in some important ways, predemocratic. Schools were initially created for the privileged classes, and practically speaking, have continued to serve as a sorting system that has persisted in excluding certain social groups. These predemocratic criteria "distort and constrain any rational debate about the democratic role of education" (Carr & Hartnett, 1996, p. 12). The problem boils down to "a contradiction between the obvious need for members of a democracy publicly to debate the social and political principles underlying its educational policies and the obvious failure of those policies to address questions about the kind of education which genuine participation in such a public debate requires" (Carr & Hartnett, 1996, p. 3).

If we hope to achieve a rich connection between democracy and education that can reconcile these tensions, we must begin with a conception of democracy consistent with educational and social aims. This chapter sketches out the ideal of critical democracy, contrasting it with other (and less robust) conceptions of democracy, and offering a justification for it as an ideal. It goes on to describe how critical democracy might take shape in contemporary education environments, including a discussion of conditions, structures, and practices that might realize this ideal.

The Unique Character of Critical Democracy

While a variety of conceptions of democracy exist, this chapter outlines the unique character of critical democracy. Let us begin by tracing its roots. Critical democracy arises primarily out of John Dewey's (1916/1966) philosophy and work, with roots in his definition of democracy as "more than a form of government; it is primarily a mode of associated living, of conjoint and communicated experience" (p. 84). Dewey viewed *associated living* as interaction that would be "equivalent to the breaking down of those barriers of class, race and national territory which kept men from perceiving the full import of their activity" (pp. 84–85). Dewey's view calls attention to the *substantive* aspect of democracy—that is, the quality and nature of participation quite apart from the procedural aspect of democracy.

Beyond Dewey's contributions, the work of Paulo Freire has strongly influenced early development of the critical-democratic ideal. Freire (1978) wrote, "Democracy requires dialogue, participation, political and social responsibility, as well as a degree of social and political solidarity ... before it becomes a political form, democracy is a form of life, characterized above all by a strong component of transitive consciousness" (pp. 28–29). As this passage emphasizes, critical democracy becomes a way of life that includes concern for meaningful engagement among citizens in all aspects of lived experience in which individuals become agents of social change. This echoes Dewey's views on associated living but includes an emancipatory component that places transformation and social change as an ultimate goal of democratic activity.

In the past two decades, the character and conditions of critical democracy have been further articulated, emphasizing personal agency, as well as fleshing out its substantive and procedural aspects. Contemporary democratic theorists and philosophers including Antonia Darder, Joe Kincheloe, Shane O'Neill, John Portelli and Patrick Solomon, Ricardo Blaug, Paul Carr, and Landon Beyer have built on these foundations set forth by Dewey and Freire.

The character of critical democracy differs from other conceptions of democracy in its requirement of a certain type of participation and a certain set of ideals. Specifically, critical democracy strives to establish a way of life that "should show us how to transform our form of life in an emancipatory manner" (O'Neill, 2000, pp. 503–504). To that end, "critical-democratic theorists seek to explore how contentious issues of moral and cultural pluralism might be dealt with in a way that minimizes the potential for oppression, alienation and violence. This means that incommensurability must not be taken as a given, or as something to be celebrated. Nor should it be brushed aside as something that will inevitably be overcome" (O'Neill, 2000, p. 505).

As O'Neill (2000) reminds us in this passage, critical democracy conceptually includes the requirements of inclusion and empowerment, with particular attention to those typically marginalized from political activity. Beyond traditional democracy's narrow concern with equality, critical democracy embraces equity as a goal with genuine and inclusive participation that "seriously and honestly acknowledges the importance of equity, diversity and social justice" (Portelli & Solomon, 2001, p. 15). *Equality* implies that all individuals have the same opportunities or distribution of goods, whereas *equity* implies that opportunities are distributed in a way that may be unequal but compensates for differences that disadvantage one group or person over another. All social conditions must allow all groups to participate as peers in all the major forms of social interaction (Travers, 2008).

Critical democracy requires a shared commitment to a particular notion of social justice. Despite its centrality in critical democracy, social justice remains a contested term with multiple meanings (Beilharz, 1989; Rizvi, 1998; Caputo, 2002). Broadly speaking, the literature reflects three dimensions of social justice: *procedural* justice or representation (concerned with the freedom to pursue goals, civil liberties); *(re)distributive* justice (concerned with the allocation of benefits and burdens); and *relational* justice (concerned with equity in all aspects of social and economic life) (Gewirtz, 1998; Caputo, 2002; Merrett, 2004). The critical-democratic conception of social justice must expand beyond distribution of goods in a society to include all aspects of institutional rules associated with relational justice (Gewirtz, 1998). In other words, social justice must permit all members of society to interact with peers equitably along all three of these dimensions. Only then can citizens achieve participatory parity (representation, redistribution, and recognition) in economic, cultural, and political aspects of life (Fraser, 2008, 2010). In this ideal, social justice is a praxis that acknowledges internalized forms of oppression[1] and privilege, and enacts practical strategies to change social institutions to overcome inequity and exclusion (Kohli, 2005; Fraser, 2010).

Despite compelling moral, religious, political, and legal arguments[2] supporting its importance, social justice is subject to criticism. First, social justice has come under scrutiny since there are so many versions that are extremely difficult to pin down. Fundamental disagreements remain about what fairness and equity are, and how to overcome them (Espinoza, 2007), though a full exploration of these is beyond the scope of this chapter.[3] Because public dialogue does not necessarily lead to reconstitution of power relations in a way that might address inequity, social justice has been called a form of "romanticized localism" (Rizvi, 1998; Vincent, 2003, p. 4). However, critical democrats would argue that without social justice as a goal, no progress can be made toward the elimination of power imbalances (Carr, 2007; Pinto, 2012).

Other, popular conceptions of democracy limit it to a form of rule that fails to go beyond narrow, government-sanctioned citizen activities such as voting. By contrast, critical democracy is a personal, social, and political experience rather than a form of government, concerned with a set of values, dispositions, and behaviours that go far beyond officially sanctioned citizen involvement.

Critical Democracy in Light of Alternate Conceptions

To better understand critical democracy, it is useful to contrast it with other forms of democracy. Let us begin with the broad concept of liberal democracy.

Liberal democracy dominates much of the Western world in the form of *representative* democracy, in which civic participation is the responsibility of elected officials, and so it is largely procedural in nature. Citizens' roles are limited to voting and the odd "town hall" consultation. Benjamin Barber (2003) describes "liberal democracy" as holding a "perceived monopoly" on forms of politics (p. 3). Similarly, Chantal Mouffe (2000a) argues that "very few dare to openly challenge the liberal democratic model" (p. 1) despite evidence of disaffection. The dominance of liberal democracy is dangerous because, when liberal democracy is thought of as the only legitimate form of government, critique is limited and alternatives for consideration become scant.

Barber's (2003) work characterizes liberal democracy as "thin," in that it privileges individual interests while undermining democratic practices upon which those individuals and their interests depend. In other words, liberalism's commitment to individual freedom forces it to view each person as "essentially identical to all others" (Graham,

2002, p. 231). This limits the possibility to explore a politics of difference, and therefore eliminates any emancipatory potential (Graham, 2002). Moreover, this conception limits democracy to a political procedure within official institutions, rather than an experience lived by all citizens. In practice, this "precarious foundation" of a procedurally oriented liberal democracy excludes citizenship, participation, and the public good (other than the occasion of voting every four years or so).

Additional critiques of liberal democracy centre on undesirable consequences such as apathy, lack of transparency, absence of trust, and inequality (Glynos, 2003). Though perhaps not as widely accepted as other conceptions of democracy, critical democracy holds promise to address some of their shortcomings and challenges. To understand these critiques and visions of alternatives and to provide a basis for comparison with critical democracy, in the following subsections I compare and describe three versions of liberal democracy: market democracy, deliberative democracy, and agonistic democracy.

Market Democracy

The literature documents the rise of market democracy (Chua, 2000; Pettit 2008; Sunstein, 1997) out of "a period of mounting enthusiasm for free markets" (Sunstein, 1997, p. 3), in which these markets and democracy appear "luxuriously compatible" (Chua, 2000, p. 378). *Market democracy* first appeared in the work of economist Joseph Schumpeter during the mid-20th century, relying on the belief that spreading markets and privatization equates with spreading democracy (Barber, 2003). In this conception, individuals in the electoral polity (formerly "citizens") divide into consumers and producers and interact within a "marketplace" to arrive at policies by spending their dollars and casting their votes (Manzer, 2003; Pettit, 2008). Thus, economic "choice" and "consumption" of public goods and services (including education) are taken to be "citizenship." These consumer-citizens register their preferences in polls (Chua, 2000; Pettit, 2008). In this way, policies attempt to track trends in voter preferences (Pettit, 2008).

Critics identify several problems with market democracy, largely focused on two areas: problems with the market analogy, and an apparent inability to address equity and justice. With respect to the market analogy, equating consumers and citizens neglects the difference in dispositions and skills associated with these two roles. As Zygmunt Bauman explained, "Consumer skills emphatically do not include the art of translating private troubles into public issues, and public interests into individual rights and duties—the art that constitutes the citizen and holds together the polity as the congregation of citizens" (as cited in Leighton, 2002, p. 15). In this way, market democracy has a "tendency to paralyze and de-legitimate political thinking as a gateway to political action," in which individuals are mistakenly thought to be "utility maximizing," rational decision makers (Birchfield, 1999, p. 30). This fails to take other factors that influence citizens' preferences and beliefs into account. For example, market criteria do not address social problems, given their narrow procedural focus that ignores issues of equity (Rizvi, 1998).

Social justice then becomes a "*non sequitur* outside the logic of markets" (Beilharz, 1989, p. 95), since the emphasis on "fairness" principles has to do only with access to choice, not recognition or redistribution. Market democracy is mediated by material, political, and ideological devices that "de-escalate the conflict between market-generated wealth disparities and majoritarian politics" (Chua, 2000, p. 290). Free markets' promises of liberty become conflated with equality under the argument that people may trade goods and services as they wish. This free market allows each person equal (but not equitable) right to transact and participate in market arrangements (Beetham, 1997). Along those lines, this "depersonalized logic of market forces" (Beetham, 1997, p. 76) leads to power imbalances, and these exacerbate problems of inclusion and social justice. Critical democracy, by contrast, seeks to deal specifically with inclusion, equity, and social justice, without concern for promoting the interests of capital in all aspects of life.

Deliberative Democracy

Tatsuo Inoue (2003) observed that deliberative democracy has become a "prevailing catchword," especially popular in the political science literature where it is an important normative theory (Dryzek, 2009; Gutmann & Thompson, 2004). *Deliberative democracy* describes several approaches to democracy that rely on a certain type of citizen participation whose goal is participation in governance through deliberation, as its name implies. It arose in response to critiques of representative democracy, especially the failure to recognize the centrality of deliberation (Dryzek, 2009).

While advocates disagree about its features and its configurations vary, two main versions of deliberative democracy exist: one put forward by John Rawls, the other by Jürgen Habermas. Both versions call for structured citizen participation in political decision making. Participation takes the form of deliberation in structured, "official" forums, with an aim of consensus or agreement that is arrived at through the "exchange of arguments among reasonable persons guided by the principle of impartiality" (Mouffe, 2000a, p. 4). This requirement of arguments is rooted in rationality—it assumes that citizens will present rational arguments and be moved to consensus by clear-cut reasons.

However, the two versions contain some important differences. The Habermasian version, based in critical theory, relies on "communicative action," in which citizens engage in discourse in good faith during "ideal speech situations" characterized by unforced argument without time constraints (Habermas, 1984). Some classify this version of deliberative democracy as procedural, since it emphasizes process over content (Gutmann & Thompson, 2004). The Rawlsian perspective has its roots in John Rawls's *Theory of Justice* (1971). Rooted in liberalism (not critical theory), this version relies on "*public reason*": rational argument in formal venues on officially sanctioned issues (Gutmann & Thompson, 2004). Its aim is rational consensus among citizens.

Political philosopher Chantal Mouffe (1997, 2000a, 2000b) rejected the inevitability of consensus central to these versions of deliberative democracy. She maintained that it is impossible to come to final, rational, and neutral decision procedures, resulting from unavoidable power structures and the plurality of values.

Agonistic Democracy

Agonism was Chantal Mouffe's (1997, 2000a, 2000b) solution to deliberative democracy's limits. Agonistic democracy has three unique features. First, it rejects rational consensus and agreement as democratic goals. At its core, agonistic democracy is founded upon Wittgenstein's critiques of rationalism—that for agreement of opinions, first there must be agreement in forms of life. What constitutes a good life, Mouffe contends, is not an absolute and so agreement and rational consensus are not always possible.

In response to the rejection of rational consensus, some criticize agonistic democracy for a reliance on irrational decision making (Dryzek, 2009; Crowder, 2006), based on Mouffe's claim that rationality cannot exist for all issues, and that passion and emotion are necessary in political matters. The failure of rationalist models and their critiques suggest, however, that Mouffe may be correct. This is supported by a general recognition within the argumentation literature that emotion can be civil and has a legitimate and positive role to play in argument (Gilbert, 1997, 1999, 2001; Carozza, 2007). From a feminist perspective, this inclusion of passion and emotion is a strength (Ruitenberg, 2009; Thien, 2007).

The inevitability of power is a second key foundation of agonistic democracy. Mouffe (2005) forcefully argues that acts of consensus are necessarily built upon exclusion and simply reinforce hegemonic power. By removing the condition of consensus, power relations are acknowledged and have the potential to be addressed. Therefore, agonistic democracy is concerned with "how to constitute forms of power more compatible with democratic values," rather than try to eliminate power (Mouffe, 2000b, p. 100). To explain how power operates, Mouffe redrew the lines of politics and the political. *Politics* are the practices, discourses, and institutions that attempt to establish order and organize human life in conditions that are always in conflict because of the political. The *political*, on the other hand, is the site of struggle in which groups with opposing interests vie for hegemony. Political conflict becomes a force to be channelled into a democratic commitment to tame the agon, rather than a problem to be overcome. This is in direct opposition to deliberative democracy's desire to eliminate conflict—and in Mouffe's view, conflict is simply a part of the democratic process, and any attempts to eliminate it lead to highly unproductive antagonism. As Claudia Ruitenberg (2009) points out, psychoanalysts have illustrated that the suppression of fundamental desires and emotions does not eliminate them, but rather delays their manifestation.

Finally, agonistic democracy requires a different way to view the "Other." It calls on citizens to view the "Other" as an adversary—"somebody whose ideas we combat but whose right to defend those ideas we do not put into question … a legitimate enemy one with whom we have some common ground" (Mouffe, 2000b, p. 102)—rather than an illegitimate enemy or opponent. Adversaries share principles of equity and liberty but disagree on the meaning and implementation of those principles. The key to the adversarial relationship is that both parties recognize that rational persuasion will not change the other's political identity. The goal of agonistic confrontation, then, becomes compromise rather than consensus—where a compromise is recognized as "temporary respite from ongoing confrontation" (Mouffe, 2000b, p. 102).

Mouffe (2005) insists that agonism makes for a more harmonious and safer society over time by taming and diffusing antagonism, such that the "enemy" would be transformed into the adversary. One might envision this functioning as in organized sport, such as a game of football (Tally, 2007). Rivals compete in an unambiguously agonistic struggle for dominance, with a clear winner and loser. Teams play by certain rules, unwilling to destroy the sport itself to achieve a particular goal. The goal is not consensus but victory for a particular match. As in agonistic democracy, clearly defined "Others" compete—the aim is to win, not to destroy the other or the sport.

While, arguably, other versions of deliberation might be adapted to reflect critical democracy, Mouffe's conception of agonistic exchanges best characterizes the sort of interaction suited to critical democracy. This agonistic approach to understanding the "Other," as well as to recognizing the permanence of conflict within politics and the political, realizes the critical-democratic ideal; moreover, mutual concern and respect among opponents supports critical democracy's aims of equity, diversity, and social justice. Recent empirical investigation points to possibilities for very civil and productive applications of agonistic democracy (Bäcklund & Mäntysalo, 2010; Goi, 2005; Pinto, 2012; Pløger, 2004) that support the possibility of achieving critical democracy in political arenas.

The Case for Critical Democracy

The aim of any democratic structure is to create a just society that is governed by the people. Regardless of the form it takes, liberal democracy fails to consider social justice as an aim or central feature of democratic action and outcomes. This leads to power imbalances where democratic inclusion is limited to "elites" rather than all citizens from a broad range of social positions (Glynos, 2003). With the exception of Mouffe's agonistic democracy, most forms of liberal democracy also fail to address very real issues of power that encompass conflicts over values, resources, and control. If we accept that social justice is a legitimate goal of a just society, and that issues of power cannot be overcome, then we must seek a democratic conception that can address the limits of liberal democracy.

Critical democracy holds promise to tackle the shortcomings just described. The centrality of social justice as an aim of procedures and outcomes places critical democracy in opposition to the individual freedoms focus of liberal democracy. By privileging social justice over individual liberty, critical democracy has the potential to actively work toward equity for all, and therefore toward a more just society where justice means equity for all. It also takes on issues of inclusion, since an aim is to ensure representation and emancipation. Obviously, the project of equity requires compromise given that disagreements are inevitable (Espinoza, 2007). To address the very real potential for disagreements, critical-democratic praxis acknowledges power imbalances and conflicts and seeks to overcome them through substantive and procedural conditions. As described earlier, Mouffe's agonism has been successfully applied to structure citizen interaction inside and outside of official structures (Goi, 2005) in ways that would be consistent with critical-democratic principles.

Beyond far-reaching social justice goals, critical democracy's commitment to equitable citizen involvement makes political sense. When law and policy is produced in ways perceived as "fair,"[4] outcomes are more likely to be considered legitimate (Gandin & Apple, 2012; Pinto, 2012; Tyler, 2000). Thus, critical-democratic procedures can have self-serving ends for governments and politicians. Participation in political matters through critical democracy also has positive benefits on citizens. Political participation has been empirically shown to result in civic learning, and a sense of community, and respect for others' perspectives (Baiocchi, 2005; Goi, 2005; Pinto, 2012) in the spirit of agonism.

What Does Critical Democracy Mean in Education?

Both Dewey and Freire envisioned the school as a fundamental venue for democracy to grow—a place of education for critical democracy. Several levels within the education system must play a role in transformation toward the critical-democratic ideal. This requires both procedural and substantive conditions at three levels: policy, governance, and in classrooms. In this section, I briefly sketch out possibilities, with particular attention to classroom practice.

At the policy level, critical democracy ought to be reflected in several ways. First, statements of educational purpose and the content of legislation and policy must address central features of social justice and substantive democracy as a way of life. Education policy content must provide spaces and opportunities for schools to be sites of democratic learning in the spirit of Dewey. Second, arriving at policy content consistent with the critical-democratic ideal must involve both substantive and procedural aspects of critical democracy in policy production: equitable inclusion of citizens' voices and perspectives, full participation, and a shared commitment to compromise (Freedman, 2007; Gandin & Apple, 2012; Pinto, 2012). Examples of structures and procedures to facilitate this type of critical-democratic policy production have been identified in the literature (Gandin & Apple, 2012; Pinto, 2012; Pløger, 2004), and it appears to be a very real possibility when political leaders and citizens will demand it.

Second, school administrators play a significant role in achieving the critical-democratic ideal, since administrative practice ought to be intertwined with research and theory "to support the type of schooling (and society) that values rather than marginalizes" (Brown, 2004, p. 77; Ryan, 2006). Educational administration has traditionally reflected a culture that marginalizes issues of social justice (Marshall, 2004), which are central to critical democracy. But, as the literature suggests, greater emphasis on social justice among school administrators is critical to change at the school level (Cambron-McCabe & McCarthy, 2005; Marshall, 2004; Shields, 2004). Unless school administrators create school environments that encourage and allow democratic practice in education, teachers and students will continue to face barriers to the lived experience of critical democracy that eliminate the possibility of schooling to prepare an active citizenry (Portelli & Campbell-Stephens, 2009). Democratic leadership practices can take many different forms, but within critical-democratic environments they must include all voices, including those typically marginalized, and include elements of agonistic exchanges in coming to understand the positions of the "Other" to arrive at compromises in school-based policy and practice. While few examples of critical-democratic leadership have been documented, Goodman's (1992) work illustrates a structure in which students and teachers can be actively involved in school-based governance and decision making. Ryan's (2006, 2007) and Ryan and Rottmann's (2009) work illustrates approaches to democratic leadership for social justice through dialogic communication that would be consistent with critical democracy in schools. Together, these examples of critical-democratic leadership in action share a commitment to thick inclusion of multiple members of the school community in decision making, shared commitment to social justice, and forms of communication that reflect agonism through respect for the "Other."

Finally, critical democracy calls on teachers to critically interrogate the practices and policies underpinning their work, and consider what other possibilities exist to foster democracy *in* education and education *for* democracy in their classrooms. If teachers share a vision of critical democracy as an ideal, it follows that they would engage their students in exploring alternative ways of constructing, resisting, and enacting education policy. By doing so, schools would provide an education *for* democracy by engaging students in learning that increases their capacities as critical-democratic citizens (Pinto, 2012; Portelli & Vibert, 2001). This constitutes a curriculum of life "that is grounded in the immediate daily world of students as well as in the larger social, political contexts of their lives" (Portelli & Vibert, 2001, p. 63). Kenneth Saltman (2005) offers specific criteria that characterize education for critical democracy:

- encourage intellectual curiosity and an understanding of the historical and global dimensions of knowledge;
- raise questions about broader structures of power in relation to interpretations of truth;
- encourage the development of intellectual tools to transform the world in ways that make a more just and democratic society;
- enhance capacities to imagine a future in which inequalities and injustices are overcome and history is not inevitable and predetermined, but rather, open to transformation;
- make hope a social and political project; and
- make individual freedom an ideal fulfilled by helping others to be free.

Among other suggestions, Saltman also calls on educators to recognize the role of a critical pedagogy to achieve these ends. At the heart of critical pedagogy is Paulo Freire's (1972, 1978) belief that education ought to empower students to recognize connections between their individual problems and experiences and social contexts in which they are embedded, within the goal of social transformation. Critical pedagogy (Giroux, 1983) contributes not only to learners' analysis of curriculum content but also to the ideal forms of curriculum enactment in the classroom to achieve a critical-democratic learning environment.

Freedman (2007) describes some practical limitations of critical pedagogy in a highly institutionalized environment where leadership and structures may not conform to critical-democratic ideals. Freedman acknowledges that a truly democratic classroom may not be possible in most schools, since institutional limitations discourage radical transformations of teachers' roles. His revision of Paulo Freire's critical pedagogy prescribes presenting "multiple positions on salient public issues, and train[ing] students in a method of analysing these positions" by "probing into the root causes of social inequalities" (Freedman, 2007, p. 467). In doing so, Freedman (2007) believes that critical-democratic education can happen within systems that are not designed to promote it.

The type of education Freedman discusses can take place in various educational spaces. For example, Claudia Ruitenberg argues that citizenship education initiatives must take the task seriously.

She proposes three areas in which political education (as a component of citizenship education) must change: educating political emotions in a way that moves against masculinist rationalism and is consistent with agonism, fostering an understanding of the political, and finally, developing political literacy to read the political landscape in a way that uncovers the social order (Ruitenberg, 2009). While this might be addressed in classrooms, student government can be reformed to become an exercise in learning critical democracy by living it (Schmidt, 2008). While most schools have some form of student government, the format and quality varies (McFarland & Starmmans, 2009). Most take the form of representative democracy where participation is limited voting. Students may complete school without having exposure to anything but representative democracy. However, participation in critical democratic student government that involves equitable representation, agonistic deliberation, and a commitment to social justice in process and outcomes would allow students to reimagine political structures and to learn the requisite civic skills for robust democratic life.

Others have pointed to approaches to critical-democratic education in other subject areas beyond citizenship. Romas (2008), an Ontario science teacher, discussed the challenges of addressing social justice: "There wasn't enough time to progress through the levels of learning, to more complex thought and analysis ... How was I going to find time to incorporate teaching for social justice if I had to race just to get through the science material?" (Romas, 2008, p. 43). To address this, he used current social issues (e.g., HIV/AIDS, water privatization, and alternative energy) as critical-democratic examples through which he taught conventional science topics. Similarly, Stocker and Wagner (2008) describe ways to address several equity issues in mathematics classrooms by using data sets to shift the focus of the curriculum toward social justice issues. They "make the invisible visible" (Stocker & Wagner, 2008, p. 72) by creating math problems for students to solve that uncover social inequities. In one example, they provide seventh grade students with data sets that invite them to compare annual spending on advertising against the (much smaller) amount of money needed to eliminate world hunger. They report students' "outrage" followed by "hope" (Stocker & Wagner, 2008, p. 73) when confronted with a problem (hunger) that initially appears insurmountable, but the data lead them to a basis for action.

In other examples, Pinto (2005, 2006) describes a critical-pedagogical approach to the study of entrepreneurship in business education, in which learners actively unpack the "cultural myths" common in business studies, with particular attention to ideologies, racial and gender equity, and power. Ngai and Koehn (2011) demonstrated that critical-democratic education need not be limited by the boundaries of the classroom. Their cross-curricular elementary school project extended to the community, allowing students to experience local Indigenous communities through visits, including ongoing interaction with tribal educators and Elders.

These examples provide a few of the many possibilities to transform educational systems in ways that promote education *for* critical democracy, and critical democracy *in* education. The possibilities for this sort of transformation are only limited by students', teachers', and educational leaders' imaginations.

Because, as Kohli (2005) reminds us, schools are primary sites for critical transformation since they reproduce inequality, they represent a starting point for realizing the critical-democratic ideal. Only when educational policy makers, leaders, and teachers commit themselves to critical-democratic transformation can we realize a more robust critical democracy inside and outside school walls.

REFERENCES

Bäcklund, P., & Mäntysalo, R. (2010). Agonism and institutional ambiguity: Ideas on democracy and the role of participation in the development of planning theory and practice—the case of Finland. *Planning Theory, 9*(4), 333–350. doi:10.1177/1473095210373684

Baiocchi, G. (2005). *Militants and citizens: The politics of participatory democracy in Porto Alegre.* Stanford, CA: Stanford University Press.

Barber, B. (2003). *Strong democracy: Participatory politics for a new age* (20th anniversary ed.). Berkeley: University of California Press.

Beetham, D. (1997). Market economy and democratic polity. *Democratization, 4*(1), 76–93. doi:10.1080/13510349708403503

Beilharz, P. (1989). Social democracy and social justice. *Journal of Sociology (Melbourne, Vic.), 25*(1), 85–99. doi:10.1177/144078338902500105

Birchfield, V. (1999). Contesting the hegemony of market ideology: Gramsci's 'good sense' and Polanyi's 'double movement.' *Review of International Political Economy, 6*(1), 27–54. doi:10.1080/096922999347335

Boler, M. (2004). *Democratic dialogue in education: Troubling speech, disturbing silence.* New York: Peter Lang Publishing.

Brown, K.M. (2004). Leadership for social justice and equity: Weaving a transformative framework and pedagogy. *Educational Administration Quarterly, 40*(1), 77–108. doi:10.1177/0013161X03259147

Cambron-McCabe, N., & McCarthy, M.M. (2005). Educating school leaders for social justice. *Educational Policy, 19*(1), 201–222. doi:10.1177/0895904804271609

Caputo, R.K. (2002). Social justice, the ethics of care, and market economies. *Families in Society, 83*(4), 355–364. doi:10.1606/1044-3894.10

Carozza, L. (2007). Dissent in the midst of emotional territory. *Informal Logic, 27*(2), 197–210.

Carr, P. (2007). Standards, accountability and democracy: Addressing inequities through a social justice accountability framework. *Democracy & Education, 17*(1), 7–16.

Carr, W., & Hartnett, A. (1996). *Education and the struggle for democracy.* Buckingham, UK: Open University Press.

Chua, A.L. (2000). The paradox of free market democracy: Rethinking development policy. *Harvard International Law Journal, 41*(2), 287–379.

Crowder, G. (2006, September 25–27). *Chantal Mouffe's agonistic democracy.* Paper presented at the Australian Political Studies Association Conference, University of Newcastle.

Darling-Hammond, L. (1996). The right to learn and the advancement of teaching: Research, policy, and practice for democratic education. *Educational Researcher, 256*(6), 5–17. doi:10.3102/0013189X025006005

Dewey, J. (1966). *Democracy and education. An introduction to the philosophy of education.* New York: Free Press. (Original work published 1916)

Dryzek, J.S. (2009). Democratization as deliberative capacity. *Comparative Political Studies, 42*(11), 1379–1402. doi:10.1177/0010414009332129

Espinoza, O. (2007). Solving the equity-equality conceptual dilemma: a new model for analysis of the educational process. *Educational Research, 49*(4), 343–363. doi:10.1080/00131880701717198

Fraser, N. (2008). Abnormal justice. *Critical Inquiry, 34*(3), 393–422. doi:10.1086/589478

Fraser, N. (2010). Injustice at intersecting scales: On "social exclusion" and the "global poor." *European Journal of Social Theory, 1*(3), 363–371. doi:10.1177/1368431010371758

Freedman, E.B. (2007). Is teaching for social justice undemocratic? *Harvard Educational Review, 77*(4), 442–473.

Freire, P. (1972). *Pedagogy of the oppressed.* London: Penguin Books.

Freire, P. (1978). *Pedagogy in process.* New York: Seabury.

Gandin, L.A., & Apple, M.W. (2012). Can critical democracy last? Porto Alegre and the struggle over thick democracy in education. *Journal of Education Policy, 27*(5), 621–639. doi:10.1080/02680939.2012.710017

Gewirtz, S. (1998). Conceptualizing social justice in education: Mapping the territory. *Journal of Education Policy, 13*(4), 469–484. doi:10.1080/0268093980130402

Gilbert, M.A. (1997, May 16–20). *Prolegomenon to a pragmatics of emotion.* Paper presented at First International Conference of the Ontario Society for the Study of Argumentation, St. Catharines, ON.

Gilbert, M.A. (1999). Language, words and expressive speech acts. In F. van Eemeren, R. Grootendorst, J.A. Blair, and C.A. Willard (Eds.), *Proceedings of the fourth international conference of the international society for the study of argumentation* (pp. 231–234). Windsor, ON: Ontario Society for the Study of Argumentation.

Gilbert, M.A. (2001). Emotional messages. *Argumentation, 15*(3), 239–250. doi:10.1023/A:1011156918137

Giroux, H. (1983). *Theory and resistance in education.* London: Heinemann.

Glynos, J. (2003). Radical democratic ethos, or what is an authentic political act? *Contemporary Political Theory, 2*(2), 187–208. doi:10.1057/palgrave.cpt.9300064

Goi, S. (2005). Agonism, deliberation, and the politics of abortion. *Polity, 37*(1), 54–81. doi:10.1057/palgrave.polity.2300005

Goodman, J. (1992). *Elementary schooling for critical democracy.* Albany: State University of New York (SUNY) Press.

Graham, K.M. (2002). Race and the limits of liberalism. *Philosophy of the Social Sciences, 32*(2), 219–239. doi:10.1177/004931032002005

Gutmann, A. (1999). *Democratic education* (2nd ed.). Princeton, NJ: Princeton University Press.

Gutmann, A., & Thompson, D. (2004). *Why deliberative democracy?* Princeton: Princeton University Press.

Habermas, J. (1984). *Reason and the rationalization of society. Vol. 2 of the theory of communicative action.* Boston: Beacon.

Inoue, T. (2003, August 12–18). *Two models of democracy: How to make demos and hercules collaborate in public deliberation.* Paper presented at IVR-2033 World Congress, University of Lund, Sweden.

Kohli, W. (2005). What is social justice education? In W. Hare & J.P. Portelli (Eds.), *Key questions for educators* (pp. 98–100). Halifax: Edphil Books.

Leighton, D. (2002). Searching for politics in an uncertain world: Interview with Zygmunt Bauman. *Renewal, 10*(1), 14–18.

Levin, B. (1998). The educational requirement for democracy. *Curriculum Inquiry, 28*(1), 57–79. doi:10.1111/0362-6784.00075

Manzer, R.A. (2003). *Educational regimes and Anglo-American democracy.* Toronto: University of Toronto Press.

Marshall, C. (2004). Social justice challenges to educational administration: Introduction to a special issue. *Educational Administration Quarterly, 40*(1), 3–13. doi:10.1177/0013161X03258139

McFarland, D., & Starmmans, C.E. (2009). Inside student government: The variable quality of high school student councils. *Teachers College Record, 111*(1), 27–54.

Merrett, C.D. (2004). Social justice: What is it? Why teach it? *Journal of Geography, 103*(3), 93–101. doi:10.1080/00221340408978584

Mouffe, C. (1997). Decision, deliberation and democratic ethos. *Philosophy Today, 41*(1), 24–30.

Mouffe, C. 2000a. *Deliberative democracy or agonistic pluralism.* Reihe Politikwissenschaft Political Science Series, Institute for Advanced Studies, Vienna. Retrieved from http://users.unimi.it/dikeius/pw_72.pdf.

Mouffe, C. (2000b). *The democratic paradox.* London: Verso.

Mouffe, C. (2005). *On the political.* London: Routledge.

Ngai, P.B., & Koehn, P.H. (2011). Indigenous education for critical democracy: Teacher approaches and learning outcomes in a K-5 Indian Education for All program. *Equity & Excellence in Education, 44*(2), 249–269. doi:10.1080/10665684.2011.559414

O'Neill, S. (2000). The politics of inclusive agreements: Towards a critical discourse theory of democracy. *Political Studies, 48*(3), 503–521. doi:10.1111/1467-9248.00272

Olssen, M., Codd, J., & O'Neill, A. (2004). *Education policy: Globalization, citizenship and democracy.* London: Sage.

Pettit, P. (2008). Three conceptions of democratic control. *Constellations (Oxford, England), 15*(1), 46–55. doi:10.1111/j.1467-8675.2008.00473.x

Pinto, L.E. (2005). The Apprentice: A critical approach to media portrayal of business in the classroom. *Orbit (Amsterdam, Netherlands), 35*(2), 31–33.

Pinto, L.E. (2006). Critical thinking and the cultural myth of the entrepreneur. *Our Schools/Our Selves, 16*(1), 69–84.

Pinto, L.E. (2012). *Curriculum reform in Ontario: Common sense processes and democratic possibilities.* Toronto: University of Toronto Press.

Pløger, J. (2004). Strife: Urban planning and agonism. *Planning Theory, 3*(1), 71–92. doi:10.1177/1473095204042318

Portelli, J., & Vibert, A. (2001). Beyond common educational standards: Toward a Curriculum of Life. In J. Portelli & P. Solomon (Eds.), *The erosion of democracy in education* (pp. 63–82). Calgary: Detselig. [See also page 223 of this volume.]

Portelli, J.P., & Campbell-Stephens, R. (2009). *Leading for equity: The investing in diversity approach.* Toronto: Edphil Books.

Portelli, J.P., & Solomon, R.P. (2001). *The erosion of democracy in education.* Calgary: Detselig.

Rawls, J. (1971). *Theory of justice.* Cambridge: Harvard University Press.

Rizvi, F. (1998). Some thoughts on contemporary theories of social justice. In B. Atweh, S. Kemmis, and P. Weeks (Eds.), *Action research in practice: Partnerships for social justice in education* (pp. 47–56). London: RoutledgeFalmer.

Romas, J. (2008). Science and social justice are not mutually exclusive. *Our Schools/ Our Selves, 17*(2), 43–52.

Ruitenberg, C.W. (2009). Educating political adversaries: Chantal Mouffe and radical democratic citizenship education. *Studies in Philosophy and Education, 28*(3), 269–281. doi:10.1007/s11217-008-9122-2

Ryan, J. (2006). Inclusive leadership and social justice for schools. *Leadership and Policy in Schools, 5*(1), 3–17. doi:10.1080/15700760500483995

Ryan, J. (2007). Dialogue, identity and inclusion: Administrators as mediators in diverse school contexts. *Journal of School Leadership, 17*(3), 340–369.

Ryan, J., & Rottmann, C. (2009). Struggling for democracy: Administrative communication in a diverse school context. *Educational Management Administration & Leadership, 37*(4), 473–496. doi:10.1177/1741143209334579

Saltman, K. (2005). *The Edison Schools: Corporate schooling and the assault on public education.* New York: Routledge.

Schmidt, S.J. (2008). Practicing critical democracy: A perspective from students. *Journal of Curriculum and Instruction, 2*(1), 38–55. doi:10.3776/joci.2008. v2n1p38-55

Shields, C.M. (2004). Dialogic leadership for social justice: Overcoming pathologies of silence. *Educational Administration Quarterly, 40*(1), 109–132. doi:10.1177/0013 161X03258963

Stocker, D., & Wagner, D. (2008). Talking about teaching mathematics for social justice. *Our Schools/Our Selves, 17*(2), 69–82.

Sunstein, R. (1997). *Free markets and social justice.* New York: Oxford University Press.

Tally, R.T. (2007). The agony of the political: A review of Chantal Mouffe, *On the political.* Faculty Publications—English. Paper 10. Retrieved from https://digital. library.txstate.edu/handle/10877/3920

Thien, D. (2007). Disenchanting democracy: Review of *On the political. Area, 39*(1), 134–135. doi:10.1111/j.1475-4762.2007.725_4.x

Travers, A. (2008). The sport nexus and gender injustice. *Studies in Social Justice, 2*(1), 79–101.

Tyler, T.R. (2000). Social justice: Outcome and procedure. *International Journal of Psychology, 35*(2), 117–125. doi:10.1080/002075900399411

Vincent, C. (2003). *Social justice, education and identity.* London: RoutledgeFalmer.

NOTES

1 Gewirtz (1998) provides a useful categorization of "five faces of oppression": exploitation, marginalization, powerlessness, cultural imperialism, and violence (p. 469).

2 Religious and moral arguments centre on doctrines that call for people to live their lives with concern for the needs of others. Legal justifications include preservations of rights and freedoms, such as those in the United States Bill of Rights, and in Canada's Charter of Rights and Freedoms. Political arguments centre on the idea that social justice builds an inclusive citizenry, and democratic

institutions thrive when economic and political inequities are minimized (Merrett, 2004).

3 Espinoza (2007) provides a detailed account of many of these disagreements. Some conceptions of fairness emphasize only distribution, ignoring the (more robust) fairness of procedure; and equity conceptions range from individual to social group issues. Which social groups are perceived to be marginalized and oppressed, and to what degree, vary and can include (dis)ability, race, religion, class, gender, sexuality, and so on (Espinoza, 2007). Moreover, how to address inequity and fairness, including goals, remains highly controversial (Espinoza, 2007).

4 Tyler's (2000) meta-analysis found increased legitimacy in outcomes where citizens based their perceptions of fairness on the following criteria: opportunities to participate; neutrality of authorities; people's trust in the motives of the authorities; and treatment of people with dignity and respect during political processes.

11

Philosophy and the Art of
Teaching for Social Justice

Kathy Hytten *

*This chapter has been reprinted from Hytten, Kathy (2007). Philosophy
and the art of teaching for social justice. In Daniel Vokey (Ed.), *Philosophy of
Education 2006* (pp. 441–449). Urbana, IL: Philosophy of Education Society.
Reprinted by permission of the Philosophy of Education Society.

Given our current social, political, and educational climate, the need
to teach in ways that help students develop the habits of democratic
citizenship and inspire them to work for social justice is increasingly important. The barriers to democracy and justice are many.
While we are at war in Iraq, at home we are implicitly called upon to
uncritically support our government in a show of unity and patriotism (Benporath, 2004). At the same time, we push neoliberal economic policies that ensure the expansion of unfettered free-market

capitalism throughout the world, resulting in devastating human and environmental costs: growing poverty and desperation, inhumane working conditions, destruction of natural resources, privatization of public goods, disruption and dislocation of Indigenous communities, and international policies and agreements that put profits before people. In terms of civil rights, the gaps between the wealthy and poor in the United States are widening, and the life prospects for marginalized citizens—especially those who are not white—are often grim. While we recently celebrated the fiftieth anniversary of the *Brown v. Board of Education* decision to end legal segregation, we have de facto segregation in almost all spheres of public life. The large majority of non-white students currently attend poorly funded majority-minority schools, and those numbers are growing (Orfield & Lee, 2004). Yet, in the face of this suffering and social injustice, many of us remain largely oblivious or indifferent. In part, this stems from the luxury of being globally privileged as citizens of the most powerful nation in the world. But more important, perhaps, our ignorance is connected to the unfulfilled promises of democratic education. Instead of schooling that helps us develop social consciousness, compassion, commitment to others, and a sense of fairness, we worship competition, individual achievement, and educational standardization, believing ultimately in education as a means to economic productivity.

Arguably, one of the most important roles for education in the US, if not the most important, is to teach the habits, dispositions, attitudes, and behaviours necessary for democratic citizenship. These include openness, tolerance, respect, humility, co-operation, accountability, moral commitment, critical thinking, and concern for the common good, including the dignity and rights of minorities (Apple & Beane, 1995). Democracy and social justice are intimately interrelated. A democratic way of life is predicated on problem solving and continually working to bring about more enriching, enabling, and just social conditions. To teach for social justice is to engage the very real struggles that exist in the world around us in classrooms and in the broader life of schools. It is to foreground issues of democracy above and beyond the more narrow educational goals of efficiency and increased tests scores that are often tied to high-stakes accountability schemes. "Teaching for social justice," writes Maxine Greene (1998), "is teaching what we believe ought to be—not merely where moral frameworks are concerned, but in material arrangements for people in all spheres" (p. xxix). It is teaching that arouses "vivid, reflective, experiential responses that might move students" to seriously engage questions of justice and to take ameliorative action in the world around them (p. xxix).

While we have some exemplar schools set up to teach for social justice, they are few and far between. Moreover, in the educational climate that surrounds No Child Left Behind, we see less and less talk of the importance of educating for more than simply greater achievement on standardized tests. Given the mounting inequities in the world around us, it seems imperative that we as philosophers of education help reinvigorate the discussion of social justice issues in schooling, and in particular, provide some visions and tools for teaching and teacher education. In her recent Philosophy of Education Society presidential address, Barbara Houston (2003) calls for us to "adopt a forward looking perspective on taking responsibility" in the face of social problems (p. 7). She writes, "we can acknowledge the problems and ask ourselves the question: what will I undertake?" (p. 7) Responding to this challenge, in this essay I offer several ways in which philosophers of education might take on the issue of educating for social justice and thereby contribute to more democratic educational and social visions. In so doing, I provide some ideas of what we might, as philosophers and educators, undertake, as well as what kinds of work still needs to be done.

There is a long tradition in philosophy of education of scholars who have prioritized addressing unjust social conditions in their work. I begin by describing some of the tools they have developed to help us to think critically about our world. In the second section, I contextualize these existing tools within the metaphor of a journey, suggesting that, although we may not know our ultimate destination, we need to act on injustices in the present so as to open up new and different possibilities for the future. Here I also respond to critiques that the kinds of critical-thinking processes that we have so often called for may actually get in the way of our social justice efforts. In the last section of the essay, I argue that we also need to create new tools for addressing injustice, particularly within the context of teacher education.

Thinking Philosophically

Critical educational theorists have compellingly demonstrated that we do not often encourage deep critical thinking in schools but instead teach toward tests and reward recall of isolated facts. Lecture style pedagogies, arguably still the most predominant method of teaching in most school settings, tend to confuse teaching with transmission, and information with knowledge and understanding.

Educational philosophers have long argued for the importance of developing critical-thinking abilities in students as they are essential to democratic participation and decision making. They are also necessary for imagining alternative possibilities, as without critical reflection, students tend to think of the status quo (including persistent inequities) as natural and inevitable. In the face of social injustice, philosophers offer us valuable tools for thinking differently. Among the most important of these tools are disrupting taken-for-granted assumptions and unsettling common sense, asking better questions that help to clarify meanings and investigate implications, and offering alternative visions and possibilities.

Perhaps one of the hallmark tools of philosophy is to uncover that which we take for granted: the assumptions that go behind our actions that we rarely explore because they are so deeply naturalized and obscured in the ways we see the world. For example, there are many practices that go relatively unquestioned because they seem simply to constitute the phenomenon of schooling: dividing students by age, fragmenting school days into distinct classes, grading competitively, and teaching only certain subjects. Schools have looked fairly similar for so long that we can easily forget the origin and rationale for current practices, and thus assume the way things are organized is either the only, or the best, way we can imagine. Patricia Hinchey (1998) maintains, "we rarely see that our customs constitute one choice among many choices. Immersed in our own culture, we think in terms of doing things the one *right* way rather than in terms of doing things in one of many possible ways" (p. 5). The consequence of not exploring our assumptions is that we then "create mental cages and inflexible rules" that seemingly control our actions (p. 6). This is the case both in schooling and in how we look at the world around us. Among other things, failure to explore assumptions can result in paralysis, stagnation, and resignation, all of which are antithetical to forwarding ameliorative social change. Alternatively, a disposition to ask why we believe what we believe, and how we have become socialized to accept certain realities, can help us to ask better questions about our social condition, challenge givens, and open up alternatives and possibilities.

About philosophical thinking, Dewey (1933/1998) writes that it is "inquiry, investigation, turning over, probing or delving into, so as to find something new or to see what is already known in a different light. In short, it is *questioning*" (p. 265). There is an art to teaching that begins in questioning, yet too often schooling is an affair of telling; "education is suffering from narration sickness," as Freire

(2000) claims (p. 71). Freire's problem-posing approach provides us with a useful model of the kind of educational questioning that opens possibilities, particularly toward the ends of greater social justice. He calls for learning that involves an existential exploration of the conditions of our lives, one that can both unveil how we often make choices that contribute to our own oppression and reveal other choices that promote our freedom. In a problem-posing approach, "people develop their power to perceive critically *the way they exist* in the world *with which* and *in which* they find themselves; they come to see the world not as a static reality, but as a reality in process, in transformation" (p. 83).

Asking probing and revelatory questions is an important tool that philosophers can bring to the task of educating for social justice. Unfortunately, we don't value questions or problems enough in schools; instead we prioritize the recalling of "right" answers. Nicholas Burbules (2000) writes that "learning how to ask a good question is in one sense the central educational task, yet one that is almost never taught explicitly, and rarely taught at all. The typical sorts of questions teachers ask are questions to which the teacher already knows the answer" (p. 184). In exploring questions, we open up possibilities for seeing the world differently. This is another tool philosophers of education offer to educating for social justice: more hopeful visions for schools and society. Greene (1995) often ties philosophy to imagination, believing that "it may be the recovery of imagination that lessens the social paralysis we see around us and restores a sense that something can be done in the name of what is decent and humane" (p. 35). One of the areas in which philosophers have offered vision is in unpacking the meanings of democracy and justice, describing the educational implications of different conceptions of democracy, and calling for more inclusive and enriching forms of democracy. We see this especially in the work of Dewey, but also in the works of many of our members, for example more recently in Nel Noddings's (2004) call for critical thinking in times of war; Ronald Glass's (2004) admonition for us to attend "to the contradictions between ... espoused ethics and theories of justice" and current social practices (p. 165); and in John Covaleskie's (2005) argument for the importance of fostering the democratic virtues of altruism, diligence, and intelligence in schools.

The Journey toward Social Justice

While philosophers of education have been calling for better critical-thinking capacities by students and more imaginative democratic visions for education for a long time, these ideas have never been widely prevalent in schools. In part, this is because we are often not very good at speaking to broader audiences, preferring instead the more theoretically sophisticated argumentation that occurs among likeminded colleagues, often in discipline-specific meetings. Moreover, though we philosophers of education may take the tools that I have been describing—uncovering assumptions, asking different questions, offering theories and visions—as given, and indeed rather mundane, it is important to address the fact that these tools, and the conceptions of democracy and justice that drive many of our visions, can themselves become barriers to our social justice efforts. This is largely because our tools are always part of our present world-views, which are inherently partial and limited. As we have seen in the large body of work done on the problem of whiteness in our diversity efforts, we cannot rely on good liberal intentions (typically grounded in "rational" thinking) to lead our efforts to disrupt racism. Instead, those of us who are part of the dominant culture need to be much more self-reflective about our own assumptions and in so doing realize that there are some things we cannot know, in large part because of our social positionalities. Only then can we learn to truly listen to, and collaborate with, marginalized others. Moreover, we need to trouble the call for abstract and decontextualized ways of questioning, reasoning, and behaving in the face of diversity. In making this point, Audrey Thompson (2003) challenges what she sees as the appeal by white liberals and progressives for universal moral principles, suggesting that the morality of the privileged "is one of the main obstacles to racial change. 'Universal' codes of ethics are the arrangements that make sense to people accustomed to privilege" (p. 18). She goes on to argue that the critical tools we have available to us now are "shaped to an important degree by the relations they are meant to disrupt," and thus we cannot rely on them alone if we are going to realize new, more socially just, possibilities for living amid diversity (p. 20).

Thompson is not alone in critiquing the tools of the liberal philosophical tradition. Feminist, poststructuralist, and postcolonialist scholars are similarly concerned with how our current ways of thinking can impede rather than further social justice efforts. For example, Elizabeth Ellsworth (1989) challenges critical educators for being blind to the ways that they "are always implicated in the very structures they are trying to change" (p. 310). Similarly, Dan Butin (2002) critiques social justice educators for assuming that their work for social and educational change is "somehow outside the potential for oppression" (p. 14). He is concerned that social justice efforts are based too heavily on a "rational discourse of overcoming" and on the myth that social transformation is largely dependent on simply changing individual actions (p. 14). Troy Richardson and Sofia Villenas (2000) question the very ideas of democracy and human rights as the bases for moral decision making and action, suggesting they are too tied to Eurocentric assumptions and the imperatives of the dominant culture and ruling class.

These are important critiques that we need to take seriously in our efforts to teach and work for social justice. Yet, there is a danger that they can become disabling, as we can lose sight of any sort of anchor in working toward the reduction of unnecessary suffering and toward the abatement of racism, classism, sexism, and heterosexism. We also risk miring ourselves in theoretical debates while the suffering around us grows. The problems of social injustice are too grave for inaction. It is essential that we address them in the here and now, even while we trouble potential solutions that we may arrive at, and even while we debate the dangers of offering visions (especially as they can become reified in metanarratives). Here is where I think we can benefit from seeing work toward social justice in relation to the metaphor of a journey, one whose ultimate destination we cannot know in advance. In writing about the disruption of social systems that overly privilege some groups of people (particularly those from the dominant culture), Allen Johnson (1997) claims that "it has to be enough to move away from social life organized around privilege and oppression and to move toward the certainty that alternatives are possible, even though we may not have a clear idea of what those are or ever experience them ourselves" (p. 147). As part of the journey toward justice, we need to use the best tools that we have available to us now, including the tools of critical thinking that philosophers so value and the models we have developed of what a just society looks like, while also troubling those tools and remaining reflexive about the ways in which our social positionalities (and the blindnesses that are necessarily part of those positionalities) limit the potential effectiveness of these tools. This balancing act can then help us to shift our perspectives, actions, relationships, and investments so that we can then create new tools for thinking and acting differently.

In his philosophical analysis of The Odyssey, Burbules (2002) alludes to the importance of balancing what we think we know with the inherent uncertainty of all knowledge. He also nicely displays the value of a journey metaphor—particularly one with unclear ends. He relates philosophical thinking and philosophical change to the kinds of experiences Odysseus undergoes in his decade-long voyage back to his home in Ithaca, which is, of course, a different place when he does eventually arrive. Burbules credits Odysseus with the virtue of *metis*: the capacity to be strategic, crafty, adaptive, and resourceful—to get by amid challenges and roadblocks. We need a similar kind of ability to get by to work for justice in the absence of certainty. The challenges Odysseus faced parallel the roadblocks faced by philosophers engaging in social justice work. Burbules argues that "philosophy requires a certain kind of binocularism, I think: the possibility of holding certain beliefs while at the same time seriously appreciating the perspectives from which those beliefs might be problematic" (p. 9). Similarly, educating for social justice requires using the critical-thinking tools we have available, recognizing how they can be limited and even problematic, seeking out alternative ways of thinking about and using these tools, and perhaps most important, developing new tools and habits for engaging social injustice. Given how long we philosophers have been arguing for more critical habits of thinking, it seems imperative that we do more than just try harder at what we have always been doing.

New Possibilities

To inspire students both to think critically and to assume the moral agency necessary to cultivate more humane and more democratic social and political relationships, we need to use and invent new forms of pedagogical engagement, which ideally can also serve as models for new forms of social engagement. These can only be developed as we experiment with different methods and with multiple ways of seeing and engaging the world around us in educational spaces. This is not to say that we do not also want to teach about already developed theories of justice, but only to acknowledge that these rarely inspire our students to challenge their ways of seeing and acting in the world. There are a variety of alternative forms of pedagogical activity that open up possibilities for social justice education and that can help us to develop some new tools for social and educational transformation. Here, I will outline two possibilities that can complement our efforts to get students to think more critically, focusing in particular on the topic of globalization (especially as it is manifest in the unfettered expansion of global capitalism, which many argue is the root of so much injustice). These are working with experiential accounts and narratives in classrooms and engaging students in performative activities.

Any of us who have worked with young kids know that stories often have much more evocative power than arguments, which can feel overly abstract and decontextual. Poems, parables, autobiographies, pictures, photographs, and videos are equally evocative representations. Greene (2003) lauds the arts for inspiring us to see the world in new ways: awakening reflectivity, defamiliarizing commonsense, provoking questions, and releasing imagination. While many of us are aware of the power of personal accounts to evoke, they are often an underutilized resource in educating for social justice. When teaching about globalization, for example, I want students to think critically about several assumptions that are offered in mainstream discourse: capitalism is the one best system, success can be best measured through economic means, free trade equals fair trade, and competition is inherently good. I want them to ask different questions and imagine different possibilities. They begin to do this well using the tools of critical thinking I described earlier, yet they are most moved, both personally and to think more critically, after stories and videos that expose the real impacts of globalization. For example, using ethnographic narratives, photographs, visual representations, and theoretical analyses, Deborah Barndt (2002) shows how the habits of first-world consumers and the livelihoods of third-world workers are fundamentally connected in the means of production. She puts a human face on the realities of transnational capitalism by describing the tomato production process, from Mexican fields to US and Canadian tables. In detailing the stories of the female workers who plant, pick, package, and sell tomatoes, often under grueling and inhumane conditions, we can't help but see the human, ecological, and spiritual costs of food systems controlled by market forces. The video *Life and Debt* (2001), a powerful account of the deleterious impact of WTO and IMF policies in Jamaica, also introduces us to the real people who provide for our desires (picking our food and assembling our clothes) as they sacrifice their own. Videos such as *This is What Democracy Looks Like* (2000), an independent media documentary of the WTO protests in Seattle, and *Affluenza* (1997), a humorous yet telling portrayal of the consequences of US-American overconsumption, also help provoke different kinds of classroom engagement. Images and metaphors from these films and stories stay with my students as they try to make sense of globalization, to critically analyze arguments from a variety of perspectives, and to consider how they are compelled to act in the face of global injustice. At the same time, we also trouble the ways in which such viewing also can be an act of consumption of the "exotic" Other, and may be colonizing as well as inspiring.

Another tool that can help students to think, feel, and act differently is performance. Performance studies scholars call for more embodied ways of knowing in classrooms, arguing against the Cartesian separation of the mind and body that is so prevalent in academic settings. They claim that our identities are constituted by a series of performances, what Judith Butler (1990) calls "a stylized repetition of acts" (p. 270). When we become aware of how these everyday, often mundane acts create our social worlds, we can then have more control over these worlds and learn to act differently, for instance, in more communal and environmentally sustaining ways. So, for example, driving to work, shopping at Walmart, eating at McDonalds, acquiring more than we need, and worshiping technology are all performative acts that help to shape and constitute the world we live in. Yet we are often not critically conscious of what these acts do for us, how they contribute to larger social dynamics, and/or how they connect us to others around the world. Using performance in the classroom can help us to see the problematic impacts of some of our choices. For example, Bill Bigelow (2002) asks his students to perform as leaders of developing countries in "The Transnational Capital Auction: A Game of Survival," where they are pitted against each other, bidding to get transnational corporations to locate in their countries by creating a climate friendly to capital (low-wage jobs, few taxes or restrictions, weak environmental laws, and no unions). In playing the game, students are forced to confront the ethics behind globalization, breathing "life into the expressions 'downward leveling' and 'race to the bottom'" (p. 131). Alternatively, students can performatively practice organizing, creating alliances, and developing transnational coalitions—all essential for combating the negative effects of globalization.

Using narratives, personal accounts, documentaries, and performances in the classroom, along with developing students' capacities to think critically, are tools that we currently have available to us in our efforts to teach for social justice. Philosophers of education can play an important role in these efforts by helping students use these tools, trouble these tools, and create new tools for engaging our social worlds. Given our current climate of growing suffering, poverty, conflict, and desperation, philosophers of education can also help to reinvigorate discussions of the importance of education for democracy and social justice: education that cultivates students' capacities to respond imaginatively and amelioratively to the world. This is hard to do through familiar, and frequently uninspiring, forms of pedagogical engagement. While using alternative textual forms such as narratives and performances in the classroom is not necessarily new, they do have the potential to open up yet unimagined spaces out of which we can create new tools to use in our social justice efforts. Ultimately, they also may help inspire the passion and vision needed to construct a more hopeful, democratic, and just future.

REFERENCES

Apple, M.W., & Beane, J.A. (1995). *Democratic schools.* Alexandria, VA: Association for Supervision & Curriculum Development.

Barndt, D. (2002). *Tangled routes: Women, work and globalization on the tomato trail.* Lanham, MD: Rowman and Littlefield.

Benporath, S. (2004). Radicalising democratic education: Unity and dissent in wartime. In K. Alston (Ed.), *Philosophy of Education 2003* (pp. 245–253). Urbana, IL: Philosophy of Education Society.

Bigelow, B. (2002). The lives behind the labels: Teaching about the global sweatshop and the race to the bottom. In B. Bigelow & B. Peterson (Eds.), *Rethinking globalization: teaching for justice in an unjust world* (pp. 128–132). Milwaukee: Rethinking Schools Press.

Burbules, N.C. (2000). Aporias, webs and passages: Doubt as an opportunity to learn. *Curriculum Inquiry, 30*(2), 171–187. doi:10.1111/0362-6784.00161

Burbules, N.C. (2002). 2001: A philosophical odyssey. In S. Rice (Ed.), *Philosophy of Education 2001* (pp. 1–14). Urbana, IL: Philosophy of Education Society.

Butin, D.W. (2002). This ain't talk therapy: Problematizing and extending anti-oppressive education. *Educational Researcher, 31*(3), 14–16. doi:10.3102/0013189X031003014

Butler, J. (1990). Performative acts and gender constitution: An essay in phenomenology and feminist theory. In S.E. Case (Ed.), *Performing feminisms: Feminist critical theory and theatre* (pp. 270–282). Baltimore: Johns Hopkins University Press.

Covaleskie, J.F. (2005). Can democracy work if it relies on people like us? In C. Higgins (Ed.), *Philosophy of Education 2004* (pp.186–193). Urbana, IL: Philosophy of Education Society.

Dewey, J. (1998). *How we think.* Boston: Houghton Mifflin Company. (Original work published 1933)

Ellsworth, E. (1989). Why doesn't this feel empowering? Working through the repressive myths of critical pedagogy. *Harvard Educational Review, 59*(3), 297–325.

Freire, P. (2000). *Pedagogy of the oppressed.* New York: Continuum.

Glass, R.D. (2004). Pluralism, justice, democracy, and education: Conflict and citizenship. In K. Alston (Ed.). *Philosophy of Education 2003* (pp. 158–166). Urbana, IL: Philosophy of Education Society.

Greene, M. (1995). *Releasing the imagination: Essays on education, the arts, and social change.* San Francisco: Jossey Bass.

Greene, M. (1998). Introduction: Teaching for social justice. In W. Ayers, J.A. Hunt, & T. Quinn (Eds.), *Teaching for social justice.* New York: The New Press.

Greene, M. (2003). In search of a critical pedagogy. In A. Darder, M. Baltodano, & R.D. Torres (Eds.), *The Critical Pedagogy Reader* (pp. 97–114). New York: Routledge.

Hinchey, P.H. (1998). *Finding freedom in the classroom: A practical introduction to critical theory*. New York: Peter Lang.

Houston, B. (2003). Taking responsibility. In S. Fletcher (Ed.), *Philosophy of Education 2002* (pp. 1–13). Urbana, IL: Philosophy of Education Society.

Johnson, A.G. (1997). *Privilege, power, and difference*. New York: McGraw Hill.

Noddings, N. (2004). War, critical thinking, and self-understanding. *Phi Delta Kappan, 85*(7), 489–495.

Orfield, G., & Lee, C. (2004). Brown at 50: King's Dream or Plessy's Nightmare. Retrieved from http://www.civilrightsproject.harvard.edu.

Richardson, T., & Villenas, S. (2000). "Other" encounters: Dances with whiteness in multicultural education. *Educational Theory, 50*(2), 255–273. doi:10.1111/j.1741-5446.2000.00255.x

Thompson, A. (2003). Tiffany, friend of people of colour: White investments in anti-racism. *International Journal of Qualitative Studies in Education, 16*(1), 7–29. doi:10.1080/0951839032000033509

12

Post-Neoliberalism, Education, and the Principles of Democratic Learning

*Emery J. Hyslop-Margison
and Samuel LeBlanc*

Introduction

Similar to many other industrialized countries, in the late 1970s Canada was influenced by a series of recessions due to an oversupply crisis in the economy. In an attempt to control the money supply and reduce inflation, banks raised interest rates, causing consumer spending to dwindle (Hyslop-Margison, 2005). When consumer demand for goods and services falls, inventories swell, the demand for labour shrinks, and unemployment rises (Posner, 2010). While layoffs mounted in both the private and public sectors, education, historically the target of revision in difficult or troubling economic times, predictably confronted calls for significant reform.

In this chapter we trace the development of neoliberal and post-neoliberal policies that followed this period of economic crisis.

We consider how these policies affect education and identify the corresponding threats they pose to democratic learning. Given the socializing responsibility of schools, teachers have a concomitant duty to prepare students as participatory democratic citizens. With this duty in mind, we propose three principles of democratic learning (Hyslop-Margison & Graham, 2001) to counter neoliberal and post-neoliberal threats to student agency and democratic citizenship: (a) democratic education respects student rationality by encouraging critique of course content, objectives, and prevailing ideas; (b) democratic education includes alternative perspectives on issues such as social, economic, and labour market structure, sustainable development, the labour movement and labour history, acceptable working conditions and globalization; and (c) democratic education emphasizes that economic, labour market, and working conditions are constructed through human agency and can be transformed through reflective action, or praxis.

Neoliberalism and Post-Neoliberalism

The 1950s and 60s were two socially progressive decades in Canada that witnessed the development and implementation of widespread welfare state policies. In the two and a half decades following the Second World War, there was significant expansion throughout the Canadian economy. The burgeoning wartime manufacturing infrastructure was rapidly transformed to satisfy the growing demand for consumer goods and, consequently, unemployment figures remained consistently low. Canada also firmly established itself as a compassionate welfare state by implementing the Canada Pension Plan, universal national health care, and a range of other programs designed to improve economic equality (Banting, 1987).

Consistent with the ebb and flow of capitalist economies, the late 1970s brought an economic crisis of significant proportions. This decline resulted from a contraction-based monetary policy introduced to control widespread inflation and the general oversupply of available goods in the economy. The buoyant economic times promoted by Keynesian supply side economics ended, as major corporations quickly downsized their workforces to protect shrinking profit margins. Rather than blaming the tightened monetary policies for causing the recession, welfare state policies, labour unions, and a general lack of economic productivity were targeted by business leaders and industry captains for causing economic decline. In classic ideological fashion, blame was effectively shifted from those who caused the economic crisis, policy makers, the banks, and industry leaders, to those who suffered its devastating consequences, the working and middle classes. This misinformation was publicly disseminated through a variety of sophisticated methods, including the corporate-controlled media and domestic politicians such as Canadian Prime Minister Brian Mulroney and Ontario Premier Mike Harris, the former neoliberal premier of Ontario.

Mike Harris rose to power in 1995 by asking citizens to join him in a "Common Sense Revolution" premised on significant cuts in four areas: taxes; government spending; barriers to job creation (including workmen's compensation premiums and progressive labour legislation); and the size of government. Harris was especially effective in transforming the province's educational agenda to one entirely focused on instrumental human capital development. Harris, Mulroney, and others inherited and adopted the ideological drive toward smaller government, sweeping economic deregulation, and creating a business-friendly environment. This is the legacy of neoliberalism, and the trickle-down economics it generated, a legacy most notably popularized through the political rhetoric and policy reform of United States President Ronald Reagan (1981–89, Reaganomics) and British Prime Minister Margaret Thatcher (1979–90, Thatcherism).

Neoliberals such as Reagan and Thatcher aggressively spread an economic ideology advanced by US economist Milton Friedman, a professor at the University of Chicago during the period. In the 1970s, Friedman challenged the popular economic theories of John Maynard Keynes, the British economist who argued that governments had a responsibility to assist capitalist economies through periods of recession. Keynes's most notable contribution, *The General Theory of Employment, Interest and Money* (1936), proposed a solution to the economic recessions of capitalism based on a government-funded policy of full employment. Keynes argued that recessions are not only cyclical in capitalism but they are also generated from within. Therefore, it was misguided policy to let capitalism self-regulate in the long term. Moreover, there was little comfort in knowing that full employment and economic growth would return in the long run, as "The *long run* is a misleading guide to current affairs. *In the long run* we are all dead" (Keynes, 1924, p. 80).

In Friedman's view, one that ultimately came to define neoliberalism, government was conversely obliged to stay completely removed from the economy and permit the free market to determine employment levels. Neoliberalism rapidly became the prevailing ideology with the assumption that policies and practices deemed effective for the market and, by extension, most beneficial to corporations were necessarily good for everyone else. By the 1980s, the "logic" of the marketplace and corresponding corporate rule became the guiding principles for public policy development, including that in public education, among virtually all industrialized nations (Hyslop-Margison & Graham, 2001).

The promise advanced by neoliberals such as Friedman, Mulroney, Harris, Reagan, and Thatcher was that economic growth could be fully restored if and only if those policies that interfered with market economy logic were rescinded. As a result, during the 1980s and 90s virtually all developed countries launched concerted attacks on social programs that allegedly interfered with the economy by tempering the negative social consequences of unfettered capitalism. For example, the Mulroney Conservative government in Canada implemented massive reductions in federal spending—25% across the board reduction—in areas such as socialized medicine, unemployment insurance, and social assistance benefits (Dobbin, 2003). Social programs were considered direct interference in the economy by skewing the labour market structure to advantage workers, thereby distorting the supply and demand principles of the labour market. Alternatively, free trade agreements such as NAFTA were aggressively pursued to dismantle barriers to economic globalization and transfer manufacturing sector production to developing economies with cheap sources of labour and lax environmental laws (Hyslop-Margison, 2005).

In spite of further recessions in the 1990s, industrialized governments, directed largely by their corporate sponsors, continued to pursue neoliberal policies, eliminate government programs, and reform education to coincide with perceived human capital demands. As a result of these policies, the gap between those doing well under neoliberalism and those suffering its devastating consequences increased dramatically. Neoliberalism proved a resilient ideology and withstood this growing disparity, although expanding citizen discontent and mass public protests, such as the Battle in Seattle[1] and the Third Summit of the Americas in Quebec City,[2] occurred with increased frequency. In spite of these sporadic public protests, the reputation of neoliberalism remained relatively unscathed until the massive global economic meltdown in 2008.

Falling on the heels of US President George W. Bush administration's final term in office, the economic crisis of 2008 resulted, in part, from the massive economic deregulation policies implemented under neoliberalism. Encouraged by various Wall Street magnates, Bush worked diligently to remove many of the checks and balances required to prevent reckless financial lending and related profiteering. The thirst for wealth, the possible fulfillment of the American dream of home ownership, and the easy access to credit, coupled with deregulation, meant that a vast number of problematic loans and mortgages were bundled together and sold by Wall Street vendors to other financial lenders around the world. When a massive number of defaults occurred, those who actually financed the bad loans by supplying the necessary capital suffered huge financial losses and housing markets correspondingly tumbled, thereby prompting the most severe economic downturn since the Great Depression (Cohen, 2009). The myth that market deregulation and neoliberalism generated endless economic growth exploded with a resounding bang, and, ironically, governments were forced to fill the economic void by bailing out with public funds the same corporate culture that previously demanded eliminating the public role in economic policy development.

Although an expectation that the economic crisis might prompt a major re-examination of neoliberal policies seemed reasonable, corporate leadership, with the political influence it enjoyed, was not prepared to relinquish control. This structural outcome was obvious soon after the US government's $700-billion bailout of the corporate sector when newly minted President Barrack Obama appointed several neoliberals as his closest financial advisors. It was business as usual on Wall Street, but the general public in industrialized countries was no longer sold on the merits of neoliberalism as the best of all possible economic worlds. This growing public discontent generated a resulting shift from the *ideological state apparatus* to the *repressive state apparatus* to sustain corporate control over public policy (Althusser, 1971; Hyslop-Margison & Leonard, 2012), a shift we refer to in this chapter as *post-neoliberalism*.

The ideological state apparatus and the repressive state apparatus are distinctions identified by critical theorist Louis Althusser (1971) to explain the mechanisms employed to sustain socially destructive capitalist states. Essentially an extension of Marx's base/superstructure analysis of society, the ideological state apparatus (ISA) includes forces such as communication platforms, schools, and popular culture designed to shape and control prevailing ideas. The ISA is the preferred method of social control to direct public opinion in favour of hegemonic interests because states are seldom sustained indefinitely through force. But with the economic collapse of 2008 and the growing loss of public confidence in neoliberal tenets, the repressive state apparatus (RSA) became a far more visible feature of industrialized nations. In countries such as Greece, Spain, and Italy, massive public protests against government "austerity" have been met with considerable police state force and violent suppression. In Canada, the emerging RSA was especially apparent during the 2010 G20 meetings in Toronto, Ontario (Hyslop-Margison & Leonard, 2012).

The Group of Twenty Finance Ministers and Central Bank Governors (G20) meeting in Toronto during the summer of 2010 provides a classic example of the RSA in several troubling ways. The G20 meeting precipitated the passing of secret legislation that afforded the police sweeping arrest and detainment powers. The province of Ontario quietly passed a law that permitted police to arrest people wandering near the G20 security zone who refused to identify themselves or allow an arbitrary police search of person and property. The legislation was passed under Ontario's Public Works Protection Act and, consequently, was not subject to interparty debate in the provincial legislature. The cabinet action came in response to an "extraordinary request" by Toronto police chief Bill Blair, who demanded sweeping powers shortly after learning the G20 was coming to Toronto. The clandestinely passed law empowered "guards" appointed under the act to arrest anyone who came within five metres of the security zone. The legislation resulted in shocking abuses of police power, "the largest mass arrests in Canadian history" (Morrow, 2012, n.p.), including unnecessary acts of violence and oppression against citizens simply exercising their democratic right to public assembly and public protest (Hyslop-Margison & Leonard, 2012; Yang, 2010). As we alluded to above, neoliberalism and, more recently post-neoliberalism, substantially impacted on public education and curriculum at all levels. In the next two sections of the chapter we identify how these conditions have affected schools, universities, curricula, and teachers.

Neoliberalism and Education

With the emergence of neoliberal political policies in the late 1970s, education in virtually all industrialized countries was targeted for massive reform. Since the inception of public education, schools afforded the ruling classes with a trenchant means to convey hegemonic ideology. Historically, education reform to advance ideological interests is often justified on the grounds that it effectively addresses various social and economic problems, including urban decay and youth unemployment, and that improved human capital education increases domestic competitiveness (Kantor, 1986).

With economic globalization comprising a key building block in the construction of a neoliberal edifice, it was fitting that the Organisation for Economic Co-operation and Development (OECD) became the major vehicle for neoliberal policy formation in education. In 1977 the OECD, a corporate-friendly institution representing the 34 most industrialized nations in the world, introduced the idea of *cross-curricular competencies* (OECD, 1977), designed to replace the specific content and understanding traditionally comprising education objectives. These competencies, including "skills" such as problem-solving and critical thinking, were intended to provide students as future workers with abilities that transfer between changing working contexts. Since neoliberalism offered no promise of employment security, it was imperative that workers be retooled to serve the new labour market demands for a flexible and transferable human resource. Although ostensibly a rational approach to education in uncertain economic times, the OECD's cross-curricular competencies initiated a major antidemocratic curricular shift. Rather than preparing students with a wide range of knowledge and understanding, and as future democratic citizens, the role of education was increasingly defined as preparing learners as human capital for a fixed social and economic reality.

In Canada OECD influence on education was most noticeable through the Conference Board of Canada (CBOC). The purpose of the CBOC's now-defunct Corporate Council on Education was to "act as a catalyst to engage business and education in partnerships that foster learning excellence and thus ensure that Canada is competitive and successful in the global economy" (CBOC, 1992, p. 3). The council drafted the *Employability Skills Profile* (*ESP*) (CBOC, 1992), an extremely influential document that identified a list of generic employment competencies: "The Employability Skills Profile is a generic list of the kinds of skills, qualities, competencies, attitudes and behaviours that form the foundation of a high quality Canadian workforce both today and tomorrow" (p. 3). The document was exceptionally influential in domestic curriculum as seven million copies of *ESP* were distributed among Canadian secondary schools and businesses following its initial publication in 1992 (Bloom, 1994).

The entire *ESP* document was heavily laden with neoliberal threats to democratic learning. For example, under the heading "Adaptability Skills," the program expected students to "demonstrate a positive attitude toward change" (CBOC, 1992, n.p.). Attitudes are not skills in any traditional semantic sense and categorizing them in this manner simply avoided providing acceptable reasons for their inclusion in public education. Furthermore, there is nothing inherently positive, or for that matter negative, in the concept of change. Any reaction to change invariably hinges on the context, implications, and consequences of the transformation in question. The expectation that students simply "adopt" a positive attitude toward abstract change represents an ideological strategy to encourage the passive acceptance of occupational instability.

In the *Construction of Social Reality*, Searle (1995) distinguishes between *brute facts* and *social facts*. Brute facts are propositions based on facts about the natural world that, although sometimes operational, cannot be transformed or reversed by human beings. For example, fresh water at sea level freezes at zero degrees Celsius, or ice and snow remain atop Mount Everest for 12 months of the year. Social facts, similar to brute facts, qualify as true propositions, but their truth value is determined entirely by human decision making rather than some pre-existing state of affairs. The contemporary features of social and economic conditions, constructed as social facts, are created entirely by the policies and practices pursued by persons and institutions. Although it may be true that contemporary labour market conditions demand worker flexibility, such observations do not denote some naturally occurring pre-existing state of affairs. Even a cursory glance at the history of economic thought reveals the extent to which theory is made to fit hegemonic socio-political interests. Hence, structural conditions that emerge from human decision making should not be described as a social or economic "reality" to students since this undermines their recognition of how human agency and praxis ultimately determine structural conditions.

Eagleton (1991) points out that the naturalization of social conditions, or the conflation of brute facts and social facts, comprises a major ideological tool in capitalist states. One need not look far in contemporary curriculum to find examples where the naturalization of social reality permeates public education. The current Ontario guidance and career education grades 11 and 12 curriculum offers a subtle but effective example:

> As they learn about the career-planning process, students set goals for postsecondary education and work and develop the knowledge and skills they need to achieve those goals. The program helps prepare students for a changing world by demonstrating that a career is not just an occupational destination but also a journey that involves lifelong learning. (Ontario Ministry of Education, 2013a, p. 5)

There are a couple of claims contained in this quote that support neoliberal precepts. The mandate of preparing students for a "changing world" implies that structural transformation is something beyond their control and, instead, their role is limited to preparation for a world created through the actions of others. The concept of "lifelong learning" within this curriculum is also reduced to an educational imperative that expects students to accept personal responsibility for job retraining in the face of neoliberal labour market instability. Social reality is depicted as something created and controlled by others, whereas students are portrayed as objects whose primary responsibility is meeting unstable workforce needs. The educational agenda that accompanies this line of thinking on lifelong learning remains silent on the possibility of social transformation, and learning is antidemocratically circumscribed by neoliberal market-driven objectives (Hyslop-Margison & Naseem, 2007).

Many public education curricular documents represent a monolithic perspective on structural design. Most documents in the area of career education reflect a corporate perspective on the labour market with little or no mention about the role and importance of labour or the labour movement. For example, the same Ontario guidance and career document cited above does not contain any meaningful information on the rights of workers, unions and/or union organization, the labour movement, or any other details that run counter to mainstream corporate and neoliberal interests. The exclusion of alternative perspectives from decisions on labour market structure or prevailing social/economic conditions represents another ideological strategy to undercut the democratic decision making and participation of students.

Post-Neoliberalism and Education

The neoliberal influence on education is often in the form of subtle discourses or strategies, such as those described above, embedded in various curricular initiatives, policies, and documents. As we indicated previously, post-neoliberalism entails far more open and confrontational attacks on teacher and student agency, and on basic democratic rights and freedoms. Indeed, the recent passing of draconian legislation in the form of Bill 115 by Ontario's McGuinty government that removed teachers' right to strike and, instead, imposed a unilateral contract settlement affords an excellent example of how legislators, representing the interests of the structural status quo, are emboldened when backed by the RSA.

The sweeping antidemocratic legislation passed by the Charest government in Quebec to terminate student protests against tuition increases is another example of post-neoliberal policy. With this legislation, student leaders suggested the Charest government violated their Charter rights and created a police state in Quebec. The president of the Federation of College Students in Quebec suggested, "This bill transforms all civil protests into a crime and transforms a state that has a tradition of openness into a police state. It is an unreasonable limit on our right to demonstrate and aims at killing our associations" (Seguin, 2012, n.p.). Another student leader, the president of the Federation of University Students in Quebec, declared the legislation "amounts to a declaration of war on the student movement" (Seguin, 2012, n.p.). A student responsible for organizing the protests maintained the Charest government sought a major right-wing transformation of Quebec society that commenced with an assault on the publicly funded health care system and universities, and now threatens democracy more generally (Seguin, 2012).

The impact of post-neoliberalism is especially obvious in higher education where professors presently confront concerted attacks on traditional academic rights such as academic freedom. The organization of presidents of Canadian universities recently issued a revised and unanimously supported statement on academic freedom that undercut many of the advances achieved by Canadian faculty over the past century (Canadian Association of University Teachers [CAUT], 2011a). The Association of Universities and Colleges of Canada (AUCC) statement removes the right of faculty to publicly criticize their institution and fails to recognize that academic freedom, as a meaningful concept, must be respected across teaching, research, and service. In their response to the AUCC statement, CAUT representatives James Turk and Wayne Peters argued, "With the growing pressures on universities to compromise their defense of academic freedom in the quest for financial support, we need a more expansive notion of academic freedom, not a more restrictive one" (CAUT, 2011a, p. A1). Universities also employ increased numbers of vulnerable part-time faculty to cut the bottom line and eliminate dissent. While representing necessary work for aspiring academics, the insecurity, turnaround, minimal pay, and last-minute contracts for part-time faculty create a docile and unorganizable workforce.

Rather than simply employing neoliberal ideology to limit Canadian universities as possible sites for democratic dissent, post-neoliberal attacks tend to be far more aggressive and explicit in nature. At the University of New Brunswick, for example, the institution's faculty association recently wrote an open letter to the university president condemning the administration's attempt to prevent union-organizing activities on campus by incorrectly deeming them "illegal" (CAUT, 2011b, A9). These types of attacks on traditional democratic rights and freedoms, supported by draconian policy and legislative revision, are consistent with those of post-neoliberal practices and the RSA. Hence, there is an urgent need to promote democratic values and citizenship in Canadian classrooms at all levels.

Principles of Democratic Learning

The *principles of democratic learning* (PDL) (Hyslop-Margison & Graham, 2001) were developed in response to threats posed by neoliberal education to the democratic citizenship of students. To reiterate from the chapter introduction, PDL include the following: (a) Education based on PDL respects student rationality, that is, the capacity of students to critique curriculum content. When students are deprived of the opportunity to question what they are learning and/or why, they become the passive objects of teaching rather than participatory subjects in democratic learning; (b) Education based on PDL provides students with alternative viewpoints and perspectives on issues relevant to social and economic experience. If students are expected to make informed, critical, and democratic choices, they require some exposure to different perspectives on social and economic issues; and (c) Education based on PDL does not depict social reality as fixed or predetermined but explicitly recognizes the democratic right of students to transform economic, labour market, and working conditions through informed political participation. Classroom teachers who understand PDL can mitigate the ideological impact of neoliberal curricula by encouraging student critique and reform of problematic practices and objectives. More generally, PDL are designed to promote student understanding that society is a dynamic and transformable human construct rather than a static and inexorable one.

We already illustrated how current curriculum in Ontario guidance and career education conflates the critical distinction between brute facts and social facts. Unfortunately, such inattention to the possible role of students in democratically reforming structural conditions is not an isolated example. For example, in the Ontario secondary school business studies curriculum, one section on "international business" (Ontario Ministry of Education, 2013b) encourages students to think about barriers and obstacles to global trade and economics. Unfortunately, there is absolutely no suggestion that students learn anything about, or consider, the deleterious affects of globalization as it relates to trade imbalances, manufacturing sector employment losses, and general working conditions.

By failing to encourage critique of globalization or to promote discussion about the more problematic implications of international free trade agreements, the business studies curriculum is manifestly undemocratic. Another section in the same curriculum encourages students to explore Canadian banks to familiarize themselves with domestic banking practices. Once again, the learning outcomes are entirely uncritical and facilitate an instrumental understanding of the Canadian banking industry. There is no imperative to critique from an ethical perspective huge banking profits in light of their disparate relationship to general economic conditions and stagnant worker wages. Any issues or perspectives that might run counter to hegemonic corporate interests are simply excluded from the document and students are left with a superficial, ideologically driven understanding of the relationship between business, economic organization, and social disparity.

By applying PDL to the Ontario secondary business studies curriculum, teachers can elevate the classroom discussion on issues such as globalization and banking to afford students a more comprehensive and critical understanding. A critique of the curriculum content, consistent with the first PDL, might be prompted by encouraging students to ask what or whose interests are primarily served by the document in its current form? What issues, organizations, or perspectives are left out of business studies and why are they left out? In response to the second PDL, the importance of including alternative perspectives, students might be asked to write a research paper that problematizes international trade and globalization, or the Canadian banking industry.

The presentation of social and economic conditions to students in curricular documents naturalizes prevailing structural conditions to students. Unlike the guidance and career education curriculum that offers no discussion of unions or union organization, the business studies curriculum invites learners to review the "changing role of unions," where the latter's role in a post-neoliberal context is portrayed as limited. Whether in labour unions or in schools, students are expected to shape their existential aspirations to the purported needs, values, and interests of a corporate-dominated society typically presented as beyond their influence. The paucity of curricular imperatives that encourage students to critique or transform the social status quo is both troubling and antidemocratic. By ignoring the distinction between brute facts and social facts, programs such as those discussed above fail to generate student understanding about their capacity to transform structural conditions through the exercise of agency and praxis. Teachers who respect PDL can overcome these hurdles by stressing the existential capacity of humans to act upon and transform their social, economic, and working conditions.

Conclusion

Neoliberalism and post-neoliberalism pose a considerable threat to the democratic citizenship rights of Canadian teachers and students and, ultimately, to all Canadians. Since the 1980s, as a major component of the ideological superstructure, public education curriculum presents students with instrumental perspectives on social and economic conditions. Students, as future citizens, are expected to adopt a passive political stance on learning that conforms to the influential interests and values of major corporations and their government allies.

Curricular documents are abstractions insofar as innovative and courageous classroom teachers can deliver them in any number of ways. Teachers equipped with PDL may successfully transform programs such as Ontario's guidance and career education and business studies into legitimate educational exercises that promote rather than delimit the future democratic citizenship of students. Although the introduction of PDL may be met with resistance in some quarters, the commitment to democracy, and the type of education required to foster it, affords teachers with a powerful argument to defend their methods.

Teachers who implement PDL allow education to achieve its full democratic potential by encouraging students and workers to critique and transform labour market, economic, and social conditions. The pedagogical approaches consistent with PDL create learning opportunities for students to explore a variety of perspectives on current issues affecting the global and regional marketplace, and to critique and evaluate labour market, economic, and social norms. Education programs respecting PDL enable our students to become politically informed subjects in the democratic construction of their social experience rather than the mere objects of neoliberal and post-neoliberal corporate interests.

REFERENCES

Althusser, L. (1971). *Lenin and philosophy and other essays.* New York: Monthly Review Press.

Banting, K. (1987). *The welfare state and Canadian federalism.* Kingston, ON: McGill-Queen's University Press.

Bloom, M. (1994). *Enhancing employability skills innovative partnerships: Projects and programs*. Ottawa, ON: Conference Board of Canada.

Canadian Association of University Teachers (CAUT). (2011a). CAUT challenges AUCC attempt to downsize academic freedom. *CAUT Bulletin, 58*(10), A1.

Canadian Association of University Teachers (CAUT). (2011b). AUNBT alleges interference in union drive. *CAUT Bulletin, 58*(10), A9.

Cohen, W. (2009). *House of Cards: A tale of wretched excess and hubris on Wall Street*. New York: Doubleday.

Conference Board of Canada (CBOC). (1992). *Employability skills profile: What are employers looking for?* Ottawa, ON: Author.

Dobbin, M. (2003). Martin sings the blues. *Rabble.ca*. Retrieved from http://rabble.ca/news/martin-sings-mulroney-tunes

Eagleton, T. (1991). *Ideology: An introduction*. London, UK: Verso.

Hyslop-Margison, E.J. (2005). *Liberalizing vocational education: Democratic approaches to career education*. Lanham, MD: University Press of America.

Hyslop-Margison, E.J., & Graham, B. (2001). Principles for democratic learning in career education. *Canadian Journal of Education, 26*(3), 341–361. doi:10.2307/1602212

Hyslop-Margison, E.J., & Leonard, H. (2012). Post neo-liberalism and the humanities: What the repressive state apparatus means for universities. *Canadian Journal of Higher Education, 42*(2), 1–12.

Hyslop-Margison, E.J., & Naseem, A. (2007). Career education as humanization: A Freirean approach to lifelong learning. *Alberta Journal of Educational Research, 53*(4), 347–358.

Kantor, H. (1986). Work, education, and vocational reform: The ideological origins of vocational education, 1890–1920. *American Journal of Education, 94*(4), 401–426. doi:10.1086/443860

Keynes, J.M. (1924). *A tract on monetary reform*. London, UK: Macmillan and Co, Limited.

Morrow, A. (2012, August 23). G20-related charges against nearly 100 protesters dropped. *The Globe and Mail*. Retrieved from http://m.theglobeandmail.com/news/national/g20-related-charges-against-nearly-100-protesters-dropped/article1758102/?service=mobile.

Ontario Ministry of Education. (2013a). Guidance and career education grades 11 and 12. Retrieved from http://www.edu.gov.on.ca/eng/curriculum/secondary/guidance1112currb.pdf

Ontario Ministry of Education. (2013b). Business studies grades 11 and 12. Retrieved from http://www.edu.gov.on.ca/eng/curriculum/secondary/business1112currb.pdf

Organisation for Economic Co-operation and Development (OECD). (1977). *Education policy and trends in the context of social and economic development perspectives*. Paris: Author.

Posner, R. (2010). *The crisis of capitalist democracy*. Cambridge, MA: Harvard University Press.

Searle, J. (1995). *The construction of social reality*. New York: The Free Press.

Seguin, R. (2012, June 18). Charest launches legislation to crack down on student protesters. *The Globe and Mail*. Retrieved from http://www.theglobeandmail.com/news/politics/charest-launches-legislation-to-crack-down-on-student-protests/article4186647/

Yang, J. (2010, June 25). G20 law gives police sweeping power to arrest people. *The Toronto Star*. Retrieved from http://www.thestar.com/news/gta/article/828367–g20-law-give-police-sweeping-powers-to-arrest-people

NOTES

1 In November 1999, Seattle, Washington, was the site of a World Trade Organization meeting to discuss international trading rules. There were massive public protests and considerable abuses of police power. The mainstream, corporate-led media coverage in the US concentrated on the violent aspects of the protests without examining the major issues such as increased corporate domination of society.

2 The Third Summit of the Americas was held on April 20–22, 2001, and featured negotiations between western hemisphere governments on a free trade area in the Americas. Similar to the Battle in Seattle, there were massive public protests and frequent abuses of police power.

13

Schooling for Democracy

*Nel Noddings**

*This chapter was originally published as Noddings, N. (2011).
Schooling for democracy. *Democracy and Education* *19*(1), 1–5.
Reproduced with permission.

Should all children go to college? There are those who insist that
the current dedication to preparing all students for college is
inspired by democratic ideals. I will argue here that such a move
actually puts our democracy at risk. We risk losing what might be
called the Whitmanesque vision of democracy—a democracy that
respects every form of honest work, includes people from every
economic and social class, and cultivates a deep understanding of
interdependence.

Conflicting Views on Democracy and Education

One view, made popular by Mortimer Adler, holds that democracy requires equal education for all children through high school, and by *equal* Adler meant the *same*. He wrote:

> We should have a one-track system of schooling, not a system with two or more tracks, only one of which goes straight ahead while the others shunt the young off onto sidetracks not headed toward the goals our society opens for all (Adler, 1982, p. 5).

Adler's objections to tracking have been echoed by many educational researchers and writers today, although some—perhaps most—do not advocate the specific one-track curriculum he prescribed. In the discussion that follows it will be important to distinguish between two senses of *tracks* and *tracking*. In one sense, when we talk about tracks, we refer to different programs such as academic (or college preparatory), vocational/industrial, and commercial. I will offer a strong defence for this form of tracking. In a second sense, we refer to the practice of assigning students to classes composed by ability groups. I won't say much about this form of tracking here, but I will suggest that if the first form were wisely designed and implemented, the second form could be reasonably recast in terms of interest rather than ability.

Current writers who oppose tracking (both forms) make a powerful argument, and it is almost frightening to suggest that they may be mistaken (Nieto, 1999; Oakes, 1995; Spring, 2000). My basic argument is that the idea of providing different programs (or tracks) for different talents and interests is a good one, fully compatible with social justice. It is the implementation of the idea that has gone badly wrong. I agree wholeheartedly with the opponents of tracking who claim that poor and minority students have been shoved into dead-end courses and, thus, deprived of anything close to equal opportunity. But different programs need not differ in quality, and forcing everyone—regardless of interest or talent—into one program is hardly democratic.

The concern that I want to explore in some depth was well expressed early in the twentieth century by Charles Eliot, when he was president of Harvard. He warned:

> If democracy means to try to make all children equal or all men equal, it means to fight nature, and in that fight democracy is sure to be defeated. There is no such thing among men as equality of nature, of capacity for training, or of intellectual power (National Society for the Promotion of Industrial Education, 1908, p. 13).

The point I want to emphasize builds on Eliot's comment that "democracy is sure to be defeated." The comment is particularly interesting because Eliot's defence of different tracks and electives represented a sharp turn-around from his earlier advocacy of the classical education recommended by the Committee of Ten (which he had chaired). During the period from about 1890 to 1910, there were strong voices recommending that high-school education be extended to all children. This seemed necessary to many for two reasons: first, the enormous influx of immigrants created a need for increased citizenship education, and second, the nation was moving away from an agricultural economy toward one based on industry. To produce good citizens and workers the country needed to expand education. But there were equally strong voices warning that many children were simply not capable of the academic work that defined high schools—classical academies—of the time.

Both groups were right. Democracy demanded the extension of secondary schooling to all children and most children were at that time incapable or uninterested in the traditional secondary education. What was to be done? The answer was ingenious: the comprehensive high school was created. The public was persuaded that this new school would offer useful courses and not just studies for future professors, preachers, and enlightened housewives. The comprehensive high school, denigrated by traditionalists then and now, made American education a model for the world. High-school education grew rapidly. By 1970, the high school graduation rate had climbed to more than 75% from its 1900 mark of 6%. This was a remarkable achievement.

Complaints against the comprehensive high school never disappeared, but they were stronger in some years than others. In the period following World War II, the objections raised against progressive education (and the comprehensive high school) reached a high point. Echoing the Committee of Ten, Arthur Bestor claimed that all students should follow the sort of program laid down by the committee, and he made his recommendations with reference to the demands of democracy. He vigorously denied that intellectual capacity was somehow lacking or diminished at lower economic levels (Angus & Mirel, 1999; Kliebard, 1995). The purpose of the school, he insisted, was to promote intellectual growth. Everything else should be subordinated to this goal. As we have noted, Mortimer Adler argued anew for the same claim 30 years later.

Without denying that intellectual growth is an important aim of education, we might respond to Bestor and Adler that other aims are equally important and that the achievement of intellectual goals is closely related to—perhaps even dependent on—the achievement of these other aims. Further, we might object to defining intellectual content as Bestor and Adler did—as a set of traditionally defined subjects long thought to be central to college preparation. Notice that we may agree with Bestor and today's opponents of tracking that intellectual capacity is not confined to one socio-economic group, race, ethnicity, or gender, but still insist that talents and interests differ across individuals. And we might also insist that the *intellectual* should not be narrowly defined in terms of traditional subjects such as algebra or history. So much hinges on this that we must address it directly if briefly.

Confusion over the Intellectual

John Dewey (1916) made it clear repeatedly that no subject is inherently more intellectual than another, and I have also made that argument in several places (Noddings, 1992, 2003, 2007). If we identify the intellectual with thinking, the algebra taught in schools is not inherently more intellectual than cooking or motorcycle repair. Calvin Woodward made the argument even before Dewey, referring to young workers in a forging shop as "young Vulcans, bare-armed, leather-aproned with many a drop of an honest sweat ... They are using their brains and hands" (as cited in Kliebard, 1999, p. 1).

Today, Mike Rose has reminded us that thinking and doing are mutually supportive, tightly connected activities. No useful activity or preparation for an occupation involving hands-on work need be simply manual labour; such work can be taught and learned intelligently, and classroom discussion can move beyond specific "doings" to matters of citizenship, mutual respect, and prospects for a satisfying personal life (Rose, 1995, 2005). Rose connects his discussion to the meaning of democracy and the centrality of respect in a growing evolving democracy. In such a democracy, honest workers are worthy of respect. One should not need a college degree to earn respect (Dewey, 1927, p. 184).

We should note, however, that Rose has recently expressed concern that his appreciative appraisal of the "mind at work" might be used to launch a renewed effort to direct minority and low-SES students away from college preparatory courses and into vocational programs. I share that concern, and I'll say more about it a bit later. But I have an even greater concern, and that centres on the high-school drop-out rate. We may comfort ourselves by bragging that we now prepare *all* students for college, but we lose a huge number before high-school graduation. Keep in mind also that my enthusiasm for vocational education rests on two essential premises: first, that we will get to work seriously in creating rich and relevant vocational programs and, second, that we will provide extensive counseling and mentoring services so that students can make intelligent choices of program. If those premises are denied or ignored, I might unhappily join my anti-tracking colleagues and do my best to stuff algebra into everyone. Well, no, as an old math teacher, I probably couldn't go that far. But I would roll up my sleeves and work with enlightened math educators to create a college-acceptable substitute for traditional algebra (Hersh & John-Steiner, 2011; Jacobs, 1970).

Whatever we devise by way of courses and programs, our products should be intellectually rich, and we should make it clear that the truly intellectual is closely related to the moral. In contrast to both those who identify the intellectual with some form of pure thinking and those who sharply separate the intellectual from the moral, Matthew Crawford (2009) insists that the two are intimately connected:

> *Any discipline that deals with an authoritative, independent reality requires honesty and humility. I believe this is especially so of the stochastic arts that fix things, such as doctoring and wrenching, in which we are not the makers of the things we tend (p. 100).*

In describing the intellectual dimension of a good mechanic's work, Crawford sees a set of virtues that connect that worker to the moral world of reality. The motorcycle mechanic must identify possible alternatives in his recommendations for repair, consider his client's resources and the purposes for which he intends to use the motorcycle, and report honestly on his analysis.

Miles Horton, too, in his work at Highlander School, saw the connection between the intellectual and the moral. Working, hiking, thinking, Horton struggled with the ideas of communism and socialism. He struggled with pacifism and its limits in advancing the good. He was clearly a well-read intellectual, but he built his life and work with working-class people and, like Paulo Freire, he believed that social justice must be achieved "with people from the bottom, who could change society from the bottom" (Horton, 1998, p. 44).

It is worth mentioning also that the philosopher Charles Sanders Peirce claimed a moral base for intellectual-scientific work. A scientist must be dedicated to the truth if he or she is to find it, and science requires commitment to continued inquiry. Thus, genuine intellectual inquiry rests on a moral foundation. One does not shut out objections to one's own position but renews inquiry in an attempt to resolve the problem and get at the truth (Thompson, 1963).

Some might argue that there are lines of work—in the financial world, for example—that do not seem to rest on a moral base and yet require vigorous mental activity. But, clearly, any work that has possible effects on the well-being of others has a moral dimension. We can recognize the mental acuity of financial wizards who betray or ignore the welfare of others, but we should hesitate to label their machinations as intellectual. Perhaps it is a matter of linguistic choice. Should we think of Professor Moriarity as a wicked intellectual or as a mental genius whose intellectual development was impaired?

In that spirit, we should admit that there are respectable thinkers who argue strongly that the intellectual is often rightly detached from the moral and even from empirical reality. The mathematician G.H. Hardy is said to have declared (bragged?), "I have never done anything 'useful'" (Newman, 1956, p. 2026). Hardy (knowing that his proclaimed uselessness was nonsense in the eyes of the world) described himself as a maker of patterns composed of ideas. The patterns, he said, must be *beautiful*, and the significance of a mathematical theorem lies not in its practical consequences but in its beauty and seriousness. For Hardy, the *intellectual* cannot be identified with the trivial even if the trivial is called *algebra*. This reminds us that the intellectual has an aesthetic dimension. When there are no obvious real-world or human effects of the work in question, judgment of its value focuses on its effects on the field of study and/or its beauty.

Some scientific work, separated from the empirical world, would pass both Peirce's moral test (truth is scrupulously pursued) and Hardy's aesthetic test (the results are beautiful and advance the field), but induce moral consternation when connected to the real world. Consider the moral agonies of Einstein, Oppenheimer, and other scientists involved in the development of the atomic bomb.

We should also recognize that intellectual work varies with respect to the objects it treats. Some intellectual work is done entirely with ideas and symbols; it does not require the body's physical participation. Other intellectual work demands the co-operation of mind and body. Traditionally, we have made the mistake of thinking that only the first sort of activity is properly called intellectual. Far worse, however, we have wrongly supposed that any sort of activity done at a desk (or computer work station) is necessarily more intellectual than work done with the hands and body in motion. In fact, much white-collar work performed in cubicles is routine, sometimes mind numbing (Crawford, 2009).

It is probably correct, however, that subjects, activities, and occupations offer a range of potential intellectual challenge. Usually, we consider as intellectuals those people who enter a field that requires devotion to thinking and working with ideas and symbols. Such work is not always directed at a specific useful outcome. It involves a substantial amount of play, and it grants ardent participants considerable delight. Hardy was being honest (if incorrect) when he said that he had never done anything useful. As educators, we should help students to understand that intellectual work (work with ideas) does indeed offer intrinsic rewards, but we need not elevate this work above all other forms of work that require varying participation of the intellect.

We must also admit that some jobs are essentially mindless and even demeaning. Digging ditches, cleaning toilets, scrubbing pots, picking beans all day, every day, are not jobs likely to engage the intellect. Utopian writers have long recognized the difficulty of reconciling economic justice and respect with the demeaning boring nature of some necessary work. Writers as different as Edward Bellamy and B.F. Skinner have explored the idea of utopian societies in which such work is shared by everyone so that no one person need spend his or her full work week in hard, dirty, mindless labour (Bellamy, 1897/1960; Skinner, 1948/1962). Others have suggested that people who do this undesirable but necessary work should be paid correspondingly more for their sacrifice or that employers be compensated for hiring more low-wage workers (Phelps, 1997).

As we plan for the future of secondary schooling, we should abandon the notion that vocational and commercial education are intellectually inferior to traditional academic subjects. Some students—for a variety of reasons, all of which should be examined sympathetically—will land in the jobs no one would choose, but the outcome should not be an accepted result of what we provide in schools. Every course offered by our schools should be rich in intellectual, moral, and aesthetic content (Noddings, 2007).

Economic Concerns

Today the most frequently heard argument for a single traditional track does not emphasize the intellectual content, but I've spent some time on it because it has been so important in the past and may be revived in the future. Instead, the main argument for preparing all students for college is economic. It is claimed that individuals who earn college degrees can expect higher lifetime earnings than those who do not, and that the nation needs more college graduates if it is to remain competitive in the world economy.

The first claim is generally true, but there are many exceptions. Recent studies have shown that, given the high cost of college, it takes many years before some graduates begin to show even a small edge in lifetime earnings, and some never do. On the second, it is not at all clear that increasing the number of college graduates will automatically increase our national competitiveness. Instead, we need to educate people well for the work they will do.

It is foolish to suppose that our economic competitiveness depends on the number of college graduates we produce. We have learned recently that China is suffering from an overload of college graduates, and many young Chinese are unable to find work commensurate with their education. It seems likely, too, that the lower rate of unemployment among college graduates in the United States is due at least in part to their acceptance of jobs that do not require a college education.

In many of the most prosperous European countries, high quality vocational education and training (VET) are deemed essential:

> Countries with strong VET systems have a different conception about learning for jobs. They make a distinction between a calling or occupation and learning the specific skills needed to weld or solve banking problems or manage the IT system in a corporation ... work is related to active citizenship and thus education and training needed for work are seen as the joint responsibility of the government and what are called nicely the "social partners" (employers and labor unions). (Hoffman, 2010, p. 1).

American educators and policymakers should renew the conversation about "callings," finding work that is satisfying in itself, and the connections among intellectual, moral, social, and aesthetic ideals.

In a recent Letter to the Editor, an angry man complained that he could no longer compare his income with professional workers. Now, he wrote, he could barely stay even with police and firemen. He ended his bitter comments with this question: Why did I go to college? Apparently, he saw only one reason for going to college—to make more money—and he is not alone in this thinking. We encourage it in our schools today.

The present emphasis on preparing everyone for college may also have an entirely different sort of economic motivation; it may not be driven entirely by a mistaken democratic commitment to social justice. Good vocational education is far more expensive than the usual college preparatory course of study. It requires more space, expensive equipment, smaller classes, a specially trained faculty, and a commitment to add new equipment regularly. It is far less expensive to place all students in regular academic courses whether or not such placement suits them. Even if we provide extra help to assist students in passing these courses, we are still ignoring their present and long-term interests. We feel justified in claiming that we have provided equal opportunity when in fact we have hurt many students doubly: We have forced them into studies at which they do not do well, and we have deprived them of courses at which they might succeed. As a result, many do not graduate from high school, and even those who do may wind up in jobs by default instead of by choice. They may well believe that they are doing this work because they are not good enough for anything else.

Toward Democratic Equal Opportunity

It is reasonable to put aside claims that children are intellectually deprived if they do not receive a college preparatory education. On the contrary, we should recognize that many students today are indeed intellectually shortchanged by the academic program forced on them. Many students suffer algebra courses that bear little resemblance to the algebra that might make it possible to study further mathematics. These unfortunate students—and their number seems to be increasing—have *algebra* listed on their transcripts, but they have learned so little that they must start all over in community college. It is not necessarily the case that their teachers are at fault. Indeed, many teachers present weak courses because they do not want their students to fail, and they know that the students would in fact fail more rigorous courses. Thus, they concentrate on teaching well-defined skills and facts—material Whitehead (1929/1967) called "inert ideas"—and omit the material essential to understanding. The intellectual is washed out.

We are now at a point very like the one educators and policy-makers faced in 1900. Should we prepare all children for college? Why? When a similar question was raised in 1900 about high-school attendance, advocates had good answers to the question. How are we answering it? One answer from many of our national leaders is that we should be first in the world in the production of college graduates. Why? We should press this question and invite vigorous debate. For example, do we really need more scientists? At present, we hold many young Ph.D.s in near-servitude for years because there is no room for them in either the academic or industrial hierarchy. The frequently voiced intention to be "number one" has become a peculiar American mania. We would do better to concentrate on the *quality* of our graduates at every level.

I think we should respond to the current question in much the same way that Eliot and others argued in the early twentieth century. They endorsed secondary education, but they redefined it. I am not arguing against post-secondary education but only against defining it in terms of a traditional college education. Further, those who can profit from *post*-secondary education must first complete *secondary* education, and many more might do so if they were given an opportunity to study material relevant to their interests and talents. Schools today claim to offer equal opportunity by forcing all students, regardless of interests, into the same curriculum. This does not meet a democratic criterion for equal opportunity. In a genuine democracy, choice is fundamental, and democratic education should provide opportunities for intelligent guided choice.

Some thoughtful critics of the approach I suggest object that teenagers are too young to make decisions that may affect their futures dramatically. However, I am not suggesting that young students be allowed to "do as they please" without guidance. And, in agreement with colleagues who wish to end tracking, I am opposed to *assigning* youngsters to tracks. The choice must be made collaboratively: counselors sharing what is revealed by tests, grades, former teachers' comments, and records; students sharing their hopes and dreams for the future. By "counselors" here I mean teachers, parents, and community mentors, as well as professional counselors; such counseling should begin early and be continuous. Moreover, if a student insists on enrolling in the college-preparatory program despite a poor prognosis, he or she should be allowed to do so. Every effort should be made to find a program suited to the student's talents, interests, and willingness to persevere. John Dewey (1916) spoke on the need for this forward-looking reflective process:

> To find out what one is fitted to do and to secure an opportunity to do it is the key to happiness. Nothing is more tragic than failure to discover one's true business in life, or to find that one has drifted or been forced by circumstances into an uncongenial calling (p. 308).

A choice made at the level of high school should, of course, be reversible. These days, middle-aged workers often change their professions, and teenagers should certainly be supported in doing so. We should rethink the idea that all high-school students must graduate in four years. The point is not simply to go straight forward to a better-paying job but, more important, to find work with which one can feel productive and reasonably content.

Charles Eliot feared that democracy would be the loser if we insisted on forcing all students into the same college-preparatory curriculum. He was right. By doing this, we ensure that either the courses will become weaker or many children will fail them. This is not because many children are incapable of good thinking or because teachers have low expectations for them. People are different, and we all do our best thinking in areas that interest us. Intellectual challenges can be introduced into any well-taught subject. Instead of working toward creating rich, relevant, and intellectually challenging courses in every program, we have endorsed the notion that a subject is automatically intellectually rich if it has regularly appeared in the traditional curriculum. When children do poorly with that curriculum, they may feel like failures, and when they fall into occupations by default, they may believe it is because they were not good enough for something better. That is the risk to democracy we invite by insisting that equal opportunity means the same curriculum for all.

John Gardner put it clearly in *Excellence* (1961). He, too, extolled the value of continued education, but he argued that this "does not mean sending everyone to college" (p. 97):

> *But scaling down of our emphasis on college education is only part of the answer. Another important part of the answer must be a greatly increased emphasis upon individual differences, upon many kinds of talent, upon the immensely varied ways in which individual potentialities may be realized (p. 99).*

Schooling consonant with genuine democracy not only recognizes differences. It respects and appreciates those differences. Walt Whitman saw all this clearly. In his beautiful "Song for Occupations," he expressed admiration and even awe at the enormous variety of work being done around him. In lines ringing with a celebration of "ordinary" people, he wrote, "the sum of all known value and respect I add up in you whoever you are," and then after praising old institutions, the Union, and the Constitution, he wrote:

> *I do not say they are not grand and good—for they are,*
> *I am this day just as much in love with them as you,*
> *But I am eternally in love with you and with all my fellows*
> *upon the earth*

(Whitman, 1982, p. 93).

Whitman reminds us here that democracy is not entirely defined by principles and processes. It is fundamentally, as Dewey (1916) said, a mode of associated living (p. 87).

As we think about shaping our schools to promote genuine democracy, we might consider vocational schools similar to those in Germany and the Scandinavian countries. They have been highly effective, but there are two possible drawbacks to this arrangement. One is the practice of assigning students to these programs instead of allowing guided choice, as I've suggested here. Another is that placing young people in separate buildings, often miles apart, undermines the possibility of making the school-place into a living democracy. Democracy is more than a set of practices, as Dewey and Whitman pointed out. The very best, small, comprehensive high schools in twentieth-century America provided real opportunities for students from different programs to act together in music, art, clubs, athletics, and student government. It is probably impractical to build and maintain such schools today. We can get ideas from many times and places, however, without trying to reproduce exactly what others have done. The road forward is rarely behind us. The question for us is how to create schools that will serve as incubators of democracy.

REFERENCES

Adler, M.J. (1982). *The paideia proposal.* New York: Macmillan.

Angus, D.L., & Mirel, J.E. (1999). *The failed promise of the American high school: 1890–1995.* New York: Teachers College Press.

Bellamy, E. (1960). *Looking backward.* New York: New American Library. (Original work published 1897)

Crawford, M.B. (2009). *Shop class as soulcraft.* New York: Penguin Press.

Dewey, J. (1916). *Democracy and education.* New York: Macmillan.

Dewey, J. (1927). *The public and its problems.* New York: Henry Holt.

Gardner, J.W. (1961). *Excellence.* New York: W. W. Norton.

Hersh, R., & John-Steiner, V. (2011). *Loving and hating mathematics.* Princeton: Princeton University Press.

Hoffman, N. (2010, August 3). Learning for jobs, not "college for all": How European countries think about preparing young people for productive citizenship. *Teachers College Record.* ID# 16096.

Horton, M. (with J. Kohl & H. Kohl), (1998). *The long haul.* New York: Teachers College Press.

Jacobs, H.R. (1970). *Mathematics: A human endeavor.* San Francisco: W. H. Freeman.

Kliebard, H. (1995). *The struggle for the American curriculum 1893–1958.* New York: Routledge

Kliebard, H. (1999). *Schooled to work: Vocationalism and the American curriculum 1876–1946.* New York: Teachers College Press.

National Society for the Promotion of Industrial Education. (1908). *Industrial education as an essential factor in our national prosperity.* (Bulletin No. 2). Charles W. Eliot.

Newman, J.R. (Ed.). (1956). *The world of mathematics* (Vol. 4). New York: Simon and Schuster.

Nieto, S. (1999). *The light in their eyes: Creating multicultural learning communities.* New York: Teachers College Press.

Noddings, N. (1992). *The challenge to care in schools.* New York: Teachers College Press.

Noddings, N. (2003). *Happiness and education.* Cambridge: Cambridge University Press. doi:10.1017/CBO9780511499920

Noddings, N. (2007). *When school reform goes wrong.* New York: Teachers College Press.

Oakes, J. (1995). *Keeping track: How schools structure inequality.* New Haven: Yale University Press.

Phelps, E.S. (1997). *Rewarding work.* Cambridge: Harvard University Press.

Rose, M. (1995). *Possible lives: The promise of public education in America.* Boston: Houghton Mifflin.

Rose, M. (2005). *The mind at work: Valuing the intelligence of the American worker.* New York: Penguin.

Skinner, B.F. (1962). *Walden two.* New York: Macmillan. (Original work published 1948)

Spring, J. (2000). *American education.* Boston: McGraw Hill.

Thompson, M. (1963). *The pragmatic philosophy of C.S. Peirce.* Chicago: The University of Chicago Press.

Whitehead, A.N. (1967). *The aims of education.* New York: Free Press. (Original work published 1929)

Whitman, W. (1982). A song for occupations. In J. Kaplan (Ed.), *Poetry and prose* (pp. 89–99). New York: Library of America.

14

Strangers in Our Midst

From Tolerance to Hospitality

*Trudy Conway**

*This chapter was first published as Conway, G. (2002). Strangers in our midst: From tolerance to hospitality. *Analytic Teaching, 23*(1), 51–57. Reproduced with permission.

The experience of the people of Le Chambon, France, during the Nazi occupation offers insight into an account of the hospitable response to strangers in our midst. The Chambonnais, at grave risk, opened their homes to Holocaust refugees, not only taking in but welcoming approximately 5,000 strangers, saved through their courageous efforts. Because of their compassionate response to the suffering of refugees, the Chambonnais were called to acts of hospitality. While most accounts of their efforts focus on their compassionate sheltering of these refugees, in this chapter I explore specific aspects of their hospitable response.[1] The Chambonnais' actions are worth our attention, for they exemplify what is required by hospitality, a virtue needed not only in dramatic circumstances in which strangers are at grave risk but in the everyday interactions of strangers within local communities. The Chambonnais provide a way of understanding how we might move from a tolerant to a hospitable encountering of the cultural Other.

The Compassionate Response of the Chambonnais to the At-Risk Stranger

The Le Chambon narrative offers a powerful account of the compassionate response to the suffering of the Other. According to the philosophical accounts of Aristotle, Rousseau, and Adam Smith on compassion, this basic social emotion is rooted in a triggering of a "fellow-feeling," tied to both our recognition of the suffering of others and our judgment that our own life is also vulnerably open to the possibility of misfortune and suffering. Through the compassionate response, we feel the pain of the Other, be it of our close family members, neighbours, distant strangers, or even enemies. Because of their own Huguenot history of persecution, the Chambonnais identified powerfully with the plight of the Jewish refugees arriving on their doorsteps. Because of this shared experience, they were able to enter imaginatively into the suffering of the refugees. Compassion entails one's perceiving of the Other's situation, one's being able to empathetically put oneself into the Other's situation and feel their pain. Compassion connects persons to each other, allowing for the intermeshing of their lives. As Martha Nussbaum (1996) states, "it is conceived of as our species' way of hooking the interests of others to our own personal goods" (p. 28). Herein, I perceive the refugees' distress, their uprootedness, and loss of shelter and support and affirm basic goods that would alleviate their condition. In doing so, I recognize the Other's good as my good. Aristotle argues that the powerful emotional response of compassion is rooted in three basic cognitive beliefs, namely, (a) that the suffering of the Other is serious, rather than trivial; (b) that such suffering was either not caused by the person's culpable actions or the suffering is out of proportion with the fault (such that the culpable person is not deserving of this degree of suffering); and (c) the belief that as a human subject I am similarly at risk of suffering. As Rousseau (1979) argues, this basic social emotion is rooted in the realization that ultimately "man is the same in all stations" (p. 225). The compassionate response of the Chambonnais to the plight of the refugee is rooted in their fundamental ability to recognize and respond to basic human needs, no matter how distant be the stranger at their doorstep. Compassion arises from the realization of a shared humanity, the recognition that we are all vulnerable beings dependent for our well-being on circumstances not fully under our control. Because of the compassionate response of the Chambonnais, they were called to acts of hospitality, to the welcoming of strangers into their homes, captured in Magda Trocmé's "abrupt, ungrudging, raucous command issued through a wide-open door: «'Naturally, come in, and come in'»" (Hallie, 1994, p. 154).

The Hospitable Response of the Chambonnais to the At-Risk Stranger

The compassionate response of the Chambonais is itself commendable and explains the powerful effect of their story on listeners. But what interests me here are some of the details of their hospitable response. According to specifics developed in Philip Hallie's book *Lest Innocent Blood Be Shed* (1994), Pierre Sauvage's documentary *Weapons of the Spirit*[2] (which chronicles his own experience as one of the harboured refugees), and discussions with Nelly Trocmé,[3] the hospitable response of the Chambonnais has the distinctive feature of affirming a human commonality, a basic identity expressed in difference. The Chambonnais recognized the refugees' suffering and welcomed them into their homes as fellow persons, sharing with them the meager goods they could manage in such trying times. But at the same time, the Chambonnais were a people with a distinct, deeply rooted identity as French Huguenots, members of a close-knit local religious community with deep faith commitments lived in distinctive practices. And yet these French Huguenots welcomed non-Christian foreigners into their homes at grave personal risk. What comes across powerfully in the Le Chambon narratives is their welcoming of these others in a way that did not require them to abandon their own identity, beliefs, and practices. Their interaction with the refugees was powerfully characterized by a mutual respecting of the Other. Although their compassionate response was rooted in strong regard for the shared humanity of the Other, their hospitable response clearly was affected by a recognition of irreducible difference. Because of this recognition, they were able to offer hospitality to those who were different from themselves, respectfully acknowledging their variant convictions, beliefs, and practices. Rather than simply tolerating their guests' differences, they respectfully affirmed them, welcoming these others into their community, encouraging them to live as practicing Jews. They sought opportunities for interactions and advances in mutual understanding of their respective traditions, the meaning-contexts of their belief and activity. In being hospitable, they welcomed the refugees into their own homes whose daily ways were shaped by a specific tradition of belief and practice. They expected the refugees to recognize the distinctive ways of their homes, while at the same time seeking to make these refugees feel "at home," such that they could live their beliefs and practices in these strangers' homes. Andre Trocmé, the pastor of Le Chambon, was adamant that his parishioners not attempt to convert the refugees to their own strongly felt and lived convictions. The refugees had to be welcomed and respected as Others with robust identities. Interviews with refugees decades after their stay in Le Chambon reveal the power of this hospitable response. They describe welcoming invitations to Jews to attend Christian religious services and supportive efforts to ensure that these Jews could maintain their own religious rituals and daily practices. The Chambonnais sought to open a space within their community for the life of these committed Jews. The power of the Le Chambon story rests in these villagers' ability to recognize and affirm a common humanity expressed in difference.

Perhaps we can learn much from the hospitality of these people; perhaps their narrative offers us a model for interactions in our multicultural local and international communities. In recognizing and respecting other persons, we must recognize and respect them both as human persons, who share a common humanity with us, *and* as persons with robust, particular identities, as German Jews, French Huguenots, Iranian Muslims, etc. Elaine Scarry (1996) writes of the need for "generous imaginings" that enable us to interact with strangers, foreigners who are different from us. In encountering the Other, I recognize him or her to be a person who shares with me basic human needs, desires, and goals. I generously recognize our commonality, our need for circumstances of prosperity, external goods that promote our flourishing. I also recognize that these human needs, desires, and goals are addressed and pursued through contexts of different ways of being human. I recognize that I and the Other are born into communities defined by distinctive beliefs, commitments, practices, and institutions that are passed down in the form of traditions.

From Tolerance to Hospitality

The hospitable response of the Chambonnais may provide insight into what is required in the everyday interactions of strangers within local communities. Contemporary philosophy and life are to a great extent distinguished by a recognition of diverse pluralistic traditions and beliefs. Postmodern thought has schematized the problem of the Other, preoccupying itself with a critique of all attempts to exclude, reduce, conceal, or assimilate the alterity of the Other, to diminish *difference* and plurality. As entailing the recognition that not all beliefs, claims, and values can be harmoniously reconciled, pluralism gives rise to a consideration of tolerance. Lack of unanimity creates conditions in which tolerance becomes possible; we find ourselves at odds with the Other and yet refraining from interference in or suppression of such alterity. But too often the postmodern celebration of pluralism, characterized by a spirit of open-mindedness extolling the virtue of tolerance, appears to be grounded in the acceptance of the groundlessness of all beliefs and claims. One is called to respect the diversity of traditions but only through recognizing their equally contingent status and lack of rational justification. Herein, the Other's stand is recognized, but only as equally arbitrary as one's own. One can neither justify his or her own stand nor provide reasons for convincing the Other to embrace this stand. With such an account, there seems to be no motive for taking the Other seriously or even oneself for that matter. It seems the basis for such tolerance is diminished esteem for what Richard Rorty (1989) calls one's own "final vocabulary" (p. 189). Rather than increasing respect for other perspectives, one's own and the Other's are diminished in esteem. All becomes levelled.

Such tolerance occasions an indifference toward the Other. This spirit of tolerance delivers a single universal appeal, namely, that we accept pluralism, simply acknowledging its inevitable existence. Such a minimalistic account requires that we "live and let live," removing all impediments to and interference in the Other's way of life. We put up with the Other so long as they do not disrupt our own way of life. Each community of discourse is left alone to pursue its own differing and competing way. It offers no reason for attending to the Other, for taking the Other seriously, for welcoming the Other into our community. Such tolerance is at best a negative, passive virtue that leads to a detached indifference to the Other, providing no motivation for seeking exchange, dialogue, or the open conversation enabled by the response of hospitality. Transformed into mutual indifference, such tolerance leaves us merely affirming pluralism without attempting any active engagement of differences.

It seems that the people of Le Chambon provide a way of conceiving the movement beyond tolerance to hospitality. They model a way of encountering the Other that bears similarities to Gadamer's (1989) understanding of an engaged response to pluralism, a response rooted in respect for persons and their seeking of truth. Gadamer's inquiry originates in an awareness of the embeddedness of the human subject in a tradition among other traditions. All human understanding takes off from inherited ways of making sense of this human world. These inherited prejudgments, which form the scaffolding of one's thought, shape one's understanding of oneself and the world. Without them there would be no understanding. Each inquirer stands committed to a view of the world that shapes what can be taken seriously and affirmed. Such confidence and partiality toward a tradition should not be mistaken for an arrogance that unreasonably presumes the superiority of one's tradition over all others. Rather, one stands confidently committed to the truth of the tradition into which one has been initiated.

Once one recognizes the centrality of beliefs, claims, and practices to the shared life of one's own community and tradition, one must reasonably extend such recognition to other communities and traditions. One may find oneself far from agreeing with or appreciating, and even outright disapproving of, alien beliefs and practices. And yet from such a distance, one must still acknowledge their centrality within the alien tradition. Tolerance is herein rooted in due respect for persons and traditions in their very diversity. But rather than resting with the mere respectful acknowledgement of such diversity, Gadamer draws one toward engagement rather than disengagement, toward dialogue rather than indifference. Herein, one seeks to understand the Other, to reasonably explore differences, to engage in a dialogue defined by a distinctive spirit of hospitality. Such dialogue is taken seriously and promoted on the basis of respect for persons and the assumption that such dialogue may disclose something of worth.

Such hospitable dialogue places demands on persons. Attending to the Other requires that we open ourselves to the Other's claims in their very alterity. Such dialogue demands more that minimal recognition of the Other and becomes possible only if we practice a cluster of hermeneutic virtues: an open-mindedness that requires that we be receptive to the disclosure of the Other, seeking to understand and do justice to what is disclosed; an imaginative empathy that allows us to conceive of the Other in his or her alterity; and a courage that allows us to risk our own prejudgments and critique our passively transmitted cultural commitments. Such response demands that rival claims be taken seriously and presented in the strongest light.

Rather than being preoccupied with discrediting the Other or winning debate, we seek to understand the Other's standpoint, so "his ideas become intelligible without our necessarily having to agree with them" (Gadamer, 1989, p. 303).

Gadamer affirms the worth of such dialogue. Only through encountering the Other does one come to true self-understanding. Being initiated into an inherited tradition, one (to use the phrase of Wittgenstein) "swallows whole" a cluster of assumptions that defines one's understanding of the world. Encountering the Other brings one to articulate and examine the tradition to which one belongs, thus occasioning a more reflective participation in that tradition. Herewith, we subject our claims to critical review, putting to test our basic prejudgments. Encountering the Other brings our tradition to articulation and prevents us from lapsing into thoughtless conformity. Dialogue with the Other discloses our entrenched prejudgments, putting them at risk before the Other, forcing us to justify our truth-claims, thereby allowing critiques of passively transmitted cultural claims.

Besides disclosing our own point of view, dialogue allows for the disclosure of that the Other as Other. Through dialogue we articulate an awareness of our own horizon, enlarged so as to include the disclosure of the Other's claims in their own respective horizon. Gadamer (1989) maintains that in this context of dialogue, a "fusion of horizons" may occur (p. 306). It seems that hospitality is the precondition of the possibility of such a fusion of horizons. Hospitality opens the possibility of our mutual attending to each other's claims, explicating of our positions, discovering of insight and oversights, agreements and disagreements, and disclosing of what was previously unseen. Hospitality opens the space of dialogue.

This interpenetration or "fusion" of horizons is only possible if both participants can enter a horizon that encompasses both self and Other. This entering is made possible by the hospitable welcoming of the Other into dialogue. Dialogue requires mutual recognition of both commonality and difference. Without such commonality in a shared form of life, there is no possibility of dialogue. Without significant difference, there is no compelling need for dialogue. For dialogue to commence, the Other must be recognized in both sameness and difference. For the dialogue to continue, the participants must neither rest content with the mere voicing of difference nor cancel differences to promote unanimity. Dialogue entails working toward mutual understanding of our very differences. The "fusion of horizons" is only possible if horizons, although limited, are not closed and are capable of being enlarged.

Entering dialogue in such a spirit of hospitality, we stand both committed to our own point of view and open to the equally committed claims of the Other. Such a posture requires an understanding of our human finitude, a recognition of our fallibilism, the insight that we may be wrong and the Other right. Hospitable dialogue is distinguished by a certain intellectual humility whereby one assumes one is not mistaken yet remains humbly open to such possibility. We take seriously the Other's truth-claims as they bear on and question ours. Herein, the Other's views are courteously acknowledged and judiciously heard. Such respect for the Other does not require that we accept their claims but that we be open to the possible disclosure of truth. We stand committed to the constellation of beliefs and claims that define our "final vocabulary" and at the same time remain open to their revision. We recognize that, as truth-claims, our judgments are worth defending and, at the same time, corrigible. We open ourselves to dialogue with the Other, avoiding both an overconfident dogmatism that refuses to subject itself to revision and a skepticism that concedes that all is groundless. Through critical dialogue we seek to reveal what is of worth. Such fallibilism presupposes there is a truth to be known.

Such dialogue requires a hospitable public space that values the articulation and engagement of our differences. Such hospitality toward the Other is rooted in and restricted by the overarching requirement that we respect persons and their beliefs and truth-claims, even when they differ from our own. It brings us to respectfully consider the significance and worth of other points of view and ways of life. The intending of dialogue in circumstances that risk misinterpretation and misunderstanding renders it a hopeful but realistic venture. We commence dialogue with the Other, acknowledging that it may not lead to unanimity, as Aristotle (1947) says, "to our living together and enjoying the same things" (N.E. 5.5 1157b. 22–23). We realistically recognize that dialogue may end with our facing a nonreducible plurality of claims. But by engaging in dialogue, we promote conversation and reasonable discourse, activities Aristotle described as fostering and sustaining friendship and civility. The contemporary recognition of strangers in our midst, of a plurality of rival traditions, places great responsibilities upon us. It seems our times call for more than the "live and let live" tolerant response to pluralism, in which we prize our autonomy and noninterference with the Other. Rather, such times call for an open hospitable dialogue engaging our differences, sensitive to both the strength and fragility of such dialogue. Such times demand that we recognize and work to eliminate situations and conditions that thwart and distort dialogue, cultivate the host of virtues bearing upon hospitality (humility, patience, courtesy, respect for persons, and truth), and work to envision and actualize ways of fostering dialogue that let that which appears so alien and foreign speak to us. Herein, we promote not tolerance as passive acquiescence to a regrettably inevitable pluralism, but hospitality, which judiciously promotes the mutuality of respect distinctive of rational persons and civil societies at their very best. Herein, foreigners entering our communities—through birth, immigration, or the seeking of refuge—are welcomed and encouraged to feel "at home," to be themselves and to participate in a civil society defined by hospitable discourse about our commonalities and differences. And thereby we may hopefully begin to understand and model the hospitality captured in the powerfully welcoming words of the Chambonnais to the strangers in their midst: "Naturally, come in, and come in."

REFERENCES

Aristotle. (1947). *Nicomachean ethics* (Modern Library Edition). (R. McKeon, Ed.). New York: Random House.

Conway, T.D. (2009). From tolerance to hospitality: Problematic limits of a negative virtue. *Philosophy in the Contemporary World, 16*(1), 1–13. doi:10.5840/pcw20091611

Gadamer, H.-G. (1989). *Truth and method* (2nd ed.). (J. Weinsheimer & D.G. Marshall, Trans.). New York: Crossroad.

Hallie, P. (1994). *Lest innocent blood be shed.* New York: Harper.

Nussbaum, M. (1996). Compassion: The basic social emotion. *Social Philosophy & Policy, 13*(1), 27–58. doi:10.1017/S0265052500001515

Rorty, R. (1989). *Contingency, irony and solidarity.* New York: Cambridge University Press. doi:10.1017/CBO9780511804397

Rousseau, J.J. (1979). *Emile: Or on education* (A. Bloom, Trans.). New York: Basic Books.

Scarry, E. (1996). The difficulty of imagining other people. In M. Nussbaum (Ed.), *For love of country, debating the limits of patriotism* (pp. 98–110). Boston: Beacon Press.

NOTES

1 See Conway (2009) for a more extended discussion of tolerance.

2 *Weapons of the Spirit* (1989) is a documentary written, produced, and directed by Pierre Sauvage. For details, see the website of the Chambon Foundation, http://www.chambon.org.

3 Nelly Trocmé is the daughter of André and Magda Trocmé, whose dedication to arranging shelter in Le Chambon for Jewish refugees is recounted in Hallie (1994).

Part IV: Standards, Efficiency, and Measurement

The popular discourse in education in the past 20 years has been replete with references to the importance of standards, efficiency, and measurement in education. Catchphrases such as "we need higher and common standards," "no progress without efficiency," and "reaching success for all by regular testing" have been frequently invoked by ministries of education worldwide. At face value such terms are usually considered to be fully acceptable. However, more and more educationalists and people from the field, including philosophers of education, have raised some very serious issues that take us back to the crucial issue of the aims of education in a democracy. The chapters in this section invite us to consider such issues by asking: What do standards in education mean? Are standards simply given and factual or do they involve a set of values? Should we have one common set of standards or a variety of standards? Should the standards be determined on the grounds of efficiency and value for money? Should educational standards rely solely on economic needs? Would the application of a restricted notion of economic needs to education lead to excessive consumerism in schools? And how should we determine whether or not standards are being achieved? Does standardized testing help or does it discourage educational and democratic aims?

In the first chapter, John Portelli and Ann Vibert analyze the concept of standards, unpack the several implications of making reference to standards, and argue that a critical democratic stance is incompatible with the colonialist mentality built into the call for common standards. Such a call rests on the hidden assumption that one size fits all is both ethically and educationally sound. If we base our curricula, pedagogy, and evaluation on a common standard, whose values and ways of life will be privileged and whose will be marginalized? Does the one-size-fits-all mentality in fact militate against the realization of equity and social justice in education? Is such a perspective based on a deficit mentality and an inherent, albeit not always explicit, set of neoliberal values (competition, individualism, narrow accountability, rigid empiricism, and marketization)? Portelli and Vibert contend that the notion of common standards is neither practical nor just. As an alternative, based on empirical work they have conducted, they strongly suggest the idea and practice of a curriculum of life, which while based on a pedagogy of hope and possibility is not seen as a panacea for all of our current educational ills.

In the second chapter, Francine Menashy focuses on the call for efficiency in education that is not just a recent issue. *Efficiency*, the ability to reach desired results with minimal problems (including financial ones), is not necessarily problematic. But are there different interpretations of efficiency? Are some of them inconsistent with educational values? Should efficiency be the primary aim of education? What are the implications of the ideology of efficiency on democracy? And what are the possible ethical implications of accepting efficiency without any critical awareness? Menashy claims that efficiency is not intrinsically bad. However, she argues that efficiency is a relational term and its meaning and force vary with the aims it is associated with as well as with the context in which it is applied. According to her, the efficiency movement is tied too closely with economic aspects to the detriment of educational, ethical, and democratic values. Efficiency is always a means to achieving something else; when it is construed as a naturally given end in itself, it turns into a cult.

As a result of neoliberal economics, we are now being faced with universal calls for economic austerity that, in turn, has exacerbated the narrow view of efficiency as the only acceptable form of accountability. One impact of this thinking gives rise to the increase of consumerism and corporate involvement in schools—an issue that is taken up in the third chapter by Trevor Norris. Is consumerism in schools necessary and is it educationally valuable? Even if corporate involvement benefits schools materially, is it in the best interest of students' education? Does it blindly reproduce capitalist values both explicitly and through the hidden curriculum? How can schools deal with the reality of consumerism without breaking ethical and educational demands? Without denying that consumption is necessary, Norris uses the works of Hanna Arendt and Paulo Freire to analyze educational concerns that arise from a consumer society that has seriously and negatively impacted educational aims in schools. While he outlines the impact of the ideology of consumerism on pedagogy and learning, he also encourages us to think about how education itself may have been complicit in unwittingly reproducing consumerist values. He urges educators to move from a pedagogy of possession to one of action and humanization.

But does the overemphasis on standardized and high-stakes testing itself hinder us from dealing in a critical way with the values associated with excessive consumerism? Does the almost exclusive focus on these types of measurement produce a citizenry that believes that these tests are the only worthwhile ones? And do these tests actually undermine the value of equity and critical consciousness, and thus negatively control and limit the critical agency of teachers and students? Do high stakes and standardized testing invariably contradict educational ends in a democracy? These are the questions that the next two chapters by Harvey Siegel and Wayne Au deal with.

Siegel argues that critical thinking, based on the view that a critical thinker is "one who is appropriately moved by reasons," is a central aim of education in a democratic society. Drawing on his analysis of an example of a current testing program in Florida, Siegel shows how high-stakes testing diminishes the importance of the ideal of critical thinking as an educational aim and other related aims such as open-mindedness, creativity, imagination, and caring. Siegel is not arguing that we should not evaluate students or that any form of evaluation is necessarily arbitrary. But he clearly demonstrates the weakness of forms of evaluation and assessment that do not take crucial educational aims into account, other than the instrumental aim of economic prosperity. His concern with the latter is twofold: it disregards wider aims of education; it reduces students to objects rather than seeing them as agents who direct their own lives.

While Siegel focuses on the lack of consideration of educational aims underlying high-stakes testing, Au focuses on the context of high-stakes testing, including the domain of policy, as well as its impact on classroom practices and learning. Based on current research, Au identifies how these tests control what is taught, how it is taught, and what is considered to be worthwhile knowledge: focusing only on what may be on the test; enacting pedagogies based on the "banking concept of education," and reproducing the primacy of what is measurable, reductionist and fragmented. All of this reflects the reality of a centralized policy based on authoritarian forms of accountability and control of teachers' and students' lives. For Au, the hidden curriculum of these policies encourages the views that teachers are not competent, diversity hinders excellence, and context is irrelevant. Like some other authors represented in this collection, Au concludes that the current predominant ideology determining most practices associated with educational institutions is not consistent with the values and way of life associated with democracy.

For very good reasons philosophers have always been uneasy with catchphrases. As Angela Y. Davis (2012), a well-known African American scholar and activist put it: "… categories always fall short of the social realities they attempt to represent, and social realities always exceed the categories that attempt to contain them" (p. 197). Unfortunately, in popular education discourse there is still the mentality that categories are given, fully objective and neutral, and fixed. As human beings we cannot communicate without reference to categories, but it is crucial to keep in mind the very limits of categories themselves. Given our human predicament we have the responsibility, especially as educators, to critically examine regulatory categories such as standards, efficiency, and evaluation, as well as think carefully about their implications. A democracy based on unthinking catchphrases is a bankrupt democracy.

REFERENCE

Davis, A.Y. (2012). *The meaning of freedom and other difficult dialogues.* San Francisco: Open Media Series/City Light Books.

15

Standardization and Equity in Education

John P. Portelli and
Ann B. Vibert*

*This is a revised and updated version of Portelli, J.P., & Vibert, A.B. (2001). Beyond common educational standards. In J.P. Portelli & R.P. Solomon (Eds.), *The erosion of democracy in education: From critique to possibilities.* Calgary: Detselig.

Educational issues, practices, and beliefs have always been of public interest. Public debates in the media have focused on such issues as bullying, LGTQ clubs, mainstreaming, whole language vs. phonics, media literacy, black-focused schools, separate schools, multiculturalism and antiracism in schools, quality, sustainability and accountability, standardized testing, and concern about educational standards. The call for common national standards, the arguments to evaluate more thoroughly students' achievements, as well as the complaints about the lowering of standards in schools, all demonstrate the need to seriously examine the issue of standards, an issue that has become so predominant in educational debate.

In this chapter we first clarify the notion of standards. We claim that common yet serious misinterpretations arise from confusions about the meaning of the concept of standards in popular discourse. Second, we offer a critical examination of the assumptions underlying popular discourse about standards, and finally, we offer alternative perspectives on educational standards and justification for these perspectives. These alternative perspectives rest on the conception of the *curriculum of life*—a curriculum that is grounded in the immediate daily world of students, as well as in the larger social political contexts of their lives. We argue that it would be more worthwhile to direct the efforts spent on establishing and monitoring common standards toward the support needed to enact a curriculum of life. Such a redirection would provide better opportunities for creating equity and social justice in schools.

We want to make it very clear at the outset that although our focus is on the issue of standards, we do not see this issue as discrete from other current and important educational, social, and, ultimately, political debates, including, for example equity, social justice, and issues of difference. In other words, we believe that the issue of standards, like any other educational issue, is not merely an educational issue but that it is also ethical and political in nature. Ultimately, there are no purely educational concerns.[1]

One of the major popular concerns is the claim that we don't have high standards in public education (Nikiforuk, 1993; Ontario Ministry of Education, 2000; Bush & Klein, 2011; Zwaagstra, 2012). There seems to be a widespread public concern that educational standards in Canada are slipping in comparison to the "good old days" when education, it is claimed, was more rigorous. Another equally pervasive concern is the fear that we do not have a common set of standards throughout the country, which is an echo of the larger plea for common, global, universal standards (Eisner, 1995; Hirsch, 2010; Mitchell, 2010). The argument seems to be that if we had common universal standards, then our quality of education would not be deteriorating, and students historically marginalized as "at-risk" would have a better chance at completing schooling. And hence the sense of urgency for schools to develop mission statements with which everyone can agree or pretend to agree. This argument is also presented as a plea for practicality: if we do not have a common set of standards, then we cannot proceed or operate well in practice; it is not practical to operate with different criteria. Moreover, we claim that having diverse criteria does not make the standard less clear.

What Are Standards?

Before we move to some critical analysis of these concerns about educational standards, it is crucial to make some clarifying remarks about the nature of standards. The term "standards" has different meanings and is used in different contexts. For example, we refer to "the standard point or complaint made," namely the typical or popular point made. But then we also say "these are the standards that we use," namely the criteria that we use to evaluate something, or in a sense, the policies that direct our actions. And we also have the Canadian Standards Association (CSA) that develops and monitors standards for commodities and production of materials. The CSA makes sure that the standards are met and that they are at least of acceptable quality. And we also use "standard" in another context when we refer to a standard as a flag or emblem, as in "standard-bearer" in the case of the military. The term is also used as a verb when, for example, we try to "standardize equipment" or even "standardize replies." In these instances, what we mean is to try to conform to an established or uniform position or specifications. Surely, in the educational context we do not mean to use all these different meanings at the same time. But the confusion about the issue of standards arises partly because of the lack of clarity.

In an educational context, as Eisner (1993) warns us, we need to distinguish between "standard as a measurement" and "standard as a value" (p. 344). An example of the first meaning would be the metre: the fact that we have conveniently agreed that a metre is 100 centimetres and that we use it as a tool to measure. In this context not many controversies arise. But there is another meaning to the word "standard," as when we say we have high educational standards. The second meaning involves values and criteria, not just an agreed-upon measurement, as in the metric example. Moreover, these criteria are value-laden and will therefore probably involve differences simply because people consider different things to be worthwhile.

It is crucial not to confuse these two very different meanings of standards, but, unfortunately, the notion of a *standard as a measurement* and a *standard as a value* are confused in the public discourse about standardized testing in Canada. The assumption is that standardized tests (the measurement) will improve educational standards (the value). Literacy and reading, for example, are treated as if they were objective facts measurable by a yardstick and not as contested, value-laden ground. We thus move to a discussion about the popular concerns raised about educational standards to raise the values issues that need to be clarified and discussed.

Falling Standards

The first concern is that of a lack of high standards. There is no doubt that this is a very loaded and serious charge, for no one really wants to promote mediocrity. But are educational standards really low? Of course, the reply will depend on the criteria and underlying values that one is using to assess the quality of education. If two people are using different and possibly conflicting criteria, then it should be no surprise that the evaluations and outcomes will be very different. The claim that standards are low is debatable. A quick glance at a high-school curriculum, for example, certainly contradicts the view that the standards have decreased from "the good old days" of educational rigour: the academic high-school curriculum of today is decidedly advanced over our curricula 35 years ago, both in terms of the quantity and quality of curriculum content, particularly in mathematics and science. On this point, Sobol (1997) contends, "of course there was no Golden Age—just the memory of our golden youth. All times are the best of times and the worst of times, because the present is always the only time we have" (p. 631). And Barlow and Robertson (1994) have argued convincingly that the popular discrediting of public education in Canada is part of a larger hidden agenda. They demonstrate how recent media reports have carefully selected and distorted evaluative data to support a view of a failing public education—a tactic designed in part to garner support for cuts to education, they argue. For example, Barlow and Robertson clearly show, by using Statistics Canada figures, that contrary to popular mythology, the dropout rate is lower than that in 1956 and 1971, and that the Economic Council of Canada information on illiteracy is mischievously distorted and inflated. The same point is made by Shannon (1996) and Berliner and Biddle (1995) for the US context. More recent Organisation for Economic Co-operation and Development (OECD) reports consistently characterize Canadian public education as among the top five to 10 countries in the world in terms of several quality and equity-of-outcome factors (OECD, 2012).

We are not suggesting here that there are no compelling problems facing public education in Canada. Quite the opposite, in fact. We are suggesting that the issues facing education presently are far more complex than the standards movement would allow. It may be that the cacophony about standards serves as a convenient distraction from far larger social, educational, and political issues facing us. As Apple (1996) puts it with regard to the issue of establishing a national curriculum in the US, the national curriculum (and in our context the establishing of common standards) could be seen as "a mechanism for the political control of knowledge" (p. 35). Moreover, as Kohn (1999) has convincingly argued, the "Tougher Standards Movement" has not given rise to higher quality, since in practice, this has amounted to "a little bit of everything and a thoughtful treatment of nothing" (p. 59). Kohn also points out that the plea for rigour or tougher standards has in fact resulted in narrowness, for "such objectives as wanting students to learn how to write persuasively or solve problems effectively are dismissed as 'mushy'" (p. 48). The emphasis has been on "long lists of facts and skills that students must acquire" (Kohn, 1999, p. 49). From our perspective, this perpetuates the predominance of a dangerous and limited conception of knowledge—one that focuses exclusively on the given rather than the critical and controversial.

Lack of Common Universal Standards

As mentioned earlier, there seem to be three reasons for the view that holds that there should be common, universal standards: (a) common standards will secure high quality, (b) they will address equity and access issues for students historically marginalized as "at-risk," (c) they will make practice more efficient and less confusing. We have to be very cautious about these seductive arguments.

Although there is no necessary or intrinsic connection between common standards and high quality, some (Adler, 1982; Hirsch, 1987; Mitchell, 2010) have proceeded from assuming such a connection to arguing that common standards therefore address equity and access issues. In the American context, for instance, Hirsch (1987) has argued that lack of a shared, common cultural curriculum—a curriculum he defines in quite traditional, Eurocentric terms—has contributed to inequities of access to educational capital for many of America's marginalized students. But Hirsch's argument hinges on several questionable assumptions concerning both curricula in American schools and teaching/learning processes. Specifically, Hirsch assumes that the reason American students do not know "what every American needs to know" is because they haven't been taught it; in other words, he mistakenly assumes a one-to-one correspondence between the formal and actual curriculum (Portelli, 1993).[2] While we would certainly acknowledge that students marginalized as "at-risk" in America experience a second-rate curriculum (see, for example, Anyon, 1981; Apple, 1992; Haberman, 1991), the content of that curriculum is, by many accounts, precisely the sort of content for which Hirsch argues (Shannon, 1992; Connell, 1994; Haberman, 1991). The problem, as Hirsch sees it, of students failing to master what he believes every American needs to know would appear not to be so much rooted in their not having been taught it as in their not having learned it.

Oversimplification of the workings of standards in this manner has given rise to movements like "outcomes-based education," which assumes agreement on issues upon which there may be little real agreement. We may agree that public schools ought to support people's ability to read critically, write clearly, and to think for themselves; however, we may mean very different things by these phrases. Agreement on outcomes desired does not guarantee that the outcomes will be achieved. Unfortunately, popular education documents have fallen victim to these kinds of problems. The most obvious case is that of the language used in these documents, including slogans like "excellence," "cooperative learning," "critical thinking," "high quality," and "good and productive citizens." This kind of rhetoric gives the impression of universality or homogeneity and hides the possibility of differences (Shannon, 1995). The language of forced consensus gives the illusion that there are no differences or that there ought to be no differences, while in fact, there are disagreements and differences among educational "experts" on what amounts to quality education (see Popkewitz, 1991; Smyth, Angus, Down, & McInerney, 2009).

The argument based on practicality is also deceptive, for even if we were to agree on a commonly held set of standards, in reality we still have to face the diversity and multiplicity that the application and interpretation of standards require. Standards are by nature subject to interpretation. For example, as teachers, even when we espouse identical standards for writing, rarely do we evaluate the same writing identically. In practice, standards are always negotiated. Therefore, in this sense, claims to common standards are artificial and enforced. Standards, given their interpretive nature, are not naturally given unquestionable facts (Shannon, 1995; Shannon, 2007).

The call for common, universal standards is problematic on other counts too. Whose standards are we going to follow? And who decides what is going to amount to common standards? If we were to arrive at a set of common standards, that would mean that some people's standards may be left out and, if so, for what reasons? Whose standards count the most and why? Who benefits from common standards?

These are vital questions that the movement for common standards does not address. However, these are the crucial questions that challenge the inequities of the status quo; as many current cultural thinkers have argued, those standards identified as "universal" inevitably re-inscribe the values and worldview of a dominant minority (Said, 1993; Smith, 1999).

A similar critique to the one we are raising is made by Apple (1996) in relation to the call to revert to a "common culture." According to Apple, "such an approach hardly scratches the surface of the political and educational issues involved. A common culture can never be the general extension to everyone of what a minority mean and believe. Rather, and crucially, it requires ... the creation of the conditions necessary for all people to participate in the creation and re-creation of meanings and values" (p. 39). Moreover, forceful emphasis on common standards contradicts popular notions of democracy that, by definition, rule out emphasis on conformity. This is ironic as only 22 years ago the popular Western criticism of the Soviet bloc and China was that these people did not allow diversity. We used to complain about their emphasis on uniformity (same clothes, same jackets, same ties, same hairstyle), which was associated with communism and totalitarianism. The West was seen as the bastion of democracy precisely because of its encouragement of diversity.[3] So, now we need to ask, how can we explain the contemporary emphasis on uniformity (as exemplified in the harsh call for common, universal standards) and still claim that we embrace democracy?

In response to our rhetorical question, one may retort that insisting on common standards will ensure that all teachers will have high expectations for all students irrespective of their cultural and/or socio-economic background. In other words, one may argue that common standards will ensure that no students will be viewed from a "deficit mentality" (Valencia, 1997). And we may be reminded that promoting high expectations for all and diminishing a negative deficit mentality are consistent with the democratic principle of equity. While we definitely agree that having high expectations for all and eliminating deficit mentality are worthwhile educational and democratic aims, the counter-argument to our stance fails to demonstrate the unique and necessary connection between common standards and maintaining high expectations for all. Will it be really profitable if we focus on high expectations while the standards that guide our practices are not suitable, inclusive, or democratically derived? What matters is not that we have common standards but that we have appropriate and fair standards. Moreover, it has been argued that higher and common standards are "used as selection devices to privilege some over others" (Kohn, 1999, p. 102). In other words, what is promoted officially as a way of securing quality for all, in fact, by implication, amounts to a hidden way of sorting out people. Linda McNeil's (2000) empirical study has established that "standardization creates inequities, widening the gap between the quality of education for poor and minority youth and that of more privileged students" (p. 3). In the same vein, Hursh (2007) notes that while the rhetoric of reforms pledges that those that have been traditionally neglected will now be taken care of as we focus on high standards, accountability, objective testing, and equality of opportunity, at the same time the "system of testing and accountability permits the state to determine the goals and output without directly intervening in the process itself, thereby reducing resistance" (p. 29). And finally, Smyth et al. (2009), commenting on the situation in Australia and the United Kingdom, remind us that standardized curricula and high-stake testing reforms "have failed to deliver on the promise of lifting achievement levels, participation rates, and student engagement for a large portion of young people" (p. 21).

Contrary to the evidence of major work on issues of race, class, gender, and sexuality by sociologists of education in the 20th century (Rist, 1970; Bourdieu, 1973, 1974; Willis, 1977; Persell, 1979; Anyon, 1981, 1997; Weis, 1990; Simon, 1992; Solomon, 1992; Dei, Mazzuca, McIsaac, & Zine, 1997), the erroneous view that having common, essential standards will translate into being able to apply them commonly assumes a meritocracy or the belief that people advance on the basis of their inherent abilities. It assumes that if we have common standards, then we can apply them fairly and in the same way to all contexts. There are at least two problems with this. First, there is a difference between having a meritocracy and assuming a meritocracy. The fact that we assume it is not the same as having it. Second, even if we had a meritocracy, evaluating fairly may imply holding different standards (Martin, 1985). As Plato argued a long time ago, fairness is not always identical to sameness. To be fair, sometimes we need to account for and acknowledge differences that do not necessarily lead to a common standard or a common solution. In other words, there is a difference between equity and equality (Martin, 1985, especially Ch. 2). As Shannon (1995) argues, "[s]et in this context, equality does not seem to be the ideal toward which we should strive; in fact, it leaves previous inequalities intact while at the same time frustrating any attempts to alter those inequalities by characterizing them as attacks on the ideal of equality. Requirements that we ignore the past and treat unequals equally mean that we can never approach true equality—that is, fairness among human beings" (p. 230). Ultimately, the plea for common standards, albeit unwittingly and unwillingly, rests on the basic colonial belief of one size fits all. Privileging one set of standards over another set of standards, by definition (i.e., beyond empirical data), marginalizes certain standards irrespective of the educational and moral reasons in support of them. Moreover, adopting a set of standards that are deemed to be universal (irrespective of contrary evidence) necessarily reproduces inequities.

Where Do We Stand?

In a nutshell, we are arguing that the public discourse around defining and maintaining common standards is ill-conceived, misleading, and fundamentally dishonest (Ohanian, 1999). Let us be very clear. We are not saying that we do not care about the quality of education. Criticizing common standards does not imply a lack of concern about quality or about standards themselves. As Eisner (1995) puts it: "To give up the idea that there needs to be one standard for all students in each field of study is not to give up the aspiration to seek high levels of educational quality in both pedagogical practices and educational outcomes" (p. 760). We are concerned about quality and what it involves, such as taking difference seriously. We urge teachers, parents, and guardians to ask the questions concerning quality that are left out by the common standards movement: Whose standards? How are these standards to be arrived at? Who is included and who is excluded from defining these standards? (Kelly, 1993; Christensen, 1995; Apple, 1996; Swartz, 1996). Why is there a real resistance to looking at these kinds of questions? Who benefits from not raising and discussing these questions?

The popular view pushed by the neoconservative world rests on the fallacy that unless standards are clear and commonly held then we have no standards. The assumption is that unless we have commonly agreed-upon standards set up and advertised, there will be no real change; mediocrity will flourish. We are arguing that it is not the agreement on standards but the discussion of them that will help bring about change. As Shannon (1995) recommends:

> we should begin with the clarification of our starting points for thinking about literacy and assessment that the standards processes seem to paper over. Just what do various groups have in mind when they use terms such as interests of the students, fair, and equitable? We must display these differences in public. It is not our dirty laundry; rather, it is our reasoned way to air the issues. (p. 232)

Media and corporate discourse about standards seems to be based on a belief that standards are very easy to define, that we have common agreement on them, and that all we need to do to improve public education is to measure students against these standards, as though measurement itself somehow improves learning (Barlow & Robertson, 1994; Shannon, 1995, 1996). As Margaret Meek Spencer (1993) reminds us, a pig will not gain weight the more often we weigh it. We need to feed the pig as well as consider the quality of the food! Our conclusion is that we need to stop the rhetoric and the unnecessary diagnosing and measuring. There is massive evidence that shows that those who are well off have a bigger chance of surviving the system (Willis, 1977; Apple, 1979, 1996; Anyon, 1981, 1997; Shannon, 1992; Curtis, Livingstone, & Smaller, 1992; McLaren, 1998; Smyth et al., 2008, 2009; OECD, 2012). Funds need to be spent on supporting teachers' work and improving the quality and climate in schools rather than on unnecessary and expensive standardized testing.

Contrary to popular belief, we are arguing that educational standards are not absolute, fixed, and naturally given facts. They are socially constructed. Even Richard Weaver (1970), a conservative rhetorician, objected to the way we continuously treat rhetorical socially contested issues as though they were physical facts about which there can be no disagreement. In other words, we are not dealing with so-called scientific laws that are expected to apply universally by definition. We cannot expect that kind of exactitude when we are dealing with the human predicament. And, hence, we need to ask who constructed these standards, for what reasons, and whose values are included and excluded from them. The public discussion on standards will continue to reproduce inequities and injustices unless these questions are dealt with seriously and differences are recognized.

This last point may give the impression that we are urging an "anything goes" mentality. We are not. We do, however, maintain that insistence on commonality and uniformity will discredit important differences, which is ultimately contrary to one of the basic values or principles of the democratic spirit, namely the acknowledgement of differences. In a democracy, for example, people should not be concerned that we have different accents, that we express ourselves differently. The urge for uniformity, on the other hand, can be seen as a fear of dealing with differences, of losing power, of change, of ambiguity and uncertainty. Yet, to be honest, we have to ask another question: Are all differences of equal worth? For example, is the view that people as human beings ought to be respected of equal worth to a view that promotes hatred toward certain people? We need to distinguish between (a) accepting that there are different values, and (b) holding that all these different values have equal worth. Democracy implies the acceptance that there are different values; it does not imply that all values are of equal worth. Acknowledging difference does not rule out the possibility of recognizing and valuing basic human rights.

Ultimately, our view rests on the belief that the either-or mentality is problematic (Dewey, 1938). We object to the view that maintains that either all values are absolute or anything goes; or that we either take an extreme conservative position or an extreme liberal position. There are other positions that go beyond this simplistic either-or way of thinking and account more fully for questions of educational equality in a pluralistic society.

More than 100 years ago, John Dewey (1900/1974), the American philosopher of education, wrote:

> We are apt to look at the school from an individualistic standpoint, as something between teacher and pupil, or between teacher and parent. That which interests us most is naturally the progress made by the individual child of our acquaintance, his [her] normal physical development, his [her] advance in ability to read, write, and figure, his [her] growth in the knowledge of geography and history, improvement in manners, habits of promptness, order, and industry—it is from such standards as these that we judge the work of the school. And rightly so. Yet the range of the outlook needs to be enlarged. What the best and wisest parent wants for his [her] child, that must the community want for all of its children. Any other ideal for our schools is narrow and unlovely; acted upon, it destroys our democracy.... . Only by being true to the full growth of all the individuals who make it up, can society by any chance be true to itself. (p. 6)

It would be very hard, if not impossible, for anyone to disagree that attempting to achieve the "full growth of all the individuals" who make up society is worthwhile and needed. The questions that arise include those about how we are going to achieve this and about which standards we should aim for. In response to the latter, Dewey offers an answer in the above quote: "what the best and wisest parent wants." We believe that this simple answer is rather dangerous. First, we are not in agreement about who is the best and wisest parent. Second, this assumes that there is only one best possible reply. In other words, this position does not allow for the possibility of having different, yet equally valuable, approaches and standards. Although we do agree on several things, it is a fact of life that human beings have different values that will be reflected in different standards.

What are some of our options when we are faced with different standards? We could try to create situations in which one set of standards will dominate or be imposed on all, irrespective of contexts and needs and values, an approach that has been described by Sternberg (as cited in Johnson, Johnson, Farenga, & Ness, 2008) as "the enemy of effective public schools" (p. 16). Or we could try to understand differences that exist and allow for different sets of standards to operate at the same time, admitting that there are differences but acknowledging that standards, although different, may be equally valuable. We argue that the latter is the option that is most conducive to sustaining, developing, and reconstructing democracy (for democracy, by nature, is never stable). Of course, acknowledging and respecting differences does not mean that everything is acceptable. The Keegstra case in Alberta clearly demonstrates this.[4] However, in a democracy, decisions about what is acceptable require serious and engaged discussions from the citizenry—and not just the few. Therefore, conditions need to be created that encourage discussion, rather than restrict it. The authoritarian approach implied by the universal standards movement, an authoritarianism that is no less dangerous because it is sometimes subtle, forecloses possibilities for broad public discourse on which standards schools should aim to achieve.

What Does All of This Have to Do with Teaching?

The debate about standards—the attempt to define and enforce appropriate academic standards in schools—is for teachers in classrooms simultaneously critically important and something of an irrelevant luxury. However the debate comes out, whichever outcomes we decide upon will have immediate and substantial consequences for curricula, determining issues like whether an educated person can continue to be defined solely by her or his knowledge of Western European traditions or whether we might justifiably expect an educated person to know something of the cultural traditions of, for instance, Aboriginal peoples. In that sense, the debate has everything to do with classroom teaching, however absent teachers' voices have been from that debate (at least at public levels). But, in another important sense, the exercise of defining common standards is very far removed from the "dailiness" of teaching actual people in actual classrooms. As one teacher put it, "They can define whatever outcomes they like; unless those outcomes are possible and sensible and purposeful for the real children in my real grade three classroom, the whole exercise will remain just an exercise."

We have argued that the rhetoric within the standards movement is misleading in several ways, including the assumption (based on little evidence) that "standards are slipping" in schools, the assumption that standards can be easily and justly defined and interpreted, and the slipshod logic that confuses measuring quality with improving quality. From the point of view of teaching, however, the standardization movement poses further problems in that it "constrain[s] teachers" (Hyslop-Margison & Sears, 2006, p. 16) and it serves as a distraction from conversations in teaching and schooling in which we, as a society, urgently need to engage ourselves—conversations about a curriculum of life.

Let us illustrate this with an example. In one of the schools we worked in, a grade 4 child, who was a beginning reader, was coded by his school as having a reading disorder. Talking to the child, his teacher discovered that for his entire school career the child had spent no more than six months in any one classroom because his father, a construction worker, had been moving all over the country in search of work. In the context of working with the child, the teacher learned that the child's "reading problem" had little to do with reading or academic ability at all and everything to do with a level of anxiety and disruption in his life that made learning to read difficult and, apparently, irrelevant. Like many educational problems, this child's learning problem was, in fact, a consequence of a much larger social problem (underemployment and the creation of surplus labour markets) manifested in schooling.

Hence, the act of teaching in increasingly diverse and increasingly underfunded classrooms graphically illustrates the manner in which education is embedded in complex social and political realities. From this vantage point, the debate about standards—the campaign to define a set of common standards that can only serve to further sanction the official knowledges of the already privileged—is entirely beside the point. Moreover, the debate, perhaps deliberately, distracts us from asking the kinds of pressing questions that teaching presently raises, questions like: Why is it that we appear unable to create just and viable schooling for all? Are teachers being prepared and supported to be able to respond to the many different and conflicting perspectives they encounter in their students? Do they have the time and the support they need to address and come to terms with the kinds of changes happening in their classrooms? The standards debate, by reducing these complexities to a simple matter of defining common standards and measuring student achievement against them, conveniently allows us to blame the individual (the student and/or the teacher) and ignore the larger social and political realities in which teachers, students, and schools are immersed. And as Maxine Greene (1995) warns us:

> *a return to a single standard of achievement and a one dimensional definition of the common will not only result in severe injustices to the children of the poor and the dislocated, the children at risk, but will also thin out our cultural life and make it increasingly difficult to bring into existence and keep alive an authentically common world. (pp. 172–173)*

Alternative Vision

What, then, are the alternatives we propose? Our critique of the pervasive current discourse about educational standards clearly implies an alternative vision for educational policy. Let us, then, be explicit about the alternatives for which we have argued above. As a conclusion, we will identify four alternatives.

First, we have claimed that the public discourse of slipping standards in education is misleading and misinformed. The alternative we are proposing here is an open and balanced public debate—a debate acknowledging educational standards as necessarily provisional, dynamic, located, interpretive, and informed by issues of politics and power. Such debate is, after all, far from new within the confines of academic and educational literature. That the central political debate is missing from our public discourse on standards in education is, at the very best, curious.

We are suggesting that several questions need to be asked, publicly, of the slipping standards claim—questions like: "Is this true?" "To what extent is this true?" "What standards are slipping and whose standards are they?" "What new standards are emerging?" "Why is this happening?" Without seriously engaging in such questions, the standards movement simply becomes "a mechanism of ideological control" (Down, 2012, p. 66).

Second, we have argued that broad-based standardized testing confuses and oversimplifies several issues of quality in education, thereby perpetuating the status quo. We have suggested that the public discourse around standardized testing and test scores fails to acknowledge thoroughly documented social inequities reproduced through such testing, and, further, that this discourse confuses "standard" as a value with "standard" as a measurement, resulting in the magical notion that we can improve quality by measuring it. We have also argued that such an approach to assessment fails to acknowledge central features of standards themselves—namely, that in practice, standards are irredeemably local and interpretive.

The alternative we are suggesting here is, of course, the development of local assessments—or, perhaps more accurately, the development of educational policy acknowledging the reality of local assessment (Eisner, 2000; Meier, 2002). We need to redeploy the enormous resources spent in developing national and regional assessments ("bigger and better mousetraps" as Jerome Harste [1992] has called them) in helping teachers to develop and engage thoughtful local assessment that acknowledges and accounts for the realities of social difference.

Third, the flurry of activity to define and measure common standards seems to us to have overlooked the obvious and essential step. If we are genuinely interested in improving the quality of education for all, surely we need to do more than define what we want and test whether we are getting it. We need to put resources into actually improving the decaying conditions in classrooms. Teachers are besieged: they lack classroom resources, they lack time for professional development, they lack social and educational support networks, they lack support for real initiative and innovation, and their class sizes are rising everywhere just as diversity multiplies and social supports for children and families erode. In short, they struggle just to do their jobs in the face of enormous cutbacks and escalating demands. We are arguing that the time, money, and resources spent on defining common standards and measuring our achievement of them would be much better spent on supporting teachers, classrooms, and schools—IF we were serious about changing schooling and improving education (Noddings, 2007).

Fourth, the general tendency of common standards and standardized testing movements is, for complex reasons, toward the production and reproduction of a mechanistic, technocratic vision of curriculum—a vision that ultimately is based on a conception of education that "may be appropriate for totalitarian societies but is incompatible with democratic ideals" (Eisner, 1995, p. 763). As Beyer and Pagano (1998) argue, such a vision of curriculum is only appropriate to industrial models of education that, they remind us, "have been thoroughly criticized over the last three decades, and teachers, curriculum designers and principals have increasingly eschewed such models" (p. 381). Defining common standards and testing against them simply leaves the flesh-and-blood reality of actual classrooms outside the issue. We are told that violence, for instance, is increasing in schools, and we don't deny this claim. Teachers and schools, however, where violence is an issue may be discouraged from making it central to the curriculum if official sanction is placed on, for instance, students' ability to commute fractions by the end of grade 6. The standards movement in its present form appears to mitigate against what we call *the curriculum of life.*

By "curriculum of life" we mean a central, organizing stance that informs pedagogy. Curriculum of life is not solely an aspect of curriculum, of the teachers' pedagogy, or of school and classroom management. In fact, the normally accepted meaning of the term "management" contradicts the spirit of a curriculum of life. Students and curriculum in this approach are not "managed" but "engaged"; that is, the aim is to actively involve them in the life of the school. Curriculum of life is an approach to pedagogy that informs and gives coherence to often disparate aspects of school life. It is implicit in curriculum, in school organization and policy, in discipline, in school/community relations, in classroom and school-wide pedagogy, in school culture. In other words, the curriculum of life is a conception of curriculum that breaks down the walls between the school and the world. Social studies, language arts, mathematics, science, and art become "disciplines" in the original sense of the word: that is, they are disciplined ways of thinking through important questions and concerns. The curriculum of life is rooted in the school and community world to which the students belong, addressing questions of who we are and how we live well together; it extends into the larger world of possibilities beyond school and community bounds; and it addresses directly questions about the larger social and political contexts in which these worlds are embedded.

The curriculum of life is grounded in the immediate daily worlds of students, as well as in the larger social and political contexts of their lives. As such, students' worlds and lives are not addressed as factors that need to be excused, pitied, mediated, or fixed to get on with the curriculum but as the vital ground of/for learning. This is an approach to curriculum that presupposes genuine respect for children's minds and experience—without romanticizing either. The connection between the curriculum of life and students is essentially an ethical one, for as Freire (1998) argued: "It's impossible to talk of respect for students, for the dignity that is in the process of coming to be, for the identities that arise in the process of construction, without taking into consideration the conditions in which they are living and the importance of the knowledge derived from life experience, which they bring with them to school" (p. 62).

Teachers are telling us that the curriculum of life—the actual, immediate, and urgent experiences, issues, and questions of children in schools—is becoming more and more the irresistible content of the classroom (Portelli, Shields, & Vibert, 2007). By failing to recognize this situation, the common standards movement cuts educators off from the very questions they most need to engage with each other, just at a time when they have no choice but to engage these questions in their daily life practice in classrooms. Maxine Greene (1984) has captured the gist of our thinking here:

> We need ... spaces for expression, spaces for freedom, yes, and a public space. By that I mean, as Hannah Arendt did, a space where living persons can come together in speech and action, each one free to articulate a distinctive perspective. ... It must be a space of dialogue, a space where a web of relationships can be woven, and where a common world can be brought into being and continually renewed. (pp. 295–296)

REFERENCES

Adler, M. (1982). *The Paideia Proposal.* New York: McMillan.

Anyon, J. (1981). Social class and school knowledge. *Curriculum Inquiry, 11*(1), 3–42. doi:10.2307/1179509

Anyon, J. (1997). *Ghetto schooling: A political economy of urban educational reform.* New York: Teachers College Press.

Apple, M.W. (1979). *Ideology and curriculum.* London, UK: Routledge & Kegan Paul. doi:10.4324/9780203241219

Apple, M.W. (1992). *Teachers in text.* Cambridge, MA: Harvard University Press.

Apple, M.W. (1996). *Cultural politics and education.* New York: Teachers College Press.

Barlow, M., & Robertson, H.J. (1994). *Class warfare: The assault on Canada's schools.* Toronto: Key Porter Books.

Berliner, D., & Biddle, B. (1995). *The manufactured crisis: Myths, fraud and the attack on America's public schools.* Reading, MA: Addison-Wesley.

Beyer, L.E., & Pagano, J.A. (1998). Democratic evaluation: Aesthetic, ethical stories in schools. In L.E. Beyer & M. Apple (Eds.), *The curriculum: Problems, politics and possibilities* (pp. 380–396). Albany, NY: SUNY Press.

Bourdieu, P. (1973). Cultural reproduction, and social reproduction. In R. Brown (Ed.), *Knowledge, education, and social change.* London, UK: Tavistock.

Bourdieu, P. (1974). The school as a conservation force: Scholastic and cultural inequalities. In J. Eggleston (Ed.), *Contemporary research in the sociology of education.* London, UK: Methuen.

Bush, J., & Klein, J. (2011, June 23). The case for common educational standards. *Wall Street Journal.* Retrieved from http://online.wsj.com/article/SB10001424052 702304070104576399532217616502.html

Christensen, L. (1995). Whose standard? Teaching standard English in our schools. In D. Levine, R. Lowe, B. Peterson, & R. Tenerio (Eds.), *Rethinking schools: An agenda for change* (pp. 128–135). New York: The New Press.

Connell, R.W. (1994). Poverty and education. *Harvard Educational Review, 64*(2), 125–149.

Curtis, B., Livingstone, D., & Smaller, H. (1992). *Stacking the deck: The streaming of working class kids in Ontario schools.* Toronto: Our Schools/Our Selves.

Dei, G.J., Mazzuca, I., McIsaac, E., & Zine, J. (1997). *Reconstructing "drop-outs": A critical ethnography of the dynamics of black students' disengagement from school.* Toronto: University of Toronto Press.

Dewey, J. (1938). *Experience and education.* New York: MacMillan.

Dewey, J. (1974). *The school and society.* Chicago: University of Chicago Press. (Original work published 1900)

Down, B. (2012). Reconceptualising teacher standards: Authentic, critical and creative. In B. Down & J. Smyth (Eds.), *Critical voices in teacher education: Teaching for social justice in conservative times* (pp. 63–80). New York: Springer. doi:10.1007/978-94-007-3974-1_5

Eisner, E.W. (1993). Why standards may not improve schools. *Educational Leadership, 50*(5), 22–23.

Eisner, E.W. (1995). Standards for American schools: Help or hindrance? *Phi Delta Kappan, 76*(10), 758–765.

Eisner, E.W. (2000). Those who ignore the past …: 12 "easy" lessons for the next millennium. *Journal of Curriculum Studies, 32*(2), 343–357. doi:10.1080/002202700182808

Freire, P. (1996). Reading the world and reading the word: An interview with Paulo Freire. In W. Hare & J.P. Portelli (Eds.), *Philosophy of education: Introductory readings* (pp. 185–192). Calgary, AB: Detselig Ent. Ltd. [See also page 403 of this volume.]

Freire, P. (1998). *Pedagogy of freedom. Ethics, democracy, and civic courage.* Lanham, MD: Rowman & Littlefield Publishers.

Giroux, H.A. (1994). Teachers, public life, and curriculum reform. *Peabody Journal of Education, 69*(3), 35–47. doi:10.1080/01619569409538776

Greene, M. (1984). "Excellence," meanings, and multiplicity. *Teachers College Record, 86*(2), 283–297.

Greene, M. (1995). *Releasing the imagination: Essays on education, the arts, and social change.* San Francisco: Jossey-Bass Publishers.

Haberman, M. (1991). The pedagogy of poverty versus good teaching. *Phi Delta Kappan, 73*(4), 290–294.

Hare, W. (1996). Propaganda in the classroom: The Keegstra case. In W. Hare & J.P. Portelli (Eds.), *Philosophy of education: Introductory readings* (pp. 149–164). Calgary: Detselig Ent. Ltd. [See also page 358 of this volume.]

Harste, J. (1992). *Evaluation and standards.* Keynote address presented at Nova Scotia Reading Association Annual Conference, Mount St. Vincent University, Halifax, NS.

Hirsch, E.D., Jr. (1987). *Cultural literacy: What every American needs to know.* Boston: Houghton Mifflin.

Hirsch, E.D., Jr. (2010). *The schools we need and why we don't have them.* New York: Random House.

Hursh, D.W. (2007). Marketing education: The rise of standardized testing, accountability, competition, and markets in public education. In E.W. Ross & R. Gibson (Eds.), *Neoliberalism and education reform* (pp. 15–34). Cresskill, NJ: Hampton Press, Inc.

Hyslop-Margison, E.J., & Sears, A.M. (2006). *Neo-liberalism, globalization and human capital learning: Reclaiming education for democratic citizenship.* Dordrecht, The Netherlands: Springer.

Johnson, D.D., Johnson, B., Farenga, S.J., & Ness, D. (2008). *Stop high-stakes testing: An appeal to America's conscience.* New York: Rowman & Littlefield Publishers Inc.

Kelly, U. (1993). Teaching "English": Who's subject to what? In D. Bogdan & S. Straw (Eds.), *Constructive reading: Teaching beyond communication* (pp. 205–213). Portsmouth, NH: Boynton Cook.

Kohn, A. (1999). *The schools our children deserve: Moving beyond traditional classrooms and "tougher standards."* Boston: Houghton Mifflin.

Martin, J.R. (1985). *Reclaiming a conversation: The ideal of the educated woman.* New Haven, CT: Yale University Press.

McLaren, P. (1998). *Life in schools: An introduction to critical pedagogy in the foundation of education* (3rd ed.). New York: Longman.

McNeil, L.M. (2000). *Contradictions of school reform: Educational costs of standardized testing.* New York: Routledge.

Meier, D. (2002). *In schools we trust: Creating communities of learning in an era of testing and standardization.* Boston: Beacon Press.

Mitchell, T. (2010, July 30). Common educational standards for common good. *San Francisco Chronicle.* Retrieved from http://www.sfgate.com/opinion/openforum/article/Common-educational-standards-for-common-good-3180461.php

Nikiforuk, A. (1993). *School's out: The catastrophe in public education and what we can do about it.* Toronto: MacFarlane Walter & Ross.

Noddings, N. (2007). *When school reform goes wrong.* New York: Teachers College Press.

Ohanian, S. (1999). *One size fits all: The folly of educational standards.* Portsmouth, NH: Heinemann.

Ontario Ministry of Education. (2000). *Learning for life.* Toronto: Ministry of Education.

Organisation for Economic Co-operation and Development (OECD). (2012). *Equity and quality in education: Supporting disadvantaged students and schools.* Paris: OECD Publishing.

Persell, C. (1979). *Education and inequality.* New York: Longman.

Popkewitz, T. (1991). *A political sociology of educational reform: Power/knowledge in teaching, teacher education, and research.* New York: Teachers College Press.

Portelli, J.P. (1993). Dare we expose the hidden curriculum? In J.P. Portelli & S. Bailin (Eds.), *Reason and values* (pp. 171–197). Calgary: Detselig Ent. Ltd.

Portelli, J.P. (1996). The challenge of teaching for critical thinking. In W. Hare & J.P. Portelli (Eds.), *Philosophy of education: Introductory readings* (pp. 55–72). Calgary: Detselig Ent. Ltd.

Portelli, J.P., Shields, C.M., & Vibert, A.B. (2007). *Toward an equitable education: Poverty, diversity, and students at risk.* Toronto: OISE.

Portelli, J.P., & Solomon, R.P. (Eds.) (2001). *The erosion of democracy in education: From critique to possibilities.* Calgary: Detselig.

Rist, R.C. (1970). Student social class and teacher expectations: The self-fulfilling prophecy in ghetto education. *Harvard Educational Review, 40*(3), 411–451.

Said, E.W. (1993). *Culture and imperialism.* New York: Vintage Books.

Shannon, P. (Ed.). (1992). *Reading instruction and social class. Becoming political: Readings and writings in the politics of literacy education.* Portsmouth, NH: Heinemann.

Shannon, P. (1995). Can reading standards really help? *Clearing House (Menasha, Wis.), 68*(4), 229–232.

Shannon, P. (1996). Mad as hell. *Language Arts, 73*(1), 14–19.

Shannon, P. (2007). *Reading against democracy: The broken promises of reading instruction.* Portsmouth, NH: Heinemann.

Shor, I. (1992). *Empowering education: Critical teaching for social change.* Chicago: University of Chicago Press.

Simon, R. (1992). *Teaching against the grain: Texts for a pedagogy of possibility.* Toronto: OISE Press.

Smith, L. (1999). *Decolonizing methodologies research and indigenous peoples.* New York: Zed Books Limited.

Smyth, J., Angus, L., Down, B., & McInerney, P. (2008). *Critically engaged learning.* New York: Peter Lang.

Smyth, J., Angus, L., Down, B., & McInerney, P. (2009). *Activist and socially critical school and community renewal.* Rotterdam: Sense Publishers.

Sobol, T. (1997). Beyond standards: The rest of the agenda. *Teachers College Record, 98*(4), 629–636.

Solomon, P. (1992). *Black resistance in high school: Forging a separatist culture.* New York: SUNY Press.

Spencer, M.M. (1993, March 27). *Memorial lecture for Patricia S. Barnes.* Delivered at Mount Saint Vincent University, Halifax, NS.

Swartz, E. (1996). Emancipatory pedagogy: A postcritical response to "standard" school knowledge. *Journal of Curriculum Studies, 28*(4), 397–418. doi:10.1080/0022027980280402

Valencia, R.R. (Ed.). (1997). *The evolution of deficit thinking: Educational thought and practice.* London: The Falmer Press.

Weaver, R. (1970). *Concealed rhetoric in scientistic sociology. Language is sermonic.* Baton Rouge: Louisiana State University.

Weis, L. (1990). *Working class without work: High school students in a deindustrializing society.* New York: Routledge.

Willis, P.E. (1977). *Learning to labour: How working class kids get working class jobs.* Westmead, UK: Saxon House.

Zwaagstra, M. (2012, October 8). Failed education fads should be buried, not resurrected. Retrieved from http://michaelzwaagstra.com/?page_id=33.

NOTES

1 For an elaboration of this point, see Shor (1992), Giroux (1994), Portelli (1996), and Freire (1996).

2 As teachers all know, there is a big difference between lesson plans and actual practice. Likewise, just saying so in a document is no guarantee that the proposed will actually take place. For example, several education documents have told us that diversity will be respected and supported. However, for example, in Halifax, when the first cuts in education were made, ESL teachers were among the first to be reduced and, in some instances, even eliminated.

3 In reality, one could argue that in the West we actually encourage individualism rather than genuine diversity; that is, while individual differences are accepted, that is not the case with social differences such as race and gender. One has to be careful not to conflate a sort of political individualism with democracy.

4 Jim Keegstra was a public school teacher in Alberta from 1968 to 1983 when his teaching license was revoked by the Alberta Minister of Education and he was expelled from the Alberta Teachers' Association. In 1985 he was convicted on the charge of promoting hatred against Jews through his teaching. For more details, see the chapter by Hare (1996) in this collection.

16

The End of Efficiency

Implications for Democratic Education

*Francine Menashy**

*This chapter was originally published as Menashy, F. (2007). The end of
efficiency: Implications for democratic education. *Journal of Educational
Thought, 41*(2), 165–177. Reproduced with permission.

The label "efficient" is rarely given as a pejorative. In fact, it is generally taken for granted as positive. When we are considered efficient,
we are celebrated; when inefficient, we are chastised. By proper definition, however, the term ought to carry no value at all. Efficiency is
a term often decontextualized and thereby problematically applied
and assumed to produce only positive outcomes. In this chapter,
I tackle this concept of efficiency and its application to current
educational initiatives and reforms. It will be shown that efficiency

movements in education are primarily based on a narrow conception of efficiency, giving rise to serious ethical implications. I begin with an examination of the term and common misconceptions of its meaning. Manifestations of the efficiency movement in education are then described, followed by the impacts of this movement on democratic education and equity. It will be concluded that the problematic consequences of efficiency initiatives in schools are primarily due to the application of an overly narrow conception of efficiency.

Defining Efficiency

Efficiency, as the term is commonly invoked in our society, implies a specific conception that is associated primarily with economic aims. If properly understood, however, *efficiency* has very general applications, meant, quite simply, to produce a desired result with minimal effort, expense, or waste. There is a widespread assumption that the term *waste* herein refers to "cost" or "resources," but this is only the case in certain circumstances. As Janice Gross Stein (2002) explains: "Efficiency clearly takes on different meanings in different spheres of human activity. The yardstick is relative and rooted in context" (p. 12). Efficiency is therefore always a means to some end. No one, or nothing, is ever merely efficient; we are always efficient *at* something. A fuel-efficient car is not simply efficient; it is efficient *at* conserving fuel. It is therefore problematic to view efficiency as an end in itself or to strive for it decontextualized from an aim. As Stein argues, efficiency has become so unproblematically valued in our society that it is often misunderstood as an "end," not as a "means." And, as will be shown, this singular end is frequently conceived of as economic in nature.

As argued by Joseph Heath, we ought to value efficiency in satisfying our various needs, but these needs are not limited to resources or production or wealth. Efficiency, for Heath (2001), is a valued means to achieving such goods as "[o]ur need for clean air, beautiful surroundings, knowledge, and even protection against risk" (p. xvi). Moreover, pursuing efficiency helps us to determine ways in which to organize our lives, attain our goals, and how best to achieve "win-win" situations (Heath, 2001, p. 24). As such, pursuing efficiency can indeed be viewed as highly valuable. However, the significance lies not in the act of being efficient but in the ends it attains.

Invoking efficiency to attain a goal is then not problematic in and of itself. In fact, it is often worthwhile. The critique I place is not on the notion of efficiency. It is instead on a narrow conception of the term that has become prevalent in our society. The widespread understanding of efficiency implies a specific end, not many. Its meaning in this sense is narrow, and a distortion with serious ethical implications.

As Heath (2001) states: "There is a strong tendency to think of efficiency only in very narrow terms—to judge it by looking at the total value of goods produced by the market. This is deeply wrongheaded" (p. xvi). The common understanding of efficiency links it inextricably to economics. The term is almost interchangeable with "cost-effectiveness," "cost cutting," "value for money," or "productivity" (Heath, 2001; Stein, 2002; Welch, 1998). Due to a decontextualizing of the term, routinely linking efficiency to "an ethos of business style principles" has become pervasive (Welch, 1998, p.157). Efficiency's value has been reduced to its contribution to economic growth. This prompts the belief that a lack of contribution to economic productivity implies "inefficiency" (Heath, 2001; Meyer, 1998; Stein, 2002).

As argued by Stein (2002), the promotion of efficiency "engenders almost blind loyalty" and in this sense can be viewed as a "cult" (p. 4). The pervasive demand for efficiency, in terms of productivity, therefore exists beyond the corporate arena and has infiltrated the provision of public goods. As will be shown, an excessively narrow conception of efficiency, limited to economics, is that which is most often applied to the realm of education.

It is this *limitation* of efficiency to economics within educational mandates that is critiqued in this chapter. Economic efficiency ought not to be presented as inherently problematic. It can be highly valuable to conserve resources. Problems arise when economic efficiency is sought *at the expense* of other aims. The objective of economic efficiency must be tempered by the pursuit of other aims of education. This chapter demonstrates that economic efficiency is often presented as the *dominant* aim of education, leading to what Susan Meyer (1998) describes as a reductionist, technicist approach to pedagogy and educational policy. There is no doubt that resources are important. However, it is possible that policy-makers can strive for a degree of economic efficiency so long as other aims are identified, pursued, and not subjugated to financial objectives (Meyer, 1998).

The Efficiency Movement in Education

The notion of efficiency as a "cult" in fact preceded Stein, and was first applied to schools by Raymond E. Callahan in his 1962 book *Education and the Cult of Efficiency*. Callahan (1962) critiqued the promotion of "modern business methods" employed to reform schools, for he felt that educational concerns were "subordinated to business considerations" (pp. 5, 246). Schools in Callahan's time were conceived of as factories, meant to provide a practical curriculum "in order to serve a business society better" (p. 18). The drive toward economic goals within schools were a result of what Callahan termed a "cult of efficiency" in education, and manifested in the application of business methods to achieve financial, more than educational, ends. Over 50 years later, the present applicability of Callahan's critique is quite notable.

For instance, Anthony Welch (1998) depicts current efficiency movements in education that are "predicated upon the idea that both individual worth and the worth of education can be reduced to economic terms" (p. 158). Educational reforms falling under "efficiency movements" have been widespread since the early 1990s and implemented in such countries as Canada, the United States, Australia, New Zealand, and the United Kingdom.[1] These reforms have been widely critiqued as neoliberal in nature (Olssen, 1996; Pinto & Portelli, 2009; Stein, 2002; Welch, 1998; Wrigley, 2003). The policies are described by critics as adhering to a specific ideology based on free-market principles that include a reduced role of government, consumer choice, and individualism. A central tenet of neoliberalism is economic prosperity as a primary aim (Freire, 2001; Olssen, 1996; Pinto & Portelli, 2009; Welch, 1998). Educational aims that are espoused in these movements are then reduced primarily in relation to economic growth. Improvements to education are defined as investments, and the student body is viewed as human capital. In this sense, education is a commodity. It is therefore only natural that business methods are readily applied to educational policies (Welch, 1998). It is apparent that in Callahan's assessment, along with those of contemporary theorists, the term "efficiency" as applied to education implies the economically narrow conception.

One manifestation of this efficiency movement is increased corporate involvement in schools. Within a Canadian context, Alison Taylor (2001) describes a common view of education "as a means for developing a highly skilled workforce and thus securing national economic prosperity" (p. 169). As such, there exists a strong impetus toward creating ties between businesses and schools. Business-education conferences have been popularized in their endeavour to promote partnerships and co-operation between corporations and schools. The Conference Board of Canada—a corporate-backed research institution—has been widely successful in sponsoring these conferences in several provinces. For instance, these conferences critique curriculum in terms of its applicability to the workplace, promoting a refocusing toward more business-oriented subjects. Also promoted are "co-operative," "apprenticeship," or "workplace learning" programs. Business leaders are increasingly involved at the policy level in education, as well, voicing their opinions on what can best make a student employable. In consistently invoking the catchphrase "Knowledge Economy," business leaders and educators inextricably link education to economic development (Taylor, 2001).

The rise in commercialism in schools further demonstrates the influence of the educational efficiency movement. As argued by Alex Molnar and Joseph Reaves (2002), while students are moulded to enter a specific workforce, they are concurrently "conditioned to express civic and economic participation through consumerism" (p. 18). Such activities that perpetuate this consumerism include allocation of school space to advertising that markets toward children, sponsoring of educational materials by corporations, and incentive programs where students or schools receive awards or funding from businesses for engaging in specific activities. According to a study conducted by Molnar and Reaves, corporate spending on marketing to youth has never been higher. They conclude: "In an ongoing quest to capture lifelong consumers, corporations are turning schools into servants of a marketing machine" (p. 48). Commercialism in schools and business involvement in educational programs are related to a limited definition of efficiency, wherein schools are viewed as a critical component of economic growth. An assumption is made that the more businesses are involved in the structure of schools, the more efficiently schools and students will contribute to the economy.

Furthermore, the curriculum ought to be not only applicable to the workplace but also "common." Efficiency is related to this standardization drive in part due to the belief that "universal standards ... will make practice more efficient and less confusing" (Portelli & Vibert, 2001, p. 66). It is assumed that this allows for easier, less time-consuming and therefore more cost-effective assessment via standardized testing. For instance, the provincial Progressive Conservative government in Ontario in the mid-1990s introduced both a common curriculum and rigid standardized testing structure that are still in place today (Dei & Karumanchery, 2001). These tests are widely viewed as efficient measures of student achievement and tend to concentrate on literacy and mathematics skills (Dei & Karumanchery, 2001; Macedo, 2000; Welch, 1998). Moreover, the increasing importance placed on standardized tests is derived from a narrow vision of the aims of education, which I argue are underpinned by a narrow notion of efficiency (Siegel, 2004).

The widespread promotion of privatization of education and school choice also reflects the efficiency movement. The push toward privatization derives from the conception of the State, as a provider of goods and services, as essentially inefficient (Stein, 2002; Welch, 1998). The privatization of schools can create competition, and there is a widely held belief that problems plaguing the public school system may be cured via school-choice initiatives. The conservative Fraser Institute has been a strong proponent of the school-choice movement in Canada. It is argued by the institute and other advocates that "an educational market will foster competition among schools, rewarding the cost-effective schools that provide quality education and punishing the failures as parents 'exit'" (Stein, 2002, p. 99). Those who advocate privatization "treat parents and their children as individual 'consumers', educators as 'suppliers', and government as the regulator of the rules of the market, not as the direct provider of public education" (Stein, 2002, p. 99).

Ethical Implications of the Efficiency Movement in Education

It is apparent that there is an impetus toward greater efficiency in schools, and that this conception of efficiency is reduced to economic aims and market ideology. Manifestations of this efficiency movement, such as corporatism, consumerism, high-stakes testing, curriculum reform, and privatization, prompt several ethical concerns. In particular, the degree to which education can be deemed democratic must be questioned, given the impacts of the efficiency movement.

For John Dewey (1997), a democratic society includes such elements as free communication and association, equal participation, and "must have a type of education which gives individuals a personal interest in social relationships and control, and the habits of mind which secure social changes without introducing disorder" (p. 99). He states that "democracy means freeing intelligence for independent effectiveness" (Dewey, 1977, p. 230). Therefore, democratic education must do more than teach students about the mechanics of political processes but also foster in them a sense of agency within this process. A school itself must also adhere to democratic principles; the classroom must be a democratic place. Students may then see that they are participants in their learning, and thereby schools can create citizens who have the capacity and drive to act toward social transformation. This moves beyond the notion of education as knowledge acquisition (Levin, 2000; Pinto & Portelli, 2009). John Portelli and Patrick Solomon (2001) advocate a meaning of democratic education that incorporates such elements as "critical thinking, dialogue and discussion, tolerance, free and reasoned choices, and public participation" (p. 17). Given these descriptions, in my view, democratic schools are meant to allow student participation in what and how they are taught, to be arenas of social change and therefore transformative toward a more democratic society. As will be shown, efficiency movements in education counter these democratic principles and aims.

For instance, corporate ties to education generally reflect not the interests of educators, parents, or children, but of business leaders. At business-education conferences, Taylor (2001) has found that business representatives identified most of the issues to be addressed and created the agendas (p. 184). One must question the degree to which these ventures are in the best interests of the students, or if they are simply furthering the interests of the business community. Furthermore, one may question if equity plays a role in this "new vocationalism" (Taylor, 2001, p. 181). In that the majority of the apprenticeships have attracted male students, to what extent do these programs reproduce gendered workplace roles? Also, many of these vocational programs are offered only to certain streams of high-school students, where there is a targeting of those deemed non-college bound. In this, are these programs contributing to the reproduction of class divisions? (Taylor, 2001) While the endeavour to create a better workforce may be argued to contribute to economic prosperity, there are serious concerns if the best interests of the students are being truly furthered by these business-education initiatives. As Welch (1998) asserts: "The current imposition of business and market principles of efficiency upon schools and universities results in predictable distortions of the principles of social justice and equality, towards ones of economics and business management" (p. 171).

Consumerism in schools raises similar concerns. Commercial ventures in schools have been found to "influence the structure of the school day, shape curricula, undermine quality education ..." (Molnar & Reaves, 2002, p. 17). The pervasiveness of commercialism in schools prompts questions concerning the perception of students as investments and the degree to which they are being socialized and targeted as consumers without their consent. Noam Chomsky (2000) argues that "[e]arly in your education you are socialized to understand the need to support the power structure, primarily corporations—the business class" (p. 17). In this sense, education is viewed primarily as a commercial venture, where, as Henry Giroux (1999) asserts, "the only form of citizenship offered to young people is consumerism" (p. 141). This counters the democratic participation of students in their own learning, treating them in an instrumentalist fashion, or as Paulo Freire (2001) has described, as objects instead of subjects. Students are more economic agents than learners and citizens with individual needs, desires, and histories.

A counterargument can be made that asks: what if students want to become economic agents? This is a fair question, for a student may democratically choose to be treated as a consumer and involved in the various initiatives of the efficiency movement. The problem, however, is that their current treatment is not their choice. If the students do not wish to be treated as consumers, they have no means to opt out. It is the lack of consent that demands critique and can be deemed unethical and undemocratic.

Further supporting the argument that the efficiency movement reduces democratic education are the implications of standardized testing and curriculum reforms. Standardized tests, despite their efficiency in assessing certain skills, support test-guided teaching that prevents students from developing other abilities that allow them to examine the world critically (Giroux, 1999; Macedo, 2000). Teaching to a test only promotes, as Freire (2001) has described it, "banking education," and hinders "true learning." As he explains: "in the context of true learning, the learners will be engaged in a continuous transformation through which they become authentic subjects of the construction and reconstruction of what is being taught ..." (Freire, 2001, p. 33). This process cannot occur when teaching is restricted in its content and guided by standardized tests. Independent thought and critical thinking are devalued and suppressed via "this form of mindless skills-based education" (Macedo, 2000, p. 4).

Critical thinking is not merely problem-solving or thinking creatively. It includes a dispositional component where individuals' actions are informed by thinking critically in given situations (Pinto & Portelli, 2009). In allowing the space and encouraging students' critical thinking, they may then learn to question the world around them, including what and how they learn in schools. In this way they may act as participants in their own education, countering "banking education" and the possibility of indoctrination (Freire, 2001; Pinto & Portelli, 2009). Critical thinking is therefore a central component of democratic education, in its fostering of participatory learning within classrooms that are democratic spaces.

Challenges to critical thinking, which in turn hinder democratic education, result from the efficiency movement, such as space and time limitations due to high-stakes standardized tests and rigid curriculum policy. The economic focus in education addresses the needs of future employers, yet is likely at the expense of other aims, such as instilling political empowerment in students. The emphasis on testing that focuses on basic literacy and mathematics limits the room in which students may engage in critical thinking. Teaching as test-preparation allows little opportunity for students to critically examine their experiences in and out of schools (Pinto & Portelli, 2009; Siegel, 2004; Wrigley, 2003). As Terry Wrigley (2003) explains:

> Students struggling to negotiate a complex set of power relationships, values and ideologies need space to explore plural and shifting identities, to critique the dominant discourses (globalization, consumerism, 'economic rationalism' and religious fundamentalisms) and work out how to position themselves within a complex intersection of power relationships and consumer identities. They need to deal creatively, at an affective as well as cognitive level, with problems of poverty, patriarchy, sexuality, racism and war (p. 108).

The absence of critical thinking that results from efficiency movements act to hinder students' abilities to understand and address important global issues and dominant ideologies. Test-based teaching, in opposition to democratic practices, only furthers the power of hegemony, repressing the critical transformative aim of education. Ideologies that likely reflect only the interests of dominant groups may be easily ingrained in students when critical reflection is suppressed. This suppression is only perpetuated when learning is restricted by a common curriculum and teaching is guided by high-stakes standardized testing. If there is no opportunity to engage critically with alternative perspectives, closed-mindedness or indoctrination may result (Chomsky, 2000; Freire, 2001; Pinto & Portelli, 2009).

The standardization of curriculum also raises equity concerns and must be problematized in terms of its design. Advocating a common curriculum, George Sefa Dei and Leeno Karumanchery (2001) argue, raises the following questions: "Who is writing these new curricula? How do the new curricula address questions of equity and social difference? Whose values, ideas, and knowledge are being represented? One must ask how outcomes are to be achieved by all when the playing field is not level" (p. 201). Similarly argued by Portelli and Vibert (2001), the standardization movement assumes a "common culture" giving little consideration to the diversity among students while emphasizing conformity (p. 69). Markets have become the models for schools and curriculum, potentially subjugating equity considerations in education. As Welch (1998) states: "The cult of efficiency often masks an economistic, technicist conception of education which resists any incursions by criteria of equity or social or individual development" (p. 171).

Furthermore, a significant characteristic of the limited conception of efficiency is its restricted applicability to that which is easily measurable; only what is empirically verifiable can be deemed efficient by economic standards. This implies that anything unquantifiable, that cannot be proven to contribute to economic aims, is often considered inefficient. Meyer (1998) employs the term *technicism* to describe the reduction of educational issues to only that which is quantifiable. Technicism, she argues, is an indicator of the hegemony of rational scientific thinking. Quantitative data, it is argued, is much easier to communicate and is more readily accepted than non-empirical arguments to support policy (Meyer, 1998). Technicism influences the emphasis on quantifiable outcomes that are stressed in the common curriculum and assessed by the associated standardized tests. This reductionist approach has repercussions for democratic education and equity issues, for there is a risk that non-quantifiable outcomes of education will be considered as secondary aims. Examples of such educational aims are fostering critical thinking, anti-racism, and other equity measures.

Finally, the drive toward privatization, with the aim of improving the cost-effectiveness of schools, raises obvious concerns surrounding equity given that access is often dependent on the socio-economic class of the student. The disempowering of the public sector in the provision of education reduces the likelihood of providing quality education to whole communities. Moreover, the said improvement of schools via competition implies that a school is the same as a business, assuming similar aims. Any responsibility that education may have to increase democratic practices is subjugated to the pursuit of efficiency (Giroux, 1999; Stein, 2002; Welch, 1998).[2]

These manifestations of the drive toward efficiency in education all demonstrate an excessively narrow conception of the term, with economic growth, market mechanisms, and cost-effectiveness at the core. There are questionable outcomes of these initiatives and reforms, in terms of equity and democratic education. Furthermore, they rest on a specific conception of the aims of schooling and the nature of the student. Concern is limited to those aims of education that can be quantified and potentially contribute to the economic base of society. The focus on efficiency has been shown to suppress various social aims of education, such as equity and democracy, yet supports other aims such as the development of human capital and consumerism. The efficiency movement also implies that there is no intrinsic worth to education, that schools are simply meant to create avid consumers and a profitable workforce. This would explain the acceptance of teaching guided by tests, where students are not meant to think critically about the world but instead to learn basic skills that can be transposed to the workplace and thereby help them "succeed" in capitalist society.

One may question the degree to which students are viewed as means to economic ends in this focus on efficiency. This raises a serious ethical concern, for there is an instrumentalist perception of students, by which their opinions, needs, desires, and independent thoughts are disregarded. Students are instead viewed as investments. Manifestations of the efficiency movement in education weaken "the role that public schools might play in keeping the experiences, hopes, and dreams of a democracy alive for each successive generation of students" (Giroux, 1999, p. 142).

Conclusion

Educational initiatives and reforms are often based on a misleading conception of the term efficiency. There is a pervasive assumption that efficiency ought to be a means to a very limited end, namely economic growth. Educators and policy-makers must be cautioned against narrow and simplistic applications of this concept (Meyer, 1998). As has been shown, this overly narrow conception influences policies and practices that give rise to ethical concerns surrounding the aims of education and the treatment of students. However, this does not discount the value of efficiency in terms of its proper use. For instance, I would advocate initiatives implemented that promote more efficient means to the end of equity, or social justice. The goal of efficiency is not problematic, if this desire is contextualized and aims at ethical ends. Even in the case where economic efficiency is pursued, it is only unethical if it is at the expense of other, likely unquantifiable outcomes. As argued by Callahan (1962) half a century ago, concerns for efficiency in education must aim at "humanist," not economic goals. We must consistently question why we continue valuing efficiency, by examining the ends at which our efficiency aims.

REFERENCES

Callahan, R. (1962). *Education and the cult of efficiency*. Chicago: University of Chicago Press.

Chomsky, N. (2000). *Chomsky on miseducation*. New York: Rowman & Littlefield Publishers, Inc.

Dei, G.S., & Karumanchery, L. (2001). School reforms in Ontario: The 'marketization of education' and the resulting silence on equity. In J. Portelli & R.P. Solomon (Eds.), *The erosion of democracy in education: Critique to possibilities* (pp. 189–215). Calgary: Detselig Enterprises Ltd.

Dewey, J. (1977). Democracy in education. In J.A. Boydston (Ed.), *John Dewey: The middle works* (Vol. 3, pp. 1903–1906). Carbondale, IL: Southern Illinois University Press. [Original work published in 1903].

Dewey, J. (1997). *Democracy and education.* New York: The Free Press. [Original work published in 1916].

Freire, P. (2001). *Pedagogy of freedom: Ethics, democracy, and civic courage.* Lanham, MD: Rowman & Littlefield Publishers, Inc.

Giroux, H. (1999). Schools for sale: Public education, corporate culture, and the citizen-consumer. *Educational Forum, 63*(2), 140–149. doi:10.1080/00131729908984404

Heath, J. (2001). *The efficient society: Why Canada is as close to utopia as it gets.* Toronto: Penguin Books Ltd.

Levin, B. (2000). Democracy and Schools. *Education Canada, 40*(3), 4–7.

Macedo, D. (2000). Introduction. In *Chomsky on miseducation.* New York: Rowman & Littlefield Publishers, Inc.

Meyer, S. (1998). Efficiency in education: the problem of technicism. *Educational Philosophy and Theory, 30*(3), 223–238. doi:10.1111/j.1469-5812.1998.tb00325.x

Molnar, A., & Reaves, J. (2002). The growth of schoolhouse commercialism and the assault on educative experience. *Journal of Curriculum and Supervision, 18*(1), 17–55.

Olssen, M. (1996). In defense of the welfare state and publicly provided education: a New Zealand perspective. *Journal of Education Policy, 11*(3), 337–362. doi:10.1080/0268093960110305

Pinto, L.E., & Portelli, J.P. (2009). The role and impact of critical thinking in democratic education: Challenges and possibilities. In J. Sobocan & L. Goroarke (Eds.), *Critical thinking education and assessment: Can higher order thinking be tested?* (pp. 299–318). London, ON: Althouse Press.

Portelli, J.P., & Vibert, A. (2001). Beyond common educational standards: Towards a curriculum of life. In J.P. Portelli & R.P. Solomon (Eds.), *The erosion of democracy in education: From critique to possibilities* (pp. 63–82). Calgary: Detselig Enterprises Ltd. [See also page 223 in this volume.]

Portelli, J.P., & Solomon, R.P. (2001). Introduction. In J.P. Portelli & R.P. Solomon (Eds.), *The erosion of democracy in education: From critique to possibilities* (pp. 15–27). Calgary, AB: Detselig Enterprises Ltd.

Siegel, H. (2004). High stakes testing, educational aims and ideals, and responsible assessment. *Theory and Research in Education, 2*(3), 219–233. doi:10.1177/1477878504046515. [See also page 271 in this volume.]

Stein, J. (2002). *The cult of efficiency.* Toronto: House of Anansi Press Ltd.

Taylor, A. (2001). Education, business, and the 'knowledge economy.' In J. Portelli & R.P. Solomon (Eds.), *The erosion of democracy in education: From critique to possibilities* (pp. 169–188). Calgary: Detselig Enterprises Ltd.

Welch, A. (1998). The cult of efficiency in education: Comparative reflections on the reality and the rhetoric. *Comparative Education, 34*(2), 157–175. doi:10.1080/03050069828252

Wrigley, T. (2003). Is 'school-effectiveness' anti-democratic? *British Journal of Educational Studies, 51*(2), 89–112. doi:10.1111/1467-8527.t01-4-00228

NOTES

1 Some have labelled similar reforms as "effectiveness" movements. See, for example, Terry Wrigley (2003).

2 For a more comprehensive examination of the complex privatization debate, see J. Stein's *The Cult of Efficiency* (2002), which provides an excellent investigation of the relationship of efficiency to privatization and school-choice movements in North America.

17

Arendt, Freire, and the Pedagogy of Possession

*Trevor Norris**

*This chapter is a revised version of Norris, T. (2005). Re-thinking re-producing consumption: Hannah Arendt, Paulo Freire and the pedagogy of possession. *Philosophical Studies in Education, 36,* 77–90. Reproduced with permission.

Three days after the attacks of September 11, George W. Bush strode across the White House lawn to a sea of cameras and microphones. He needed to provide reassurance, strength, and direction to a disoriented American people. His inspiring words galvanized a nation and reflected what has become the defining spirit of the American people. Joining a long tradition of great orators in times of struggle, he looked confidently into the cameras and called upon the American people to go shopping.[1]

Amid the tumult and distress of those shocking days, the peculiarity of this statement was easily overlooked and forgotten. That it would be the responsibility of a democratically elected leader to call upon the people to shop is surely a perversion of the meaning of political leadership. It is radically different from the slogans of World War II about courage, frugality, and the virtue of investing in war bonds. Today a trip to Walmart is said to perform the same political function and express equivalent love of country. But for Dick Cheney it is not only an act of patriotism but also an act of military aggression: within a week of the event, he described shopping as a way for ordinary citizens to "stick their thumbs in the eye of the terrorists" (Gosselin & Vieth, 2001). And on September 24, NBC's Tom Brokaw insisted that "Americans need to go out and spend" (Jackson, 2001). Grieving and consuming are in turn conflated.

While international politics increasingly takes on the tone of apocalyptic fervour, some have argued that the centrality of consumption to the American way of life is itself responsible for widespread resentment and anti-Western sentiment. In *Jihad vs. McWorld*, democratic theorist Benjamin Barber (2001) asserts that the proliferation of Western consumerism constitutes a new "soft" power of "McWorld's assiduously commercialized and ambitiously secularist materialism" (p. xxvi) and "inadvertently contribute[s] to the causes of terrorism" (p. xi). All too often the West has been more successful at spreading consumer goods and values than the institutions and practices of democracy.

In its quest to establish new markets and satiate our own consumer society, the Western world extends its reach globally and draws all nations into its orbit. But consumer society is not only a new force in the evolving international system. It can also be considered a colonial force in our backyard—or rather in our schoolyards. The inroads made by advertisers into the school environment to gain access to the student body are possibly the most compelling evidence of the fact that our society has become a consumer society. It is undeniable that today's youth market is worth billions, and advertisers are aggressively pursuing this target audience through *school-business partnerships*, by which schools become an opportunity to secure a new market of consumers. Education is ideally considered a means of critically intervening in society, constructively enabling the development of a robust democracy and active citizenry. Consumerism, however, *undermines* the critical task of education, reducing it to a process by which students become increasingly *acquisitive* yet decreasingly *inquisitive*.

I shall begin this chapter by exploring the rise of consumer society and proposing a theory of consumption based on the notion of "possession." I will then turn to the inroads made by corporations and advertisers into the educational environment and their problematic impact on pedagogical practices and models of learning. I will then consider two significant contemporary thinkers, a political philosopher and a philosopher of education: Hannah Arendt (1958) outlines the rise of the private concerns of consumption that she links with labour and work, while Paulo Freire (1970) identifies "possessive consciousness" as a central characteristic of the oppressors, which in turn is a feature of the "banking model of education." Both thinkers recognized fundamental problems inherent to the direction of modern industrial society. Their works are well known for this recognition but have never before been used together specifically to critique *consumer* society.[2] Connecting their analyses of consumerism will better illuminate this trend and its implications for educational theory and practice. In essence, consumerism's penetration into education must be tempered, as it negates education's critical and liberatory possibilities.

Consumption and Consumer Studies

In this chapter I argue that consumerism entails the institutionalized production of need and the invention of new desires, the systematic inculcation of inadequacy and yearning for completion through material gratification. Yet consumption entails more than the mere fiscal transaction of physical acquisition. I will critique, but not stop at, this common understanding of the term and will examine it instead as an archetypal activity of contemporary society by which the model of consumerism extends itself into all aspects of human life, from the teacher-student relationship to our experience of citizenship. In this sense, consumerism constitutes a process that expands beyond the purchasing of a product to include the transformation of all things in the world into objects for human consumption.

There is wide debate among theorists of consumer society about the origin of consumerism. Some scholars argue that it has always been an integral part of human social existence since the earliest stages of history. Yet it was a marginal issue in perhaps the most important and influential text on political economy of the 18th century, Adam Smith's (1936) *The Wealth of Nations*, where there is only one reference to consumption in its 900 pages (p. 625). Centuries later Marx emphasized the importance of labour and production to the formation of human consciousness. Like Smith, Marx focused his analysis of capitalism and political economy primarily on the political importance of human labour, arguing that the material conditions of production were the primary determinants of human consciousness and political order. Marx argued that we produce ourselves through our labour because human consciousness and political structures are determined by the ownership of the modes of production. Consumption is barely mentioned in his (1867/1906) magnum opus *Das Kapital.*

Others point to distinctive features associated with the emergence of modern capitalism during the Industrial Revolution, when consumption was considered a response to the homogenizing forces of mechanization and technology caused by industrialization and growing urbanization (Aldridge, 2003). People began to consume as a principal mode of self-expression, a common language through which we communicate and interpret shared cultural signs and meanings. Others have argued that consumerism is a 20th-century phenomenon associated with the rise of mass communication, growing affluence, and the monolithic modern corporation (Galbraith, 1968; Achbar, 2004). Several theorists have argued that there has been a gradual shift this century from the political and cultural importance of the production of goods to the production of needs, and that the modern subject is thus experiencing a shift in forms of identity and its expression from the workplace to consumption (Bell, 1976). People decreasingly identify themselves with respect to traditional work-related social groupings and more so with consumer products and the messages and meanings conveyed about them. For example, Thorstein Veblen (1899/1931) proposed "conspicuous consumption" as a way to express affluence. Several theorists have also pointed toward an important distinction between the consumer and the customer, the latter of whom embraced a more personalized set of long-term relationships rooted in familial and communal contexts and who is being eclipsed by the former (Bocock, 1993).

Perhaps a deeper understanding of this activity can be pursued through an etymological account. The English word "consume" can be in part derived from two distinct Latin verbs. The first is *consummare*, from *summa*, which means to complete, sum up, or fulfill in a teleological culmination, as in "to consummate." The second is *consumere*, from *sumere*, meaning to take in, or be taken up by. We can speak of being consumed by anger, that it has taken possession of us and we are swept up and compelled toward action. But it also implies that it has overtaken us, and by extension has negated our autonomy. We could say that we are consumed by consuming, or possessed by consuming. Today even time itself is being consumed: we often speak of activities as being "time-consuming." My concern is that we are not only consuming products but selling out something fundamental within ourselves and essential to our social existence and pedagogical practices such that in our pursuit of possession we experience absence rather than completion.

Consumerism and the pursuit of possession have been linked to two key features of liberalism: contract and choice. In *The Political Theory of Possessive Individualism*, noted Canadian political philosopher C.B. Macpherson (1962) argues that the very birth of modern liberalism in the early British social contract theorists John Locke and Thomas Hobbes was based largely on the drive toward private acquisition. For these thinkers, humans are compelled to enter into civil society and submit to a social contract largely because the state of nature is characterized by great uncertainty concerning the protection of private property. Yet while the notions of possession and private property were originally construed as a way to protect oneself against the power of the state, many liberal critics argue that this attempt at protection has radically different implications. Macpherson asserts that "the original seventeenth-century individualism contained [a] central difficulty, which lay in its possessive quality" (p. 3). The liberal emphasis on the importance of the individual is bound up with the "possessive quality" of that individual; the liberal theory of politics is intended to safeguard the autonomous sphere of the possessing individual. This emphasis is also associated with the capacity to autonomously assess one's needs and deliberate rationally about one's desires, and to make choices on the basis of this autonomous deliberation. Autonomy and deliberation, desire and needs are construed as existing before society as inherent features of the individual preoccupied with the consumer activities of choice and the satisfaction of ideologically defined personal preferences. The philosopher of education Ruth Jonathan (1997) argues that liberalism is "a social philosophy defined by the *priority given to preference satisfaction*" (p. 6).

In addition to the links with liberalism, consumerism presents new challenges to the notion of citizenship: just as the political categories of democracy, the public realm, and citizenship are being eroded, corporate institutions are gaining political status: corporations have been humanized as "persons" and now speak of themselves as "corporate citizens." This humanization of the corporation as citizen parallels the decline of active "human" political citizenship—we are asked to shop as a means of supporting our country in a time of need—and the transformation of human relations into consumer relations. The consumer replaces, or rather even "consumes," the citizen.

Consuming Schooling

Having surveyed the historical rise of consumerism and explored its various theoretical underpinnings, I will now turn to trends in contemporary schooling. Once a relatively protected and decommodified public good, education is being swept up by globalizing forces, transformed into a commercial enterprise, and reoriented toward a thoroughly integrated relationship with commercial interests. This is not to evoke a golden era when schooling and society were not impacted by consumerism but rather to suggest that constructing young consumers has become a growing element of the socialization process and a central component of the educative project. Schoolchildren are daily exposed to thousands of advertising images, and the educational environment is itself now drawn into this trend as desperate schools turn to corporate advertisers for revenue. To mention two examples, one Philadelphia school board president and self-proclaimed "director of corporate development" talks about "peddling the naming rights to the district's only school on eBay" and "instituting a school uniform policy and selling ads on the uniforms" (Graham, 2004). In some cases, corporations have sought to directly influence teachers: General Mills offered teachers $250 per month to act as "freelance brand managers" and promote its products in the classroom (Sandel, 2004). These examples may explain why according to the Millward Brown Global Market Research Agency, "nowhere else in the world [but America] are 8- to 12-year-olds more materialistic or more likely to believe that their clothes and brands describe who they are and define their social status" (Schor, 2004).

Corporations seek access to public schools for several reasons. First, youth spent in excess of $170 billion in 2002 (Greenspan, 2003). Second, advertisers face the challenge of how to effectively reach a market in an environment of growing "clutter" from other advertisers. Schools provide a much more targeted market than that available to TV broadcasters; they contain not only a specific age group but also reflect the local ethnicity and economic status of the surrounding population. Third, children exert tremendous sway over their parents' spending habits and become corporate representatives within the family. Schooling is thereby used not only to access youth but also their parents through what marketers term the "nag factor" or "pester power." Children become the "Trojan Horse" of the home market, and influenced total family purchases to the tune of $500 billion in 1999 (Campbell & Davis-Packard, 2000). Lastly, youths have been called "consumers in training"; they are developing "brand loyalties" that may last for their entire lifetime and may include lifelong addictions to tobacco, cola, and other physical substances.

While corporations might describe their relations with schools as "partnerships," and might emphasize the advantages schools reap, they are motivated only by profit. This is not corporate benevolence: First, the cost of school advertising is factored into the price of the consumer product; it is we who pay for it. Second, corporate involvement in education is done only if they expect to make more money than they pay. Furthermore, corporations will prevent any opposition or criticism within schools.[3] This dynamic blurs the line between educating students and acquiring new consumers, between schools as commercial spheres and educational environments.

In his analysis of trends in school commercialism, Alex Molnar (2003–2004) differentiates between "selling to schools, selling in schools, and finally, the selling of schools and of education as a marketable commodity" (p. 35). In *The Educational Cost of Schoolhouse Commercialism*, the 14th annual report on schoolhouse commercializing trends 2010–11, Molnar, Boninger, and Fogarty (2011) show that corporate intrusions into schools create significant educational harms. Molnar et al. identify four types of harms resulting from school commercialism: psychological, educational, health, and financial cost. For example, regarding educational harms, there is significant incompatibility between commercial values and the promotion of critical thinking: "It is not in the interest of corporate sponsors to promote critical thinking. Far from it: their interest is in selling their products or services or 'telling their story.' Encouraging children to learn to identify and critically evaluate a sponsor's point of view and biases, to consider alternative points of view or products and services, or to generate and consider solutions to problems other than the ones sponsors offer would, from a corporate point of view, be self-defeating" (p. 8). The report emphasizes the deep incompatibility between the aims and values of education and the aims and values of commercial interests. The commercial emphasis on short-term gratification, hyperstimulation, materialism, and individualism are values that are often in tension with what teachers aim to promote in their classrooms. "When for-profit corporations are involved in schools, irrespective of what the particular surface aspects of a given relationship may be, the heart of the relationship is mis-educative. This is because for-profit corporations must maintain a focus on the bottom line—they must make a profit. The mission of the school, on the other hand, is to provide educative experiences for students" (p. 8).

Chris Arthur (2012) describes how, following the credit crisis of 2008, the struggle over the representation of the crisis and strategies to divert attention away from Wall Street led to an initiative to emphasize the centrality of personal financial mismanagement and overspending as the causes of the credit crisis. In Ontario, Canada, Financial Literacy Education is promoted as a way to protect citizens from irregularities in the economy. Arthur shows how such strategies in fact "individualize" economic responsibility and leverage schools as places to access and influence new young consumers.

A survey of commercial trends in Canadian schools reveals that "32 per cent of schools reported the presence of advertising in or on the school," and notes that the "issues of commercialism and privatization of K–12 education are a growing concern for Canadian educators and education organizations focused on the need to ensure access to a publicly-funded inclusive education system without commercial or corporate influence" (Froese-Germain, Hawkey, Larose, McAdie, & Shaker, 2006, p. 19). For example, in Canada a McDonald's-sponsored fitness program (the "Go Active! Olympic Fitness Challenge," which has the blessing of the Canadian Olympic Committee) has the burger corporation partnered with 445 schools (nearly 50 in Ontario) involving some 50,000 students in nearly every province and territory except Quebec and Newfoundland/Labrador; McDonald's is offering schools a $200 credit toward the purchase of gym equipment (to a maximum of $500 per school) for participating schools (p. 22).

Contemporary experiences of childhood and adolescence are increasingly the construct of consumer culture. Schools and parents are portrayed as the negative "Other" and resented as authority figures, while the icons of consumption and entertainment are elevated as symbols of rebellion to identify with and emulate. What has been referred to as Generation X or Y could in fact be increasingly called the branded generation. In *Consuming Children: Education-Entertainment-Advertising*, Jane Kenway and Elizabeth Bullen (2001) outline the changing conceptions of the child and find that the prevalence of consumer culture has dramatically altered the contemporary project of schooling. In eroding the demarcations between education, entertainment, and advertising, it has brought schooling into what they call the "age of desire" (p. 59).

Through the influence of consumerism, student empowerment is translated into strengthening purchasing power, and the development of self-esteem is reduced to the development of consumer confidence. And yet the prevalence of consumerism and the inroads made into the educational environment not only influence spending habits, but in fact alter the entire educational experience. First, the student body itself becomes represented as a "consumable" that is sold as a commodity to advertisers. Second, the student is increasingly described as a "consumer" of educational services, purchased in a financial transaction in which the classroom becomes a site of commercial exchange. The student's self-understanding becomes that of a consumer of educational services, as implied in the discourse of "school choice." Fourth, knowledge becomes a "consumable" and learning itself an act of consumption.

The Disneyification (Giroux, 1999), McDonaldization (Boyles, 1998; Ritzer, 2001), and Coco-colonization[4] of contemporary schooling reinforces students' role as consumers, spectators, and passive citizens. As Deron Boyles (1998) argues, this trend "reduce[s] searching, being, and thinking to objectified and reductionistic particulars" (p. xv). Consumerism may lead students to no longer value their own curiosity and learning for its contribution to a richer democratic society and instead focus on stimulation and extrinsic material rewards. Thus, consumerism reduces education to the reproduction of private accumulation, turns social resistance into political apathy, and transforms human relations into commercial transactions of calculated exchange. When corporations go to school, what they learn is how to undo schooling; schools thereby facilitate the transformation of our culture into a *consumer* culture.

Hannah Arendt: The Eclipse of Political Life

I now consider how an influential political philosopher and a philosopher of education have theorized consumerism, beginning with Hannah Arendt's (1958) *The Human Condition*. In this work she documents the historic ascent of consumption to a place of political dominance and the resulting eclipse of what she terms the "public realm." Arendt holds a unique place among contemporary philosophers for her compelling and insightful critique of modern society. She has become of growing interest to philosophers of education in recent years, beginning with the work of Maxine Greene (1988) and continuing with the recent publication of Mordechai Gordon's (2001) collection of essays. Although *The Human Condition* contains a section called "The Consumer Society," the concept has been often overlooked by Arendt scholars. I will outline the place of this key concept within her work and connect it to contemporary trends in education.

Arendt develops a distinction between public and private, drawn from three key human activities. Within Arendt's typology, these are labour, work, and action. Labour is grounded within what Arendt calls the human condition of life, the biological life process to which we are bound simply by virtue of being human, compelled to submit to and preoccupy ourselves with species preservation. *Labour*, "the source of all property" (1958, p. 101) is the interaction between the human and nature, the endless taking from nature and returning to it through consumption. It is the private activity that provides for the biological continuation of life, in which the human body "concentrates on nothing but its own being alive" (p. 115). Because none of the products of human labour are lasting, she describes labour as "futile," while privacy implies "privative," or deprivation. We remain isolated within ourselves so long as we are bound up within this process and restricted to our own privacy, deprived of engagement in political action in the realm of human affairs. We are pulled into the cyclical process of consumption and exist in a "mere togetherness" where we are neither seen nor heard in our full humanness.

Between action and labour Arendt situates *work*, the activity that corresponds to the human capacity to build and maintain those physical things essential for political life. Work differs in terms of duration: its products last long enough to provide the physical stability required for the public realm to emerge. However, in a consumer society the products of work are increasingly "consumed," and no longer provide a lasting and stable structure for political community. The form of community that arises from work is a community motivated by "the desire for products, not people," where humans express themselves "not [as] persons but producers of products" (p. 209). Human relations become mediated through objects, and we only appear to—and through—our objects, and human community becomes merely "an organization of property-owners" (p. 68). The activities of labour and work are thus antipolitical, and eclipse—even consume—the public realm.

In contrast, action expresses our highest potentialities, through which we are known by others and participate in something larger than ourselves. It is through *action* that our uniqueness can be disclosed and made known to others, through which we "insert ourselves into the human world" of the public realm (p. 176). In contrast to work and labour, the "products" of action are not objects to be consumed but rather constitute the very fabric of human relations, which depends upon "the constant presence of others who can see and hear and therefore testify to their existence" (p. 95). Thus, action is not lost to decay or the maintenance of life but rather constitutes the process by which we present ourselves and appear to others.

For Arendt, the public and private realms and their corresponding activities are not historically static: that is, they may change in relative importance throughout history. The rise of labour and consumption to a place of political dominance "began when Locke discovered that labor is the source of all property" (p. 101). What emerged in the place of the public realm is a community centred around consumption in which human self-understanding became based on possession, action reduced to acquisition, and self-disclosure reduced to consumption. Instead of experiencing action in the public realm, humans were reduced to mere adjuncts of the cycle of consumption.

Within Arendt's framework there is thus a hollowness to this transitory character of possession, as objects rapidly become irrelevant and "unfashionable," passing through use into decay. In a consumer society, the pursuit of possession means that the products of fabrication no longer provide the lasting and durable physical world within which humans can engage in politics and self-disclosure but are instead themselves consumed. This becomes a self-perpetuating dynamic: just as the rise of consumption erodes the public realm, consumerism is strengthened when we are denied meaningful political life. We are no longer Aristotle's *zoon politikon*, or political animal, but live as if merely *zoon*: according to our possessive proclivities. Work and labour are mistakenly thought to transcend the imperatives of biological preservation, and political life is replaced by the accumulation of goods rather than political action. It is for these reasons that Arendt observes, "it is frequently said that we live in a consumer society" (p. 126).

Paulo Freire: Pedagogy of Possession

As a political philosopher, Hannah Arendt provides an account of how the public sphere itself has been consumed and political action reduced to consumption. Yet a critique of consumerism can also be gleaned from perhaps the most influential educational thinker of the second half of the 20th century and a contemporary of Hannah Arendt. Paulo Freire (1970) provides a compelling account of the dialectical relationship between the oppressed and oppressors in his influential *Pedagogy of the Oppressed*. It might seem odd to discuss this work in this context, as consumerism does not initially appear as a central concept. Yet in a footnote on the first page can be found a reference to our "consumer civilization." I will link the notion of consumerism to several key concepts in this text, including possessing, having, and being, which suggest important links with Arendt's critique of politics as possession and the consumption of the public realm.

A central attribute of Freire's account of the oppressors is their "possessive consciousness" that their entire being is oriented around and dependent upon the experience of possession, that the oppressors are compelled to possess: "without possessions they would lose contact with the world" (1970, p. 40). Freire is worth quoting at length on this matter:

> *In their unrestrained eagerness to possess, the oppressors develop the conviction that it is possible for them to transform everything into objects of their purchasing power ... For the oppressors, what is worthwhile is to have more-always more-even at the cost of the oppressed having less or having nothing. For them, to be is to have and to be the class of the "haves." (p. 40)*

For the oppressor, being is contingent not only on having but also on the process of transforming objects into possessions. Freire outlines how paradoxically in their compulsion to possess, in their objectivizing orientation toward the world, oppressors in fact negate themselves: "in the egoistic pursuit of *having* ... they suffocate in their own possessions and no longer *are*; they merely *have*" (p. 41). Thus, while those characterized by possessive consciousness must *have* to *be*, they in fact *become* what they *have*, undermining the very possibility of being. In their attempt at ontological affirmation they have in fact negated themselves—they no longer *are*, in a world they have in turn consumed. Their "having" negates their own being, their being is consumed by having. But their possessive orientation toward the world is not limited to physical objects. It includes an entire category of persons: the possession of the oppressed: "the oppressed feel like 'things' owned by the oppressors" (p. 48). Thus for Freire, possessive consciousness entails an ontological negation of both the oppressor and the oppressed.

Yet Freire's analysis is not limited to a discussion of this ontological and dialectical relationship of possession; he considers its presence within pedagogical practices and relationships. The trait of possessiveness is apparent when knowledge becomes a "consumable" to be possessed as an object by the learner, and when teaching becomes the delivery of measurable bits of information. Thus emerges Freire's notion of the *banking model of education*, within which learning "becomes an act of depositing, in which the students are the depositories and the teacher is the depositor" (p. 53). This model encourages a passive role for the student: "The more complacently they accept the passive role imposed on them, the more they tend simply to adapt to the world as it is and to the fragmented view of reality deposited in them" (p. 54). The banking model "transforms students into receiving objects," turns ideas into "consumables," learning into consuming, and pedagogy into possession (p. 58). Ultimately, "the educators' task is ... to 'fill' the students by making deposits of information," simply digested by students in a passive process of consumption (p. 57). Freire contrasts this model of the teacher-student relationship with the dialogical relationship of problem-posing education, which "cannot ... become a simple exchange of ideas to be 'consumed' by the discussants" (pp. 70–71). Problem-posing education offers the possibility of a humanized mode of relating to others, a way of promoting an understanding of the self and others that empowers, humanizes, and enlivens the subject in pedagogical pursuits and broader social relations.

Pedagogy of the Oppressed is concerned with the unveiling of systemic oppression, with drawing the human subject as a being of possibility into the world, working toward humanization through critically intervening in reality. For Arendt, action is how we disclose our uniqueness and "insert ourselves into the human world" of the public realm. By linking these two thinkers, we see pedagogy as a form of political action, the communicative insertion of the subject into the world. Today this unveiling, transformation, and insertion, as described by Arendt and Freire, is profoundly compromised by the conflation of schooling and consuming and the invasion of the educational environment by commercial interests.

Conclusion: Resistance and Discomfort

Consumerism is today our new ideology, the paradigm of postmodernity. The commodity and the brand can be considered our new idolatry. From Arendt to Freire, consumerism has been identified as corrosive of political life, a deformation of human consciousness, and a reduction of pedagogy to possession. Consumption is thus a process by which the human being is dehumanized and depoliticized, an active citizenry replaced with complacent consumers, and engaged learners with passive and possessive spectators. Globalization and the commodification of all aspects of human life, the "Malling of America," are increasingly the unchallenged assumptions of our times, accepted as inevitable and irreversible (Baird, 2009). Consumption has become our primary language, literacy the interpretation of commercial symbols, and the act of consumption our primary mode of insertion into the world. We internalize the act of purchasing and translate this experience onto all other human activities and aspects of our social existence, from political engagement to pedagogical practices.

Yet consumption is not action, and consumer society is not a public realm. Consumerism imposes a profound passivity under the illusion of political action and emphasizes individual gratification at the expense of collective action. The expansion of consumer choice is paralleled by the contraction of the public realm. This narrowed vision of political life and contracted understanding of pedagogy profoundly changes our cultural landscape and radically alters the unfolding of democracy.

Although the images of commercial culture are a part of the daily life of students of all ages, the classroom can be a place for their analysis and critique rather than complicit incorporation. Concrete pedagogical action such as "culture jamming" can allow students to engage in activities to decode and deconstruct the messages they are continually bombarded by (Lasn, 1999). This enables students to creatively express their daily experiences with the images of consumption and thereby become active producers of meanings, contributing to culture rather than merely consuming it. The development of "critical media literacy" allows students to break out of the monologue of advertising and initiate a dialogical response based on the students' own creative appropriation and subversion of the messages of consumption. Such practices allow schools and the classroom to remain sites of critical engagement and political resistance rather than simply smooth the progress of accelerating consumerism. However, the classroom is not only a site for opposition and resistance but one in which opposition and resistance will itself be encountered by any teacher who attempts to challenge internalized commercial values. Megan Boler (1999) explores the dynamics of resistance and refusal in her account of the "pedagogy of discomfort," which "begins by inviting educators and students to engage in critical inquiry regarding values and cherished beliefs" (p. 176). Not all students will be receptive to a critique of their way of life and may themselves resist knowing the extent to which they are caught up in this process and have internalized its values.

It could be said that consumer culture is the consumption of culture. But it is also the consumption of the next generation at the hands of schools. Yet it is inadequate to simply argue that we should stop spending, never go shopping, live without money, and have no possessions. Rather, I hope to have revealed certain political and pedagogical problems consumerism creates so as to draw attention to the dangers of various trends occurring in contemporary schooling, problems that Freire and Arendt anticipated and articulated. The "epoch" of consumerism calls the entire project of modernity into question, revealed as a process of possession rather than action or humanization. If schooling assists the students' subjugation to the images and values of consumerism, and is appropriated and undermined by consumer values, then critical pedagogy and political action are jeopardized. Ultimately, we must rethink the extent to which education is complicit in the reproduction of a society centred around consumption so that our era is not remembered as one so insightfully described by Freire as a "consumer civilization."

REFERENCES

Achbar, M. (2004). *The corporation: The pathological pursuit of power.* Toronto: Viking.

Aldridge, A. (2003). *Consumption.* Cambridge, UK: Polity Press.

Arendt, H. (1958). *The human condition.* Chicago: University of Chicago Press.

Arthur, C. (2012). *Financial literacy education: Neoliberalism, the consumer and the citizen.* Rotterdam, The Netherlands: Sense Publishers. doi:10.1007/978-94-6091-918-3

Baird, S.H. (2009). The malling of America: The selling of America's public parks and streets—the economic censorship and suppression of First Amendment rights. Retrieved from http://www.buskersadvocates.org/saamall.html

Barber, B. (2001). *Jihad vs. McWorld: Terrorism's challenge to democracy.* New York: Ballantine Books.

Bell, D. (1976). *The cultural contradictions of capitalism.* New York: Basic Books.

Bocock, R. (1993). *Consumption.* London, UK: Routledge. doi:10.4324/9780203313114

Boler, M. (1999). *Feeling power: Emotions and education.* New York: Routledge.

Boyles, D. (1998). *American education and corporations: The free market goes to schools.* New York: Garland Publishing.

Campbell, K., & Davis-Packard, K. (2000, September 18). How ads get kids to say, I want it! *Christian Science Monitor.* Retrieved from http://www.csmonitor.com/2000/0918/p1s1.html

Duarte, E.M. (2000). Thinking together as one: Freire's rewriting of Husserl. *Philosophy of Education Yearbook, 180*–188. Retrieved from http://ojs.ed.uiuc.edu/index.php/pes/article/view/1968/674

Freire, P. (1970). *Pedagogy of the oppressed.* New York: Continuum.

Froese-Germain, B., Hawkey, C., Larose, A., McAdie, P., & Shaker, E. (2006). *Commercialism in Canadian schools: Who's calling the shots?* Ottawa: Canadian Teachers' Federation.

Galbraith, J.K. (1968). *The affluent society.* New York: Penguin.

Giroux, H. (1994). *Disturbing pleasures: Learning popular culture.* New York: Routledge.

Giroux, H. (1999). *The mouse that roared: Disney and the end of innocence.* New York: Rowman and Littlefield Publishers.

Gordon, M. (2001). *Hannah Arendt and education: Renewing our common world.* Boulder, CO: Westview Press.

Gosselin, P.G., & Vieth, W. (2001, September 17). As markets reopen, US seeks to prop up economy. *L.A. Times.* Retrieved from http://articles.latimes.com/2001/sep/17/news/mn-46648

Graham, K.A. (2004, February 22). Is this any way to pay for public education? *The Philadelphia Inquirer.* Retrieved from http://www.commercialalert.org/news/archive/2004/02/is-this-any-way-to-pay-for-public-education

Greene, M. (1988). *The dialectic of freedom.* New York: Teachers College Press.

Greenspan, R. (2003, September 16). The kids are alright with spending. *ClickZ Demographic Statistics*. Retrieved from http://www.clickz.com/clickz/news/1708006/the-kids-are-alright-with-spending

Jackson, J. (2001, November 1). Patriotic shopping: "Neither caring nor moral." *Fairness and Accuracy in Reporting (FAIR)*. Retrieved from http://fair.org/extra-online-articles/patriotic-shopping/

Jonathan, R. (1997). *Illusory freedoms: Liberalism, education and the market*. Oxford, UK: Blackwell Publishers.

Kenway, J., & Bullen, E. (2001). *Consuming children: Education-entertainment-advertising*. Philadelphia: Open University Press.

Kincheloe, J., & Steinberg, S. (Eds.). (1997). *Kinder culture: The corporate construction of childhood*. Boulder, CO: Westview.

Klein, N. (2000). *No logo: Taking aim at the brand bullies*. Toronto: Vintage Canada.

Lasn, K. (1999). *Culture jam: The uncooling of America*. New York: Eaglebrook.

Macpherson, C.B. (1962). *The political theory of possessive individualism*. Oxford, UK: Oxford University Press.

Marx, K. (1906). *Das kapital: A critique of political economy*. New York: Modern Library. (Original work published 1867)

Molnar, A. (2003–2004). *Virtually everywhere: Marketing to children in America's schools—the seventh annual report on schoolhouse commercialism trends*. Tempe, AZ: Commercialism in Education Research Unit, Education Policy Studies Laboratory, Arizona State University.

Molnar, A., Boninger, F., & Fogarty, J. (2011). *The educational cost of schoolhouse commercialism*. Boulder, CO: Commercialism in Education Research Unit.

Norris, T. (2011). *Consuming schools: Commercialism and the end of politics*. Toronto: University of Toronto Press. doi:10.1007/s11217-010-9217-4

Ritzer, G. (2001). *The McDonaldization of society*. Thousand Oaks, CA: Pine Forge Press.

Sandel, M. (2004, November 1). *Are we still a commonwealth?* Retrieved from http://masshumanities.org/f04_awsc

Schor, J. (2004, September 11). Those ads are enough to make your kids sick. *Washington Post*. Retrieved from http://www.washingtonpost.com/wp-dyn/articles/A13374-2004Sep11.html

Smith, A. (1936). *The wealth of nations*. New York: Modern Library.

Veblen, T. (1931). *The theory of the leisure class*. New York: Modern Library. (Original work published 1899)

NOTES

1 I explore this conflation of political speech and commercial discourse, as well as the nature of consumerism and its impact on education, more thoroughly in Norris (2011).

2 In a paper at the Philosophy of Education Society Conference, Eduardo Duarte (2000) describes dialogical parallels between Arendt's account of thinking and Freire's "critical consciousness."

3 Numerous examples of how corporations enforce their presence, from suspending students who criticize the corporations to preventing teachers from turning off Channel One, can be found in Boyles (1998), Giroux (1994), Kincheloe and Steinberg (1997), and Klein (2000).

4 None of these three terms are my own. To learn more about the origin and use of these three terms, simply type them into any search engine.

18

High-Stakes Testing, Educational Aims and Ideals, and Responsible Assessment

*Harvey Siegel**

*This chapter was originally published in *Theory and Research in Education* (2)3, 219–233. Copyright © 2004 by Sage Publications. Reprinted by permission of Sage.

Introduction

Why engage in testing in general and in high-stakes testing in particular? There are many answers to this question: to monitor student performance, to measure teacher and/or school effectiveness, to ensure accountability, etc. Some reasons for such testing are good, others not. But a key question, not often asked, concerns the relation of testing to our considered educational ideals. In what follows, I will briefly discuss a relatively uncontroversial aim of education, namely that of fostering critical thinking, after which I will consider the degree to which current high-stakes testing practices contribute to the achievement of that aim. I will argue that while some testing is perfectly legitimate, current high-stakes testing practice is largely inimical to the achievement of our most defensible educational ends.[1]

What Are Our Educational Aims and Ideals?

The history of educational thought is littered with suggested aims of education. Fostering creativity, producing docile workers or good citizens, maximizing freedom or individual happiness, developing religious faith and commitment, and fostering ideological purity are just some of the many educational aims that serious educational thinkers have proposed. This is not the place to offer a systematic analysis and evaluation of the multitude of proposed educational aims. Instead, I will briefly articulate an aim that is widely accepted in our current educational *milieu*: that of critical thinking.

On the conception of critical thinking I have defended elsewhere,[2] the critical thinker is one who is *appropriately moved by reasons.* Critical thinking involves skills and abilities that facilitate or make possible the appropriate assessment of reasons. It also involves dispositions, habits of mind, and character traits. Let us briefly consider these two dimensions of critical thinking in turn.

A critical thinker is one who has significant skill and ability with respect to the evaluation of reasons and arguments. For to say that one is *appropriately* moved by reasons is to say that one believes, judges, and acts in conformity with the probative or evidential force with which one's reasons support one's beliefs, judgments, and actions. In order properly to evaluate beliefs, actions, and judgments, and the reasons that are thought to support them, a critical thinker must have both a solid understanding of the principles of reason assessment and significant ability to utilize that understanding. This dimension of critical thinking may be called the *reason assessment* component of critical thinking.

There are at least two general sorts of principles of reason assessment: general, or *subject-neutral*, principles and *subject-specific* principles. General, subject-neutral principles are the sort that apply and are relevant to many different contexts and types of claims; their applicability is not restricted to some particular subject area. Principles of logic—both formal and informal—are subject-neutral principles, as are most of the principles typically taught in traditional critical-thinking courses. Using statistical evidence well, properly evaluating observational evidence and causal claims, and recognizing instances of fallacious reasoning such as begging the question all involve subject-neutral skills and abilities of reason assessment. To the extent that a student/person is a critical thinker, she is the master of a wide variety of subject-neutral principles of reason assessment.

Unlike these subject-neutral principles, some principles apply only to rather restricted domains; in those domains, though, they are central to proper reason assessment. Such principles are subject specific: they guide the assessment of reasons, but only in their local domain. The critical thinker must have some knowledge of the subject-specific principles operative in various domains in order properly to assess reasons in those domains. The grasp and utilization of subject-specific principles of reason assessment typically requires subject-specific knowledge as well. For example, to evaluate the claim that my symptoms provide evidence that I have malaria, I must know something about medicine. To evaluate the claim that because the sun is in position P I should use shutter speed S, I must know something about photography. The principle "yellowish tinged skin indicates liver malfunction" will properly guide judgments and decisions in the doctor's office but not in the banana section of the local produce market; "The failure of premises to entail their conclusion constitutes a defect in an argument" properly guides argument evaluation in deductive logic classes but not in most scientific contexts. In general, then, principles of reason assessment can be both subject neutral and subject specific, and the critical thinker manifests a mastery of both sorts of principle. This is because the ability to assess reasons and their warranting force is central to critical thinking.

In addition to skills and the grasp of principles of reason assessment, the critical thinker must also have certain attitudes, dispositions, habits of mind, and character traits. This complex can be called the *critical spirit* component of critical thinking. It is not enough that a person be *able* to assess reasons properly; to be a critical thinker, she must *actually engage* in competent reason assessment and be generally disposed to do so. She must habitually seek reasons on which to base belief and action, and she must genuinely base belief, judgment, and action on such reasons. She must, that is, be appropriately *moved* by reasons. Given that there are compelling reasons to believe, judge, or act in a certain way, the critical thinker must be moved by such reasons to so believe, judge, or act. She must have habits of mind that make routine the search for reasons. She must be disposed to base belief, judgment, and action on reasons according to which they are sanctioned. The critical thinker must *value* reasons and the warrant they provide. She must be disposed to reject arbitrariness and partiality.[3] She must *care* about reasons, reasoning, and the living of a life in which reasons play a central role.

Thus far, I have tried to emphasize two points. First, reasons have *probative* or *evidential force*—that is, they support the beliefs or claims for which they are reasons to some degree or other—and the critical thinker must be proficient at evaluating the probative force of reasons, that is, the degree to which they support the relevant beliefs or claims. This is required for the critical thinker to be *appropriately* moved by reasons. Second, reasons have what might be called *normative impact*: they guide rational belief, judgment and action, and the critical thinker must be so guided if she is to be appropriately *moved* by reasons. Probative force and normative impact are both key features of reasons. They are each captured by this conception of critical thinking, according to which the critical thinker is appropriately moved by reasons. On this conception, both skills and abilities of reason assessment and the attitudes, dispositions, habits of mind, and character traits constitutive of the critical spirit are crucially important dimensions of critical thinking.

In *Educating Reason* (1988, Ch. 3) I offered four reasons for thinking that critical thinking, as just conceptualized, constitutes a fundamental educational ideal: respect for students as persons, self-sufficiency and preparation for adulthood, initiation into the rational traditions, and democratic living. I will not review the discussion of these four reasons here, except to say that in my view the fundamental justification for regarding critical thinking as an educational ideal is the first, moral one: conceiving and conducting education in ways that do not take as central the fostering of students' abilities and dispositions to think critically fails to treat students with respect as persons, and so fails to treat them in a morally acceptable way.[4]

But it is worth pointing out, before leaving this section, that taking the aim of critical thinking seriously has important implications for citizenship and democratic society, since it suggests that matters of public concern be decided in free and open deliberation, on the basis of relevant reasons. In this respect taking critical thinking seriously as an educational aim is especially appropriate in democratic societies such as our own (Scheffler, 1989; Sirotnik, 2002).[5]

The Alleged Arbitrariness of Judgment

What subjects or items of knowledge are worth studying and learning? What counts as acceptable or unacceptable pedagogy? How should we assess student learning? How should we assess our own educational practices?

Such questions as these, which are fundamental to the enterprise of schooling, are notoriously difficult to answer in a way that a clear and substantial majority of parents, teachers, and citizens find compelling. Part of the reason for the difficulty is that answering them requires appeal to *criteria*, which can themselves be controversial. For example, if a school-board member argues that the high-school science curriculum should include units on astronomy but not astrology—or, more dramatically, evolution but not "creation science"—both fellow school-board members and unconvinced parents might disagree that an appeal to the criterion of *contemporary scientific opinion* is legitimate, since some might contend that that criterion privileges the worldview of atheistic "secular humanism." Similar cases can readily be found of curricular controversy over literature/language arts curricula whose choice of texts—for example, *Fahrenheit 451, The Adventures of Tom Sawyer,* or a book by Judy Blume—is made on the basis of criteria that are rejected by others. Other cases concern criteria for student performance. For example, some hold, but others deny, that *the ability to read at grade level* or *the ability to write "standard English"* are appropriate criteria for promotion or graduation.

Even if questions concerning criteria could be resolved without controversy, further difficult issues would remain. Suppose, for example, that a community reaches a consensus that one criterion for awarding a high-school diploma is the ability to read. Once we agree that ability to read is a relevant criterion, we immediately face the question: *How well* must the student read in order to graduate? That is, what *standard* of reading competence must the student meet? What counts as "meeting" the relevant standard?

Questions concerning criteria (i.e., the considerations deemed appropriate and relevant for educational decisions) and questions concerning standards (the degree to which, or level at which, the criteria are deemed to have been satisfactorily met) are controversial. This is at least in part because such decisions seem be a matter of *judgment*, and judgments such as these are often thought to be inherently and unavoidably *arbitrary*. As we have seen, at least two distinct sorts of arbitrariness threaten: arbitrariness concerning the determination of appropriate criteria, and arbitrariness concerning the determination of appropriate standards or levels at which the criteria must be met. All such determinations rely on judgment. Is such judgment inevitably arbitrary?

An affirmative answer to this question poses a grave threat to the practice of testing. For if such basic educational judgments as these are problematically arbitrary, then both the results of testing and the uses to which they are put will also seem arbitrary. Can grades and test scores, or decisions to keep students from promotion or graduation or to "track" them into particular streams, be justified, if the basis on which such decisions are made is arbitrary? It appears not. So advocates of testing have a vital interest in overcoming the charge of arbitrariness.

I believe that the charge of arbitrariness can be overcome; educational judgments concerning both criteria and standards can be non-arbitrarily justified. But the charge cannot be overcome in a way that will bring comfort to advocates of high-stakes testing. Judgments concerning both criteria and standards (and so decisions based on them) can be justified non-arbitrarily by relating them to appropriate educational aims and ideals. And judgments concerning those aims and ideals can themselves be justified non-arbitrarily by appeal to relevant arguments concerning the nature and aims of education. But advocates of high-stakes testing defend such testing by appeal to educational aims and ideals that fail to be adequately supported by such arguments. The result is that such testing is defeated, not by arbitrariness, but by its resting on indefensible aims and ideals, and by its concomitant failure to be informed by more worthy and fundamental ideals.

Let us consider this alleged arbitrariness of judgment concerning standards and criteria in the context of a particular test, the Florida Comprehension Assessment Test (FCAT). Doing so will help us see that the real problem is not arbitrariness but rather the striking "disconnect" and incompatibility between our testing practices and our considered educational aims and ideals.

A Brief Case Study: Florida's FCAT

The FCAT[6] is a descendent of earlier minimum competency tests[7] (*FCAT Briefing Book*, 2001, p. 18). It tests students in several areas and at several grade levels, and passing it is required for both promotion to the next grade (passing the reading portion of the test in grade 3 is required for promotion to grade 4) and receipt of a high-school diploma. Its aim, as articulated by the Florida Commission on Educational Reform and Accountability and adopted by the State Board of Education, is to "assess ... student learning in Florida" in a way that will "raise educational expectations for students and help them compete for jobs in the global marketplace" (*FCAT Briefing Book*, 2001, p. 18). Passing the FCAT requires meeting the standards articulated in the *Sunshine State Standards*:[8]

The FCAT content is derived from the Sunshine State Standards adopted by the State Board of Education. The Standards are broad statements of what students should know and be able to do, and they are subdivided into smaller units called "benchmarks." The FCAT measures certain of these benchmarks in reading, writing, and mathematics. (FCAT Briefing Book, 2001, p. 7; examples of these benchmarks appear here)

The FCAT is now a central component of Florida's Student Assessment Program, the primary purposes of which are "to provide information needed to improve the public schools by enhancing the learning gains of all students and to inform parents of the educational progress of their public school children" (*The 2002 FL Statutes*, Title XLVIII, K-20 Education Code, Ch.1008, Assessment and Accountability: 1). As Charlie Crist, the former Commissioner of Education of the State of Florida, put the point:

it is important to remember that the FCAT is not an end in itself, but a means to an end. The result is an improved education for Florida's children and increased accountability for its schools. (FCAT Briefing Book, 2001, p. 2)

Students are required to take the FCAT because:

Florida students are increasingly expected to display high-level learning and perform complex problem solving. Today, the job market requires people who are proficient in advanced mathematics and who can read and construct meaning from difficult and technical texts. The FCAT is given to measure achievement of the Sunshine State Standards that are being taught to and learned by Florida students. (FCAT Briefing Book, 2001, p. 5)[9]

The passages just cited mention several aims or purposes of the FCAT. The test is intended to: assess student learning; raise the educational expectations of students; enhance student job competitiveness; ensure that successful students (i.e., those who pass the test) are minimally competent in reading, writing, and mathematics in virtue of their meeting the benchmarks set out in the *Sunshine State Standards*; provide information needed to improve the public schools and the education students receive in them; inform parents of the educational progress of their public-school children; increase accountability for Florida public schools; and ensure that successful students are proficient in advanced mathematics and can read and construct meaning from difficult and technical texts, because the "job market requires" such people.

There are well-known objections to high-stakes testing programs, most of which have been made regarding FCAT. One is that it is discriminatory because members of certain groups fail the test at higher rates than others.[10] Another is that the FCAT has become so dominating a concern of school and district administrators, because student performance fundamentally affects school funding, that administrators sacrifice valuable aspects of the curriculum and require teachers to "teach to the test."[11] A third is that such testing contributes to teacher demoralization and attrition (Sirotnik, 2002, p. 662), at a time when Florida is experiencing a severe teacher shortage. While these objections are in my view extremely serious, I will not discuss them here. Instead, I want to focus on the just-cited explicit aims of the test.

These stated aims reveal a conception of the aims of education that is worth spelling out a bit. That conception is largely *economic*: the aim of public education in Florida is overwhelmingly that of ensuring that students are able to attain gainful employment and function adequately in the local, state, national, and global economies. The more specific content aims mentioned, such as meeting the benchmarks in reading, writing, and mathematics set out in the *Sunshine State Standards*, are justified in terms of the broader economic conception of the aim of education articulated: it is important for students to meet these standards because if they do not they will not be able to compete in the global economy in which they find themselves.

The rationale for the test is also importantly *political*: we require students to take the FCAT because we want to hold schools accountable and make sure our tax dollars are well spent, that we taxpayers are getting our money's worth. But this political rationale is itself understood ultimately in economic terms. We hold schools accountable in accordance with our standards: our schools are doing well enough when enough of our students pass the FCAT and other tests because we think that passing the tests ensures that they have a reasonable chance of succeeding, or at least surviving, economically.

To be clear, I am not suggesting that the State of Florida explicitly or officially conceives of all the aims of the FCAT, or of public education more generally, in wholly economic terms. As we have seen, several of the articulated aims of the FCAT involve non-economic matters involving levels of student mastery of specific subject matter, student expectations, etc. But the offered rationale for such non-economic aims is itself economic: it is important for students to achieve such mastery because their successful functioning in the marketplace depends upon it.

This economic conception of the aim of education is *instrumental*: do well in school so you can have a good job and have a decent place in the state, national, and global economies when your school days are finished. While there is perhaps nothing wrong with wanting students to have good jobs and the benefits that go with them, this is a remarkably narrow view of education. It is narrow in at least two ways.

First, it ignores the whole host of broad aims of education articulated in the history of educational thought. In doing so, it ignores widely acknowledged and more fundamental aims of education—for example, enhancing knowledge and understanding, fostering rationality and good judgment, opening minds and overcoming provincialism and close-mindedness, enlarging the imagination, fostering creativity and caring, and so on. While I do not claim that all aims articulated in the history of educational thought are worthy of our embrace, I do claim—although I cannot argue the point here—that at least the specific aims just mentioned are indeed so worthy, and that an education that ignores them does so at its peril.

I immediately concede that the aims just mentioned are difficult to test for. But that they are difficult to test for is a weakness of our tests, not of those aims. Israel Scheffler (1989) decries the too common practice of focusing on "externals," such as test results, "because they are easier to get hold of than the central phenomena of insight and the growth of understanding" that should be our primary educational concern; Scheffler urges us to keep our educational eye on those central phenomena, rather than casting our gaze on less important but more easily tested matters (p. 90). And he cites a highly relevant passage from William James (1958), to which defenders of high-stakes testing should pay particular heed:

> Be patient, then, and sympathetic with the type of mind that cuts a poor figure in examinations. It may, in the long examination which life sets us, come out in the end in better shape than the glib and ready reproducer, its passions being deeper, its purposes more worthy, its combining power less commonplace, and its total mental output consequently more important. (p. 101; as cited in Scheffler, 1989, p. 91)

Richard Pring (1999) offers a more recent articulation of the point, with specific reference to the *moral* dimensions of education:

> [T]he control of education by government of what children should know and how they should learn, sustained by an all-pervasive system of assessment, leaves little room within the schools for that deliberation of what is worthwhile and for that forming of a moral perspective which is essentially unpredictable, not to be captured in a detailed assessment profile … The grave danger is that, in making schools more 'effective' in reaching the goals laid down by government and its agencies, this central moral goal of education finds no place. (p. 159)

And in words reminiscent of James and Scheffler, Pring (1999) tellingly suggests that tests and assessment regimes of the sort we have been considering "necessarily have to promote the trivial, for that alone is measurable, and to ignore that which is most important" (p. 165). While the point may be somewhat overstated, since it has not been shown that only the trivial is measurable, Pring's insistence that a focus on testing tends to distract educational efforts from the most important educational matters is well worth our attention, for this does indeed appear to be a basic flaw of the FCAT and other current high-stakes testing efforts. The fundamental aims mentioned above are harder to test for and to measure than the knowledge and skills tested for by the FCAT, to be sure. But they are nevertheless our most fundamental aims. Losing sight of them and focusing our tests instead on more easily tested items is rather like looking for our lost keys under the streetlight even though we know we lost them in the poorly illuminated bushes (Sirotnik, 2002, p. 666).

Second, and perhaps more important, the instrumental, economic view of the aims of education underlying the FCAT conceives of students as little more than future "workers" or, more generously, future "economic agents"—that is, as little more than cogs in an all-encompassing economic engine. In so doing, it manifests a wholly inadequate view of students because it fails to recognize them as ends-in-themselves rather than as mere means, with interests other than the economic ones emphasized by their institutions of public education.

There is, of course, nothing wrong with a strong economy. But to see education in strictly instrumental, economic terms is to do a great disservice to students (Sirotnik, 2002, p. 664). It is to treat them immorally because it fails to treat them with respect, as autonomous agents whose desires, needs, and interests ought not to be subordinated to economic or other imposed ends (Siegel, 1988, Ch. 3).

It cannot and should not be denied that education is highly valuable in both economic and other, broadly social ways. It plays an important and productive role in securing a whole host of public goods, including its important contributions to fostering and maintaining community, civility, tolerance for alternative worldviews and ways of life, *and* a productive economy. But these are not the only, or even the most important, dimensions of education's value. It is also valuable in virtue of its contributions to student knowledge, understanding, open-mindedness, independence of thought, and autonomy, things that are good independently of their acknowledged economic and social payoffs. It is this central dimension of education—and a corresponding view of students as persons, rather than as merely economic agents—that a focus on high-stakes testing ignores.

The point is most easily seen by considering our earlier discussion of critical thinking. If our educational aim is to foster in students the skills, abilities, dispositions, habits of mind, and character traits of the critical thinker, an education focused on the aims articulated by the State of Florida, to which the FCAT is the means, would be at best sorely lacking in attention to those aspects of a student's education that are crucial to the achievement of critical thinking. There is a tremendous disparity between the conceptions of education offered by the State of Florida in its articulated rationale for the FCAT and that suggested by the ideal of critical thinking. For the former, education is essentially concerned with helping students to become competent masters of a range of linguistic and computational skills, able eventually to garner occupational skills sufficient for maintaining a place in the existing economic order. For the latter, education goes far beyond such considerations by seeking to inculcate the skills, abilities, dispositions, habits of mind, and character traits constitutive of the critical thinker, and in so doing ensuring and honouring the student's autonomy. This is a far deeper conception of education and its aims.

That education should be concerned with fostering students' autonomy is a philosophically very important point, one that has enormous practical ramifications as well. In an education that takes autonomy seriously, we do not strive to determine students' future life trajectories, for we take that to be the prerogative of the student, and we recognize that the years of public education end far too quickly for such determination. Indeed, insofar as we embrace that aspect of the ideal of critical thinking that highlights student autonomy and self-sufficiency, we recognize that students' futures are essentially always open. We educate so as to enable the student to *create* her future, not to submit to it.[12] The aim of education is not to shape the mind of the student or to prepare the student for predetermined roles in the social and economic orders. It is rather to *liberate* the mind by enabling the student both to envision possibilities and to evaluate their desirability intelligently (Scheffler, 1989, pp. 143–144). It is far from clear that an education built upon the economic, instrumental conception of the aims of education will do much to further that liberatory end.

I do not mean to argue that the FCAT, or high-stakes testing more generally, is inimical to critical thinking. I have no doubt that some of the knowledge and skills for which the FCAT tests is of positive value from the point of view of the development of critical thinking. But I do want to suggest that that ideal is given very short shrift in an education focused on high-stakes testing. In such an education, the autonomy of the student and the liberation of her mind are largely ignored. The degree to which a student emerges from such an education as a critical thinker is neither an aim of that education to maximize nor of testing to reveal. The instrumental, economic aims of education that the FCAT strives to foster and measure are exceedingly narrow and shallow, as judged from the vantage point of philosophical reflection on education and its proper aims.

Conclusion: Toward Responsible Assessment

So, is the FCAT arbitrary? It is not, in my view, problematically so. While establishing precise pass/fail levels might be a matter of judgment, and in that unproblematic sense arbitrary, the knowledge and skills articulated by the Sunshine State Standards, taught in the classrooms of Florida public schools and tested for by the FCAT, are not arbitrary. Their weakness, rather, is that they are informed by a very narrow and philosophically uninformed vision of the aims of education. A well-educated person is much more than a person who is able to function successfully in the marketplace. But the latter is, for all intents and purposes, the full vision of the well-educated person conceived by the State of Florida and its educational visionaries. It is the paucity of that vision that renders the FCAT problematic. The narrow conception of education and its aims presupposed by the FCAT, and by other, similar, high-stakes testing initiatives, is inadequate. So, too, therefore, is the education for which the FCAT and similar tests are the chief measures of minimal competence.

From the point of view of critical thinking, the FCAT is not arbitrary. It is, rather, inadequate and indefensible, both as educational practice and as an embodiment of a serious conception of education. Responsible assessment must be informed and guided by our richest, deepest, and philosophically most defensible educational ideals. Its failure to be so informed and guided is the FCAT's most fundamental flaw.

I trust it is clear that I am not arguing against testing per se. Responsible assessment of student learning and understanding is educationally both legitimate and important. But responsible assessment must be conducted in a way that furthers, or at least does not frustrate, our considered educational aims and ideals (Sirotnik, 2002). High-stakes testing, like Florida's FCAT, unfortunately does not further our efforts to graduate students who are good critical thinkers. Indeed, it is typically conducted without any attention either to that or to any other defensible and fundamental educational ideal. This is the basic flaw of much educational practice, including that involving high-stakes testing like the FCAT.

ACKNOWLEDGEMENTS

This article was presented at a symposium organized by the Association for Philosophy of Education on "School Accountability and High Stakes Testing" at the Eastern Division meeting of the American Philosophical Association in Washington, DC, in December 2003. I am grateful to James Dwyer for the invitation to participate in the session and to him, the other speakers, Randall Curren and Francis Shrag, and the commentators, Catherine Z. Elgin and Nel Noddings, for their excellent criticisms and suggestions. I dedicate this article to Don and Barbara Arnstine and the late Jim McClellan, three friends who have taught me much about the deficiencies of high-stakes testing. I regret my failure to address important problems caused by the *standardization* and neglect of *individualization* imposed by such testing. For a brief discussion, see Sirotnik (2002, p. 666; 669–670). Sirotnik's (2002) call for systems of accountability to "honor the professional judgment of educators" (p. 669) and his project to develop a more effective approach to "responsible accountability" are I think extremely important. This article was originally written at Sirotnik's invitation and appears (in a version focusing more than this one on matters of accountability and the place of high-stakes testing within broad systems of accountability) under the title "What ought to matter in public schooling: judgment, standards, and responsible accountability," in Kenneth A. Sirotnik (Ed.) (2004). *Holding Accountability Accountable: What Ought to Matter in Public Education* (pp. 51–65). New York: Teachers College Press, © 2004 by Teachers College, Columbia University. All rights reserved. I am grateful to Sirotnik both for the invitation and for his insight, advice, and guidance with respect to the literature on accountability.

REFERENCES

Bailin, S., & Siegel, H. (2003). Critical thinking. In N. Blake, P. Smeyers, R. Smith, & P. Standish (Eds.), *The Blackwell guide to the philosophy of education* (pp. 181–193). Oxford: Blackwell.

Curren, R. (1995). Coercion and the ethics of grading and testing. *Educational Theory, 45*(4), 425–441. doi:10.1111/j.1741-5446.1995.00425.x

FCAT Briefing Book (2001) Florida Department of Education. Retrieved May 2003 from http://www.firn.edu/doe

James, W. (1958). *Talks to teachers on psychology; and to students on some of life's ideals.* New York: Norton.

Law about the FCAT (2002). The 2002 Florida Statutes. Retrieved May 2003 from www.flsenate.gov

Lessons Learned—FCAT, Sunshine State Standards and Instructional Implications (2002) Florida Department of Education. Retrieved May 2003 from http://www.fldoe.org

Pring, R. (1999). Neglected educational aims: moral seriousness and social commitment. In R. Marples (Ed.), *The aims of education* (pp. 157–172). London: Routledge.

Scheffler, I. (1989). Moral education and the democratic ideal. In I. Scheffler (Ed.), *Reason and teaching* (pp. 136–145). Indianapolis: Hackett.

Siegel, H. (1988). *Educating reason: Rationality, critical thinking, and education.* New York: Routledge.

Siegel, H. (1997). *Rationality redeemed? Further dialogues on an educational ideal.* London: Routledge.

Siegel, H. (1999). What (good) are thinking dispositions? *Educational Theory, 49*(2), 207–221. doi:10.1111/j.1741-5446.1999.00207.x

Siegel, H. (2003). Cultivating reason. In R. Curren (Ed.), *A companion to the philosophy of education* (pp. 305–319). Oxford: Blackwell. doi:10.1002/9780470996454.ch22

Sirotnik, K.A. (2002). Promoting responsible accountability in schools and education. *Phi Delta Kappan, 83*(9), 662–673.

Technical Report: For Operational Test Administrations of the 2000 Florida Comprehensive Assessment Test (2002). Florida Department of Education, 27 March. Retrieved May 2003 from http://www.fldoe.org

---

NOTES

1 I do not, in what follows, address more general questions concerning the ethics of testing and grading. (For an excellent discussion, see Curren, 1995.)

2 Siegel (1988, 1997, 2003) and Bailin and Siegel (2003). The following several paragraphs are taken, with some changes, from the introduction to Siegel (1997).

3 I offer an account of thinking dispositions in Siegel (1999).

4 This alleged justification is "Enlightenment" or "modernist" in its individualistic orientation, just as the conception of critical thinking allegedly justified by it is equally modernist in its valorization of rationality. Criticisms of this dimension of my conception of critical thinking, and the case for regarding it as a fundamental educational ideal, are systematically addressed in Siegel (1997, Part 2; 2003) and Bailin and Siegel (2003).

5 It is also worth noting that while critical thinking is the only educational aim I have briefly defended here, the criticism of current high-stakes testing practice offered below does not depend on the acceptance of that particular aim.

6 As Nel Noddings rightly suggests, it is important to understand the broader political context in which current high-stakes testing takes place and, in particular, the role of the federal No Child Left Behind Act. I regret my inability to discuss these further here, though I should note that minimum competency tests, of which the FCAT is a descendant, considerably predate that act. The information concerning the FCAT presented below is taken from the State of Florida's, and especially the Florida Department of Education's, own publications and web resources.
I am grateful to my student Ana Cristancho for help in finding, evaluating, and assembling these and other relevant resources, and for helpful advice on an earlier draft.

7 It is consequently not surprising that the FCAT shares many of the problems that plagued the earlier minimum competency tests, including those involving alleged arbitrariness (Siegel, 1988, Ch. 7).

8 *Sunshine State Standards.* Available at http://sunshinestatestandards.net/.

9 A somewhat fuller description of the FCAT and the process that led to it—and that makes clear its status as a minimum competency test—is given by the State of Florida:

In 1996 the Florida education community identified a core body of knowledge and skills that all Florida students should have. This body of knowledge, called the Sunshine State Standards, *spanned seven content areas (language arts, mathematics, science, social studies, health and physical education, foreign language, and the arts). The* Sunshine State Standards *were divided into four grade-level clusters (Pre-K–2, 3–5, 6–8 and 9–12) that were further subdivided into benchmarks. By adopting the* Sunshine State Standards *in May 1996, the Florida Board of Education defined a clear set of standards upon which to build an equitable system of student assessment and school accountability.*

In 1995 and 1996 the Florida Educational Reform and Accountability Commission recommended the development of a statewide assessment system. These recommendations, called the Florida Comprehensive Assessment Design, led to development of the Florida Comprehensive Assessment Test (FCAT). The FCAT was designed to augment the existing language arts assessment in writing at Grades 4, 8, and 10 (the Florida Writing Assessment Program) by adding an assessment of reading at the same grade levels. In addition, an assessment of mathematics was added at Grades 5, 8, and 10. The reading component of FCAT would assess the reading-related elements of the Sunshine State Standards *in language arts and the mathematics component would assess as many of the benchmarks in the Mathematics* Sunshine State Standards *as appropriate for the selected grade levels. The Comprehensive Assessment Design also specified other features for the new assessment, including application of skills in cognitively challenging situations and inclusion of constructed-response questions (performance tasks) that require students to demonstrate their understanding instead of just choosing a correct answer. (*Lessons Learned—FCAT, Sunshine State Standards *and* Instructional Implications, *2002)*

10 African-American students do significantly less well on the FCAT exams than Hispanic-American students, who in turn do significantly less well than White non-Hispanic students. (For some relevant data, see *Technical Report: For Operational Test Administrations of the 2000 Florida Comprehensive Assessment Test,* 2002, pp. 10–13). In May 2003 the press reported that more than 12,500 Florida high-school seniors—mainly African-American and Hispanic-American—were expected to leave high school without obtaining their diplomas because of their failure to pass the FCAT, despite their having met all other requirements for graduation. In addition, more than 40,000 third-graders in Florida (approximately 23% of the total) would not be promoted to fourth grade because of their failing FCAT scores. Needless to say, the issue is politically extremely contentious.

11 The State of Florida vigorously denies that FCAT encourages teachers to "teach to the test"; anecdotal and other data (including the experience of my daughter, at the time of writing about to complete eighth grade) suggest otherwise. For the state's defense, see the *FCAT Briefing Book,* p. 6, and other documents posted at the Florida Department of Education website.

12 The preceding three sentences are taken, with changes, from Siegel, 1988, p. 122.

19

The Idiocy of Policy

The Antidemocratic Curriculum of High-Stakes Testing

Wayne Au*

*This chapter was first published as Au, W. (2010).
The idiocy of policy: The anti-democratic curriculum of high-stakes testing.
Critical Education, *1*(1), 1–15. Reproduced with permission.

Introduction

Public education in the United States is currently dominated by policies centred upon systems of high-stakes, standardized testing. As part of a broader political agenda, and despite the persistent production of inequality (e.g., Au, 2009b; Ladson-Billings, 2006), such policies have been advanced based upon a consistent rhetoric of democracy, couched in terms of individual choice, individual equality, equal opportunity for achievement, and offering the promise of leaving no child behind (Apple, 2006; Gay, 2007). In this chapter I seek to interrogate the relationship between education policy predicated on high-stakes testing and democratic ideals, particularly as they are communicated through policy structure. I begin here by defining high-stakes testing and providing a short history of the modern-day, high-stakes testing movement in the United States. I then move on to discuss the research on how these tests operate as a form of control over classroom practices and learning. Such control, I argue, is a product of education policy structure itself, which makes use of high-stakes testing to assert "bureaucratic control" (Apple, 1995) within systems of education. When viewed through the lens of democratic education, particularly Parker's (2005) discussion of the need to teach against idiocy through the encouragement of diversity and deliberation in schools, I conclude that policies based on systems of high-stakes testing teach teachers and students a curriculum of anti-democracy vis-à-vis policy structure.

High-Stakes Testing in the United States

High-stakes tests are a part of a *policy design* (Schneider & Ingram, 1997) that "links the score on one set of standardized tests to grade promotion, high school graduation and, in some cases, teacher and principal salaries and tenure decisions" (Orfield & Wald, 2000, p. 38). As part of the accountability movement, stakes are also deemed high because the results of tests, including the ranking and categorization of schools, teachers, and children by test results, are reported to the public (McNeil, 2000). "High-stakes testing" thus simultaneously implies two things: (a) standardized testing as the technology and tool/instrument used for measurement, and (b) educational policy erected around the standardized test results that attaches consequences to test results.

While the history of standardized testing in the United States reaches back to the IQ, eugenics, and scientific management movements in education of the early 1900s (Au, 2009b), the modern-day, high-stakes, standardized-testing movement can effectively be traced to the publication of *A Nation At Risk* (National Commission on Excellence in Education, 1983). This Reagan-era report sounded an alarm within public education in the United States, and despite that much of the report's education crisis was found to be manufactured (Berliner & Biddle, 1995), the report had a tremendous impact on educational policy. Fifty-four state-level commissions on education were created within one year of the report's publication, and within three years of publication 26 states raised graduation requirements and 35 states instituted comprehensive education reforms that revolved around testing and increased course loads for students (Kornhaber & Orfield, 2001). By 1994, 43 states implemented statewide assessments for K–5, and by the year 2000, every US state but Iowa administered a state-mandated test (Jones, G.M., Jones, & Hargrove, 2003). The high-stakes, standardized-testing juggernaut continued during then Vice President George H. Bush's campaign for the presidency, and as president, he carried this agenda forward into his Summit on Education, which laid the groundwork for Bush's America 2000 plan—focusing on testing and establishing "world class standards" in schools. Then President Bill Clinton and Vice President Al Gore subsequently committed themselves to following through on the goals established by Bush's America 2000 plan, including the pursuit of a national examination system in the United States, and within the first week of taking office in 2001, President G.W. Bush advocated for federal Title I funding to be tied to test scores (Kornhaber & Orfield, 2001).

In 2002 the US government passed the No Child Left Behind Act (NCLB) into law (US Department of Education, 2002). As a policy, NCLB originally mandated that all students be tested in grades 3–8 and once in high school, in reading and math, with future provisions that students be tested at least once at the elementary, middle, and high-school levels in science. If student test scores do not meet "Adequate Yearly Progress" (AYP) in subgroups related to race, economic class, special education, and English language proficiency, among others, schools face sanctions, such as a loss of federal funding or the diversion of federal monies to pay for private tutoring, transportation costs, and other "supplemental services" (Burch, 2006, 2009). Under NCLB, all students in all subgroups are also expected to be testing at 100% proficiency by the year 2014 or face the above-mentioned sanctions (US Department of Education, 2002). Thus, high-stakes, standardized testing has become *the* policy tool for enforcing educational reform in the United States. The election of President Barack Obama has only intensified the use of high-stakes, standardized tests within education policy in the US. Nowhere is this more evident than in President Obama's selection of Arne Duncan to lead the Department of Education and the subsequent promotion of the federal "Race to the Top" program, which included monies for more testing as part of a broader education reform package promoting the flawed use of tests to evaluate teachers (Baker et al., 2010), attacks on teachers unions' right to collective bargaining, and the proliferation of charter schools (Kumashiro, 2012).

High-Stakes Testing and Classroom Control

The bulk of educational research on the effects of systems of high-stakes testing on the classroom practices of teachers, as well as the classroom experiences of students, finds that these tests are essentially controlling what knowledge is taught, the form in which it is taught, and how it is taught (Au, 2007, 2009a). Within the policy context of systems built around high-stakes testing such as NCLB, this means at least three immediate things. One, the content of instruction is being determined by relevancy to the tests themselves: if subjects are not included on the tests, then the subjects are not being taught in the classroom. Thus, subjects such as social studies, science, art, among others, are being greatly reduced and sometimes even cut completely within high-stakes testing environments (see, e.g., Center on Education Policy, 2007; Renter et al., 2006). Second, in teaching to the tests, teachers are also catering their instruction to the form and presentation of knowledge included on the high-stakes tests. What this implies is that, in addition to the content being shaped to meet the norms of the tests, the very form in which such knowledge is being communicated—often times in small, isolated, decontextualized pieces of information—is also being controlled by the tests as teachers seek to improve their students' scores through the simple reproduction of test-styled knowledge in their instruction (see, e.g., Luna & Turner, 2001). Third, in response to high-stakes testing, teachers are shifting their pedagogy relative to changes in both curricular content and form of knowledge being taught. What this means is that teachers are increasingly moving toward lecture and more rote-based, teacher-centred pedagogies to meet test-based content and knowledge form demands (see, e.g., Clarke, M., et al., 2003; Vogler, 2005). Thus, we see systems of high-stakes testing exerting forms of control over knowledge content, knowledge form, and knowledge communication (pedagogy) in classroom practice. This control, however, is only made possible through policy structure itself, and, as such, it illustrates another type of control made possible via the use of high-stakes testing in US education policy: bureaucratic control.

High-Stakes Testing, Bureaucratic Control, and Performativity

The fact that high-stakes testing exerts so much control over classroom practice is evidence of the existence of hierarchies of institutional power. Indeed, high-stakes tests hold so much power because their results are tied, by policy, to rewards or sanctions that can deeply affect the lives of students, teachers, principals, and communities. High-stakes testing thus manifests bureaucratic control, or control "embodied within the *hierarchical* social relations of the workplace" (Apple, 1995, p. 128). I employ "bureaucracy" here, in the sense of Weber (1964), as an organization that relies upon

> *a complex rational division of labor, with fixed duties and jurisdictions; stable, rule-governed authority channels and universally applied performance guidelines; a horizontal division of graded authority, or hierarchy, entailing supervision from above; a complex system of written record-keeping, based on scientific procedures that standardize communications and increase control; ... predictable, standardized management procedures following general rules; and a tendency to require total loyalty from its members toward the way of life an organization requires. (Ferguson, 1984, p. 7)*

Bureaucratic control is evident in education polices structured around high-stakes testing. Research consistently finds that systems of high-stakes, standardized testing centralize authority at the top of federal, state, and district bureaucracies and generally take control away from local decision makers and local contexts by shifting power up the bureaucratic chain of command, holding those "on the bottom" accountable to those "on top" within administrative hierarchies (Apple, 2000; McNeil, 2000; Natriello & Pallas, 2001; Sunderman & Kim, 2005). In discussing the system of high-stakes testing in Texas (the blueprint for NCLB), McNeil (2005) explains that

> *The accountability system is an extreme form of centralization. The controls hinge on a standardized test. Through a simple set of linkages, the centralized educational bureaucracy of the state has established a test that must be taken by all children, in key subjects in key grades. The state then rates each school according to the test scores of the children in the school. School districts are rated by the scores of all their schools. Set up as a hierarchical system, each layer of the bureaucracy is held accountable to the one above it. The rules are set at the top and there can be no variations in their implementation, nor can schools or districts opt out if they prefer a different method of evaluating children's learning or assessing the quality of their schools. (p. 59)*

Within the bureaucratic control of high-stakes testing, upper-level authorities in the state or federal governments determine standards and tests. Student test scores are publicly reported, and state authorities use those scores to hold districts, schools, administrators, teachers, and students "accountable" for increases in those scores—handing out sanctions or rewards depending on student performance. Within these systems, McNeil (2005) continues:

The decisions are made centrally, and at the top of the bureaucracy. The lower levels of the bureaucracy, where teachers and children reside, are not invited to create variations or improvements on this system or to offer alternatives to it. They are, rather, intended to merely comply. They are to be accountable to those above them. (p. 60)

The structure of systems of accountability based on high-stakes, standardized tests pulls decision-making power away from the classrooms and schools and puts it into the hands of technical "experts" and bureaucrats who operate with their own political agendas far away from local contexts (Apple, 1995; Jones, G.M., et al., 2003; McNeil, 2000).

The power in this model, then, is located in the upper echelons of institutional bureaucracies that maintain the authority to determine the assessment, determine the criteria for what counts as passing or failing, and determine the sanctions and punishments for those who do not meet their criteria for passing. In these ways, high-stakes testing programs are an extremely effective tool for government agencies to use their regulatory power to influence what happens at the classroom level (Goodson & Foote, 2001; Natriello & Pallas, 2001). Through such regulation, these agencies can be seen as successfully tightening the loose coupling between policy makers' intentions and the institutional environments created by their policies (Burch, 2007). Educational policy constructed around high-stakes, standardized testing thus represents a form of "steerage from a distance" (Menter, Muschamp, Nicholl, Ozga, & Pollard, 1997; see also, Apple, 2006), where the state uses its regulatory power to guide the actions of local actors from afar.

While the empirical research surrounding bureaucratic structures associated with high-stakes testing and the control of teachers' labour is undeniable (see, e.g., Au, 2007), it is important to recognize that bureaucratic control is, in a sense, taking on different forms under neoliberalism that also draw on forms of neoliberal individualism that do not always require institutional, bureaucratic structures to operate. Under these forms, as an extension of the neoliberal managerial state (Clarke, J., & Newman, 1997), and as an expression of the habitus (Bourdieu, 1984) of the professional, managerial, new middle class (Apple, 2006; Au, 2008), centralized authority is often exercised vis-à-vis individualized, self-interested performativity (Ball, 2003) that does not necessarily require the existence of the institutionalized bureaucratic form. However, given the realities presented by the empirical research, where formal bureaucratic hierarchies of power are directly wielded in efforts to discipline teachers within contemporary systems of accountability (Vinson & Ross, 2003) that at times directly result in policy-based punishments such as loss of employment (Crocco & Costigan, 2007; Jaeger, 2006), it could be argued that in the US the structural, bureaucratic form of control either functions in concert with, or perhaps provides the operational basis for, the neoliberal form of control associated with performativity.

The Curriculum of High-Stakes Testing Policies

Let us shift focus here by thinking about education policy as a form of curriculum, one that communicates particular ideas, concepts, and lessons about educational practices, power, and decision making to students and teachers alike. Such a shift allows us to ask a simple question: what does our education policy teach us? Based on the research evidence discussed above, we could then say NCLB and systems of high-stakes testing teach us a few key lessons.

Lesson 1: Teachers Are Not Competent

The first lesson of high-stakes, test-based education policy is that teachers cannot be trusted, as professionals, to effectively determine the best ways to educate and assess students. Rather, echoing the application of "scientific management" of Taylorism to education (Kliebard, 2004)—where managers (administrators and policy makers) determine the "best" and most efficient methods of production (ways to teach students)—teachers are compelled within systems of high-stakes testing to adopt teaching methods strictly for the tests (Au, 2007, 2011), and oftentimes against their own judgment of what constitutes best practice (Abrams, Pedulla, & Madaus, 2003). In the process, teachers are thus feeling what Ball (2003) refers to as the "terrors of performativity" (p. 218) as their identities become increasingly defined by the test scores themselves, being labelled as "good" or "bad" teachers (and, by extension, even "good" or "bad" people) depending on whether or not their students perform well on high-stakes tests (Lipman, 2004; Smith, 2004). Consequently we see teachers' sense of powerlessness has increased in the face of such testing, with subsequent dips in morale (Nichols & Berliner, 2005).

Lesson 2: Diversity Is Bad

The second lesson of the high-stakes, test-based education policy is that diversity, in various forms, is detrimental to education. For instance, as discussed above, research has found that subject-matter diversity, as well as the diversity of instructional delivery, has decreased as a result of high-stakes testing. In this sense, knowledge and pedagogy is becoming standardized and homogenized under the influence of high-stakes testing (Au, 2007; McNeil, 2000). One extension of this process is that nontested, multicultural knowledge is likewise being squeezed out of the curriculum (Agee, 2004; Au, 2009a; Bigelow, 1999; Darder & Torres, 2004). Thus, we see high-stakes tests functioning to force schools to adopt a standardized, nonmulticultural curriculum that ultimately silences the "voices, the cultures, and the experiences of children" (McNeil, 2000, p. 232), particularly if those voices, cultures, and experiences fall outside the norms of the tests. In this way, students' lives, in all their variation, are effectively thrown out, as schools press to structure learning to fit the standardized curricular norms established by the tests, literally making their schooling subtractive (Valenzuela, 1999). In addition, under NCLB, policy has been structured so that the more subgroups a school has, the more opportunities a school has to fail to meet AYP. Thus, as schools feel pressures to meet policy mandate, homogeneity is favoured over heterogeneity, and more racially integrated and diverse schools are more likely to be penalized within the law (Darling-Hammond, 2007; Schwartz, Stiefel, & Chellman, 2005).

Lesson 3: Local Conditions Are Unimportant

The third lesson of the high-stakes, test-based education policy is that locality doesn't matter. Or, put differently, local contexts and local voices are not valued within high-stakes tests. This lesson is most apparent in the bureaucratic control of high-stakes testing, discussed above. Here, local actors—in this case teachers and students—have significant amounts of their power evacuated by policy regimes of high-stakes testing, as school, district, state, and federal policy makers and administrators above them in the institutional hierarchies use their authority to both surveil (Hanson, 2000; Vinson & Ross, 2003) and control what is happening in classrooms (Apple, 1995; Au, 2007; McNeil, 2005).

In addition to policy structure, systems of high-stakes testing also eschew localities vis-à-vis the standardized tests themselves. This is apparent in the way that such tests not only rely on the need to standardize knowledge but also rely on the need to simultaneously standardize the measurement of students so that comparisons can be made functional within education policy (De Lissovoy & McLaren, 2003). The logic is as follows: standardized test results are validated based on the assumption that they can be universally applied to different populations, thus enabling the supposedly fair and objective comparison of individuals across different contexts. In order for such comparisons to be meaningful, however, standardized tests have to deny certain amounts of local context, local variability, or local difference, thus establishing a common measurement that can reach across localities. Otherwise it would be impossible to compare student A to student B, school C to school D, district E to district F, state G to state H, and country I to country J (Au, 2009b).

Hence, standardization has to assume that local, individual conditions and local, individual factors make no difference in student performance, teacher performance, or test-based measurement. Indeed, the assumed validity of objective measurement provided by standardized tests rests upon this denial of individual differences: the tests are considered objective because they supposedly measure all individuals equally and outside of any potential extenuating circumstances (McNeil, 2000). Thus, when students, teachers, schools, districts, states, and countries are measured by standardized testing and compared to other students, teachers, schools, districts, states, and countries, they are necessarily decontextualized to make such comparisons possible. It is a process where

> Students, as well as teachers, with all their varied talents and challenges, were reduced to a test score. And schools, as well as their communities, in all their complexity—their failings, inadequacies, strong points, superb and weak teachers, ethical commitments to collective uplift, their energy, demoralization, courage, potential, and setbacks—were blended, homogenized, and reduced to a stanine score. (Lipman, 2004, p. 172)

This process of abstracting a number with which to define students in relation to other students requires that their individuality be omitted, that their variability be disregarded and reduced "to one or two characteristics common to the larger universe of objects" (McNeil, 2005, p. 103). Standardized tests, thus, by definition, literally decontextualize students for comparison. Subsequently, we can see how both policy structure, as well as the high-stakes, standardized tests such policies are built upon, serve to deny locality in two ways: policy structure serves to disempower local actors and empower centralized authorities, while the standardized tests simultaneously serve to deny the power of local contexts to inform meaning, due to their deference to a universalized and singular standard.

The Idiocy of Policy

Having explored what I have framed as the curriculum of education policy that is based on systems of high-stakes testing, we can now ask the follow-up question: given the United States' rhetorical commitment to democratic government, what kind of democratic education do high-stakes, test-centred policies provide? Parker's (2005) formulation of what he sees as the requirements for democratic education and the role of such education in "teaching against idiocy" proves useful for this analysis. As Parker explains, "idiocy" has its root in the Greek *idios*, meaning private, self-centred, selfish, and separate. Thus, for Parker, the overarching goal of democratic education is teaching *against* idiocy and teaching *for* a more public, unselfish, common, and deliberative identity.[1] In doing so, Parker optimistically asserts that schools are positioned to teach against idiocy (or, rather, teach for democracy) and that to do so requires educators to take up three key actions. Parker's first suggested key action is to "increase the variety and frequency of interaction among students who are culturally, linguistically, and racially different from one another" (p. 348). The underlying point being that diversity is good and necessary for fostering democratic education, and that such diversity would be reflected in a school experience where students could learn about each other in all of their differences. Parker's second and third key actions for democratic education revolve around the deliberation of common social and academic problems. Deliberation, he explains, is

> discussion aimed at making a decision across these differences about a problem that the participants face in common. The main action during a deliberation is weighing alternatives with others in order to decide on the best course of action. In schools, deliberation is not only a means of instruction (teaching with deliberation) but also a curricular goal (teaching for deliberation), because it generates a particular kind of social good: a democratic community, a public culture. (p. 348)

Parker distinguishes the second and third key actions related to deliberation thusly: create the conditions where diverse groups can deliberate common issues; and distinguish between what he refers to as "blather" and deliberation, as well as between inclusive/open and exclusive/closed deliberation.

Based upon the evidence I've provided regarding the effects of high-stakes, test-based policy on classroom practice, the "curriculum" of our policy effectively works against all three of Parker's (2005) key actions for developing democratic education. Given the decline of multicultural education, the standardization of classroom knowledge, the standardization of teaching and learning, and the policy pressures for less diverse student bodies (both numerically and culturally), it is reasonably clear that high- stakes, test-based education policies work against the promotion of diversity. Indeed, as

I've discussed here, policies constructed upon systems of high-stakes, standardized testing do the exact opposite: they work toward homogeneity and stasis. Further, looking at policy structure and classroom control associated with high-stakes testing, especially that of bureaucratic control (Apple, 1995; Au, 2009b), we can see an absolute absence of open or public deliberation of any form. Teachers, vis-à-vis testing, are essentially being told by outside "experts" how to best teach, with little to no public deliberation (or at least deliberation actively including teachers, students, or parents) about what should constitute best practice and whether or not such testing should be involved. As such, education policies associated with high-stakes testing, such as NCLB, might be seen as a closed deliberation among politicians, policy makers, and those corporations reaping profits from education policy (Au, 2009b; Burch, 2006, 2009). Thus, in the sense of Parker's (2005) framing, education policy that maintains a myopic focus on high-stakes, standardized testing and, by extension, sustains a self-centred disregard for diversity, local context, and teacher and student input in policy operation, is literally idiotic and structurally antidemocratic.

Conclusion

In this chapter, I have made a simple argument: based on the findings of research on the effects of education policies built upon systems of high-stakes testing in the US, educators and students alike are essentially being "taught" a curriculum that is antidemocratic. This can be seen in the various ways teaching and learning have been restructured by such systems of high-stakes testing to control teachers, to restrict diversity, and to ignore local contexts and voices. Further, using Parker's (2005) key tasks for democratic education, I have argued here that we can see that systems of high-stakes testing are literally idiotic in that they are self-centred, closed, and do not welcome open democratic deliberation. Teachers, students, and the public simply do not learn about democracy from education policies erected around high-stakes testing. Rather, they learn antidemocracy, as the curriculum of such policies works against diversity and deliberation and instead teaches bureaucratic control and autocratic, centralized authority over education.

Indeed, Dewey (1916/1966) recognized the undemocratic nature of educational systems where, as is the case with policies associated with high-stakes testing, the aims of education are being imposed by external authorities. He remarked that

The vice of externally imposed ends has deep roots. Teachers receive them from superior authorities; ... The teachers impose them upon children. As a first consequence, the intelligence of the teacher is not free; it is confined to receiving the aims laid down from above. Too rarely is the individual teacher so free from the dictation of authoritative supervisor, textbook on methods, prescribed course of study, etc., that he can let his mind come to close quarters with the pupil's mind and the subject matter. This distrust of the teacher's experience is then reflected in lack of confidence in the responses of pupils. The latter receive their aims through a double or treble external imposition, and are constantly confused by the conflict between the aims which are natural to their own experience at the time and those in which they are taught to acquiesce. Until the democratic criterion of the intrinsic significance of every growing experience is recognized, we shall be intellectually confused by the demand for adaptations to external aims. (pp. 108–109)

Dewey's analysis would be prophetic if it were not for the fact that he was addressing the rise of scientific management in US education in the early 1900s (Kliebard, 2004). Instead, his words stand as a sad testament to some of the ways that our current education policy harkens back to key issues of power and control (and inequality) associated with corporate models of schooling that originated in the 20th century (Au, 2009b). The aims of education are increasingly being imposed by external authorities with growing forcefulness and consistency, and students are feeling this double or treble external imposition as they are being told what and how to learn by teachers, who themselves are being told what and how to teach by policy makers.

Thus, even though it would be naively romantic to think that schools were particularly democratic pre-NCLB and before the hegemony of high-stakes testing—indeed, they were not (see, e.g., Anyon, 1997; Apple, 1986). In a Deweyan sense, we still might say that one of the overarching objectives of the "curriculum" of modern-day regimes of high-stakes, test-centred policy is increased pressures for the acquiescence of teachers, teacher educators, students, and student communities alike. This central critique of regimes of high-stakes testing also points to a problem that extends beyond schools: *the current hegemony of high-stakes testing not only subverts democratic deliberations of teaching, learning, and multicultural education, it also undermines democratic thinking more generally by narrowing the conversations that students, teachers, and communities can engage in as potentially active participants in the content and direction of schooling relative to broader social relations.*

Given the policy pressures to acquiesce to the expectations of high-stakes tests, it is important to recognize that the increased control over classroom practice and increased bureaucratic control are not the "unintended" consequences of high-stakes testing, as some scholars assert (see, e.g., Jones, B.D., 2007; Jones, G.M., et al., 2003; Nelson, 2002; Stecher & Barron, 2001), because policies of "accountability" built upon high- stakes, standardized tests are *intended* to control and regulate what happens in education (Madaus, 1994). As noted policy conservative Moe (2003) explains quite clearly,

> *The movement for school accountability is essentially a movement for more effective top-down control of the schools. The idea is that, if public authorities want to promote student achievement, they need to adopt organizational control mechanisms— tests, school report cards, rewards and sanctions, and the like—designed to get district officials, principals, teachers, and students to change their behavior in productive ways. … Virtually all organizations need to engage in top-down control, because the people at the top have goals they want the people at the bottom to pursue, and something has to be done to bring about the desired behaviors. … The public school system is just like other organizations in this respect. (p. 81)*

Thus, it is important to remember that policies are designed (Schneider & Ingram, 1997) and that they require active intent with regards to particular structures and particular outcomes. The intentions of promoters of policy regimes reliant upon high-stakes testing are clear in the structures and outcomes of current education policy in the United States, which are designed to negate "asymmetries" between classroom practice and the test-score-related goals of those with political and bureaucratic power (Wößmann, 2003). From this perspective, the curriculum of education policy based on systems of high-stakes testing is simply antidemocratic by design.

REFERENCES

Abowitz, K.K., & Harnish, J. (2006). Contemporary discourses of citizenship. *Review of Educational Research, 76*(4), 653–690. doi:10.3102/00346543076004653

Abrams, L.M., Pedulla, J.J., & Madaus, G.F. (2003). Views from the classroom: Teachers' opinions of statewide testing programs. *Theory into Practice, 42*(1), 18–29. doi:10.1207/s15430421tip4201_4

Agee, J. (2004). Negotiating a teaching identity: An African American teacher's struggle to teach in test-driven contexts. *Teachers College Record, 106*(4), 747–774. doi:10.1111/j.1467-9620.2004.00357.x

Anyon, J. (1997). *Ghetto schooling: A political economy of urban educational reform.* New York: Teachers College Press.

Apple, M.W. (1986). *Teachers and texts: A political economy of class and gender relations in education.* New York: Routledge & Kegan Paul.

Apple, M.W. (1995). *Education and power* (2nd ed.). New York: Routledge.

Apple, M.W. (2000). *Official knowledge: Democratic education in a conservative age* (2nd ed.). New York: Routledge.

Apple, M.W. (2006). *Educating the "right" way: Markets, standards, god, and inequality* (2nd ed.). New York: Routledge.

Au, W. (2007). High-stakes testing and curricular control: A qualitative metasynthesis. *Educational Researcher, 36*(5), 258–267. doi:10.3102/00131 89X07306523

Au, W. (2008). Between education and the economy: High-stakes testing and the contradictory location of the new middle class. *Journal of Education Policy, 23*(5), 501–513. doi:10.1080/02680930802148941

Au, W. (2009a). High-stakes testing and discursive control: The triple bind for non-standard student identities. *Multicultural Perspectives, 11*(2), 65–71. doi:10.1080/15210960903028727

Au, W. (2009b). *Unequal by design: High-stakes testing and the standardization of inequality.* New York: Routledge.

Au, W. (2011). Teaching under the new Taylorism: High-stakes testing and the standardization of the 21st century curriculum. *Journal of Curriculum Studies, 43*(1), 25–45. doi:10.1080/00220272.2010.521261

Baker, E.L., Barton, P.E., Darling-Hammond, L., Haertel, E., Ladd, H.F., Linn, R.L., & Shepard, L.A. (2010). *Problems with the use of student test scores to evaluate teachers* (Vol. Briefing Paper #278). Washington, DC: Economic Policy Institute.

Ball, S.J. (2003, March–April). The teacher's soul and the terrors of performativity. *Journal of Education Policy, 18*(2), 215–228. doi:10.1080/0268093022000043065

Berliner, D.C., & Biddle, B.J. (1995). *The manufactured crisis: Myths, fraud, and the attack on America's public schools.* Reading, MA: Addison-Wesley.

Bigelow, B. (1999). Why standardized tests threaten multiculturalism. *Educational Leadership, 56*(7), 37–40.

Bourdieu, P. (1984). *Distinction: A social critique of the judgment of taste* (R. Nice, Trans.). Cambridge, MA: Routledge & Kegan Paul Ltd.

Burch, P. (2006). The new educational privatization: Educational contracting and high stakes accountability. *Teachers College Record, 108*(12), 2582–2610. doi:10.1111/j.1467-9620.2006.00797.x

Burch, P. (2007). Educational policy and practice from the perspective of institutional theory: Crafting a wider lens. *Educational Researcher, 36*(2), 84–95. doi:10.3102/0013189X07299792

Burch, P. (2009). *Hidden markets: The new education privatization.* New York: Routledge.

Center on Education Policy. (2007). *Choices, changes, and challenges: Curriculum and instruction in the NCLB era.* Washington, DC: Author.

Clarke, J., & Newman, J. (1997). *The managerial state: Power, politics and ideology in the remaking of social welfare.* London: SAGE Publications.

Clarke, M., Shore, A., Rhoades, K., Abrams, L.M., Miao, J., & Li, J. (2003). *Perceived effects of state-mandated testing programs on teaching and learning: Findings from interviews with educators in low-, medium-, and high-stakes states.* Boston: National Board on Educational Testing and Public Policy, Lynch School of Education, Boston College.

Crocco, M.S., & Costigan, A.T., III. (2007). The narrowing of curriculum and pedagogy in the age of accountability: Urban educators speak out. *Urban Education, 42*(6), 512–535. doi:10.1177/0042085907304964

Cunningham, F. (1987). *Democratic theory and socialism.* Cambridge, UK: Cambridge University Press.

Darder, A., & Torres, R.D. (2004). *After race: Racism after multiculturalism.* New York: New York University Press.

Darling-Hammond, L. (2007). Race, inequality and educational accountability: The irony of "No Child Left Behind." *Race, Ethnicity and Education, 10*(3), 245–260. doi:10.1080/13613320701503207

DeLissovoy, N., & McLaren, P. (2003). Educational "accountability" and the violence of capital: A Marxian reading. *Journal of Education Policy, 18*(2), 131–143. doi:10.1080/0268093022000043092

Dewey, J. (1966). *Democracy and education.* New York: The Free Press. (Original work published 1916)

Ferguson, K.E. (1984). *The feminist case against bureaucracy.* Philadelphia: Temple University Press.

Gay, G. (2007). The rhetoric and reality of NCLB. *Race, Ethnicity and Education, 10*(3), 279–293. doi:10.1080/13613320701503256

Goodson, I., & Foote, M. (2001). A sword over their heads: The standards movement as a disciplinary device. In J.L. Kincheloe & D. Weil (Eds.), *Standards and schooling in the United States: An encyclopedia* (Vol. 2, pp. 703–709). Denver, CO: ABC-CLIO.

Gutmann, A. (1990). Democratic education in difficult times. *Teachers College Record, 92*(1), 7–20.

Hanson, A.F. (2000). How tests create what they are intended to measure. In A. Filer (Ed.), *Assessment: social practice and social product* (pp. 67–81). New York: RoutledgeFalmer.

Jaeger, E. (2006). Silencing teachers in an era of scripted reading. *Rethinking Schools, 20*(3), 39–41.

Jones, B.D. (2007). The unintended outcomes of high-stakes testing. *Journal of Applied School Psychology, 23*(2), 65–86. doi:10.1300/J370v23n02_05

Jones, G.M., Jones, B.D., & Hargrove, T.Y. (2003). *The unintended consequences of high-stakes testing.* New York: Rowman & Littlefield.

Kliebard, H.M. (2004). *The struggle for the American curriculum, 1893–1958* (3rd ed.). New York: RoutledgeFalmer.

Kornhaber, M.L., & Orfield, G. (2001). High-stakes testing policies: Examining their assumptions and consequences. In G. Orfield & M.L. Kornhaber (Eds.), *Raising standards or raising barriers? Inequality and high-stakes testing in public education* (pp. 1–18). New York: Century Foundation Press.

Kumashiro, K. (2012). *Bad teacher! How blaming teachers distorts the bigger picture.* New York: Teachers College Press.

Ladson-Billings, G. (2006). From the achievement gap to the education debt: Understanding achievement in US schools. *Educational Researcher, 35*(7), 3–12. doi:10.3102/0013189X035007003

Lipman, P. (2004). *High stakes education: Inequality, globalization, and urban school reform.* New York: RoutledgeFalmer. doi:10.4324/9780203465509

Luna, C., & Turner, C.L. (2001). The impact of the MCAS: Teachers talk about high-stakes testing. *English Journal, 91*(1), 79–87. doi:10.2307/821659

Madaus, G.F. (1994). A technological and historical consideration of equity issues associated with proposals to change the nation's testing policy. *Harvard Educational Review, 64*(1), 76–95.

McNeil, L.M. (2000). *Contradictions of school reform: Educational costs of standardized testing.* New York: Routledge.

McNeil, L.M. (2005). Faking equity: High-stakes testing and the education of Latino youth. In A. Valenzuela (Ed.), *Leaving children behind: How "Texas-style" accountability fails Latino youth* (pp. 57–112). Albany: State University of New York.

Menter, I., Muschamp, Y., Nicholl, P., Ozga, J., & Pollard, A. (1997). *Work and identity in the primary school.* Philadelphia: Open University Press.

Moe, T.M. (2003). Politics, control, and the future of school accountability. In P.E. Peterson & M.R. West (Eds.), *No child left behind? The politics and practice of school accountability* (pp. 80–106). Washington, DC: Brookings Institution Press.

National Commission on Excellence in Education. (1983). *A nation at risk: The imperative for educational reform.* Washington, DC: United States Department of Education.

Natriello, G., & Pallas, A.M. (2001). The development and impact of high-stakes testing. In G. Orfield & M.L. Kornhaber (Eds.), *Raising standards or raising barriers? Inequality and high-stakes testing in public education* (pp. 19–38). New York: Century Foundation Press.

Nelson, R.J. (2002). *Closing or widening the gap of inequality: The intended and unintended consequences of Minnesota's basic standards tests for students with disabilities* (Unpublished doctoral dissertation). University of Minnesota, Minneapolis, MN.

Nichols, S.L., & Berliner, D.C. (2005). *The inevitable corruption of indicators and educators through high-stakes testing* (No. EPSL-0503-101-EPRU). Tempe: Education Policy Research Unit, Education Policy Studies Laboratory, College of Education, Division of Educational Leadership and Policy Studies, Arizona State University.

Orfield, G., & Wald, J. (2000). Testing, testing: The high-stakes testing mania hurts poor and minority students the most. *Nation (New York, NY), 270*(22), 38–40.

Parker, W. (2005). Teaching against idiocy. *Phi Delta Kappan, 86*(5), 344–351.

Renter, D.S., Scott, C., Kober, N., Chudowsky, N., Joftus, S., & Zabala, D. (2006). *From the capital to the classroom: Year 4 of the No Child Left Behind Act.* Washington, DC: Center on Education Policy.

Schneider, A.L., & Ingram, H. (1997). *Policy design for democracy* (1st ed.). Lawrence: University of Kansas.

Schwartz, A.E., Stiefel, L., & Chellman, C. (2005). Subgroup reporting and school segregation. *Education Week, 24*(28), 31.

Smith, M.L. (2004). *Political spectacle and the fate of American schools.* New York: RoutledgeFalmer. doi:10.4324/9780203465554

Stecher, B.M., & Barron, S. (2001). Unintended consequences of test-based accountability when testing in "milepost" grades. *Educational Assessment, 7*(4), 259–281. doi:10.1207/S15326977EA0704_02

Sunderman, G.L., & Kim, J.S. (2005, November 3). The expansion of federal power and the politics of implementing the No Child Left Behind Act. *Teachers College Record.* Retrieved from http://www.tcrecord.org/printcontent. asp?contentID=12227

US Department of Education. (2002). *No child left behind: A desktop reference.* Washington, DC: US Department of Education, Office of the Under Secretary.

Valenzuela, A. (1999). *Subtractive schooling: US Mexican youth and the politics of caring.* New York: SUNY Press.

Vinson, K.D., & Ross, E.W. (2003). Controlling images: The power of high-stakes testing. In K.J. Saltman & D.A. Gabbard (Eds.), *Education as enforcement: The militarization and corporatization of schools* (pp. 241–258). New York: RoutledgeFalmer.

Vogler, K.E. (2005). Impact of a high school graduation examination on social studies teachers' instructional practices. *Journal of Social Studies Research, 29*(2), 19–33.

Weber, M. (1964). *The theory of social and economic organizations.* New York: Free Press of Glencoe.

Wößmann, L. (2003). Central exit exams and student achievement: International evidence. In P.E. Peterson & M.R. West (Eds.), *No child left behind? The politics and practice of school accountability* (pp. 292–324). Washington, DC: Brookings Institution Press.

NOTE

1 I want to recognize that much of the discourse surrounding democratic education is framed around the concept of democratic "citizenship" (see, e.g., Gutmann, 1990; Parker, 2005). While I clearly am supportive of democratic values, particularly those associated with "thick democracy" (Cunningham, 1987), I also have to recognize that discourses of "citizenship" are often problematically linked to official membership or allegiance to a particular nation-state (Abowitz & Harnish, 2006). It is for this reason that I am choosing here to focus on democratic education more generally, while avoiding a full engagement with concepts of citizenship within democratic education.

● ● ● ● ● ● ● ● ● ● ● ● ● ● ● ● ●
Part V: Rights, Freedoms, and Conflicts in Education

This section addresses certain cases and practices that raise difficult questions about rights and freedoms in democratic societies; it concludes with a chapter that identifies the seemingly insuperable challenges that stand in the way of achieving mutual understanding and appreciation when groups differ over value judgments and matters of principle. How are we to balance different rights and freedoms when they come into conflict in education? How are we to determine how much weight to give a certain principle in a particular context? Are there ways in which we can reach the kind of moral understanding that transcends difference?

Frances Kroeker and Stephen Norris critically examine the prevalent belief that religious schools constitute a threat to such goals of liberal education as the promotion of critical thinking, autonomy, and tolerance, and they challenge various arguments advanced by philosophers against religious schools. Kroeker and Norris concede that such criticisms may apply in certain cases of religious schooling, but they argue that such examples do not amount to a general argument against religious schooling as such. The stakes are high in this debate because the outcome may well influence government policy with respect to funding religious schools, and numerous questions arise in light of this discussion that call for careful consideration. Have liberal educators demonstrated that religious schooling is harmful in the ways suggested? Is religious education compatible with critical reflection and independent thinking? What reasons might parents and guardians have to choose religious schooling for their children? Is the danger of indoctrination and bias any greater in religious schools than in secular schools? Are there good reasons for thinking that religious schools play a valuable role in promoting fundamentally important educational aims?

Related issues and arguments concerning liberal education are taken up in the following chapter. Dianne Gereluk examines an amendment introduced in 2009 to the Alberta Human Rights Act that requires schools to notify parents and guardians when religion, human sexuality, and sexual orientation are explicitly addressed in the classroom, and which permits them to withdraw their children from those classes if they so choose. Gereluk argues that this provision in the Alberta legislation conflicts with the aim of promoting student autonomy because it means that students who are withdrawn from the classes in question will not be encouraged to think about different values and lifestyles, with the result that their ability to make thoughtful decisions about such matters later in life will be adversely affected. She further argues that exemption from such classes threatens the development of virtues such as tolerance, respect for others, and a sense of justice that are vital to the health of a democratic society. Difficult questions emerge for consideration: How much authority should parents and guardians have in such matters? If we support, or oppose, the Alberta amendment, on what grounds do we justify our decision? Does the amendment in question achieve an acceptable compromise and succeed in balancing competing rights appropriately or not?

The matter of balancing rights is also very much at issue in the chapter by Paul Clarke and Bruce MacDougall. They review the decision in a recent Canadian case to suspend the teaching certificate of a schoolteacher who on various occasions had letters published in a local newspaper in which he made discriminatory remarks concerning homosexuality. Clarke and MacDougall argue that the suspension was warranted to safeguard the rights of gay and lesbian students to equal treatment, and also because the teacher failed to conduct himself in a way that would set a suitable example for his students with respect to fundamental educational norms. The Kempling case raises numerous questions and issues that teachers will surely wish to consider. Was the suspension of his teaching certificate justified, and, if so, on what grounds? Should our view be affected by the fact that the comments in question were made outside the school context? How do we determine what constitutes unacceptable teacher conduct beyond the classroom and school? How should a democratic society weigh the rights of gay and lesbian students to protection from discrimination against the right to freedom of expression and freedom of religion? This chapter invites teachers and student teachers to reflect on the principles that are relevant to arriving at a defensible conclusion on these and related matters.

William Hare revisits a notorious case in which a teacher used his classes to spread anti-Semitic ideas. Some of Keegstra's supporters appealed to the ideal of open-mindedness to justify his teaching practices, but it is crucial, Hare argues, to ask what is really involved in an open-minded presentation of ideas. Others appealed to the principle of tolerance, but this raises the question: what limits should be placed on tolerance? It has also been suggested that the first rule of teaching is sincerity, but this case forces us to ask if being sincere in one's beliefs can in any way justify an approach to teaching that involved a dogmatic presentation of deeply offensive views. The Keegstra case soon came to be seen as one that involved indoctrination, but this was not apparent at the time to many who were familiar with what was occurring. Several questions are worth exploring. What steps can teachers take to help students defend themselves against indoctrination? Are there ways in which teachers can avoid or minimize bias in their presentation of material? Why was Keegstra seen by so many as a good teacher?

Dwight Boyd explores several issues concerned with morality and moral education with a particular focus on the idea that diversity and conflict are inescapable elements of human relationships. He argues that there are very significant obstacles to achieving an understanding of moral views and practices across the divide created by difference, and he shows very clearly how these obstacles arise: serious consideration of moral views held by others is simply abandoned because we assume that we already have clear and settled answers to moral questions; we gloss over the fact of different cultural traditions and begin to think that everyone basically subscribes to the same set of values as we ourselves do; and those who occupy a position of privilege inevitably fail to truly appreciate the condition of other groups of people who are oppressed. Teachers may profitably ask: How do we keep our minds open to the fact of pluralism with respect to moral values? Is it ever possible for someone in a position of privilege to see things from the perspective of someone who is oppressed? Are there ways in which we can overcome the problems Boyd identifies, or reduce their impact? Boyd offers many helpful suggestions to those engaged in moral education but cautions against believing that there are any easy answers to these complex problems.

In trying to determine what our own views should be on these contentious issues, we must proceed, as our contributors do, by weighing the arguments and counter-arguments in light of what we know about the facts involved, and, in Socrates's words, follow the argument where it leads (Plato, 1959, 394d). There is no possibility of avoiding the difficult ethical questions these essays deal with by simply appealing to familiar moral rules or principles that spell out the answer for us. R.M. Hare (1981) makes this clear and also shows why it is important to learn to think about such cases and problems in a critical manner:

> *Since any new situation will be unlike any previous situation in* some *respects, the question immediately arises whether the differences are relevant to its appraisal, moral or other. If they are relevant, the principles which we have learnt in dealing with past situations may not be appropriate to the new one. (p. 39)*

REFERENCES

Hare, R.M. (1981). *Moral thinking: Its levels, method and point.* Oxford: Oxford University Press. doi:10.1093/0198246609.001.0001

Plato. (1959). *The republic* (H.P.D. Lee, Trans.). Harmondsworth: Penguin Books.

20

An Unwarranted Fear of Religious Schooling

Frances M. Kroeker and Stephen P. Norris*

*This chapter was first published as Kroeker, F.M, & Norris, S.P. (2007). An unwarranted fear of religious schooling. *Canadian Journal of Education, 30*(1), 269–290. Reproduced with permission.

A primary goal of public education is the preparation of citizens who support and sustain liberal democracy. To meet this goal, it is necessary to create a sense of identification with the state, prepare citizens to participate in the democratic process, and communicate shared liberal values. Although varying models of democratic civic education have been proposed, most liberal philosophers of education identify the key characteristics of liberal education as the development of tolerance for diversity, a focus on the capacity for critical reasoning and democratic deliberation, and a commitment to the development of autonomous citizens (Callan, 1997; Gutmann, 1999; Macedo, 2000).

Liberals who argue for tolerance, critical reflection, and the development of autonomy as the goals of civic education tend also to assume that religious schooling that attempts to teach civic education from a religious perspective will thwart this aim. This position has determined public policy in at least some parts of Canada and in other Western societies. The province of Ontario, for example, has resisted appeals for funding of religious schools (with the exception of Roman Catholic schools whose funding is guaranteed by Section 93 of the Constitution Act) on the grounds that "if it were required to fund religious schools, this would have a detrimental impact on public schools and hence on the fostering of a tolerant, multicultural, non-discriminatory society in the province" (International Covenant on Civil and Political Rights [ICCPR], Sixty-Seventh Session, 1999, 4.4.3). Funding religious schools, according to the government, would undermine Ontario's "very ability to create and promote a tolerant society that protects religious freedom" (ICCPR, 1999, 4.3.4). In the words of one of Canada's chief justices, "The denial of funding to separate schools is rationally connected to the goal of a more tolerant society" (Chief Justice McLachlin in *Adler v. Ontario*, 1996, 219). Nor is tolerance the only liberal virtue considered to be at risk. Liberal educators and philosophers commonly assume that religious schooling also will hinder the development of critical-reasoning skills and thus the future autonomy of children (Callan, 1997; Dwyer, 1998; Macedo, 2000).

One liberal scholar who takes this position is Harry Brighouse (2000). His particular statement of liberal concerns serves as a useful focus for making some general arguments against this widespread liberal assumption. Brighouse situates his examples within the context of religious schooling in the United Kingdom and the United States, and, although the educational contexts of both these countries differ from Canada's, the philosophical issues are identical. Indeed, we locate this chapter within a debate about religious schooling that transcends national and jurisdictional boundaries. The issues are about religious schooling in general, and about the possibilities that it opens and forecloses no matter what the particulars of school organization and governance. Brighouse argues that religious schooling is unlikely to provide children with the education for autonomy to which they are entitled and which justice demands they receive. Religious parents and schools, in his view, are likely to protect children from outside influences and limit the development of rationality, failing to provide either the conditions or the skills necessary to support autonomy. Brighouse maintains that religious schooling will cause children to be culturally marginalized, unprepared for the "social milieu they will have to negotiate as adults" (p. 74) or for the "complex demands of modern economies" (p. 110). He makes it clear that he regards religious schooling as inferior and "repressive" (p. 71), and suggests that one of the roles of public education is to act as a defence against efforts of religious parents to control their children. Brighouse does appear sometimes to distinguish some religious schools or parents from others, but does not do so consistently. He leaves the impression that he judges all religiously based schooling and all religious parents with suspicion as threats to the future autonomy of children. It is our contention, however, that Brighouse and other liberal scholars err in making this generalization, and that many and perhaps even most religious parents and religious schools provide an education that encourages autonomous choice.

In general, Brighouse's claims regarding the importance of education for autonomy are not unlike those held by many other liberal scholars. Unlike some liberals, however, Brighouse suggests a somewhat cautious approach to education for autonomy, claiming that the liberal state has a responsibility to provide an education that facilitates autonomy, but must stop short of promoting autonomy. Brighouse's understanding of the requirements of an education for autonomy rest on this distinction between facilitation and promotion, and from one point of view, autonomy facilitation would seem to provide religious schooling a better chance of passing his test of liberal acceptability, although Brighouse uses it to try to undermine certain arguments in favour of religious schooling.

In the first section, we provide a brief discussion of autonomy facilitation and promotion and the essential skills Brighouse believes children must develop. Throughout, Brighouse exhibits a fear of religion in defending three main claims with regard to religious upbringing: that religious schooling will shield children from an awareness of other ways of life, that religious parents and educators do not want children to think for themselves, and that religious parents and communities cannot claim a right to raise their children in a particular culture. None of these assertions can be adequately defended. In the second section, we challenge Brighouse's assumptions with regard to the inadequacy of religious schooling by addressing each of these three claims in turn. We argue, first, that religious families and schools are unlikely to be as isolated from society as Brighouse suggests, or their children as unprepared for modern life as he purports. We go on to demonstrate that religious ways of thinking need not preclude rational thought or critical reflection, and argue that most religious parents and schools want children to learn these skills. Finally, we show that to be raised in a particular culture, religious or otherwise, provides children with a necessary sense of identity and a stable moral environment from which to explore the world, something all parents and schools have an obligation to provide. In the concluding section, we claim that religious schooling is much more compatible with an education for autonomy than Brighouse presumes. Consequently, although there are religious groups who rear their children in objectionable ways, liberals need not fear that religious schooling as a general rule will undermine the goals of democratic education.

Autonomy Facilitation

Brighouse (2000) holds that education for autonomy is the "fundamental value that should guide the design of educational policy" (p. 65) and that all children, including those from religious families, must have the opportunity to become autonomous adults. Justice, he claims, requires that all children have the opportunity rationally to compare different ways of life and choose for themselves from a range of options a life that they can "endorse from the inside" (p. 69). To deny children an education for autonomy is to deprive them of "skills that are of great value in working out how to live well" (p. 70). Brighouse makes it clear from the outset that he considers the rights of parents to control their children's education to be circumscribed narrowly, justifiable only on the basis of the interests of the children themselves. He holds that giving parents choice in education must not be allowed to prevent children from receiving the autonomy-facilitating education they deserve.

Although he views education for autonomy as a matter of justice, Brighouse makes a distinction between autonomy promotion and facilitation, claiming that the goals of liberal civic education must be to facilitate, but not actually to promote, autonomy. Brighouse differs from many liberal theorists in his stance on this issue. However, the majority of liberals would support his more general claim regarding the desirability of education for autonomy (Callan, 1997; Gutmann, 1999; Macedo, 2000; Taylor, 1994). Those who do offer objections to education for autonomy tend to claim that promoting autonomy in children can discourage them from choosing to live in certain cultural communities (Galston, 1989, 1995; Lomasky, 1987). Thus, an education for autonomy can lead to an erosion of diversity by undermining ways of life that do not value autonomy as a primary good. As a consequence, it may be claimed that in giving children an education for autonomy, the state is throwing its weight behind a particular way of life, something that is contrary to liberalism's commitment to free choice.

Although Brighouse does not frame his position around the protection of diversity, he uses a similar argument in rejecting autonomy-promoting education. He writes: "If the state helps form the political loyalties of future citizens by inculcating belief in its own legitimacy, it will be unsurprising when citizens consent to social institutions they inhabit, but it will be difficult to be confident that their consent is freely given, or would have been freely given" (Brighouse, 1998, p. 719). An autonomous life can be considered truly autonomous only if it is chosen without coercion. Thus, education must "not try to *ensure* that students employ autonomy in their lives ... autonomy must be facilitated, not necessarily promoted" (Brighouse, 1998, p. 734). The liberal state, he says, must not promote autonomy because civic education that deliberately inculcates certain values undermines autonomous choice and, consequently, liberal legitimacy.

For Brighouse, autonomy facilitation has an additional, pragmatic benefit. He suggests that autonomy facilitation will overcome the difficulties created by religious objections to education for autonomy. He reasons that although it is possible to argue against education for autonomy on the basis that such an education predisposes children to think in certain ways or that it may cause them to reject parental ways of life, such arguments cannot succeed against autonomy facilitation. An autonomy-facilitating school program would continue to present traditional, content-based academic curricula, but in addition would teach children how to identify fallacious arguments and present students with a range of religious, nonreligious, and antireligious ethical views, thus providing the skills and conditions necessary for autonomy. According to Brighouse (2000), autonomy facilitation does not require that children be encouraged to consider pursuing a life different from that of their parents but "merely aims to enable children to take different ways of life seriously if they wish" (p. 108). Brighouse claims that autonomy facilitation will not threaten religious ways of life in the same way that autonomy promotion presumably does, and that for this reason, religious parents may be persuaded to accept autonomy-facilitating education.

Is it possible, however, for any parent to differentiate between autonomy facilitation and autonomy promotion? Brighouse (2000) himself concedes this difficulty: "It is hard to see how a teacher could impart the skills associated with autonomy without simultaneously communicating some norms concerning the virtue of autonomy ... in practice the policies will be difficult to distinguish" (pp. 197–198). This difficulty is not enough, however, to convince Brighouse to abandon the distinction. He insists that "although the skills associated with autonomy are taught, children are not encouraged by the state to live autonomous lives any more than children who are taught how to speak French are encouraged to live French-speaking lives" (pp. 94–95). Why are children taught to speak French if it is not for the purpose of speaking the language or, in other words, to live French-speaking lives at least some of the time? Certainly, in the process of teaching a skill one seems necessarily to be promoting its practice. We choose to teach children to read or write or to speak French because we believe it is important for them to learn to do so. In the process of teaching them, we encourage them to use the skills they are learning. Indeed, we do more. It is difficult to imagine, for instance, how to teach students particular forms of critical thought without at the same time saying to them, explicitly or implicitly, that this is good thinking. It is even more difficult to imagine broadcasting this message without also sending the message that this is a form of thought that is good to employ. Why else, the students reasonably would ask, is it a part of educational goals, part of instruction, and part of what is assessed?

Children who learn the skills necessary for autonomy, who have been exposed to diversity, and who have learned to reflect critically on the choices presented to them can still choose to live their parents' way of life. However, because of the autonomy-facilitating skills they have learned, they cannot fail to be aware that this choice is not the only way of life available to them. Children who consciously choose to live a particular way of life are autonomous, whether or not the education they received was intended to promote, or merely facilitate, autonomy. In effect, there can be no difference between autonomy promotion and facilitation.

In spite of a lack of clarity regarding the distinction between autonomy promotion and facilitation, Brighouse continues to view autonomy facilitation as a useful means of ensuring that children of religious parents are given the opportunity for future autonomy. On these grounds, however, Brighouse's distinction is largely unnecessary, because religious parents are much less likely to object to education for autonomy than Brighouse fears, a point we explore in the following section. Religious parents' educational choices are likely to have more to do with providing a spiritual dimension to their children's education than with a desire to prevent their future autonomy.

Measuring Up To Brighouse's Standards

Exposure to Diversity

Brighouse (2000) holds that "autonomy with respect to one's religious and moral commitments requires exposure to alternate views" (p. 75). Given religious parents' presumed refusal to engage in deliberation with rival views, Brighouse is skeptical that they will be able to provide the necessary education for autonomy. If we allow religious parents to exempt their children from autonomy-facilitating education, the children will not be prepared for a life outside the community in which they are raised, leaving only those children who happen to be suited for their parents' way of life any opportunity of living well. This, says Brighouse, constitutes a "strong prima facie injustice" (p. 73). Brighouse argues that a right to exit does not by itself mitigate this injustice. Children who do exit will be even worse off than those who stay because they will not have been prepared for the social milieu of modern society.

Brighouse refers to religious parents variously as deeply religious, fundamentalist, or sectarian. As noted earlier, it is not entirely clear whether he is concerned with a particular segment of the religious population to whom these terms might apply, or whether he believes any schooling of a religious nature poses a difficulty with regard to autonomy. Certainly, it is hard to conceive of any community, except perhaps the Amish, to be as isolated from society as Brighouse imagines religious families to be. Parents who waive autonomy-facilitating education, he says, "typically live in tight-knit communities which limit the opportunities for exposure to other ways of life and for the development of critical faculties" (Brighouse, 2000, pp. 70–71), leaving children unprepared to engage in the economic and social organization of mainstream society. Except perhaps for a tiny minority, this fear, however, is scarcely reasonable. Modern culture is, as one writer describes it, "dominant, pervasive, and unavoidable" (Salomone, 2000, p. 212), and few families would be truly able to isolate themselves from it even if that were their aim. The majority of deeply religious parents live, not in separate communities like the Amish, but in neighbourhoods that are not segregated by religion. Most religious families engage in the activities of the larger community and many initially send their children to local public schools, only later seeking accommodations or withdrawing to religious schools. Many are active in politics, perhaps to the chagrin of those who, like Brighouse (2000), lament the fact that "in the US, fundamentalist Christianity remains a strong cultural force, and even a remarkably strong political force" (p. 207). Nor is religion or religious schooling an impediment to preparation for a mainstream career or a hindrance to engaging in the complex economic activities of modern society. Brighouse must realize that religious parents are themselves engaged in a range of economic activities and would want their children to be prepared for a successful future as well. As Raz (1994) notes, members of all communities inhabit the same economy and must possess "the same mathematical, literary, and other skills required for effective participation" (p. 173). Given the number of scientists, entrepreneurs, educators, and other professionals who were raised in religious homes and schools, and who are nevertheless highly successful in their chosen fields, a religious schooling does not seem to be a barrier to acquiring and using those skills. Brighouse highly exaggerates the isolation experienced by children from religious families, and children in religious schools are no doubt better prepared for modern society than he acknowledges.

What of the curricular objectives Brighouse argues must be met to ensure the exposure to diversity that is required for autonomy with respect to one's religious and moral commitments? Brighouse suggests children must be taught about a range of religious, non-religious, and antireligious views and the ways in which secular and religious thinkers have dealt with moral conflict. However, there are serious limitations in Brighouse's educational model. Regardless of how serious any advocate may be, to be addressed by the proponent of a particular view in the "controlled environment of the classroom" (Brighouse, 2000, p. 75) is not the same as seeing a way of life lived out. It is very unlikely that a series of classroom presentations would have any significant role in children making a meaningful choice with regard to religion. Because of its limitations, a classroom presentation is an unlikely means of conveying the mystical or spiritual nature of religion or the full implications of committing oneself to a "road less travelled." As a means of exposing children to diversity, this approach is necessarily limited because few schools would have the resources to present any more than a small selection of views in any comprehensive way. In anything but urban schools, this limitation would be even more acute. Neither would this proposal satisfy religious parents because it fails to present children with a deep understanding of any one religious choice and may in fact omit the parents' particular perspectives entirely. Thus, even in a common school that attempted to include some religious views, the choices made available to children would be limited substantially. Any upbringing and any education, religious or secular, will predispose children to select some options and reject others, while remaining ignorant of yet other possibilities. Brighouse's proposal is no exception to this rule and suffers in addition from other shortcomings.

Religious schooling, then, may not limit a child's choices with regard to religion any more than any schooling does. Although religious schooling is likely to familiarize a child deeply with only one religion, it is improbable that a secular education will give a child a deep understanding of any religion. Yet a deep understanding of one religious way of life may help the child to understand more fully the implications of choosing any religious way of life because most religions challenge many of the practices of a predominant consumer society and adopt a spiritual perspective on life in the world. At the same time, although most religious schools focus on a single religious perspective, they need not limit children's choices in other respects. If religious schools have the necessary resources, they can as readily as common schools present a broad range of courses for students, presenting everything from arts to sciences as fascinating areas of study, and can as well as other schools prepare students for careers in a wide variety of fields, from business to politics. In a liberal society that respects religious freedom, deeply religious persons, to use Brighouse's term, are free to engage fully in the social, political, and economic worlds that surround them, and a religious schooling need not in any way restrict their freedom to do so. Religious families are unlikely to be as isolated as Brighouse imagines, and religious schooling need not restrict children's awareness of the world around them.

Critical Reflection

Brighouse holds the view that religious parents want to control their children's thinking and that religious education would prevent the development of critical-reasoning capacities, a view that is not uncommon among liberal education theorists (Curren, 2000; Dwyer, 1998; Macedo, 2000). No doubt, there are religious parents who, like many nonreligious parents, desire to control what their children think and believe. However, Brighouse is making an unfair assessment of religious parents and religious schooling in general. Although most religious parents would want their children to accept their particular way of life and to embrace it as their own, few would want them to do so unthinkingly. It is not a desire to prevent critical reflection that leads parents to choose religious schooling. Rather, religious schools are chosen by parents who want their children to learn the skills of discernment and reasoning from within the traditions of their particular religion and not from a secular perspective.

Parents who want their children to think in religious ways would no doubt be skeptical that this goal could be achieved in common schools. Historically, public schools in North America have included some recognition of religion, even if it was only in the opening of the school day in prayer. Today, prayer and other religious observances no longer form part of the common school practice in North America. Although there is good reason to remove sectarian religious exercises from public schools in a religiously pluralistic society, the absence of religion in schools can be interpreted as a message about the insignificance of religion for daily life. Religious parents who do not fear critical reflection itself may nonetheless be concerned that the deliberation encouraged in common schools will undermine their belief system because religious ways of thinking are given no consideration.

We accept that in religious schooling it is likely that certain beliefs will not be subjected to trenchant critical scrutiny: for instance, the belief in God as Creator and the belief that the demand for respect for others is grounded in the equality of all people in the eyes of God. Such practice might be seen as indoctrinative. By way of contrast, some liberal theorists, such as Macedo (2000), argue that schools must leave all religious questions aside and teach children that important public issues can be deliberated without considering the religious question (p. 122). Is this practice also inherently indoctrinative? "Whatever is done or said in the classroom conveys an inescapable and powerful non-neutral message to children that convention and authority are behind a specific practice" (Salomone, 2000, p. 204). The message the school communicates by leaving the religious question aside is that secular views have more validity than religious perspectives and that religion has no bearing on one's public life. Yet parents whose religion is deeply meaningful to them would want to see their religion's views inform the education their children are receiving in order that their children may also understand the vitality and applicability of those views. The obvious worry for religious parents may be, as Callan (2000) points out, that religious identity will be lost before it is even found, "because without yet understanding the life of faith, children come to feel it is something that is odd or shameful in a world whose predominant values declare it to be so" (p. 62).

In the end, neutrality is an improper standard for judging whether any school is indoctrinative. Education cannot take place in a context where no stance is taken on anything. The question, as always, comes down to which stances are reasonable within a liberal democratic society.

Religious schooling need not prevent the development of critical-thinking skills. Shelley Burtt (1994, 1996) contends that religious parents are not opposed to critical thinking in general, but simply to the nature of the critical thinking prescribed in secular schools. Burtt claims that fears that religious education will impair a child's ability to reason are unfounded and consequently supports parental authority over a child's education. She argues that the state must take into consideration "religiously grounded ways in which children might learn to choose well in civic and moral matters" (Burtt, 1996, p. 413). According to Burtt, conflicts that arise between religious parents and public schools are often framed as debates over whether children will receive an education that encourages critical reflection and civic competency or one that will not, when in fact the question is whether the children will receive an education for personal reflection and civic responsibility grounded in religious faith or based on secular reasoning. She challenges the assumption that is embedded "in most recent philosophical considerations of critical rationality that to reason from the basis of God's word as reflected in Scripture is somehow to abandon the exercise of critical rationality," noting the "long and distinguished traditions of religious scholarship which reflect critically on the requirements of one's own (perhaps unquestioned) fundamental commitments" (Burtt, 1996, p. 416). By way of example, Burtt cites Arneson and Shapiro (1996), who assume that Amish parents deliberately limit critical thinking so that their children will accept things on faith rather than through reflection. Burtt (1996) argues that the Amish may not be opposed to the development of critical-thinking skills but rather to the materials used by secular schools to teach those skills (p. 416). Burtt's defence of religious scholarship may bring to mind names such as Augustine or Aquinas, but no doubt most of us could name at least one contemporary scholar who is able to conduct rational inquiry with his or her faith intact, effectively confirming that religion and critical reflection are not necessarily inimical.

Religious parents, then, are likely to choose religious schooling not because of an aversion to instruction in critical-thinking skills, but rather because they want to teach these skills in an environment that is respectful of, and informed by, their particular religious perspectives. As McLaughlin (1992) points out, "It is clear that every cultural group and tradition will value and embody certain forms of reason and individual thought" (p. 127). The secular version of critical reflection adopted by common schools is not necessarily the only approach to rationality. Jane Roland Martin (1992) describes very different approaches to critical thinking from masculine and feminine perspectives and participatory and distant thinkers. Martin could well have added two more distinct categories of thinkers, the secular and the religious, showing how they differ in their approach to problems that require reflection and thought. Menachem Loberbaum (1995), writing from the perspective of the Jewish faith, says that

> traditions provide a range of acceptable and authoritative argumentation and discourse, but also "traditions when vital, embody continuities of conflict" (MacIntyre, 1984, p. 222). Within the Jewish tradition, the Talmud supplies both. It is a wide-ranging source of argumentation; indeed its literary structure is of a rhetoric that celebrates argumentation. (pp. 116–117)

Loberbaum demonstrates that an education that teaches critical reflection need not disassociate the individuals from their religious beliefs but that skills of reasoning and reflection can be developed from within religious traditions.

Liberal educators fear that children raised in such religious traditions will be so indoctrinated that they are unable critically to evaluate other choices. Most children will no doubt view the religion in which they were raised as a more credible option than other choices they may encounter, and even the capacity for rational deliberation is not likely entirely to overcome this bias. However, it is impossible not to create a bias of some sort, regardless of the tradition in which a child is raised, and a religious upbringing is unlikely to lead to a greater or more limiting bias than a nonreligious upbringing. A child raised by parents who practice no religion at all and educated in a secular common school, for example, is unlikely to view a religious way of life as a serious option, although, of course, the possibility is not entirely closed off. It would be nearly impossible for any parents to raise their children from a morally neutral perspective and it is not advisable to attempt to do so. Children are not, after all, born with the capacity for critical reflection and must for a time be given guidance with respect to what is demanded of virtuous and moral persons. The fact that children are taught from a particular perspective does not preclude rational evaluation of this way of life at a later time. Critical reflection on a particular way of life may in fact be more meaningful if a child has first gained a deep understanding of that way of life and what is at stake in rejecting or accepting it as one's own. An understanding of a particular way of life is also likely to give one a starting point for reflection and comparison that is unattainable when all options are regarded from the beginning as neutral and equal, a condition that is, as we have already noted, not realistically attainable or educationally desirable.

Consider an argument made by Randall Curren (1998, 2000). Curren, who views religious schooling as highly indoctrinative, denies similar charges against his own recommendations that children receive a moral education in particular virtues. Curren (1998) claims that children who learn to think about moral virtues "will become morally serious and committed critical thinkers, motivated by conceptions of themselves as both moral and devoted to truth" (p. 6). Curren argues that although children necessarily will form certain perceptions and sentiments as a result of such an education, this does not preclude future examination of those beliefs. A similar argument could be made with regard to religious education. Certainly, religion stimulates consideration of some very significant aspects of human existence and encourages children to think more deeply about their own lives than they may otherwise have done. Learning to think about important and serious matters is likely to develop, not impair, one's capacity for critical reflection. If this is the case, then religious education is much more compatible with the development of critical-thinking skills than Brighouse and many other liberal theorists assume it to be and should not be so quickly dismissed as a barrier to children's future autonomy.

Cultural Identity

School choice is sometimes defended on the basis of parents' rights to protect their particular ethnic or religious culture from erosion and to enable them to pass their way of life on to their children. However, inasmuch as he considers an upbringing in such particular ways of life harmful to the development of autonomy, Brighouse argues that parents have no right to raise their children from within their particular culture or religion or to send them to religious schools. Unlike Taylor (1994), who argues that governments can both be liberal and also "weigh the importance of uniform treatment against the importance of cultural survival and opt sometimes in favour of the latter" (p. 61), Brighouse doubts that liberal governments should take measures to ensure the survival of threatened cultures. According to Brighouse, parents cannot claim the right to their culture as a basis for controlling their children's education or denying them an education for autonomy. Brighouse (2000) claims that even if children are raised exclusively in their parents' culture, "there is no guarantee that that will be their culture in adulthood" (p. 101). Brighouse says,

> Fundamentally children do not have a culture. Ensuring that children are being raised exclusively in the culture of their parents is not granting them their right to culture because they do not have their own culture. To suggest that they do is to suggest that they are the kinds of beings that can evaluate and assess options available to them, which they are not. (p. 101)

Brighouse's claim here is most curious. In this passage, he seems to suggest that culture is something that one does not have until one chooses it after critical reflection on the available options. However, this seems scarcely credible. Is Brighouse suggesting that, upon maturity, one chooses one's ethnicity or religion, having until that point lived without any cultural affiliation? Certainly adults can, after reflection, choose to abandon cultural customs and traditions and to reject certain moral virtues held in their childhood. Conversely, they may choose to adopt the traditions or the language of a new culture. Such choices seem to require the adaptation or rejection of cultures of which they are already members. How did they attain that original membership? Did it become theirs only on achieving adulthood, or could they claim it as their own from childhood?

Brighouse would agree for the most part, we believe, that individuals are born into particular cultures. Cultural communities, says Van Dyke (1995), are "groups of persons, predominately of common descent, who think of themselves as collectively possessing a separate identity based on race or on shared cultural characteristics, usually language or religion" (p. 32). Membership in these cultural communities is seldom chosen but rather assumed because of the circumstances of one's birth and the acculturation experienced as one grows up within the group into which one is born. Margalit and Raz (1995), in considering group rights and group membership, argue that cultural membership is largely involuntary:

> To be a good Irishman, it is true, is an achievement. But to be an Irishman is not. Qualification for membership is usually determined by non-voluntary criteria. One cannot choose to belong. One belongs because of who one is. One can come to belong to such groups, but only by changing, e.g., by adopting their culture, changing one's tastes and habits accordingly—a very slow process indeed. (pp. 85–86)

We are Irish or French, Catholic or Jewish, because of the circumstances of our birth. Whether we would have chosen that culture given the chance to do so, we would be very surprised during our growing up years to find it was not our culture, just as we would be surprised to find out the family we were born into and grew up in was not our family. Children develop an identity in a dialogical relationship with the family and the particular group surrounding the family. They participate from early childhood in family activities, including religious observances, and find stability and comfort in the traditions the family maintains. It is only natural that as children share in the cultural, perhaps religious, life of their parents that they will come to identify with that culture as their own. This point is reiterated by Colin Macleod (2002), who points out that "children come to have a sense of self partly by locating themselves in a distinct family history and ongoing participation in the practices identified as valuable by the family" (p. 215). When parents share with children the history, beliefs, and traditions of their culture, they provide them with a sense of identity and security in a place that is uniquely theirs.

If, for the most part, individuals belong to a cultural group because they have been born and raised in that culture, then it is reasonable to assume that the culture of the group is theirs from the time they first become, even if not by choice, a member of that group. It is rather pointless and wrong-headed to claim that children do not have culture of their own simply because they have not autonomously chosen membership in a particular group, when for the most part cultural membership is involuntary. Likewise, it is pointless to distinguish between being a part of, or member of, a cultural group, which is an undeniable social fact for most children, and having one's own culture, which is what Brighouse denies to children. We cannot discern the difference. If children do have their own culture, as we believe they do, then, contrary to what Brighouse claims, cultural claims can be made on behalf of the children who are members of those groups. Any argument in defence of group protection is as much for the benefit of the children as for the adult members of the group.

Even if Brighouse were to concede this point, it may not affect his claim that parents must prepare their children to live in cultures other than the one in which they are raised. Because children may quit their parents' culture, Brighouse argues that we must prepare them to live well in whatever culture eventually will be theirs. Whereas elsewhere he expresses regrets about the isolation experienced by religious families, Brighouse, in making this argument, suggests that all children are to some degree exposed to mainstream culture, and that it is therefore essential that they be equipped to scrutinize both their own way of life and others they encounter. Although they may seldom entirely abandon the culture of their birth, it is true that as children reach maturity and gain life experience, they tend to reject at least some aspects of their ancestral culture and adopt patterns of behaviour from new cultures they encounter. This is an inevitable result of the multicultural nature of much of the Western world. Until children reach some degree of maturity, however, we would be wise to encourage parents in their efforts to raise their children in a stable moral environment. This encouragement may include support for school choice and religious schooling because without such support some cultural and religious communities may be unable to protect their communities from erosion by pervasive secular and consumer societies. Brighouse, of course, claims that there is no reason to take measures to ensure that cultures continue to exist, in part because evidence shows that people can adapt easily to changing cultures. This may be true. However, it is not an argument against supporting communities in their attempts to preserve some aspects of their particular cultures. People are able to adapt to all manner of situations, some of them tragically unfortunate. That we are adaptable does not suggest that we should allow cultures to disappear, if options exist to preserve ways of life that are meaningful to families and their children. If reasonable options such as school choice allow the preservation of particular religious or other communities, such choice should be a legitimate possibility for these communities. Far from being harmful, growing up in a distinctive community can provide children with the sense of identity crucial to engaging in a self-fulfilling, autonomous future, including the self-assured adoption of another community later in life if that is their choice.

Conclusion

We do not doubt that Brighouse and others, who are so quick to label religious schooling as harmful, have at least some basis for their conclusions. Most of us are aware of religious groups that bring up children in ways that we abhor, and to whose educational efforts we would not lend support. Knowledge of the objectionable practices of some religious groups sometimes makes it difficult to defend support for any religious schooling. Concerns about some religious practices have led to a rather unreasonable fear of religious schooling in general. It is much too hasty, however, to assume that all or even most religious communities raise their children in ways that would impair their future autonomy or harm them in any way. We would not presume to make broad judgments about particular religious groups based solely on their identity as fundamentalist, orthodox, or even liberal religious organizations. Within any of these groups, one may find educational practices that do not in any way undermine democracy. For the most part, the theorists and citizens who built our liberal society had religious roots and upbringings, and most of schooling was at one time sectarian in nature. This did not impede the development of autonomous individuals or societies devoted to justice. Religious families care deeply about their children and generally raise them in caring and responsible ways. Many, perhaps most, religious groups are concerned about individual rights and freedoms, including the rights and interests of their own children and the children of those whose parents think differently from them. Brighouse and other liberal educators cannot make any general and conclusive claims about the harm religious education imposes on children. Many religious parents and religious schools offer children an education that encourages and supports their future autonomy and does not in any way undermine the goals or aims of civic education in liberal democracies.

Such a conclusion has important implications for public policy. We have already referred to arguments made by the government of Ontario in resisting appeals for the funding of religious schools. That province, in more than one case, has claimed that religious schools would undermine the goals of liberal democracies (*Adler v. Ontario*, 1996; ICCPR, 1999), fears very similar to those expressed by Brighouse. In its response to religious claimants in *Adler v. Ontario* (1996), for example, the province argued that funding religious schools would stand in the way of the goal to build a more tolerant society, a claim that at least one justice upheld. Chief Justice McLachlin argued, in this case, that "the encouragement of a more tolerant harmonious multicultural society" (p. 10) was reason enough to deny funding to religious schools. Like Brighouse, McLachlin claims that religious schooling diminishes the multicultural exposure of children and that this "lack of exposure, in turn, would diminish the mutual tolerance and understanding of Ontarians of diverse cultures and religions for one another" (215, 217). However, we have shown that these fears are unwarranted and that religious schooling need not result in isolation or intolerance or undermine children's future autonomy. If, as we have suggested, religious schooling is not necessarily, or even in most instances, a barrier to a satisfactory civic education, the fears expressed by Brighouse and other liberals are largely unwarranted. It would be reasonable, then, to consider the possibility that religious schools have a legitimate place in the liberal democratic state.

REFERENCES

Adler v. Ontario. (1996). 3 S.C.R. 609.

Arneson, R.J., & Shapiro, I. (1996). Democratic autonomy and religious freedom: A critique of Wisconsin v. Yoder. In R.J. Arneson & I. Shapiro (Eds.), *Nomos 38: Political order* (pp. 365–411). New York: New York University Press.

Brighouse, H. (1998). Civic education and liberal legitimacy. *Ethics, 108*(4), 719–745. doi:10.1086/233849

Brighouse, H. (2000). *School choice and social justice.* New York: Oxford University Press.

Burtt, S. (1994). Religious parents, secular schools: A liberal defense of an illiberal education. *Review of Politics, 56*(01), 51–70. doi:10.1017/S0034670500049500

Burtt, S. (1996). In defense of Yoder: Parental authority and the public schools. In I. Shapiro & R. Hardin (Eds.), *Nomos 38: Political order* (pp. 412–437). New York: New York University Press.

Callan, E. (1997). *Creating citizens.* Oxford: Clarendon Press. doi:10.1093/0198292589.001.0001

Callan, E. (2000). Discrimination and religious schooling. In W. Kymlicka & W. Norman (Eds.), *Citizenship in diverse societies* (pp. 45–67). New York: Oxford University Press. doi:10.1093/019829770X.003.0002

Curren, R. (1998). Critical thinking and the unity of virtue. In S. Tozer (Ed.), *Philosophy of education 1998* (pp. 158–165). Urbana, IL: Philosophy of Education Society.

Curren, R. (2000). *Aristotle on the necessity of public education.* Lanham, MD: Rowman and Littlefield.

Dwyer, J.G. (1998). *Religious schools v. children's rights.* Ithaca, NY: Cornell University Press.

Galston, W. (1989). Civic education in the liberal state. In N. Rosenblum (Ed.), *Liberalism and the moral life* (pp. 89–102). Cambridge, MA: Harvard University Press.

Galston, W. (1995). Two concepts of liberalism. *Ethics, 105*(3), 516–534. doi:10.1086/293725

Gutmann, A. (1999). *Democratic education.* Princeton, NJ: Princeton University Press.

International Covenant on Civil and Political Rights (ICCPR). (1999, October 18–November 5). Human Rights Committee, sixty-seventh session. CCPR/C/67/D/694/1996. Retrieved from http://www.unhchr.ch/tbs/doc.nsf/0/b3bfc541589cc30f802568690052e5d6

Loberbaum, M. (1995). Learning from mistakes: Resources of tolerance in the Jewish tradition. In Y. Tamir (Ed.), *Democratic education in a multicultural state* (pp. 115–126). Oxford: Blackwell.

Lomasky, L. (1987). *Persons, rights and the moral community.* New York: Oxford University Press.

Macedo, S. (2000). *Diversity and distrust: Civic education in a multicultural democracy.* Cambridge, MA: Harvard University Press.

Macleod, C.M. (2002). Liberal equality and the affective family. In D. Archard & C.M. MacLeod (Eds.), *The moral and political status of children* (pp. 212–230). New York: Oxford University Press. doi:10.1093/0199242682.003.0012

Margalit, A., & Raz, J. (1995). National self determination. In W. Kymlicka (Ed.), *The rights of minority cultures* (pp. 79–92). New York: Oxford University Press.

Martin, J.R. (1992). Critical thinking for a humane world. In S.P. Norris (Ed.), *The generalizability of critical thinking* (pp. 163–180). New York: Teachers College Press.

McLaughlin, T.H. (1992). The ethics of separate schools. In M. Leicester & M. Taylor (Eds.), *Ethics, ethnicity, and education* (pp. 114–136). London, UK: Kogan Page.

Raz, J. (1994). *Ethics in the public domain.* New York: Oxford University Press.

Salomone, R. (2000). *Visions of schooling: Conscience, community, and common education.* New Haven, CT: Yale University Press.

Taylor, C. (1994). The politics of recognition. In A. Gutmann (Ed.), *Multiculturalism* (pp. 25–74). Princeton, NJ: Princeton University Press.

Van Dyke, V. (1995). The individual, the state, and ethnic communities in political theory. In W. Kymlicka (Ed.), *The rights of minority cultures* (pp. 31–56). New York: Oxford University Press.

21

Parental Rights and the Aims of Education

Teaching Religion, Human Sexuality, and Sexual Orientation in Schools

Dianne Gereluk*

*This is a revised and expanded version of a paper previously published as Gereluk, D. (2011, Spring). When good intentions go awry: Limiting toleration and diversity through Bill 44. *Canadian Issues (Special Issue of the Comparative and International Studies Society),* 75–79. Reproduced with permission.

Under section 11.1 of the Alberta Human Rights Act, teachers are required to give prior written notice to parents when subject matter concerning religion, human sexuality, or sexual orientation is primarily and explicitly addressed in class. Failure to comply may mean a teacher being held accountable before the Alberta Human

Rights Commission. This chapter is divided into two sections. The first section will provide the lead up to the legislation that called for increased parental discretion over morally controversial topics. The second section will consider the competing values between parental rights and the aims of education. I argue that the aim to create more transparency and parental discretion undermines the aims of public education in two significant ways. First, it inhibits children's ability to understand, discuss, and debate a range of competing perspectives on how to lead one's life specifically regarding religion, human sexuality, or sexual orientation. Second, section 11.1 undermines the very purpose of reducing discriminatory behaviour toward sexual orientation by allowing parents to opt their children out of conversations that are not congruent with their private views. To understand the underpinning philosophical argument, let us first turn to the lead up to the legislation.

Lead Up to the Legislation

On September 1, 2010, section 11.1 of the Alberta Human Rights Act came into force throughout Alberta. Section 11.1 states in part:

> *A board as defined in the School Act shall provide notice to a parent or guardian of a student where courses of study, educational programs or instructional materials, or instruction or exercises, prescribed under that Act include subject matter that deals primarily and explicitly with religion, human sexuality or sexual orientation. (Alberta Human Rights Act, R.S.A. 2000)*

The Alberta government had two reasons for passing section 11.1: to provide greater transparency to parents regarding what takes place within schools, and to make explicit parental control over topics that children might be exposed to in classrooms. To understand the rationale and justification for section 11.1 of the Alberta Human Rights Act, the discussion must be positioned within the competing political values of the right not to be discriminated against for reasons of sexual orientation, and the rights to freedom of conscience and religion in relation to their expression within the family and its relationship to public education. Specifically, we turn to three cases that are arguably instrumental in the discussion leading up to section 11.1: *Vriend v. Alberta (1998)* [*Vriend*], *Chamberlain v Surrey District (2002)* [*Chamberlain*], and the *Correns Agreement* (Province of British Columbia, 2006). A brief recitation of the facts of these cases and their influence on the creation of section 11.1 follows.

In 1988 Delwin Vriend was given a permanent contract as a laboratory coordinator at King's College, a private religious college in

Alberta. In 1990 he informed the college that he was gay. In 1991 the college created a position statement that homosexuality was contrary to the religious doctrine of that institution and consequently asked Vriend to resign from his position. Upon his refusal, the college dismissed him. Vriend appealed the decision to the Alberta Human Rights Commission but was denied on the basis that homosexuals were not protected under the provincial legislation. As it stood, the Individual's Rights Protection Act (IRPA) in Alberta offered no protection on the basis of sexual discrimination (Macklem, 1999, p. 201). Vriend argued that the omission of protecting one's sexual orientation was a breach of section 15 of the Canadian Charter of Rights and Freedoms. The Alberta Court of Queen's Bench agreed, but it was appealed to the Alberta Court of Appeal, which overturned the decision. In a seven to one decision, the Supreme Court of Canada ruled in favour of Vriend, stating that a legislative omission can still lead to a Charter violation in which the IRPA resulted in a denial of "equal benefit and protection of the law on the basis of sexual orientation which was sufficient to conclude that discrimination was present and there had been a violation of s. 15" (*Vriend v. Alberta*, 1998). Since this decision, sexual orientation has been protected despite any explicit mention in Alberta legislation at the time.

The need to amend the Alberta provincial legislation to include protection not to be discriminated against due to sexual orientation is reflected in the preamble to Bill 44 in the spring of 2009. The preamble states:

> *WHEREAS it is recognized in Alberta as a fundamental principle and as a matter of public policy that all persons are equal in: dignity, rights and responsibilities without regard to race, religious beliefs, colour, gender, physical disability, mental disability, age, ancestry, place of origin, marital status, source of income, family status or sexual orientation. (Bill 44, Human Rights, Citizenship, and Multiculturalism Amendment Act 2009)*

Ten years after the Vriend decision, sexual orientation is now a protected right in Alberta legislation.

Given this protection, the constitutional right not to be discriminated against due to one's sexual orientation comes into a value conflict with the statutory right of parents to be the chief determiners of the education of their children in so far as religious matters are concerned. Because the latter issue includes various faith-based understandings of what is appropriate human behaviour, which may not be the same as a secular understanding, conflict can arise as the institutional presentation of sexual orientation is more than merely a pedagogical experience. It is at this point that the contested nature of section 11.1 of the Alberta Human Rights Act comes into play. While the inclusion of sexual orientation was being addressed at one level in the act, schools would now be required to give prior written notice to parents whenever religion, human sexuality, or sexual orientation would be primarily and explicitly addressed in the curriculum. The argument put forth during the second reading of Bill 44 in the legislature highlights the rationale for the inclusion of a parental opt-out clause in Alberta human rights legislation. The Education Minister at the time, David Hancock, stated:

> There are topics of human sexuality, which have always been issues of concern to parents about how their children are instructed in those areas. Many parents want to know when that instruction happens, and they want to be able to know either that their child could be excluded from that or included. … We would encourage parents to be involved in their children's education, to understand what's in the curriculum, and to have the opportunity, where they object, to have their child opt out. (The 27th Legislature, Second Session, 13 May 2009, 927)

Furthermore, in developing an argument about transparency, the Conservative government drew upon Article 26 of the Universal Declaration on Human Rights (1948), which states, "Parents have a prior right to choose the kind of education that shall be given to their children." In referring to Article 26 of the declaration, the debate shifts beyond the transparency argument to arguing that parents are the final moral arbiters in their children's education. Never was this clearer than when the Honourable Member for Airdrie-Chestermere, Rob Anderson, spoke regarding the need for the parental opt-out clause. He states:

> The day that we undermine the central and critical role of parents and family in the fabric of our society is the first day of the decline of this province and of this country. Committed and thoughtful parenting is the key to positively shaping the lives of our next generation for the better, and there is no more effective parental arrangement than a committed mother and father working side by side for the benefit of their child. (The 27th Legislature, Second Session, 13 May 2009, 1009)

The comments made here by Hon. Anderson suggest a moral argument commonly applied to the view that parents have the ultimate right and final discretion to educate their children in a particular manner when major contested moral, religious, and sociopolitical issues are concerned. Such issues that commonly lack consensus in the public sphere are to be left in the hands of the family unit. Following this line of reasoning, parents become the final arbiters in their children's education.

This became more apparent when Liberal Opposition member Kevin Taft further questioned why Hon. Anderson felt that the parental opt-out clause needed to be in the Alberta Human Rights Act when similar clauses existed in the School Act. In response, Anderson stated his concern:

> If I look to our neighbours in British Columbia, there is no doubt that right now there is a movement under way to take that very right that parents have in British Columbia away from them so that they cannot opt their children out of these specific courses. So I think that it's important to enshrine that in this legislation. (The 27th Legislature, Second Session, *13 May 2009, 1010*)

It is at this point that we begin to understand the concerns that Hon. Anderson had in relation to recent decisions regarding inclusive education in British Columbia. The *Chamberlain v. Surrey School District No. 36* Supreme Court of Canada case and the Correns Agreement make this clear.

In *Chamberlain*, the plaintiff sought permission to use three supplementary reading texts that depicted same-sex parental relationships for use in the kindergarten and Grade 1 family values unit. The Surrey School Board did not approve the request, stating that the books "would engender controversy in light of some parents' religious objections to the morality of same-sex relationships ... [that] children at the K-1 level should not be exposed to ideas that might conflict with the beliefs of their parents; that children of this age were too young to learn about same-sex parented families; and that the material was not necessary to achieve the learning outcomes in the curriculum" (*Chamberlain v. Surrey School District No. 36*, 2002). The majority of the Supreme Court, however, ruled that in the board's concern over those families who might object to same-sex relationships, it failed to consider the legal rights of same-sex families and their children who are entitled to equal respect and recognition in the school system.

The family values unit requires that children discuss a variety of family models, which also includes that of same-sex relations. The court ultimately decided, "The Board must act in a way that promotes respect and tolerance for all the diverse groups that it represents and serves" (para. 25). In the wake of this decision, the Surrey School District became the first district in British Columbia to offer an inclusive curriculum that includes discussion of same-sex relationships.

Following the *Chamberlain* decision, the provincial government amended the education curricula such that they became inclusive of diverse relationships regardless of one's sexual orientation.

The second incident refers to the more recent Correns Agreement that was implemented in British Columbia (Province of British Columbia, 2006). Peter and Murray Correns, a homosexual couple, argued before the BC Human Rights Tribunal that public schools in British Columbia discriminated against homosexuals by failing to include representation of same-sex relationships in curricula and that the lack of such representation amounted to systemic discrimination. The tribunal accepted their case; however, as the hearing approached in 2006, the provincial government negotiated a settlement with the Correns known as the Correns Agreement. The province committed itself to review the inclusivity of school curricula and introduce a new elective course on social justice that would include sexual orientation, race, ethnicity, and gender issues.

The *Chamberlain* judgment and Correns Agreement both required that the provincial government amend the education curricula such that they become inclusive of diverse relationships regardless of one's sexual orientation. For Rob Anderson, his legislative allusion to the decisions made in British Columbia suggested they were arguably troublesome in the delineation between the private and public sphere regarding morally contentious issues.

In Alberta, after 36 days of debate, section 11.1 was passed on June 2, 2009, and came into effect in the fall of 2009, with one year's grace given before implementation on September 1, 2010. This provided Alberta Education and school districts with the time necessary to consider the implications of section 11.1 and the requisite requirements that would be demanded of teachers and schools.

In sum, the Alberta government appeared to create section 11.1 in response, at least in part, to the concern that there was a potential conflict between two sets of rights. The first was the right of Albertans not to be discriminated against due to their sexual orientation and that, as a pedagogical corollary in furtherance of that right, sexual orientation should be articulated and explained in schools. The second was the right of Albertan parents to instruct their children in their family's religious beliefs, including the derivative right to have prior notice of classroom activities or discussions that might by their nature deal with matters related to those beliefs at least in so far as sexual orientation was concerned. Section 11.1 was arguably the government's answer to balancing those rights in consideration of the implications associated with them. Efforts to balance these competing rights continue to play out. Since the passing of section 11.1, the Supreme Court of Canada has recently determined that balancing religious rights and the state's interest in public education is indeed a delicate balance. In the Drummondville case (*S.L. c. Commission scolaire des Chenes*, 2012) the issue of parental religious rights and the state's interest in public education was held in favour of the state's overriding interest. Mr. Justice Deschamps, speaking for the majority of the court, said,

> *Parents are free to pass their personal beliefs on to their children if they so wish. However, the early exposure of children to realities that differ from those in their immediate family environment is a fact of life in society. The suggestion that exposing children to a variety of religious facts in itself infringes their religious freedom or that of their parents amounts to a rejection of the multicultural reality of Canadian society and ignores the ... government's obligations with regard to public education. Although such exposure can be a source of friction, it does not in itself constitute an infringement of s. 2(a) of the Canadian Charter ... (para. 40)*

While the decision in the Drummondville case has sided with the role of schools to address the broader aims of public education, the Alberta Human Rights Act has erred on the side of providing greater parental control with the aim of providing more transparency of what is taught inside schools.

The justification offered for this section is to provide transparency between schools and parents when controversial and sensitive issues are discussed. Yet, in trying to create a particular transparency between schools and parents, the legislation creates several practical challenges and concerns, and, at a more theoretical level, it also challenges some of the fundamental aims and purposes of public education. Given the political and legal debates that informed the lead up to this legislation, let us now turn to the broader philosophical implications regarding parental rights and the aims of public education.

Fundamental Aims of Education Challenged

The daily challenges and obstacles that section 11.1 places on teachers and schools are notable (Gereluk, 2011)[1]. At a more fundamental level, the repercussions of implementing this act undermine some primary aims of education in liberal pluralist societies: that of fostering personal autonomy and developing civic dispositions necessary in civil society. The fostering of personal autonomy is compromised in that every individual ought to be exposed to alternative perspectives to develop the ability to make informed judgments about how they wish to lead their life. This in turn has negative repercussions from a societal perspective in compromising individuals' ability to deliberate and live together among other members of society who may have vastly different lifestyles and perspectives. Let us address each issue in turn.

The autonomy argument focuses primarily on the concern that parents may not expose their children to alternative ways of life counter to their upbringing. Allowing parents to have the primary say in a child's upbringing may limit significantly the child's exposure to alternative values, beliefs, and experiences. This includes challenging the assumed beliefs and values of their own families, and deciding for themselves how they wish to lead their lives.

A primary aim of education is to provide a multitude of opportunities that both support and challenge one's assumptions. Harry Brighouse (2006) argues:

> *Autonomy-facilitation requires a modicum of discontinuity between the child's home experience and her school experience, so that the opportunities provided by the home (and the public culture) are supplemented, rather than replicated, in the school. (p. 22)*

For Brighouse, the role for schools is not just supporting and extending the family's belief system but also providing opportunities to deliberate about different perspectives, particularly those that are incongruent with one's family values. Children's critical judgment and informed decisions rely on the ability to understand and pursue various experiences that may not be afforded to them within the family unit. Levinson (1999) more boldly states that:

> *it is difficult for children to achieve autonomy solely within the bounds of their families and home communities—or even within the bounds of schools whose norms are constituted by those held by the child's home community. If we take the requirements of autonomy seriously, we see the need for a place separate from the environment in which children are raised, for a community that is defined not by the values and commitments of the child's home, whatever they happen to be, but by the norms of critical inquiry, reason and sympathetic reflection. (p. 58)*

It is not a mere preference that children should be exposed to different experiences to secure autonomy, but a necessity. This exposure must be located in a school that challenges the established values and norms of the community. While the role of public education is not to assimilate and inculcate certain values that may be hostile to particular communities, the role of public education is arguably to expose children to different ideas beyond that of their private sphere. If we consider a person who is homosexual in such a closed religious community, the lack of understanding and acknowledgement of different sexual orientations will fundamentally impinge on that particular individual's freedom. Lest we be too quick to protect community values, we ought to attend to those individuals in those communities who may be marginalized, oppressed, or abused.

Participation in varied experiences and alternative ways of living help to secure individuals' capacities to lead a life of their own choosing as adults. If left to parents, children will have differing levels of exposure and opportunities. And while schools will not level this out, providing a school system that attends to several different experiences will reduce such inequalities. If a primary aim of education is to promote autonomy in children then arguably it is imperative that a school system be developed that supports this aim. The Alberta Education Commission on Learning Report (2003) clearly states these aims in its preamble:

> [E]ducation is the most important investment we can make as a society. Our education system not only shapes individual students' lives, it shapes the very nature of our society. A strong and vibrant public education system—a system that values each and every individual, instills positive values, and builds tolerance and respect—is critical to develop social cohesion and the kind of civil society Albertans want for the future. (p. 4)

If indeed the aims and objectives of Alberta Education are to foster these aims, then section 11.1 is in direct contravention in allowing parents to exempt their children from lessons dealing with religion, human sexuality, and sexual orientation. To secure children's abilities to make informed judgments and choices about how they wish to lead their lives, both in the present and in the future, it seems misguided to assume that all parents will provide sufficient exposure to alternative lifestyles, or conversely, that parents should have the right to limit the exposure of such essential topics (albeit potentially controversial and sensitive) under the guise of protecting their personal belief system.

Rather than broadening conversations that address religion, human sexuality, and sexual orientation, the Alberta Human Rights Act reduces this possibility. It takes a regressive step with respect to developing dispositions of inclusion and toleration for individuals in a plural society, and reduces the ability of students to make informed judgments about how to lead flourishing lives as adults.

If one of the aims of public education is to develop children's ability to make informed judgments about how to lead one's life under a notion of autonomy, schools have a second broader democratic objective. Schools have the duty to develop civic virtues that are necessary for the sustainability of a vibrant political society. The vitality of a democratic state depends on "an education adequate to participating in democratic politics, to choosing among (a limited range of) good lives, and to sharing in the several sub-communities, such as families, that impart identity to the lives of its citizens" (Gutmann, 1987, p. 42). Amy Gutmann argues that developing civic virtues in children is not a mere ideal or preference but is vital if we are to preserve and foster democratic sovereignty. Letting parents and families cultivate such virtues is problematic because the human tendency is to have natural biases toward certain preferences and orientations creating certain prejudices in their children. Schools have the ability to provide a political education that could teach all children the civic virtues necessary for them to participate in and shape the political structure and stability of society as future adults and citizens.

Schools as an institution are integral to preserving the political culture necessary for a liberal democracy to thrive. Understanding and participating in a political culture is not something one just comes to know; it encompasses certain habits, skills, and dispositions that each individual must be inducted into in a meaningful way. Eamonn Callan (1997) makes this point when he states that public institutions play a vital role in the way that we induct individuals into the larger political sphere:

> it is a shared way of public life constituted by a constellation of attitudes, habits, and abilities that people acquire as they grow up. These include a lively interest in the question of what life is truly and not just seemingly good, as well as a willingness both to share one's own answer with others and to heed the many opposing answers they might give; and active commitment to the good of the polity, as well as confidence and competence in judgement regarding how that good should be advanced; a respect for fellow citizens and a sense of common fate with them that goes beyond the tribalisms of ethnicity and religion and is yet alive to the significance these will have in many people's lives. (p. 3)

Taken together, this encompasses a demanding type of education, not to be left to chance by parents. It requires a logical and coherent political education, deliberately considered and developed in children—not through mere osmosis or exposure but through active and deliberate thought processes and engagement about civic virtues and the political structures in society. It is not simply a dilemma between parental choice and civic education but parental choice and the basic individual interests of the child. "Success in state-sponsored civic education depends crucially on the broad diffusion of public virtue and understanding throughout the citizenry and across the major cleavages of interest that might divide some groups from others" (Callan, 2006, p. 266). Schools have a duty to develop particular dispositions that will foster the ability of individuals to deliberate, critically engage, and respect those who may have drastically different moral, religious, or political viewpoints.

Discussions about religion or human sexuality are integral to the way in which people live their lives; potentially removing these debates from the classrooms minimizes the ways in which individuals are able to address substantive pressing issues that are relevant in society. Further, discussing issues about the different perspectives and values inherent in religion and human sexuality provides an educational opportunity for teachers (and schools) to critically debate and model the dispositions children need to be exposed to in order to address such topics as future citizens.

If educators are sincere about developing a capacity for a sense of justice, limiting discussion or removing potentially contentious issues that may cause offence or debate seems antithetical to fostering dispositions of inclusion and toleration. Learning how to contend with substantive issues such as religion and human sexuality that are present and real in students' day-to-day lives is something schools should address and confront rather than shy away from. To be a good citizen also requires inculcating a notion of respect for oneself and for others. And learning how to critically and rationally debate the merits and complexities inherent in discussions related to human sexuality and religion are central to the skills and habits that should be a part of learning to develop a sense of justice. Section 11.1 places unwarranted authority and decision-making in the hands of parents. Unfortunately, such parental discretion not only has repercussions for the children of those who wish to opt out but also for the stability and cohesiveness of civil society.

Conclusion

The Alberta Human Rights Act has arguably moved the pendulum away from the democratic purposes of schooling in teaching about autonomy and citizenship toward increased parental discretion in how children should be educated. Parents now are able to exempt their children from any discussion related to religion, human sexuality, or sexual orientation at the expense of those particularly at risk of having a closed belief system in their private families. Further, the new legislation limits the ability of children to have access to information and issues that are timely, relevant, and essential to the way in which they must make decisions about their own lives. It further compromises the ability of individuals to understand, acknowledge, and respect others who may have drastically different perspectives than their own. In its attempts to concede to greater parental discretion, the Alberta provincial government has compromised individual rights both on an individual and societal level. Section 11.1 creates a chill in the classroom by curtailing discussions related to religion, human sexuality, and sexual orientation.

REFERENCES

Alberta Commission on Learning (2003) *Every child learns, every child succeeds: Report and recommendations*. Alberta Education. Retrieved from http://education. alberta.ca/media/413413/commissionreport.pdf

Alberta Human Rights Act, R.S.A. 2000, c. A-25.5, Alberta Queen's Printer Law Online. Retrieved from http://www.qp.alberta.ca/documents/Acts/A25P5.pdf

Alberta, Legislative Assembly, *The 27th Legislature Second Session, 41e* (13 May 2009) at 1163 (K. Kowalski), Debates of the Legislative Assembly. Retrieved from http:// www.assembly.ab.ca/ISYS/LADDAR_files/docs/hansards/han/legislature_27/ session_2/20090513_1930_01_han.pdf

Bill 44, *Human Rights, Citizenship, and Multiculturalism Amendment Act 2009*, Second Session, 27th Legislature, Alberta, 2009. Legislative Assembly of Alberta. Retrieved from http://www.assembly.ab.ca/ISYS/LADDAR_files/docs/bills/ bill/legislature_27/session_2/20090210_bill-044.pdf

Brighouse, H. (2006). *On education*. New York: Routledge.

Callan, E. (1997). *Creating citizens: Political education and liberal democracy*. Oxford, UK: Clarendon Press.

Callan, E. (2006). Galston's dilemmas and Wisconsin v. Yoder. *Theory and Research in Education, 4*(3), 261–273. doi.org/10.1177/1477878506069113

Chamberlain v. Surrey School District No. 36, [2002] 4 S.C.R. 710, 2002 SCC 86.

Gereluk, D. (2011). When good intentions go awry: Limiting toleration and diversity through Bill 44. *Canadian Issues, Spring*, 75–79.

Gutmann, A. (1987). *Democratic education*. Princeton: Princeton University Press.

Lavallée c. Commission scolaire des Chênes, 2009 QCCS 3875.

Levinson, M. (1999). *The demands of liberal education*. Oxford, UK: Oxford University Press.

Macklem, T. (1999). Vriend v. Alberta: Making the private public. *McGill Law Journal, 44*, 197–230.

Province of British Columbia (28 April 2006). Settlement agreement between Murray Corren and Peter Corren (Complainants) and Her Majesty the Queen in Right of the Province of British Columbia, Ministry of Justice, British

Columbia. Retrieved from http://www.equalparenting-bc.ca/adobe-pdfs/
2006-04-27_corren-agreement.pdf

School Act, R.S.A. 2000, c. S-5, s. 39(1)(a).

S.L. c. Commission scolaire des Chênes (2012) SCC 7.

Vriend v. Alberta [1998] 1 S.C.R. 493.

NOTE

1 For a few of the practical challenges that are associated with the implementation
of this act, see Gereluk, 2011.

22

Crossing the Line

Homophobic Speech and Public School Teachers

Paul Clarke and Bruce MacDougall*

*This chapter was first published as Clarke, P., & MacDougall, B.
(2004, Fall). Crossing the line: Homophobic speech and public school
teachers. *Encounters/Encuentros/Rencontres on Education, 5,* 125–140.
Reproduced with permission.

The Problem

The issue of a teacher's expressed views outside the classroom and
how those can be taken to affect his position as a teacher in a public
school system came up again in the *Kempling* case. There, a secondary school teacher, who was also a guidance counsellor, made several
public statements over an extended period, most notably in letters
to a local newspaper, condemning homosexuality. In his letters to

the local newspaper, Kempling "consistently associated homosexuals with immorality, abnormality, perversion, and promiscuity" (*Kempling v. British Columbia College of Teachers*, 2004, para. 34). He also regularly identified himself as a teacher and a mental health professional. The teacher had a long and unblemished teaching career and a notable record of community service. The matter was taken up by the BC College of Teachers (BCCT), the organization that licenses teachers in the province of British Columbia. They decided that Kempling was guilty of conduct unbecoming a member and suspended Kempling's professional teaching certificate for one month (BCCT, 2003, p. 6). The British Columbia Supreme Court dismissed an appeal. Holmes J., the judge in that case, gave detailed reasons for dismissing the appeal, reasons based in both administrative law and constitutional law.[1]

The case raises an issue of the competition among various rights claims and how a tribunal or court ought to resolve such a competition. The case raises issues involving the role of a teacher (in this case also a guidance counsellor) in society, what it means to say that a teacher is a role model, and how the rights of a teacher might be constrained in ways that are not for others. Also raised is the question of the nature of state action and the extent to which a teacher can be said to be performing a government function, even outside the particular hours of government employment. The case raises issues about the extent to which the entitlements of students vis-à-vis their teachers extend to what the teacher does outside of the classroom. The case also raises issues of the nature and extent of the right of nondiscrimination on the basis of sexual orientation and the rights of freedom of expression and freedom of religion. Given that in Canada all of those are entitled to constitutional protection from state action, the question is how they can be balanced or to what extent they can be impinged upon so as to provide some sort of accommodation for all.

In this case, the particular issue arose in the context of expression about homosexuality, but the case has much larger implications. The comments could just as easily have been about the race, ethnicity (as was the all-important 1996 case of *Ross*[2]), religion, health, age, and sex of others. In a multicultural, pluralistic society such as Canada, all those are factors to which government and government actors must be alive. They are also factors that ought to be treated with equal seriousness and concern by tribunals and courts. But they are not necessarily categories where the impact of hostile expression can be assessed in identical ways and so there ought not to be a ritualistic approach to assessing harm that applies in all cases. There is no constitutional basis for setting up a hierarchy of rights and entitlements, such that, for example, the evidence of discrimination usual in one situation (e.g., ethnic prejudice) is exactly the sort of evidence that must be provided so as to prove discrimination in a different context (e.g., homophobia).

Kempling argued that the BCCT's decision to discipline him violated his constitutional rights as set out in four provisions of the Charter: ss. 2(a) and (b), guaranteeing freedom of religion and freedom of expression; s. 7 guaranteeing "the right to life liberty and security of the person"; and s. 15(1) guaranteeing equality to "every individual" and "the right to the equal protection and equal benefit of the law without discrimination and, in particular, without discrimination based on ... religion, ..." (*Canada Act*, UK, 1982). The judge, however, summarily dismissed the teacher's arguments based on ss. 7 and 15(1). We will not, therefore, engage these provisions in terms of Kempling's position. We will examine first the issues relating to the teacher's claims of freedom of religion and freedom of expression. Then we turn to look at the equality arguments against Kempling's stance. We argue that his constitutional rights to freedom of expression and freedom of religion should be restricted for two main reasons. First, it is unlikely that the teacher's discriminatory speech and religious beliefs (as manifested through his writings) are consistent with the underlying rationales of the two "freedoms." Second, the exercise of Kempling's freedoms is inconsistent with his educational obligations to act as a public school teacher. In the context of the interests competing with those of the teacher, we argue that lesbians and gays, particularly lesbian and gay students, have a claim to equality in the context of their education and that this claim can be satisfied only if gays and lesbians are accorded all of the components of full equality for the members of a minority group, namely, compassion, condonation, and celebration. For a school official, identifying himself as such, to have prevailing constitutional entitlements to make statements negating all of those elements of equality entails a denial of equality itself.

Homophobic Speech and the Undermining of Values Associated with Freedom of Expression and Freedom of Religion

As to whether imposing sanctions on Kempling infringed his constitutional freedom of religion and expression, Holmes J. ruled that he had no constitutional right, under s. 2(b) of the Charter, to express "strictly personally-held, discriminatory views with the authority of or in the capacity of a public school teacher/counsellor"[3] (*Kempling v. British Columbia College of Teachers*, 2004, para. 73). He clarified the distinction between Kempling speaking out qua private citizen and Kempling expressing himself qua public servant: "The appellant was at all times free and remains free to express his views on homosexuality in a non-violent manner qua private citizen"[4] (*Kempling v. British Columbia College of Teachers*, 2004, para. 54). What Kempling could not do was to use his authority or capacity as a public school teacher and counsellor to back his discriminatory views. Consequently, the judge held that there was no infringement of the teacher's freedom of expression[5] (*Kempling v. British Columbia College of Teachers*, 2004, para. 77). Holmes J. applied a similar logic when considering an alleged infringement of Kempling's freedom of religion under s. 2(a) of the Charter: "In other words, there is no authority for the proposition that s. 2(a) guarantees freedom to state or manifest one's strictly personal beliefs with the purported authority or capacity of one's professional status" (*Kempling v. British Columbia College of Teachers*, 2004, para. 80).

Even though the judge held that no violations of ss. 2(b) and 2(a) had occurred, he still considered a second question, namely, if Kempling's constitutional rights were infringed, was the infringement justified under s. 1 of the Charter, where constitutional protections are "subject only to such reasonable limits prescribed by law as can be demonstrably justified in a free and democratic society"? Holmes J. answered this in the affirmative.

In his s. 1 analysis, the judge noted that "close attention must be paid to contextual factors" in ascertaining what constitutes "reasonable limits" to constitutionally guaranteed rights (*Kempling v. British Columbia College of Teachers*, 2004, para. 87). The judge examined the following contextual factors: the vulnerability of children, the need to protect gays and lesbians as an historically disadvantaged group, the need to maintain professional standards of conduct, and the nature/value of Kempling's expression (*Kempling v. British Columbia College of Teachers*, 2004, paras. 87–99). In light of these factors, the judge concluded that "considerable deference should be shown the BCCT and a less stringent application of the [s.1] test is warranted" (*Kempling v. British Columbia College of Teachers*, 2004, para. 99).

Holmes J.'s s. 1 approach is more consistent with the Supreme Court of Canada's large and liberal approach to interpreting fundamental freedoms, including those protected by ss. 2(b) and 2(a).[6]

Hence, our analysis proceeds on the assumption that the disciplinary action taken against Kempling constituted a prima facie violation of his constitutional rights under ss. 2(b) and 2(a) of the Charter. We argue, however, that Holmes J. was correct in holding that these Charter rights could be restricted under a s. 1 analysis. One of our key arguments is that the very public expression of the teacher's homophobic and discriminatory beliefs strayed some distance from the core values that justify freedom of expression and freedom of religion.

Freedom of Expression

In all cases involving free speech claims under the Charter, Canadian courts invariably identify three basic values that justify the constitutional protection of freedom of expression. In *Ross v. New Brunswick School District No. 15* (1996), a unanimous Supreme Court of Canada stated: "The purpose of the guarantee is to permit free expression in order to promote truth, political and social participation, and self-fulfilment" (para. 59). Given the centrality of freedom of expression to a democratic society, it is understandable, as the Court in *Ross* intimated, that this right "should only be restricted in the clearest of circumstances" (para. 60).

Although not explicitly considered in the judgment, it is not difficult to conceive of (at least some of) the arguments Kempling might have made to maintain that his controversial speech was consistent with the values of truth, political participation, and self-realization that underscore s. 2(b). From a truth perspective, the teacher could have claimed that he sincerely believes that homosexuality is immoral, abnormal, and perverse. This position squares with his personal and subjective truth that heterosexuality is the only acceptable and legitimate form of sexual orientation and expression—even if scientific and contemporary thinking do not support this perspective. After all, as most of the Supreme Court of Canada held in *R. v. Zundel* (1992), freedom of expression protects "minority beliefs which the majority regard as wrong or false" (p. 752).

Kempling may also have argued that democracies protect speech that is unpopular or that reflects minority or controversial perspectives. To shut him down simply for expressing these views would preclude his participation in the Canadian polity. Finally, he might have alleged that expressing himself in the ways he did was important to allow him to fulfill his potential as an educator, writer, and defender of conventional norms of sexual orientation. In his eyes, this expression was arguably necessary for his personal growth and self-realization. Kempling might have relied on McLachlin J.'s view in *R. v. Keegstra* (1990) that: "If the guarantee of free expression is to be meaningful, it must protect expression which challenges even the very basic conceptions about our society" (p. 842).

Notwithstanding the arguments put forward by Kempling, Holmes J. rejected them. He, in fact, noted that the teacher's homophobic expression was "of low value, being in conflict with the core values behind the s. 2(b) guarantee of freedom of expression" (*Kempling v. British Columbia College of Teachers*, 2004, para. 95). First, the judge stated, "Discriminatory speech is incompatible with the search for truth" (*Kempling v. British Columbia College of Teachers*, 2004, para. 96). He did not flesh this out. In *Ross* (1996), however, a unanimous Supreme Court of Canada explained why racist speech was unlikely to promote the search for truth:

> This Court has held that there is very little chance that expression that promotes hatred against an identifiable group is true. Such expression silences the views of those in the target group and thereby hinders the free exchange of ideas feeding our search for political truth. … However, to give protection to views that attack and condemn the views, beliefs and practices of others is to undermine the principle that all views deserve equal protection and muzzles the voice of truth. (para. 91)

Racist speech refuses to accept people for who they are because of their racial and ethnic origins. Similarly, homophobic speech refuses to accept people for who they are because of their sexual orientation. Hence, one can argue that homophobic speech is analogous to racist speech and, for the very reasons cited in *Ross*, is unlikely to facilitate the search for truth. Outspoken homophobes like Kempling are likely to silence many gays and lesbians who live in fear and are often reluctant to come out of the closet because of the social costs associated with full disclosure. In addition, on a purely scientific or medical level, there is no credible evidence to suggest that homosexuality is related to "immorality, abnormality, perversion, and promiscuity," as claimed by Kempling. On the contrary, the best evidence shows that homosexuality, just like heterosexuality, is a legitimate and natural form of sexual orientation.

Second, as Holmes J. observed, discriminatory speech precludes gays and lesbians from reaching goals of individual self-realization: "The appellant's publicly discriminatory writings undermine the ability of members of the targeted group, homosexuals, to attain individual self-fulfilment" (*Kempling v. British Columbia College of Teachers*, 2004, para. 96). Kempling's speech helps to silence and to marginalize gays and lesbians by undermining their ability to be true to themselves and to others. In this way, his expression precludes self-fulfillment for this vulnerable sexual minority. Finally, as Holmes J. concluded, homophobic speech is inimical to the political process rationale that also justifies freedom of expression: "Discriminatory speech stifles the speech and societal participation of others, in particular members of the targeted group" (*Kempling v. British Columbia College of Teachers*, 2004, para. 97). If the personal is political, silencing of the personal because of one's sexual orientation makes the political impossible. Furthermore, the closeted students are unlikely to advocate for the rights and interests of other gays and lesbians (if they so choose) and in this way lose an opportunity to participate in the larger polity to which they belong.

The demonization of gays and lesbians is a particularly cruel, yet highly effective, means of ensuring that this vulnerable minority is precluded from having a political voice in the communities in which they find themselves embedded. People will rarely listen, let alone allow others to speak, if they consider them to be illegitimate. Kempling's speech is thus successful in frustrating the political process rationale as it applies to gays and lesbians, most particularly the young lesbians and gays who are his students.

Freedom of Religion

In *R. v. Big M Drug Mart Ltd.* (1995), Chief Justice Dickson of the Supreme Court of Canada underscored the importance of freedom of religion, and defined its central characteristics, in the following language:

> The essence of the concept of freedom of religion is the right to entertain such religious beliefs as a person chooses, the right to declare religious beliefs openly and without fear of hindrance or reprisal, and the right to manifest religious belief by worship and practice or by teaching and dissemination. (p. 336)

In *Kempling* (2004), Holmes J. acknowledged that the "publication of views informed by sincerely held religious beliefs is protected by s. 2(a), and the Court may not question the validity of those views"[7] (para. 79).

While the exact arguments made by Kempling that the disciplinary action taken against him infringed on his freedom of religion are not set out in the judgment, the arguments would probably be strikingly similar to those advanced by the anti-Semitic teacher in *Ross* who challenged a board of inquiry's order removing him from the classroom. The Supreme Court of Canada in that case summed up the teacher's position vis-à-vis s. 2(a) in this fashion:

> *In arguing that the order does infringe his freedom of religion, the respondent submits that the Act is being used as a sword to punish individuals for expressing their discriminating religious beliefs. He maintains that "[a]ll of the invective and hyperbole about anti-Semitism is really a smoke screen for imposing an officially sanctioned religious belief on society as a whole which is not the function of courts or Human Rights Tribunals in a free society." In this case, the respondent's freedom of religion is manifested in his writings, statements and publications. These, he argues, constitute "thoroughly honest religious statement[s]," and adds that it is not the role of this Court to decide what any particular religion believes.* (Ross v. New Brunswick School District No. 15, *1996, para. 70*)

Kempling may well have argued that it is not up to the courts, or anybody for that matter, to dictate to him his views about homosexuality. Notwithstanding the validity of this claim, the justification of the holding and the expression of his homophobic opinions, under the guise of s. 2(a), serves to undermine the very foundation upon which freedom of religion is built. While defining the essence of freedom of religion, Chief Justice Dickson reminds us in *Big M Drug Mart* (1995) that "Freedom must surely be founded in respect for the inherent dignity and the inviolable rights of the human person" (p. 336). It is hard to imagine how the manifestation of religious belief through writing that describes homosexuality as "abnormal, immoral or perverted" respects the "inherent dignity and the inviolable rights of the human person." Unlike the racist teacher in *Ross*, Kempling did not (technically speaking) attack the religious beliefs of gays and lesbians. Nonetheless, his systematic denigration and defamation of this group, solely on the basis of its sexual orientation, undercuts the very values on which s. 2(a) is founded.

In sum, the conveyance of homophobic and discriminatory expression in a visibly public manner undercuts the very values that help account for freedom of expression and freedom of religion. Holmes J. was therefore right to conclude that an infringement of Kempling's constitutionally protected rights, under s. 1 of the Charter, could be justified as constituting "reasonable limits" upon the teacher's fundamental freedoms. One of the key reasons he gave to explain this infringement was the nature of the Charter rights themselves in the specific circumstances of the *Kempling* case. As Holmes J. noted: "The low value of the appellant's expression is a factor militating in favour of a less stringent application of the [s.1] test" (*Kempling v. British Columbia College of Teachers*, 2004, para. 98).

The Education Context: Further Justification for Restricting Freedoms

Like all employees, teachers must act honestly, cooperatively, loyally, and obediently (Brown & Beatty, 1988). Yet public school teachers are different from other employees because of the nature of their work and the status of their position. First, and foremost, teachers are educators who work with our children. Yet, in the process of educating, teachers may also influence students through the formal and informal curriculum. Thus, their position as role models is vitally important. Furthermore, teachers have the status of being professionals, in large measure by virtue of their education, training, and expertise. Although teachers are employees, they are also educators, role models, and professionals.[8] When Kempling engaged in discriminatory speech and conduct, his actions could not be reconciled with the specific educational roles he was called to perform.

In his analysis, Holmes J. focused on the professional aspect of teaching. After all, the BCCT disciplined Kempling following charges of professional misconduct or other conduct unbecoming a member. The judge framed the issue in these terms: "The question before the Panel was whether the making and publication of those statements in the circumstances and context in which it was done fell below acceptable standards of professional conduct" (*Kempling v. British Columbia College of Teachers*, 2004, para. 39). As a professional, Kempling was expected to act in accordance with the educational system's core values. In this regard, Holmes J. observed: "Non-discrimination which includes recognizing homosexuals' right to equality, dignity, and respect, is one of the[se] core values" (*Kempling v. British Columbia College of Teachers*, 2004, para. 5). Kempling's homophobic writings negated any possibility of equality, dignity, and respect for gays and lesbians. Consequently, Holmes J. went on to hold that "a finding that those writings were of a discriminatory and derogatory nature can properly form part of the basis of a determination of conduct unbecoming" (*Kempling v. British Columbia College of Teachers*, 2004, para. 39). It should come as no surprise that a hate-monger such as Kempling could not fulfill the requirements of acting in a professional manner.

Although not considered in Holmes J.'s analysis, we suggest that Kempling's behaviour rendered him equally unfit to carry out his duties as both an educator and a role model. To educate comes from the Latin *educare*, which means to "cause to grow." As educators, teachers are supposed to help their students to develop cognitively, emotionally, and psychologically by fostering an open mind, an inquisitive spirit, a critical edge, and a caring disposition. In fact, Kempling did just the opposite. He blatantly abused his position of responsibility and authority as a public educator to promote his own distorted personal agenda. Had he innocuously claimed the moon was made of green cheese, nobody would have cared. Instead, the stakes were much higher. Kempling spread lies, promoted intolerance, and fomented hatred against a visible minority. Although he was careful not to express his controversial views in the classroom, the educative dimension of his writing did not escape notice because of his highly visible profile in the community. Furthermore, in conjunction with his writing, he expressly identified himself as a teacher and a counsellor as if to lend greater credibility to his teachings.

Teachers are not only educators. They also have a legal duty to act as role models for their students. Section 76(2) of British Columbia's School Act states that teachers must "inculcate the highest moral standards" (*School Act*, RSBC 1996). The case law likewise recognizes the role of the teacher as exemplar. In *Attis v. Board of Education of District 15 et al.* (1994), for example, Ryan J.A. declared: "A teacher teaches. He is a role model. He also teaches by example. Children learn by example"[9] (p. 35). The basic idea central to role-modelling is that teacher behaviour has some effect on student behaviour. In other words, consciously or unconsciously, students may look to their teachers to learn what conduct is appropriate and what conduct is not. Whatever teacher behaviour is on display cannot undermine the values of the school community. Furthermore, whether the studied deportment occurs on school property or not is largely irrelevant. As a unanimous Supreme Court of Canada explained in *Ross* (1996):[10]

> The conduct of a teacher is evaluated on the basis of his or her position, rather than whether the conduct occurs within the classroom or beyond. … teachers do not necessarily check their teaching hats at the school yard gate and may be perceived to be wearing their teaching hats even off duty. (para. 44)

If Fenstermacher (1990) is right in saying that "Children do not enter the world compassionate, caring, fair, loving, and tolerant" (p. 132), then who will teach them the moral virtues of living? In part,[11] students will informally learn about morality by scrutinizing the conduct of their teachers, both inside and outside the classroom. Let us never forget that teachers have the potential to exert significant sway over others, including students. Consequently, we hold teachers to account with more rigorous standards because we entrust them with our most valuable resource—our youth. As the Supreme Court of Canada in *Ross* (1996) stated:

> *It is on the basis of the position of trust and influence that we hold the teacher to high standards both on and off duty, and it is an erosion of these standards that may lead to a loss in the community of confidence in the public school system. (para. 45)*

Kempling failed to act as an appropriate role model. His actions violated the public trust placed in him by the educational community and the teaching profession. His claim that ss. 2(b) and 2(a) of the Charter offered him constitutional immunity for his homophobic writings and beliefs must be rejected for compelling educational reasons. Because of the important role-model position of the teacher, there are constraints on what a teacher can express in an active way outside the classroom. This is particularly the case if, as in *Kempling* (2004), the teacher is "linking his private, discriminatory views of homosexuality with his status and professional judgment as a teacher and secondary school counsellor" (para. 46). Then, as Holmes J. says, the teacher calls "into question his own preparedness to be impartial in the fulfillment of his professional and legal obligations to all students, as well as the impartiality of the school system. That in itself is a harmful impact on the school system as a non-discriminatory entity" (*Kempling v. British Columbia College of Teachers*, 2004, para. 46).

The Competing Equality Interests of Gays and Lesbians

Competing with Kempling's expression and religion interests will be equality interests of the students, in particular those of gay and lesbian students, but also those of gays and lesbians generally. It is important to stress the interests of gay and lesbian students in this context because often their very existence is overlooked. Indeed, even in the BCCT's report on the *Kempling* decision, gay and lesbian students were not specifically mentioned (BCCT, 2003, p. 6). In most other cases[12] where gay and lesbian rights issues have been adjudicated upon in the education context, the focus has been on gay and lesbian adult interests. The invidious position of gay and lesbian students should not be underestimated and very occasionally a judge is alive to it[13] (*Trinity Western University v. British Columbia College of Teachers*, 2001, para. 81).

One of the most striking aspects of Holmes J.'s reasons in the British Columbia Supreme Court case is the fact that he did, at several points, specifically mention the impact of speech such as Kempling's on homosexual students. He said that student and public confidence in him and the public school system would be undermined by Kempling's expression and "It would also be reasonable to anticipate that homosexual students would generally be reluctant to approach him for guidance counseling" (*Kempling v. British Columbia College of Teachers*, 2004, paras. 48, 97, 102). This concern for queer students is unusual in Canadian case law (MacDougall, 2004).

There are, it is true, a very few other cases where gay and lesbian students have had some direct input in the legal process. Probably the most significant is *Hall (Litigation guardian of) v. Powers* (2001), where a high school graduate wanted to take his same-sex date to the prom (MacDougall, 2003). But, in fact, that case highlights the difficult position of a gay or lesbian student. The publicity surrounding the *Hall* case was intense. Hall was fortunate that he lived in a reasonably supportive environment and his composure and resolution in the face of the media glare is a testament to his fortitude. But it is hardly a situation that school students should be put in to defend their equality and education interests. This is especially true in the case of a smaller community where queer students will, as Holmes J. said in *Kempling* (2004), "likely be deterred from openly espousing opposing views or being public about their sexual orientation" (para. 97).

In this difficult context for young people,[14] this age of exploring and fixing who they are and trying to conform as best they can, it is hardly an equal contest when they are expected to fight against the interests of an adult such as Kempling, a guidance counsellor, at that, the very person whose job it is to advise them on the appropriate course their lives should take. It must be acknowledged that even now in society—and especially outside the largest cities—gays and lesbians will hardly be the most popular minority groups. Individuals like Kempling will, in their "traditional values" position, have the support of their well-organized and influential religious groups. Similarly, they will often have the support of politicians and other elected officials, as *Chamberlain v. Surrey School District No. 36* (2002) made clear in the context of the Surrey school board. In considering a contest between these competing interests, Kempling's religion/expression interests and the interests of gay and lesbian students, a court or a tribunal should consider the uneven playing field on which the competition starts.

The equality argument that would be made in this case is that gays and lesbians—students, teachers, and others in society—are not being afforded the same atmosphere of respect, inclusion, and celebration that is afforded to heterosexuals. A school's acceptance of

Kempling, given his expression activity, would constitute a tolerance of such views and the creation of an environment tainted by them for those who must work with, and most especially learn, from him. His avowed hostility to homosexuality thus constitutes an impairment of the right of those who are homosexual to be treated equally.

Given that gays and lesbians are entitled "to the equality protection and equal benefit of the law without discrimination" under s. 15 of Canada's Charter of Rights and Freedoms,[15] what does this mean? One of us has argued elsewhere that the contents of true equality must be satisfied on different levels. In order for there to be real legal equality for the members of a given group, the state and its actors must show toward the members of the particular group compassion, condonation, and celebration (MacDougall, 2000–01, p. 252). Absent satisfaction of any one of those elements and the members of the group might have partial equality but not complete legal equality.

To satisfy the requirement for compassion, the basic principle of nondiscrimination must exist. In the Kempling situation, gays and lesbians are expected to be taught by, and get guidance from, an individual who clearly despises the essence of who they are. They are thus being treated differently from their heterosexual counterparts. This situation is particularly difficult for gay and lesbian students. In many cases, the parents will be hostile to the issue of homosexuality, so this discrimination is not cushioned by, or carried together by, a supportive family unit.

Likewise, the second level of equality—condonation—is hardly satisfied in this situation. Kempling might argue that it is not homosexuals he has a "problem" with but homosexual activity. Condonation, however, involves an acceptance of activity involving the members of a particular minority group. This aspect of a homosexual student's equality can hardly be said to be respected if a schoolteacher or official who is supposed, by his very actions, to help guide the actions of a student is instead dedicated to trying to prevent homosexual activity. Similarly, the interests of gay and lesbian adults are also affected, as the schoolteacher or official will be taken to be condemning their activity as gay and lesbian adults. The state can hardly be said to be condoning gay and lesbian actions if its officials are arguing against them.

The final aspect of equality, namely celebration, is also negated in the Kempling situation. When celebration is respected, the state and its agents are actively promoting the value of the members of a particular group. In the context of homosexuals, it means including gay and lesbian material in curricula, proclaiming gay pride days, and celebrating gay and lesbian marriage. Kempling's actions represent the very antithesis of this, for they condemn gays and lesbians and their activities. At the student level, celebration will facilitate gay and lesbian students seeing themselves represented positively in school actions and activities. It will foster their feeling good about themselves as gays and lesbians, a very difficult thing to do given the atmosphere of hostility toward, and denigration of, gays and lesbians in the schoolyard. Kempling's actions only validate such exclusion, marginalization, and inferiorization. They represent the opposite of celebration. How could gay or lesbian students feel valued by the school or positive about their sexual orientation when one of their teachers, again one specifically designated to instruct them as to guidance, is actively arguing that what they are and what they do is wrong?

It might be argued in *Kempling* that Kempling is simply stating his beliefs and not acting on them, just the same situation as in *Trinity Western University* (2001), where the majority of the Supreme Court of Canada said that homophobic statements prospective teachers made when applying for admission to start their education studies did not constitute acts of discrimination. The *Kempling* case can be distinguished, however, on the basis that the Kempling situation is much more invidious than a situation where would-be students sign a statement upon admission to study at an institution. Here is a teacher with some years' experience who actively and continuously makes statements prejudicing the equality interests of gays and lesbians, including his own students. These statements are not a mere formality, such as is, it might be argued, signing a document giving admission to a degree program. Kempling's statements were made as a teacher.

Furthermore, to find an infringement of the equality interests of gays and lesbians, it should not be necessary to prove actual instances of homophobic acts in the school that follow from Kempling's writings. In *Ross* (1996), the Supreme Court of Canada thought important the evidence of anti-Semitism in the school where Ross worked and tied that evidence to Ross's expression (paras. 40, 101). La Forest J. said: "where a 'poisoned' environment within the school system is traceable to the off-duty conduct of a teacher that is likely to produce a corresponding loss of confidence in the teacher and the system as a whole, then the off-duty conduct of the teacher is relevant" (*Ross v. New Brunswick School District No. 15*, 1996, para. 45).

However, in the case of homophobia, gay and lesbian students face so much of this, it would be difficult to attribute it specifically to Kempling's actions. Furthermore, especially given the absence of parental and family support, gay and lesbian students will be more than a little hesitant to bring specific complaints forward. Parents may well not care either. The court must not expect the same degree of direct connection between a teacher's action and a discriminatory environment in the case of homophobia that it might expect in other situations. Given the pervasiveness of homophobia, it is very easy for a homophobic teacher to hide within, or blend into, the pervasive homophobia and avoid specific attribution of the consequences of his actions on the discriminatory environment. It would be tragic if the courts, in essence, throw their hands up and say equality cannot be protected and homophobic expression not stopped in the schools because of the difficulty of pinning responsibility for a particular homophobic act on a particular teacher's particular expression.

Fortunately, Holmes J. in the British Columbia Supreme Court did not accept that speech cannot constitute discrimination as a matter of law or that conduct must be directed against a particular individual to constitute discrimination (*Kempling v. British Columbia College of Teachers*, 2004, para. 38). The British Columbia Human Rights Code itself brings certain publications within the scope of the discriminatory (*Human Rights Code*, RSBC 1996, ss. 1, 7). Furthermore, Holmes J. said that the fact that there was no evidence in this case of a "poisoned" school environment or specific complaints against Kempling did not mean that Kempling could not be disciplined (*Kempling v. British Columbia College of Teachers*, 2004, para. 42). This approach to the finding of discrimination is much more consonant with objectives of equality protection and it is to be hoped that this open approach sets the tone in future cases.

Resolving the Competition

Of primary importance in resolving the tension between interests in the *Kempling* case is the fact that the students involved have much less choice in the whole process than does Kempling. The students cannot really opt to go to a different school. Even if the students were geographically situated so as to make that possible, then they could only do that with the consent of their parents. Raising the issue would mean in many cases outing themselves. It would mean explaining the move to friends and neighbours. In the hostile environment that exists for many students, that is simply not a fair or appropriate expectation. Furthermore, many students will not, in fact, be sure about their sexuality or there may be other factors that mean that decisions cannot be based solely or even mainly on their sexual orientation.

Courts and tribunals should be alive to the particular difficulties faced by children in any sort of rights assertion process. Holmes J. in *Kempling* was particularly so alive. It is important to find a way for children to be comfortable bringing these issues of sexual orientation before the institutions of the law or having others bring them. Courts and tribunals ought not to make demands in terms of evidence or expect the same clarity of position in the case of children involved in legal issues. Courts have to accept that gay and lesbian children may not speak about the issues relating to their homosexuality in a way so direct as an adult might or with the same precision and certainty. An outside adult, not necessarily related, might have to speak for a gay or lesbian child on an issue of homosexuality. A court has to be better at anticipating these issues that affect gay and lesbian children, at being sensitive to potential harm. The courts must not assume that homosexuality is not an issue just because the person in front of the court or implicated in the case before the court is not being as clear or direct about the matter as an adult might be. Holmes J. was able to put himself "in the shoes" of a queer student in Kempling's school.

Of particular importance in this balancing of rights and freedoms is the constraint on the child in terms of participating in the education system. Also, as we have argued, important is the fact that the Kempling situation, if permitted, denies all aspects of a gay or lesbian child's equality interests. On the other hand, Kempling has much more flexibility in terms of options. He knows that, upon becoming a teacher, there are certain expectations and that he is seen as a holder of multiple roles, namely, professional, educator, and role model. While he might not properly be constrained from having certain views, the espousal of those views in particular public ways, especially qua teacher, is rightly regulated. He has other options than being a schoolteacher and he has options in the context of being a schoolteacher. While this resolution unquestionably puts constraints on individuals like Kempling that other positions in society do not, the gay or lesbian student, by contrast, has no real choice at all and is infinitely the more vulnerable of the two.

The BCCT clearly made the right decision in its resolution of the issues and the British Columbia Supreme Court rightly upheld that resolution. By engaging in homophobic expression in the manner in which he did, Kempling crossed the line and was justifiably disciplined. The question remains, however, why the homophobic statements of Kempling warranted only a one-month suspension of his teaching certificate, while the Supreme Court of Canada specifically approved the 18-month suspension in *Ross* (1996) for anti-Semitic expression. Could it be that homophobia is still not treated as so egregious as other forms of discrimination, even by so progressive a body as the BCCT?

REFERENCES

Attis v. Board of Education of District 15 et al., [1994], 142 N.B.R. (2d) 1 (C.A.).

BC College of Teachers (BCCT). (2003). *Report to members, 14*(4).

Black, W. (2003). Grading human rights in the schoolyard: Jubran v. board of trustees. *University of British Columbia Law Review, 36*, 45–55.

Brown, D.J.M., & Beatty, D.M. (1988). *Canadian Labour Arbitration* (3rd ed.). Aurora, ON: Canada Law Book.

Canada Act, U.K., 1982, c. 11, Schedule B. Retrieved from http://laws-lois.justice. gc.ca/eng/Const/page-15.html >

Chamberlain v. Surrey School District No. 36, 2002 SCC 86.

Clarke, P.T. (1998). Canadian public school teachers and free speech: Part I—an introduction. *Education & Law Journal, 8*, 295–314.

Egan v. Canada, [1995], 2 S.C.R. 513.

Fenstermacher, G.D. (1990). Some moral considerations on teaching as a profession. In J.I. Goodlad, R. Soder, & K.A. Sirotnik (Eds.), *The moral dimensions of teaching* (pp. 130–151). San Francisco: Jossey-Bass.

Hall (Litigation guardian of) v. Powers, 2001, 59 OR (3d) 423 (SCJ).

Human Rights Code, RSBC 1996, c. 211. Retrieved from http://www.bclaws.ca/ EPLibraries/bclaws_new/document/ID/freeside/00_96210_01>

Irwin Toy Ltd. v. Quebec (Attorney General), [1989], 1 S.C.R. 927.

Jubran v. Board of Trustees, 2002, BCHRT 10, 42 CHRR D/273 (BCHRT).

Kempling v. British Columbia College of Teachers, 2004, BCSC 133.

MacDougall, B. (2000). *Queer judgments: Homosexuality, expression and the courts in Canada.* Toronto: University of Toronto Press.

MacDougall, B. (2000–01). The celebration of same-sex marriage. *Ottawa Law Review, 32*(2), 235–267.

MacDougall, B. (2003). The separation of church and date: Destabilizing traditional religion-based legal norms on sexuality. *University of British Columbia Law Review, 36*, 1–27.

MacDougall, B. (2004). The legally queer child. *McGill Law Journal, 49*, 1057–1091.

Morin v. Prince Edward Island Regional Administrative Unit No. 3 School Board, 2002, 213 D.L.R. (4th) 17 (S.C.—A.D.).

North Vancouver School Dist. No. 44 v. Jubran, 2003, BCSC 6.

R. v. Big M Drug Mart Ltd., [1985], 1 S.C.R. 295.

R. v. Jones, [1986], 2 S.C.R. 284.

R. v. Keegstra, [1990], 3 S.C.R. 697.

R. v. Zundel, [1992], 2 S.C.R. 731.

Reyes, A. (1995). Freedom of expression and public school teachers. *Dalhousie Journal of Legal Studies, 4*(37), 35–72.

Ross v. New Brunswick School District No. 15, [1996], S.C.J. 40.

School Act, RSBC 1996, c. 412.

Trinity Western University v. British Columbia College of Teachers, 2001 SCC 31.

Vriend v. Alberta, [1998], 1 S.C.R. 493.

Walker v. Prince Edward Island, 1993, 107 D.L.R. (4th) 69 (P.E.I.S.C.—A.D.).

Walker v. Prince Edward Island, [1995], 2 S.C.R. 407.

NOTES

1 The decision was upheld on appeal: *Kempling v. British Columbia College of Teachers*, 2005 BCCA 327, 43 B.C.L.R. (4th) 41.

2 The *Kempling* case is strikingly similar to the *Ross* case, where a teacher was removed from his teaching position because he had made public anti-Semitic writings and statements while he was off-duty as a teacher. The Supreme Court of Canada in that case made some important statements about the position of a teacher. It found that while Ross's freedom of expression, protected under s. 2(b) of the Charter, had been infringed, that violation was demonstrable justified under s. 1 of the Charter. The *Ross* case will be important in resolving the *Kempling* case, though there are some differences.

3 In his writings to the local newspaper, Kempling identified himself on three separate occasions as a teacher and counsellor and explicitly linked his personal views to his professional standing as a teacher and counsellor.

4 Here the judge relied on the 1993 case and 1995 appeal of *Walker v. Prince Edward Island*.

5 Holmes J. refused Kempling's claim that his conduct was similar to that of a fellow teacher in the case of *Morin v. Prince Edward Island Regional Administrative Unit No. 3 School Board* (2002). In *Morin*, the school principal forbade a teacher to show a film on religious fundamentalism to his grade 9 class. The court ruled that this infringed the teacher's s. 2(b) rights. Holmes J. distinguished *Morin* on the following grounds: "In Morin, the prohibition was on the showing of the film itself to the students. Here, the sanction by the BCCT goes really to the appellant's wrongful public linking of his professional position to the off-duty expression of personally-held discriminatory views in order to lend credibility to those views, as well as addressing the resulting harm to the school system" (*Kempling v. British Columbia College of Teachers*, 2004, para. 77).

6 In *Ross* (1996), for instance, the Supreme Court of Canada stated: "[T]his Court has adopted a two-step enquiry to determine whether an individual's freedom of expression is infringed. The first step involves determining whether the individual's activity falls within the freedom of expression protected by the Charter. The second step is to determine whether the purpose or effect of the impugned government action is to restrict that freedom" (para. 61).
In *Kempling* (2004), the teacher's expression fell within the ambit of s. 2(b) because it "conveyed meaning" (para. 73, see also *Irwin Toy Ltd. v. Quebec [Attorney General]*, 1989) and was not articulated in a "physically violent form" (para. 73, see also *R. v. Keegstra*, 1990). Furthermore, the purpose and effect of the BCCT's suspension was to restrict the teacher's freedom of expression. The Supreme Court of Canada has also held (in *Ross*) that a public school teacher's right to make virulently anti-Semitic statements, when not on the job, received prima facie protection under ss. 2(b) and 2(a) of the Charter. In *Ross*, the local community certainly knew that the person making anti-Semitic comments (in his writings and through the media) was a well-known educator even if he never signed his work as a teacher or linked his personal views to his professional rank.

7 The judge's authority for this proposition comes from the Supreme Court of Canada's decision in *R. v. Jones* (1986).

8 One of the authors has examined elsewhere how these various roles relate to teachers' claims to free speech in both an employment law and constitutional law context. See Clarke (1998).

9 Even though Ryan J.A. wrote for the dissent, the majority did not challenge this legal principle.

10 The Court's reference to the teacher as medium is borrowed from the work of Alison Reyes (1995), who considers the importance of teachers in the education process and the impact that they bear upon the system. As Reyes notes: "Teachers are a significant part of the unofficial curriculum because of their status as 'medium.' In a very significant way the transmission of prescribed 'messages' (values, beliefs, knowledge) depends on the fitness of the 'medium' (the teacher)" (p. 42).

11 Other important sources of morality include family and religion.

12 Most notable, of late, are *Trinity Western University v. British Columbia College of Teachers* (2001) and *Chamberlain v. Surrey School District No. 36* (2002).

13 See, for example, L'Heureux-Dubé J. in *Trinity Western University* (2001), where she said: "lesbian, gay, and bisexual youth ... do not enter the school environment with the same level of family support and understanding that other members of minority groups do" (para. 81). On judicial (lack of) understanding about queer issues, see MacDougall (2000).

14 See, for example, *Jubran v. Board of Trustees* (2002), *North Vancouver School Dist. No. 44 v. Jubran* (2003), and Black (2003).

15 See, for example, *Egan v. Canada* (1995) and *Vriend v. Alberta* (1998).

23

Propaganda in the Classroom

The Keegstra Case

William Hare*

*This chapter is a revised version of Hare, William (1990). Limiting the freedom of expression: The Keegstra case. *Canadian Journal of Education, 15*(4), 375–389. Reproduced with permission.

Introduction

It is now 30 years since the Keegstra case[1] first came to the attention of the general public in Canada.[2] Throughout the 1980s and early 1990s, as the legal proceedings against James Keegstra unfolded, teachers across the country learned about the case from the media, and there was much discussion in teacher-education programs about the issues involved. This was all to the good since the case raised important matters of principle that teachers need to think about, and there was considerable confusion about what lessons were to be drawn. The Keegstra case, however, has long since faded from the headlines and, as time goes on, it is increasingly likely that teachers and student teachers will be unfamiliar with these events or have only a vague recollection of what was involved. At the time, the case quickly came to be seen as a clear instance of indoctrination, as indeed it is, but we should follow Socrates in seeking more than a clear example. It is important to understand why Keegstra's classroom teaching constituted miseducation and why attempts to characterize it as fostering open-mindedness are quite misguided.

The essential facts of the case can be briefly stated and are not generally in dispute. Influenced by anti-Semitic propaganda in books such as the infamous *Protocols of the Learned Elders of Zion*, published at the beginning of the 20th century,[3] Keegstra had come to hold an unshakable belief in the existence of an international Jewish conspiracy to establish a world government. This belief was the main idea in Keegstra's interpretation of historical events and permeated his teaching of history throughout the school year. The alleged conspiracy was appealed to to explain to students why they would not expect to find information about it in textbooks and other sources. Every aspect of Keegstra's teaching, from classroom instruction to the notes he provided, displayed and fostered anti-Semitic attitudes, with the result that students referred to Jews in derogatory and abusive terms in their written work and attributed much of the evil in the world to their actions. When students made such remarks about Jews in their essays, Keegstra reinforced these ideas. Student essays went so far as to argue that it was necessary to rid the world of dangerous Jews.[4] Keegstra's determination to present and defend his views arose from a profound conviction that his beliefs were both important and indubitable.[5]

Disclosure of these teaching practices shocked Canadian society and prompted the Province of Alberta to set up a Committee on Tolerance and Understanding in June 1983, which presented its final report in December 1984. The chairperson of the committee, Ron Ghitter, remarked optimistically that "shocking revelations can become the catalyst from which flow a myriad of positive responses" (Committee on Tolerance and Understanding, 1984, p. 3). If teachers are not to shun controversial issues in the classroom, however, we need to guard against several confused responses.

Comments were made, for example, about the value of open-mindedness in teaching, and it was suggested that Keegstra championed free inquiry. Keegstra himself claimed that he was helping his students to discriminate among alternatives. He insisted that he had presented an alternative point of view to make his students think (Bercuson & Wertheimer, 1985, p. 113), and he maintained that he advised his students that the position he defended "was only a theory" (Appeal to Board of Reference, 1983, p. 18), and not widely accepted. Some of Keegstra's former students came to believe he was silenced because the authorities were not committed to open inquiry. One student is quoted as saying that "perhaps people are scared he's stumbled onto the truth, and they don't want to know about it." Another remarked: "I'm trying so hard to be open-minded and they're close-minded" (Lee, 1985, pp. 45, 46).

The charge of bias came up frequently in discussions about the case. One commentator, however, in making the point that the students were not offered "well-articulated alternatives" (Podmore, 1985–1986, p. 17), adds the qualification that "the problem of biased teaching will arise with every teacher" (Podmore, 1985–1986, p. 17). A student is quoted as saying he had abandoned the idea of a career in teaching because he might slip up, say something inappropriate, and land in jail (Mertl & Ward, 1985, p. 133). The idea lurking behind both of these reactions is that bias is inevitable and that all teachers are similarly vulnerable.

"Freedom of speech" became something of a rallying cry among supporters and certain others involved in the case. His lawyer was reported as saying that the case would be "the greatest test of freedom of speech this country has ever seen" (Legge, 1984, p. 29). The Alberta Teachers' Association (ATA) representative assigned to help Keegstra answer the various charges brought by the school board also insisted that Keegstra's freedom of speech was being curtailed (Bercuson & Wertheimer, 1985, p. 107). Canadian civil libertarians utterly rejected Keegstra's views, of course, and applauded his removal from the classroom, but were very much concerned about the principle of free speech and the related problem of censorship in society (Dixon, 1986). Freedom of expression is an important principle in the context of school teaching, but its application is far from straightforward and it cannot be used to justify Keegstra's teaching in any way.

Keegstra was widely regarded by students, colleagues, and the Alberta Teachers' Association as a good teacher.[6] The principal at the time of Keegstra's dismissal testified that Keegstra did "a very thorough job" of classroom preparation and that he had never heard Keegstra "call down another group except maybe Communists or Zionists" (Schwartz, 1986, p. 13). A former principal commented that

Keegstra's first qualification as a teacher was his "command of discipline" (Schwartz, 1986, p. 13). Keegstra's classroom management skills have earned near universal praise. The superintendent who pursued the case against Keegstra said that the issue was not Keegstra's competence as a teacher (Bercuson & Wertheimer, 1985, p. 200).

There is enough confusion in these various reactions and comments to warrant a careful examination of the assumptions they reveal. We shall see that some who have shed light on this affair have also added to the confusion. Furthermore, there are ideas in circulation, advanced by philosophers who may never have heard of this case, which come to grief in the light of this sorry episode. An examination of the case shows that Keegstra cannot be seen as an "honest heretic" (Hook, 1968, p. 89) teaching unpopular ideas in an open-minded manner.

An Honest Heretic?

A liberal in the tradition of John Stuart Mill might experience some tension in considering this case. Mill (1947) writes:

> If all mankind minus one, were of one opinion, and only one person were of the contrary opinion, mankind would be no more justified in silencing that one person than he, if he had the power, would be justified in silencing mankind. (p. 16)

Yet, effectively, Keegstra was silenced, as a teacher, since the revocation of his teaching license removed a necessary condition of his employment. Where, in the words of Justice Holmes, is that "free trade in ideas" that ought to characterize education? Have we abandoned the idea that "the best test of truth is the power of the thought to get itself accepted in the competition of the market" (as cited in Hook, 1968, p. 87)?

In some ways, moreover, Keegstra does resemble the honest heretic rather than the furtive conspirator. Sidney Hook's classic distinction revealed differences showing why the heretic must be tolerated and the conspirator suppressed. The liberal, Hook (1968) wrote, "stands ready to defend the honest heretic no matter what his views against any attempt to curb him" (p. 89). Like the heretic, Keegstra did not shrink from publicity. In the words of one commentator, "furtiveness is alien to him" (Mazurek, 1988, p. 58). Keegstra joined the Canadian League of Rights (Bercuson & Wertheimer, 1985, p. 42) and obtained much of his material from this group, but there is every reason to agree that Keegstra saw himself as a solitary soldier (Bercuson & Wertheimer, 1985, p. 16). The telltale signs of conspiracy are not to be found and not because the tracks have been covered.

Although no conspirator, Keegstra is only in part an honest heretic. Concerning the frank admission of the content of his views, he is the honest, forthright individual generally portrayed (Mazurek, 1988, p. 58). Keegstra did not conceal what he had been teaching when cross-examined at the Board of Reference inquiry, and his claim to have been teaching the required curriculum was not a lie but a mistaken belief. He also alerted his students to the fact that his theories were not widely shared and may even have advised them of the importance of examining different points of view (Bercuson & Wertheimer, 1985, p. 50). When we consider Keegstra's classroom practice, however, the ascription of honesty becomes immediately suspect.

First, Justice McFadyen established that none of the sources to which Keegstra directed his students contained a different point of view on the theory of history he propounded (Appeal to Board of Reference, 1983, p. 19). It is inconceivable that Keegstra was unaware of any such. Second, when students ventured to draw on sources other than those Keegstra approved, sometimes their work was not assessed at all or assessed adversely (Bercuson & Wertheimer, 1985, p. 61). Keegstra believed that sources critical of his position have been censored to conceal the truth, but failed to offer his students an honest account of alternative views in terms which the defenders of those views might accept as full and fair (Montefiore, 1975, p. 18). Third, Keegstra encouraged sweeping generalizations by his students by making comments calculated to confirm or support such views (Lee, 1985, p. 38). This makes a mockery of Keegstra's claim to have been fostering the ability to discriminate between alternatives and think for themselves (Bercuson & Wertheimer, 1985, p. 202).[7]

Keegstra fails to qualify as an honest heretic in the classroom and forfeits the protection otherwise due. Appeal to the notion of a marketplace of ideas collapses in this case because Keegstra's classes were systematically biased to inculcate the Jewish conspiracy theory at every opportunity. The decisive point is that the ground was cut from under the feet of any opposition by making the theory immune to counter-evidence. Potential counter-evidence was taken as further evidence of the conspiracy, portrayed as controlling the sources of evidence, namely textbooks, the media and so on. Conspiracies can occur, of course, and it is doctrinaire to dismiss such claims a priori. We need evidence that one exists, however, and refutation must be possible in principle. In frustrating the falsification challenge (Flew, 1975, p. 55),[8] Keegstra revealed the disingenuous character of his teaching.

These criticisms are consistent with support for that strong tradition in philosophy of education that encourages students to become involved in the critical examination of controversy.[9] John Passmore (1967) has pointed out the limitations of teaching for critical thinking when criticism is reserved for "those who do not fully adhere to the accepted beliefs" (p. 197). Bertrand Russell advocated (1939) "the most vehement and terrific argumentation on all sides of every question" (p. 529) and maintained that there must be no requirement that teachers express only majority opinions. Strong enthusiasms, Russell said, are perfectly appropriate (Russell, B. & Russell, D., 1923, p. 255). In protecting his own, one-sided view from criticism, however, Keegstra subverted the educational ideal of open-minded inquiry.

It is important to keep in mind that Keegstra did not attempt to foster a marketplace of ideas, and it would be a mistake to suggest, as some have done, that this case shows the inappropriateness of the marketplace ideal in public schooling:

> *The elementary and high-school systems are not viewed by civil libertarians as part of the public forum we seek to protect from censorship. We doubt it makes sense to apply a notion such as "censorship" when we judge the professional wisdom of what is chosen for the attention of not yet fully-fledged minds. (Dixon, 1986, p. 7)*

First, however, the "not yet fully-fledged minds" include young adults in grade 12, or equivalent, many of whom will soon be university students and all of whom need to be able to think critically and in an open-minded way about important issues. A rigid division between different educational levels is arbitrary and, as Russell (1939) argues, students at school need to engage with arguments on all sides of the question. Second, there is no reason to think that the concept of censorship does not apply in the school context. When books are removed from the school library and words deleted from school textbooks to accommodate complaints, censorship exists and it constitutes a threat to open inquiry. We need to recognize censorship when it occurs in the context of schooling if we are to determine whether or not it is justified in a particular case.

Inquiry vs. Persuasion

It has been suggested that Keegstra's error can be understood in terms of a distinction between fostering inquiry and engaging in persuasion, what we might think of as the difference between teaching and preaching. J. Anthony Blair (1986) distinguishes two uses of argument to illustrate what he sees as the defect in Keegstra's approach. He distinguishes between (a) argument used to *convince* and (b) argument used to *inquire*, and Keegstra emerges as having attempted to convert students to his position rather than showing them how to employ argument to test ideas. Keegstra's use of argument to convince, Blair claims, is very different from the attempt to foster open-mindedness.

First, however, we should notice the either/or nature of Blair's suggestion. The implication is that a teacher must opt for the second use of argument, i.e., to inquire, since argument used to convince "will often be perceived by those untutored in its deployment as an instrument of coercion" (Blair, 1986, pp. 161–162). Certainly, teachers who take a stand on some question and attempt to convince their students must also teach the use of argument as a tool of inquiry if the students are to have the wherewithal to assess the teacher's position critically. But the use of argument to convince is not in itself a violation of educational principles. What matters is how the argument is *conducted*, and Keegstra's approach was a travesty of the Socratic ideal of following the argument where it leads. The obvious danger in Blair's analysis, however, is that we are close to embracing teacher neutrality as an absolute principle.[10]

Second, open-mindedness does not require neutrality. Blair (1986) glosses open-mindedness as "withholding judgment until one has thoroughly canvassed alternatives and seriously considered points of view other than one's own" (p. 162). Though popular, this is inadequate as a general account. What matters is how one's convictions are held (Hare, 1979; Hare, 1985). Here the central question is whether or not they are regarded as revisable in the light of emerging evidence and fresh argument. Keegstra is no champion of open-mindedness, not because he held, and defended, certain convictions, but because these were not revisable. Teaching is not preaching, but this point is consistent with teachers employing argument in the attempt to convince.

Keegstra's student who claims to be open-minded (Lee, 1985, p. 46) is typical of those John Dewey (1966) criticized (pp. 175–176) who naively think that open-mindedness is shown even when ideas are adopted uncritically. Ironically, since this student is prevented from rationally reviewing his own beliefs by coming to think all contrary evidence is necessarily untrustworthy, he cannot be regarded as open-minded. That would require being willing to revise his views in the light of evidence and argument, but he has come to dismiss all objections and criticisms in advance.

Indoctrination

Despite endless debate in philosophy of education over the analysis of indoctrination, it is reassuring that the parent responsible for initiating the complaint that eventually led to decisive action against Keegstra closed her letter to the superintendent with the words: "As our children are being sent to school for education, not indoctrination, I appeal to you to dismiss Mr. Keegstra from teaching those classes in which our children will be enrolled" (Bercuson & Wertheimer, 1985, p. 206). This is, of course, the appropriate distinction to draw because the students were adopting beliefs in such a way that rational criticisms were defused. Many professionals close to the scene were not able to articulate or even recognize the distinction in question. Some students did eventually start to question what they had come to believe following certain extraordinary steps including, for some, a trip to Dachau. The crucial point, however, is not that the students' beliefs could never be dislodged, but that a pattern of thinking had emerged inimical to evidence and argument.[11]

Allen Pearson (1986) fears that certain presuppositions in the teaching context helped bring about the undesirable consequence of closed-minded allegiance to irrational beliefs. The logic of the teaching situation, he argues, is that any teacher must be considered rational otherwise there would be no point attending to him or her: "One cannot be a learner if one does not accept that the teacher is acting rationally" (p. 5). Teachers like Keegstra, Pearson adds, have difficulty with cynical or very skeptical students, but these are hardly desirable traits (p. 6).

Pearson's pessimism is, I think, premature. Cynicism and skepticism are not the only defences against an irrational teacher. Pearson fails to mention *critical reflection*. If schools developed critical ability in students, and discouraged deferential acceptance, learners would not be so vulnerable. Few philosophers have noted that students need to be trained to resist indoctrination,[12] but Keegstra's approach shows how important such an ability is. Keegstra was unable to recognize his own teaching as indoctrination. The psychology of the classroom is often such that uncritical acquiescence results (Mackenzie, 1988), but there is no logical barrier to success as Pearson implies. One can learn from teachers even if one fails to agree with their ideas, or suspects that the ideas presented are spurious. One can understand what the beliefs are and why some people hold them, and resolve to assess their merits. Typically, we presume that the teacher believes what he or she is saying, but we need not, and must not, assume that the claims are true. Pearson overlooks provisional agreement where we accept "for the sake of argument" but reserve the right to subject the beliefs in question to later critical examination. We expect to learn something valuable from our teachers, but expectations are not always fulfilled.

Tolerance

The Province of Alberta moved soon after the Keegstra revelations to establish a Committee on Tolerance and Understanding. Its interim report maintained that a basic aim of education is to instil in children "an appreciation of our democratic traditions, symbolized by an attitude of tolerance, understanding and respect for others, *no matter what their origins or values may be.*"[13] In the final report, however, these concluding words were omitted when the committee set out the principles which guided its work (Committee on Tolerance and Understanding, 1984, p. 16); elsewhere in the report (pp. 58, 129), however, they are reintroduced. It is difficult to make sense of this in light of the circumstances that gave rise to the committee's work. Were tolerance required *no matter what a person's values,* then Keegstra's intolerance would itself have to be tolerated.

Some who were involved in the case came close to that view. The Alberta Teachers' Association representative who defended Keegstra at the early hearings said he, being a fairly tolerant person, could accept different points of view. He maintained that Keegstra had advanced a different point of view as was his right (Bercuson & Wertheimer, 1985, p. 118). This exemplifies the confusion mentioned earlier that leads some to see Keegstra as a champion of free inquiry silenced by an intolerant society.[14] To appeal uncritically to the principle of tolerance is to risk extending tolerance to indoctrination. The school board, on the other hand, was clearer that tolerance had limits. Keegstra's right to discuss alternative points of view and to include controversial ideas was not challenged by the school board, but it was not going to tolerate what it viewed as a "very slanted and one-sided" presentation (Bercuson & Wertheimer, 1985, p. 198). In this letter to Keegstra, the superintendent recognized Keegstra's academic freedom but emphasized that all positions were to be presented "in as unbiased a way as possible" (Bercuson & Wertheimer, 1985, p. 197). The wording on bias used by the superintendent avoids the naive position that a completely *bias-free* presentation is possible without suggesting that the amount and nature of bias is quite beyond our control.

The problem of biased teaching may indeed arise with every teacher, as some have suggested, but not in the same way nor to the same degree. Although teachers can slip into bias, a measure of tolerance is appropriate when teachers display a willingness to review their performances and the judgment of others critically and attempt to address the problem. Keegstra sincerely believed his own position was correct, but he could and should have been aware that he was not presenting other views impartially. If we tolerate the systematic distortion of issues in teaching, we cannot claim to have a serious concern for our students' education.

The Keegstra case is useful in philosophy of education as a touchstone for testing philosophical generalizations (cf. Feinberg, 1973, p. 3). If we have confidence in a particular judgment, we can ask how a certain general principle fares when viewed in the light of that judgment. Mary Warnock (1975) argues, correctly in my view, that a teacher is not invariably required to remain neutral on controversial issues, and it would be a pity if confusion resulting from the Keegstra case gave undeserved support to the idea that teachers *must* remain neutral on controversial issues. Russell, as noted earlier, saw clearly that a teacher could display strong enthusiasms but there remains an obligation to give an impartial account of what really happened. Mary Warnock, however, exaggerates the benefits of non-neutrality, thereby risking undue teacher influence on students. She maintains there is only benefit in the contemplation of someone who has principles: "The first rule of teaching is sincerity, even if one's sincerity is dotty or eccentric" (Warnock, 1975, p. 170). Concerning the danger of winning over students too easily, she assures us that time will remedy this, if remedy is needed (Warnock, 1975, p. 170). Mary Warnock was not commenting on Keegstra's teaching, but how do her comments stand up in the light of this case?

Several points should be made. First, it is clear that we cannot say that Keegstra has no principles. He does not have, as J.L. Mackie (1977) once put it, a new principle for every case (p. 156). Keegstra has his own principles and will not abandon them for convenience or advantage. But although we may admire his sincerity, it is not true that there is *nothing but benefit* in contemplating his actions. His principles are flawed from an educational perspective. Keegstra's concern for truth, which he often stressed, amounted to an all-consuming desire that his students believe what he accepted as true. In Russell's (1985a) language, the will to believe overshadowed the wish to find out (p. 117). This desire was not tempered by a concern to help students weigh evidence and formulate independent judgments.

Second, in characterizing perverse sincerity as eccentric or dotty, we may overlook more serious harms. We smile at eccentricity or dottiness, but these friendly descriptions hardly capture the situation in this case. Having students think of Jews as "gutter rats" (as cited in Bercuson & Wertheimer, 1985, p. 63) cannot be airily dismissed as eccentricity. When a student writes that we must get rid of every Jew in existence, we have gone beyond the dotty. The case shows a failure to take into account the forms perversity can take. Furthermore, this case makes one less sanguine about time affecting a remedy. Bercuson and Wertheimer (1985) express the fear that Keegstra's students may become the bearers of medieval myths in the future (p. 190). Mary Warnock had not envisaged a case where the beliefs acquired were not open to falsification, so that the passage of time would make no difference or even make matters worse.

We should be reluctant to embrace the level of tolerance suggested by Mary Warnock's comment. Should we even tolerate the *inclusion* of ideas such as the Jewish conspiracy theory? Most people will surely find the theory offensive and it is widely regarded as totally implausible. As noted earlier, however, there is a powerful tradition in philosophy of education that supports the inclusion of controversial material and open discussion of related issues. It is very doubtful, however, that the Jewish conspiracy theory properly counts as a controversial historical thesis at all. Reputable historians simply do not take it seriously. A few people dispute the opinion held by experts, but they have not succeeded in making the matter controversial. From the perspective of historical research, the theory is a non-starter.

Should it also be ignored in teaching? Surely, it might be said, the school might give the theory unwitting support by deeming it worthy of mention.[15] Its exclusion, however, might fuel the suspicion that the theory has some credibility, a suspicion actually voiced by some students, as we saw earlier. If suppression of such a view could be effectively carried out in society as a whole, this danger would disappear, but that is not a realistic possibility quite apart from considerations of moral acceptability. Given this dilemma, a compromise might be proposed, namely to ignore the theory unless it is brought up by the students. This strategy, however, presupposes that students genuinely feel comfortable raising issues, otherwise they might be privately nursing their suspicions. We need to remember here that some research suggests that students raise few questions of any kind in class (Dillon, 1988).

The traditional response to the dilemma invokes the ideal that truth should emerge in open discussion. There is no need to exclude the theory, the argument holds, since its absurdity can be demonstrated. We can explain that it is included not because it is important, interesting, or plausible but simply because students may encounter it. Doubt, however, has been cast on the so-called argument from truth:

> The argument from truth is very much a child of the Enlightenment, and of the optimistic view of the rationality and perfectibility of humanity it embodied. But the naiveté of the Enlightenment has since been largely discredited by history and by contemporary insights of psychology. People are not nearly so rational as the Enlightenment assumed, and without this assumption the empirical support for the argument from truth evaporates. (Schauer, 1982, p. 26)

Schauer reminds us that truth has no inherent ability to gain general acceptance (p. 26). The argument from truth may also involve the dubious assumption that the search for truth is the supreme value (p. 33).

It is not clear, however, that these points carry weight in the context of education. In tolerating open discussion of reprehensible views, the assumption is not that students are thoroughly rational. Rather, one of the central aims of education is to further their development as rational agents. To curtail discussion in schools because people are not always rational would deprive students of the very practice that might lead to the development of rational abilities. If it is true now that people are not particularly good at distinguishing truth from falsity, it is especially important for schools to look for ways in which this ability can be developed. The study of bad arguments and discredited theories is an important part of learning to argue effectively (cf. Russell, 1939, p. 529), and prior practice in this area would have served Keegstra's students well.

If we tolerate the discussion of such a theory, should we also tolerate a teacher indicating personal support for it? Keegstra's own approach was obviously unacceptable, and we might note Russell's (1985b) point that when the experts agree, the opposite opinion cannot be regarded as certain (p. 12). This alone would condemn Keegstra's teaching as profoundly misleading. What, however, of the teacher who avoids that error, presents all views fully and fairly, but at the same time reveals a personal inclination to accept a theory that is both discredited and offensive?

Let us distinguish this case from two others. Consider, first, the fact that various groups may find certain aspects of the school curriculum offensive. An example might be a reference in history classes to atrocities carried out in the past by a certain group or country. Here, it is vital to ask if the atrocities are indeed part of the historical record. If so, we would distort historical inquiry[16] were we to allow our preferences to dictate what enters our history books or lessons (cf. Russell, 1954, p. 43). There is a positive obligation to be faithful to the discipline and report what happened. There is also a moral obligation to try to ensure that such facts do not lead to prejudice against those associated with the country or group in question.

Consider, second, the debate over "creation science." This position is utterly discredited in contemporary science, but it is not in itself morally offensive whatever one may think of the tactics sometimes employed in its defence. One simply reveals naiveté in subscribing to such views. If a teacher reveals sympathy for "creation science," appeal to eccentricity will probably suffice to justify tolerance *if* the teacher at the same time manages to present orthodox science as it would be presented by a teacher who personally regards conventional science as compelling.

The Jewish conspiracy theory, however, is both discredited and offensive. A teacher who reveals that he or she accepts it necessarily alienates all those students, not only Jews, who take offence at others being falsely accused of general wickedness. In ordinary life, we can usually avoid those who utter offensive remarks, but "reasonable avoidability" (Feinberg, 1973, p. 44) does not exist at school. Students are obliged to attend and not normally permitted to choose which section of a course they will take, and therefore which teacher they will have, when multiple sections are available. I conclude that in such cases the expression of the teacher's personal view should not be tolerated.

Concluding Comment

Recall that Keegstra was widely hailed as a "good teacher." This suggests the dispiriting conclusion that this appraisal was in danger of losing its essential meaning. The judgment was based on the fact that Keegstra maintained discipline and was totally unrelated to any consideration of the knowledge, skills, and attitudes being learned by his students. Possibly this case will lead us to think out more carefully what it means to be a good teacher (Hare, 1993). In doing this, we will be stimulated, I think, by an observation from Russell (1938) that might have applied to this very case:

> Love of power is the chief danger of the educator, as of the politician; the man who can be trusted in education must care for his pupils on their own account, not merely as potential soldiers in an army of propagandists for a cause. (p. 304)

REFERENCES

Appeal to Board of Reference. (1983, April). Transcript of reasons for decision. Presided over by Justice McFadyen. Edmonton: N.p.

Benton-Evans, R. (1997). Just before you close the book on Keegstra. … Does he exist in every classroom? *Journal of Educational Thought, 31*(2), 123–136.

Bercuson, D., & Wertheimer, D. (1985). *A trust betrayed: The Keegstra affair.* Toronto: Doubleday Canada.

Blair, J.A. (1986). The Keegstra affair: A test case for critical thinking. *History and Social Science Teacher, 21*(3), 158–164.

Chomsky, N. (1975). Toward a humanistic conception of education. In W. Feinberg & H. Rosemount, Jr., (Eds.), *Work, technology, and education* (pp. 204–220). Urbana: University of Illinois Press.

Committee on Tolerance and Understanding: *Final report* (1984). Calgary, AB: N.p.

Dewey, J. (1966). *Democracy and education.* New York: The Free Press.

Dillon, J.T. (1988). The remedial status of student questioning. *Journal of Curriculum Studies, 20*(3), 197–210. doi:10.1080/0022027880200301

Dixon, J. (1986, April). The politics of opinion. *Canadian Forum, 66*, 7–10.

Feinberg, J. (1973). *Social philosophy.* Englewood Cliffs, NJ: Prentice-Hall.

Flew, A. (1975). *Thinking about thinking.* Glasgow: Fontana/Collins.

Hare, W. (1979). *Open-mindedness and education.* Montreal: McGill-Queen's.

Hare, W. (1985). *In defence of open-mindedness.* Montreal: McGill-Queen's.

Hare, W. (1993). *What makes a good teacher.* London, ON: Althouse Press.

Hare, W. (1995). Content and criticism: The aims of schooling. *Journal of Philosophy of Education, 29*(1), 47–60. doi:10.1111/j.1467-9752.1995.tb00340.x

Hook, S. (1968). Heresy, yes—conspiracy, no. In H.K. Girvetz (Ed.), *Contemporary moral issues* 2nd. ed (pp. 87–97). Belmont: Wadsworth. (An extract from a book by Sidney Hook with the same title.)

Lee, R.M. (1985, May). Keegstra's children. *Saturday Night*, 38–46.

Legge, G. (1984, 25 June). Hatred goes on trial. *Maclean's,* 29.

Mackenzie, J. (1988). Authority. *Journal of Philosophy of Education, 22*(1), 57–67. doi:10.1111/j.1467-9752.1988.tb00177.x

Mackie, J.L. (1977). *Ethics: Inventing right and wrong.* Harmondsworth: Penguin Books.

Magee, B. (1975). *Popper.* Glasgow: Fontana/Collins.

Mazurek, K. (1988). Indictment of a profession: the continuing failure of professional accountability. *Teacher Education, 32*, 56–69.

Mertl, S. & Ward, J. (1985). *Keegstra: The issues, the trial, the consequences.* Saskatoon: Western Producer Prairie Books.

Mill, J.S. (1947). *On liberty* (A. Castell, Ed.). New York: Appleton-Century-Crofts.

Montefiore, A. (Ed.) (1975). *Neutrality and impartiality: The university and political commitment.* London: Cambridge University Press.

Passmore, J. (1967). On teaching to be critical. In R.S. Peters (Ed.), *The concept of education* (pp. 192–211). London: Routledge and Kegan Paul.

Pearson, A.T. (1986). Teaching and rationality: The case of Jim Keegstra. *Journal of Educational Thought, 20*(1), 1–7.

Podmore, C. (1985–1986). Our freedoms of expression: reflections on the Zundel and Keegstra affairs. *Humanist in Canada, 18*(4), 16–17.

Russell, B. (1938). *Power: A new social analysis.* London: George Allen & Unwin.

Russell, B. (1939). Education for democracy. *Addresses and Proceedings of the National Education Association, 77*, 527–534.

Russell, B. (1954). The place of science in a liberal education. In B. Russell (Ed.), *Mysticism and logic* (pp. 38–49). Harmondsworth: Penguin Books.

Russell, B. (1985a). Free thought and official propaganda. In B. Russell (Ed.), *Sceptical Essays* (pp. 112–128). London: Unwin.

Russell, B. (1985b). Introduction: On the value of scepticism. In B. Russell (Ed.), *Sceptical Essays* (pp. 11–21). London: Unwin.

Russell, B., & Russell, D. (1923). *Prospects of industrial civilization.* New York: Century.

Schauer, F. (1982). *Free speech: A philosophical enquiry.* London: Cambridge University Press.

Schwartz, A.M. (1986). Teaching hatred: the politics and morality of Canada's Keegstra affair. *Canadian and International Education. Education Canadienne et Internationale, 15*(2), 5–28.

Siegel, H. (1988). *Educating reason: Rationality, critical thinking, and education.* New York: Routledge.

Warnock, M. (1975). The neutral teacher. In S.C. Brown (Ed.), *Philosophers discuss education* (pp. 159–171). London: Macmillan.

NOTES

1 The most useful analysis of the case from a historical and educational perspective is Bercuson and Wertheimer (1985). A detailed account of the 1985 trial is given in Mertl and Ward (1985). The reactions and attitudes of Keegstra's students are examined in Lee (1985).

2 Much of the credit for bringing the case to national attention must go to the documentary *Lessons in hate* shown on CBC's *The Journal,* May 2, 1983.

3 An account of Keegstra's anti-Semitic views, and information about the *Protocols* and its exposure as a hoax, can be found in Bercuson and Wertheimer (1985, chs. 1 & 2).

4 Sample essays can be found in Bercuson and Wertheimer (1985, pp. 213–23), and in Mertl and Ward (1985, pp. 5–8).

5 Keegstra was dismissed from his teaching position, effective January 1983. This decision was upheld in a Board of Reference ruling in April 1983, and Keegstra was subsequently expelled from the Alberta Teachers' Association and his teaching license revoked. In July 1985, he was convicted under section 281.2 of the Canadian Criminal Code of wilfully promoting hatred against the Jews, and fined $5000.00. The Alberta Court of Appeal overturned the conviction in 1988 on the grounds that the law in question violates the Canadian Charter of Rights and Freedoms, but in 1990 the Supreme Court of Canada ruled that the law against promoting hatred is constitutional. Following a second trial, Keegstra was again found guilty, but this conviction was also struck down on appeal. In a unanimous ruling in 1996, the Supreme Court of Canada restored the conviction on the charge of promoting hatred, and reaffirmed its 1990 ruling that the hate law is constitutionally valid.

6 For further discussion of Keegstra as a teacher, see Hare (1993).

7 The reference is to a letter from Keegstra to Superintendent Robert David, March 18, 1982, in Bercuson and Wertheimer (1985, p. 202).

8 Flew is drawing on arguments developed by Karl Popper on the distinction between science and non-science. For an excellent introduction to Popper, see Magee (1975).

9 It should be noted, however, that a surprising number of philosophers and educational theorists do not see the school as involving a marketplace of ideas, taking the view that the schools should primarily concern themselves with teaching content rather than critical inquiry (Hare, 1995).

10 For further discussion of teacher neutrality in connection with the Keegstra case, see Benton-Evans, 1997.

11 The testimony of the teacher who had the unwelcome task of succeeding Keegstra at Eckville High and of counteracting his efforts is clear. See *The Globe and Mail* (April 11, 1985, 1–2).

12 An exception is Chomsky (1975).

13 A portion of the interim report was published in *Canadian School Executive* (4(2), 1984, p. 34). Emphasis mine.

14 Unfortunately, Bercuson and Wertheimer inadvertently add to the confusion. In making it clear that Harrison, the ATA's representative, had *not* defended Keegstra's right to teach the Jewish conspiracy theory as a *fact* of history, they add (as a criticism of the short clip of a longer interview with Harrison shown on CBC television) the comment that the public perception was that Harrison had defended "Keegstra's right to teach his students about a Jewish conspiracy" (Bercuson & Wertheimer, 1985, p. 119). But, of course, Harrison *had* defended this, and the school board had never challenged it. The wording blurs the distinction needed between teaching as a *fact* and teaching *about* a claim.

15 It would surely be relevant to refer to the theory in connection with the study of anti-Semitic episodes in history.

16 On the ethical obligation not to distort the history of science in science education, see Siegel (1988, pp. 106–107).

24

Moral Education within Difference

Impediments to Appreciating the Moral Other

Dwight Boyd*

*This chapter was originally a plenary session paper presented on October 25, 2011, at the international conference, Cultivating Morality: Human Beings, Nature, and the World, *Journal of Moral Education* 40th Anniversary Conference; Association for Moral Education 37th Annual Conference; Asia Pacific Network for Moral Education 6th Annual Conference, Nanjing, People's Republic of China.

Introduction

I grew up on a farm in the American Midwest. So, I know something about cultivating actual crops such as soybeans and corn. I want to start by sharing with you some of the lessons I learned from my experience working on this farm. I want to share these with you because they have parallels in how I will approach the topic for this chapter. The core lesson that grounds all the others is my understanding that there never has been, and never will be, "*the perfect crop*." A much more effective goal of cultivation is close attention to *what can get in the way* of producing the *best crop possible*—under whatever negative, impeding conditions one faces. Such conditions would include, for example, poor soil preparation and weeds that need removal.

This change in how one thinks of goals is then supported by a perspective on what is possible in cultivation efforts. Part of this perspective is the realization that there are many conditions that affect success but that are entirely out of one's control. In the American Midwest bad weather is chief among these. However, I also learned that what *does* remain somewhat in one's control all requires *hard work*. Further, *effectiveness* in this work requires focus on the effort to *minimize the likelihood of failure.*

To many, this may appear to be a pessimistic orientation. To me, it reflects the reality of "cultivation." Furthermore, I think it applies to thinking about morality in much the same way it does to cultivating crops such as soybeans and corn.

When I think about morality, I do so primarily as a philosopher. Philosophers tend to start with problems or worries. Thus, I will shape my comments around a set of related problems in thinking about morality. I have been working in moral education for close to 40 years and I remain committed to it as essential to improving society. But over the years I have become increasingly aware of its dangers. There are *so* many ways moral education can go wrong and do considerable harm, while masking these harms behind good intentions. In this chapter, I want to focus on three harmful ways of thinking about morality in the context of social difference. I think of them as "impediments." By *impediments*, I mean things that get in the way of going somewhere or doing something—like too many weeds in your soybean field that get in the way of producing the best crop possible. I see these ways of thinking about morality as harmful because they get in the way of full appreciation of the moral Other. By thinking critically about them, I seek to minimize the likelihood of failure in this essential moral task. I call them (a) epistemological closure, (b) cultural arrogance, and (c) relations of oppression.

Contextualizing Starting Points

Before I discuss these problems directly, I need to identify four major assumptions that I am making. Please understand: these are not just unnecessary preamble. Rather, they are essential aspects of my arguments.

1. The first assumption that underlies everything else is that the social location from which anyone views the moral realm is *never* a neutral one. Rather, it inevitably shapes what one sees and how one thinks and feels about moral concerns—even what *counts* as a "moral concern." That applies to me, here today, in what follows. So, I want to explicitly acknowledge some aspects of my own location that undoubtedly shape what you will hear from me.

I speak today from a social location of considerable privilege that many people do not share. As a tenured faculty member of a major university, I have never really had to worry about where my next pay-cheque was coming from or about losing my job. Even now, retired, I am financially protected by a good pension program and benefits through the university. More generally, this university is located in a city and country both of which are governed, more or less success-fully, by democratic principles and traditions. Both also entertain public commitments to supporting the cultural diversity of their citizens. In the case of Toronto, this diversity is quite remarkable—with 500 "ethnocultural groups," each with at least 5,000 members! Located as I am within this diversity as a *white, middle-class, educated, heterosexual man*, I enjoy the privileges of a safe space to reflect criti-cally on the kind of problems that I discuss in this chapter, of not worrying about how my comments might reflect on me, and, per-haps, of having my voice heard relatively more than others not so located.

When I say that my social location is never "neutral," I mean not only that it shapes my moral vision. Rather, in addition, with the acknowledgement of my relative privilege, I mean to point out that the location—and thus the outcome of moral vision itself—is never *politically* neutral. With this characterization, I mean to emphasize that none of the markers of my location that I noted stand on their own, independent of a power relationship to other individuals and groups marked by contrasting terms. (I will elaborate on this point in the last part of the chapter.)

2. My second important assumption places high value on diversity. Diversity is now widely accepted by scientists as a *fact* of a healthy bio-sphere—of "nature," if you will. I think this claim regarding diversity also applies to the human social sphere. Acceptance of this fact then entails *also accepting* the implication that some degree of conflict is inevitable in the social sphere as it is in the biosphere.

3. I see my third assumption as following from the second. This assumption consists of a set of beliefs about the aims of morality. The first such belief is that one of the core aims of morality must be to regulate the interaction of humans within the diversity and conflict just noted. One implication of this belief is that morally good regulation of this interaction will include the best possible effort to fully appreciate the moral Other. A second implication is the need to pursue the goal to *minimize failure* in this effort. That is, thinking critically about morality includes the effort to see when a belief in superficial unity can block perception of important difference and thus impede appreciation of the moral Other who really *is* different.

4. Finally, I think a fourth assumption follows from the preceding ones. Like Socrates, I am convinced that some degree of critical *self*-reflection is a good thing, one that usually enhances human flourishing. Of course, this might not be true in all circumstances. But I believe that it definitely enhances the possibility of better appreciation of the moral Other—or at least decreases the likelihood of going seriously wrong in this appreciation. The reason for this is quite simple: I do not think one can begin to appreciate the moral Other—especially in the context of the kind of social diversity that I support—without first understanding as much as possible about oneself.

The Problems

With these starting points, I turn now to a discussion of the three impediments that I think can get in the way of moral understanding across difference. To remind you, these are: (a) epistemological closure, (b) cultural arrogance, and (c) relations of oppression. Despite the differences among the three impediments, I see a similarity in that each is a dangerous kind of "blind spot" to accurate perception of the moral Other in the context of difference. For this reason I will try to make my abstract argument more concrete by offering a visual metaphor for each impediment that suggests how one can imagine the problem. I will also provide examples of how the impediment can affect moral education and how it might be avoided, *or at least minimized.*

Epistemological Closure

By the term "epistemological," I simply mean to draw attention to how some kind of knowledge claim is involved in moral judgment. And by "closure" I am referring to how open one is to ongoing thinking about whether one's judgment is really correct. Psychologically, I think this impediment hinges on the degree of certainty that one attaches to moral judgments *and* on how fast one feels the need to assert that certainty to support one's moral position. It seems to me that many people think they have no problem identifying moral truth, and doing so with certainty. For these people, all we really need to learn how to do is to *apply* what we know with certainty to how we act. Indeed, this position can easily be found in the field of moral education.

Let me give you one very good example from the literature. Here is what Thomas Lickona (2004) says on this matter:

> The content of good character is virtue. Virtues—such as honesty, justice, courage, and compassion—are dispositions to behave in a morally good way. They are objectively good human qualities, good for us whether we know it or not. (p. 7)

He then identifies 10 "essential" virtues that are supposed to be "objectively good" in this way. There is no room for difference and disagreement on the content of this list. Rather, he is just *certain* that "they are affirmed by societies and religions around the world" (Lickona, 2004, p. 7). I must emphasize that Lickona is not alone in holding these beliefs. In fact, he has a huge following in the practice of what is known as "character education" in North America.

Keeping in mind my starting assumption about the good of critical self-reflection, I would counter Lickona's view by agreeing with what Thomas Nagel (1986) has said about this epistemological perspective:

> It is evident that we are at a primitive stage of moral development. Even the most civilized human beings have only a haphazard understanding of how to live, how to treat others, how to organize their societies. The idea that the basic principles of morality are known *and that the problems all come in their interpretation and application is one of the most fantastic conceits to which our species has been drawn. (p. 186)

From my point of view, what is going wrong here amounts to a premature *closure* of the thoughtful search for something that might be, at best, *closer* to the truth, but clearly not *all* the truth. (In terms of my lessons from the farm, it is like assuming that unless we have "the perfect crop," we have no crop at all.)

Referring to this way of thinking about morality as a kind of distortion of the aim of objectivity that he labels "objectivism," Max Deutscher (1983) puts it this way:

> Objectivism is the view that would have us forget that it is a view; the objectivist is a subject who would forget and have others forget that he [sic] is a subject. There is only what is viewed; the viewing of it is passed over. (p. 29)

In visual metaphorical terms, this kind of epistemological closure is like thinking the best way to walk across a city square crowded with people would be by taking one quick look at the destination on the other side of the square … and then closing one's eyes and walking that way across the square. It is blindness to the almost infinite points of view inhabited by other people. It is an *absence* of adequate critical self-reflectivity. It is a failure to remain open to *un*certainty—to keep in mind that one can never have more than *a view* of the truth. As such, by *not* seeing that one is engaged in the activity of seeing, one simply can't see that *others* are *also* so engaged and may see matters quite differently. In a very real sense, the moral Other ceases to exist.

Now, if we consider this way of thinking about morality to be a serious impediment to appreciating the moral Other in the context of difference—what might we do in moral education? I have here two related suggestions. The first suggestion is to pay more attention to the epistemological aspects of moral judgment in both curriculum and teaching. They need to be made much more visible and more central to moral education efforts. As such, they themselves need to be objects of ongoing, shared, critical reflection. The second suggestion is (surprise! surprise!) to build much more philosophy into how we think of good moral education. Some might think that this would not be possible at the elementary level, or even in secondary schools. However, I think the worldwide success the Philosophy for Children movement has had shows this concern to be unfounded. What is important here is that we get better at helping children learn how to *think about their thinking*.

Cultural Arrogance

I turn now to the second of the three impediments that I want to discuss, what I call cultural arrogance. It amounts to a particular—and particularly deep—way in which one can fail to see difference in viewpoint and thus fail to truly appreciate the genuinely different moral Other.

My discussion of this impediment obviously depends heavily on my starting assumption about the value and nature of diversity in the social sphere.

The focus here is on cultural diversity in a broad sense. Focusing on cultural difference in the way I understand it means attending to the complex, relatively stable, substantive traditions or "ways of life" around which large groups of individuals over long periods coalesce and differentiate themselves from others. The relevant differences here are not superficial matters, such as food preferences or styles of dress. Rather, ultimately they refer to different values, and particularly sets of moral values, that constitute the heart of different "ways of life." It is at this level that cultures are truly unique and different from each other in ways that can cause conflict because the *moral* values promoted within one cultural community will not always be compatible with those of another. In short, to truly accept cultural diversity is to accept the reality of the genuine *moral pluralism* that it entails. That is, there are many different moral points of view in the world—and they *cannot* be reduced to just one.

However, this is not a conclusion that many people can comfortably accept. Why? The reason is that the culture in which we grow up shapes us in multiple and pervasive ways—especially the moral aspects of that culture. Thus, we tend to think of it as "*natural*"—not just *a* way of life but *the only* way of life ... the *moral* way of life. We identify with it; in a very real sense it identifies *us*. As Jim Garrison (1996) has put it so nicely, "Cultural traditions have us before we have them" (p. 494). Thus, they *matter* to us because, to a very large extent, they *are* us. A threat to our primary cultural identification is then often felt as a threat to our very existence.

But note: most people have this deep identification with their cultural traditions—even those who have moral beliefs that are *really* different from ours, including some that are truly incompatible with ours. Losing sight of this fact is a serious impediment to even making an effort to understand the culturally moral Other. The impediment that I am calling cultural arrogance, then, represents a failure to sincerely accept the fact of this moral pluralism part of diversity and thus the limitations of one's place within it. On the surface, many people may give the appearance of *seeming* to accept the multicultural nature of the world. But I believe that this too often amounts to appearance only. The person who exhibits cultural arrogance really thinks that deep down we are all the same—and that the moral part of this sameness just happens to be exactly what *that person* believes about morality.

One way this impediment shows up in moral education is revealed in the quotations I used earlier from Lickona. Remember: the virtues he has in mind are said to be "good for us whether we know it or not." Another example can be found in a program currently promoted across all schools in my province of Ontario, one called "Character Matters!" It acknowledges Lickona's work as one of its main sources. Indeed, it promotes a similar short list of virtues that are characterized as "common to all." But it *appears* to not so blindly ignore the existence of real cultural diversity. That is, this list of virtues was generated from a series of public meetings in which there was considerable effort to include representatives from different cultures. However, in my view, this was appearance only. The reason for this evaluation is that any discussion of *disagreement* about what should go on the list—or about the *meaning* of what is left on it—was not entertained. If anyone *disagreed* with the suggestion to put a particular virtue on the approved list, it was simply removed, end of the matter. The surviving 10 items were then *said* to have been arrived at through "consensus." However, in the end this approach amounts to just another route to cultural arrogance because the *definitions* of the virtues that come with the list were written by a small, nonrepresentative committee *after* the list was finalized. Even a quick glance at them reveals that they represent primarily the dominant culture.

The visual metaphor that I think best matches this impediment is the following. Imagine many people looking at the same piece of abstract sculpture. Some are up close; some, farther away. Some from the left, some from the right, or front, or back, and some from above. Some with poor eyesight; some with perfect vision. Finally, some from outside the building housing the sculpture and through a distorting window; and some from outside with *no view* of the piece at all. Each location represents a view from a particular culture and a particular place within moral pluralism. Now imagine that the sculpture has been entitled by the artist—an *unknown* artist, by the way—"An Inherently Important Moral Something." The many viewers are then given the task of describing the "Something" to each other, including what it means and why it might be important. Approaching this task as if everyone has exactly the same view of the sculpture is clearly a mistake. It is also a good metaphor for the impediment of what is going wrong in cultural arrogance. Cultural arrogance in the sense I mean it is, then, the blind spot of assuming that if everyone, regardless of their cultural perspective, just focused their moral vision more carefully, they would come to the same view of what is right and wrong—*and* the same view as the person making the assumption. It is a failure to sincerely accept moral pluralism—and the limitations of one's place within it.

So, what can we say about moral education if we have in mind as an impediment this blind spot? First, I want to offer a note about what should be *avoided*. We should be especially careful to *not* transfer any form of epistemological closure—the first blind spot—into intercultural contexts. In Toronto—and I suspect in many other parts of the world today—this means into any discussion about education in general, but especially about *moral* education. I think both Lickona and

"Character Matters!" exhibit this mistake. Lickona commits it simply by the certainty of his assertion about what makes a person truly virtuous, whatever his or her culture. "Character Matters!" commits it by not accepting the fact of disagreement and conflict that is inevitable in any adequate appreciation of the cross-cultural moral Other. In both cases, the claim of "universals" and "consensus" produces a false—and very harmful—unity that simply reinforces the dominant culture. (To return to my earlier reflections about cultivating crops on a farm, I think this mistake is like really believing that only your own crop needs to be cultivated ... and others' crops are themselves impediments to this aim.)

Then, more positively, I think we need to build the acceptance of cross-cultural moral diversity and disagreement *into* how we think about the goal of moral education. This acceptance is essential to cultivating "the best crop possible" under the circumstances of moral pluralism. There are many ways that this could be done, but I will just mention three. First, I think this is one place where good literature can really help. I do *not* mean literature that preaches some moral lesson. On the contrary, literature that is good in this context illustrates in a vivid way *the problem itself*, showing what it looks like from different cultural perspectives. Then, second, I think it is quite possible to dream up engaging exercises promoting critical self-reflection by students on their own cultural embeddedness and thus limited view. An example would be through the use of metaphors such as the sculpture-viewing exercise just offered. And then, at a more general level, I think we should work hard at building into content, method, and teacher preparation ways that critical discussion of moral difference based in cultural identification can be respectfully approached, encouraged, and engaged. One way of interpreting this suggestion is to follow John Dewey (and Larry Kohlberg) in seeing a democratic way of life as an essential part of moral education.

Relations of Oppression

I turn now to the third of my three worrisome impediments to appreciating the moral Other, what I call relations of oppression. I think it is very clear that this problem has received very little attention in the field of moral education, at least in the English-language literature. I think it is also clear that this blind spot is probably the most harmful of the three. For these reasons, I want to emphasize the importance of understanding it.

Perhaps the best way of identifying what is at issue here is to draw a contrast between what the phrase "relations of oppression" means and what tends to dominate attention in Western moral and political thinking. I think it has been well established that since the Enlightenment the philosophical tradition known as "liberalism" has had an impact on our thinking that is very difficult to overestimate. At the conceptual core of this tradition lies the unshakeable belief that all moral and political thinking must start with a focus on the discrete, unique *individual*. Pretty much everything else depends on this starting point. In short, it is very hard for most people in the West to even imagine a viable alternative, let alone entertain it seriously. (And note that, given the way Western thinking throws its weight around throughout the world, this fact constitutes a good example of both epistemological closure and cultural arrogance.) I *do* believe that this tradition has given rise to some good ways of thinking about some kinds of human relations, e.g., by grounding and promoting principles of liberty, respect for persons, and distributive justice within democracy. However, I also think it fails to adequately address some kinds of pervasive and extremely harmful human relations. And it is those kinds of human relations in which the third impediment is located.

These are relations that are primarily between *groups* of people.[1] Individuals are caught up in these relations *as members of those groups*, not as discrete, unique social entities as liberalism would have it. Indeed, from the perspective of liberalism, all groups are just different kinds of ways individuals can *choose* to join together with other individuals. But this is simply not true for some kinds of groups. If we think of racial relations, gender relations, or class relations, for example, what one needs to focus on for an adequate picture is *not* primarily individuals in relationship with other individuals but on the groups that such categories point to.

These are groups that differ significantly from those that can be seen from the point of view of liberalism. In particular, as Young (1990) notes, in these cases the groups come first and individuals *find themselves* belonging to them whether they want to or not; in other words, groups of this sort are partly constitutive of individuals, exactly the opposite of liberalism's perspective. The significance of our being located in these groups is huge: in multiple ways they affect our life prospects. Moreover, as Young (1990) also emphasizes, the groups *do not exist* except in relationship to at least one other group. If we return to the markers that I used to identify part of my relevant "social location" at the beginning of this chapter, I am "white" only insofar as others are deemed "of colour," and vice versa; I am "masculine" only insofar as others are deemed "feminine," and vice versa;

and I belong to the "middle class" only insofar as others belong to the working class or upper class, and vice versa.

Finally, and especially important to my worry about the third impediment, the relationship between the two contrasting sides is not one of equality or complementarity, as liberalism would have it, but of oppression. It is a hierarchal relationship in which the first side—think "white, masculine, or middle class"—is constituted by forms of systemic, structural power and privilege in relations with those in the contrasting side. These forms of power and privilege are *oppressive*. That is, they function in multiple, interlocking ways to *restrict* and *diminish* those moral Others in terms of the development and exercise of their capacities and an effective voice in public decision making. Focusing on individuals as independent of their social group membership effectively blocks the capacity to see these extremely harmful oppressive relations.

Now, although I have used my own social location to illustrate the conceptual framework of what I am calling relations of oppression, I do not mean that those markers will be relevant in the same way in all societies or cultures. But I think it would be very difficult, if not impossible, to find a society that is not structured in part by these *kinds* of group relations. In fact, psychologists in the specialization known as social dominance theory strongly support this claim:

> Regardless of a society's form of government, the contents of its fundamental belief system, or the complexity of its social and economic arrangements, human societies tend to organize as group-based social hierarchies in which at least one group enjoys greater social status and power than other groups. (Pratto, Sidanius, & Levin, 2006, p. 271)

Thus, although the way I shall talk about the blind spot in what follows may not apply to everyone in the audience today, I think that it *will* apply to *some* in your society.

So what makes relations of oppression such a significant impediment to appreciating the moral Other? In my understanding of this problem I am depending heavily on a remarkable paper by Iris Marion Young (1997) entitled "Asymmetrical Reciprocity: On Moral Respect, Wonder, and Enlarged Thought." She answers this question through a convincing argument against the *possibility* of the goal underlying liberalism's picture of how individuals should seek to better understand the moral Other. This goal consists of seeking *complete reversibility of positions* or standpoints, what she calls the goal of "symmetrical reciprocity" (p. 44). In English, the folk-way of expressing this idea is often the advice to "walk a mile in the other person's shoes," that is, to learn to take the other's perspective *as your own*. Young argues that this goal is impossible—not just contingently impossible because we are all so bad at doing it—but *impossible in principle*. This is how she summarizes what makes this an impossible goal:

> The reciprocal recognition by which I know that I am other for you just as you are other for me cannot entail a reversibility of perspectives, precisely because our positions are partly constituted by the perspectives each of us has on the others. … Who we are is constituted to a considerable extent by the relations in which we stand to others, along with our past experience of our relations with others. Thus the standpoint of each of us in a particular situation is partly a result of our experience of the other people's perspectives on us. (p. 47)

It is important to understand here that Young is making this claim for *any* relations, even those between individuals for the most part similarly located in social terms.

However, what is even more important to my purposes in this chapter—and to Young—is how this problem looks in the context of relations of oppression. When one adds to the picture the kind of relational, asymmetrical, oppressive difference of membership in groups constructed in racial or gender terms, for example, the possibility of "walking a mile in the other person's shoes" disappears entirely. As Young (1997) puts it bluntly, "It is ontologically impossible for people in one social position to adopt the perspective of those in the social positions with which they are related in social structures and interaction" (p. 44). Moreover, as she also notes, when this is attempted by those in the dominant, privileged position, it is usually "politically suspect" and capable of inflicting great harm on members of the oppressed group (p. 47). In fact, it is one of the many ways that the privileged have to support and maintain their privilege. Here's Young's (1997) explanation:

> The social fact of structural privilege and oppression … creates the possibility of falsifying projection. … When members of privileged groups imaginatively try to represent to themselves the perspective of members of oppressed groups, too often those representations carry projections and fantasies through which the privileged reinforce a complementary image of themselves. (p. 48)

In other words, there is a blind spot built into the position of domination and privilege. Even worse, the blind spot functions to protect that very relation of domination and privilege.

Here I think I probably have a conclusion that is even more radical than that of Young's. By using the temporal qualifier "too often" here, she seems to me to imply that it is possible to avoid the "projections and fantasies" *sometimes.* I think this is highly unlikely, if not actually impossible. The metaphor that I want to use here to illustrate this point is the existence of the very real blind spot in *actual* human vision. In medicine this physiological flaw has the technical name of a "scotoma." Not many people seem to know this, but all humans have a literal blind spot right in the middle of their visual field in each eye. If you don't believe me, just enter "blind spot" in a web search engine such as Google and you will see a description of this blind spot and why it exists. In addition, you will also find an online simple test that you can try on your computer to verify that, yes, you do have it.

The reason I find this to be an appropriate metaphor for the blind spot in the moral vision of dominant, privileged people is the following. Even though most people do have two eyes that are coordinated in their visual capacity, the eyes can never see exactly the same thing because of their spatial separation. There is still something missing. What happens is the mind fills in what it "thinks" you should be seeing. And it can be wrong. But you always think you're seeing exactly what is actually there.

As we have seen in the case of privileged people trying to "see" from the position of anyone in an oppressed group, the mind fills in "projections and fantasies" that you are *supposed* to see because you are privileged. And this is almost always wrong. Moreover, the *denial* that you have this flaw serves to legitimate the false picture and maintain the harm that is inflicted on others through the domination and privilege. (Think again about that folk-wisdom advice to "walk a mile in the other person's shoes." When you are located on the dominant side of one of these oppressive group relations, the result is most likely to just be that you have their shoes and you're a mile away from the person.) In this sense, appreciation of the oppressed moral Other is severely limited, maybe even impossible. To my way of thinking, this is a very sobering conclusion, one that we should take very seriously in moral education.

So, then the question arises: what do I have to say about how *this* impediment might be countered in moral education? I will make only two suggestions, the first about some conceptual content that needs to be included in any satisfactory approach to moral education in this context, and the second, a very personal reflection.

The first suggestion is that we need to question the overwhelming tendency to assume that we can adequately conceptualize moral education as addressing only individuals and their relationships to other individuals. As I have argued, this starting point actively prevents attention to moral aspects of oppressive relations. Instead, we need to develop pedagogical strategies for helping young people see how much of human relations is structured through groups of this specific kind. Even from my experience of trying to do this with adult graduate students, however, I know that this is not easy to accomplish. But not to try is, in my opinion, morally reprehensible.

Then, second, I want to share something personal that came out of my experience of writing my paper for the 40th Anniversary Special Issue of the *Journal of Moral Education*. I titled this paper "Learning to Leave Liberalism ... and Live with Complicity, Conundrum, and Moral Chagrin" (Boyd, 2011). It is a personal account of how I learned over many years to see more clearly and accept the kind of blind spot identified in this third impediment—*and* to accept that I have it. As a way of concluding, I want to share with you the way I ended this paper. One reason for doing this is that it "works" for me, reflectively. But the second reason is very important and more generalizable. This reason is that I think it is very dangerous to be too positive about how easy it might be to face and address this blind spot in moral education. It is dangerous because far too often those in dominant, privileged positions maintain their moral innocence by believing and promoting superficial answers to deep social and political problems. In fact, in North America, part of the very *meaning* of "being white," for example, is seeing oneself as a good moral person through these kinds of superficial answers to such problems. One of these is character education programs that try to improve the moral character of those who are, in fact, victims of oppression.

So, instead, I want to end with a set of injunctions that I address first and foremost to myself. They are in the form of some warning signs of how my future thinking could easily go wrong. They take the following form:

(1) *Never assume you are symmetrically positioned with regard to anyone. You aren't.*

(2) *Never assume you can fully understand another. You can't.*

(3) *Never assume you can speak for everybody. You can't.*

(4) *Never conduct research or write as if what you're doing is politically innocent. It isn't.*

(5) *Never pretend what you have to say won't harm anyone. It will.*

(6) *Never conclude that working through these difficulties is not worth the effort. It is.*

It is with moral chagrin that I face the fact of not having earlier taken these injunctions to heart in my own work. It is my sincere hope that others might. (Boyd, 2011, p. 336)

REFERENCES

Boyd, D. (2011). Learning to leave liberalism ... and live with complicity, conundrum, and moral chagrin. *Journal of Moral Education, 40*(3), 329–337. doi:10.1080/03057240.2011.596334

Deutscher, M. (1983). *Subjecting and objecting.* St. Lucia, Australia: University of Queensland Press.

Garrison, J. (1996). A Deweyan theory of democratic listening. *Educational Theory, 46*(4), 429–451. doi:10.1111/j.1741-5446.1996.00429.x

Lickona, T. (2004). *Character matters.* New York: Touchstone.

Nagel, T. (1986). *The view from nowhere.* New York: Oxford University Press.

Pratto, F., Sidanius, J., & Levin, S. (2006). Social dominance theory and the dynamics of intergroup relations: taking stock and looking forward. *European Review of Social Psychology, 17*(1), 271–320. doi:10.1080/10463280601055772

Young, I.M. (1990). *Justice and the politics of difference.* Princeton, NJ: Princeton University Press.

Young, I.M. (1997). Asymmetrical reciprocity: On moral respect, wonder, and enlarged thought. In I.M. Young (Ed.), *Intersecting voices: dilemmas of gender, political philosophy and policy* (pp. 38–59). Princeton, NJ: Princeton University Press.

NOTE

1 In what follows, I am deeply indebted to Iris Marion Young's work, particularly in her book *Justice and the Politics of Difference* (1990). My understanding of the notion of oppression and my way of articulating that understanding both follow Young closely.

Part VI: Conceptions of Education and Teaching

The chapters in this concluding section encourage teachers to consider the problems and challenges they face in their own particular context in the light of certain broader perspectives on education, teaching, and teacher education. Such philosophical conceptions prompt us to question our conventional ways of thinking about teaching and education and help to reveal shortcomings in views we rarely question. Educational ideals, principles, and goals stand out more clearly; and teachers and teacher educators can find insights, guidance, and inspiration in these ideas that will carry over to their own schools and classrooms.

Maxine Greene develops an account of literacy that goes far beyond a narrow view that focuses on the acquisition of basic skills. Her own account, by contrast, includes the notion of young students coming to think independently, to develop their imagination, to explore their own ideas, and to engage in an ongoing attempt to make sense of their experience. This view of literacy is deeply connected, Greene argues, to an education in literature and the arts. It also requires a certain conception of teaching, one that takes seriously the aim of students becoming empowered to teach themselves and develop what she and other philosophers call "wide-awakeness." What kind of teacher is likely to be successful in achieving these aims? Greene believes we need teachers of literacy who are genuinely committed to reflection, critical thinking, openness, and discovery, and determined to resist any tendency to allow teaching to degenerate into a process that leaves students feeling powerless. Greene provokes teachers to ask themselves: How seriously do we take the idea of our students showing an independent spirit and taking charge of their own learning? Do we teach in such a way that we encourage our students to recognize, as she puts it, that there is always more to understand and more to discover?

Paulo Freire invites us to consider a general conception of education as liberation that aims at students learning to recognize, question, and make their own critical assessment of what he labels the "dominant ideology," namely all those beliefs, assumptions, and practices one encounters in the course of growing up that serve to limit one's freedom. This influential account of education involves an approach to teaching in which teachers see themselves as "teacher learners," ready to join with their students in dialogue and open-minded inquiry; closely connected also is a conception of reading as a form of critical interpretation that seeks, in Freire's words, "to unveil what is hidden in the text" and to explore the connections between the "word" and the "world." Freire's ideas leave teachers with many challenging questions. If education is never neutral, as he suggests, how are teachers to convey their own ideals and values to students without fostering uncritical agreement with the teacher's views? Is it possible to show humility in teaching, revealing a lack of certainty about many things, and at the same time be seen by students as knowledgeable and well prepared? In what sense does reading involve "rewriting" what is read, and what does this mean for the teaching of reading? Which attitudes and virtues will serve teachers well as they seek to encourage the curiosity and creativity in their students that Freire values so highly?

Jane Roland Martin reminds us that we continue to blur the important distinction philosophers such as John Dewey have drawn between education and schooling, rarely questioning the general assumption that education occurs exclusively at school or the assumption that the aims and ideals of education can be equated with schooling. Such conceptual confusion leads us to overlook the fact that numerous organizations and institutions are engaged in educational activities, and that the lessons many such groups teach, intended or otherwise, are often opposed to the ideals of democratic society. Students arrive at school having already learned such lessons making it vital that schools properly recognize what Martin identifies as "education writ large" if they are to adequately address the problem of democratic education. Many questions arise from this discussion that teachers need to consider. What steps can schools take to offset the miseducative influences at work in general society? What would it mean in practice for a school to become what Martin calls "a site of democratic culture"? Does contemporary schooling take seriously the idea of educating the whole person? Can schools and other agencies learn to work together despite differences and disagreements? Can these other agencies be brought to see that they have a vital role to play in fostering democratic education?

Fittingly, in the final chapter in this collection, Gert Biesta redirects our attention to a conception of education and teaching that he believes should inform our general perspective on the education of teachers but that tends to be neglected in contemporary policy documents. Biesta suggests that we free ourselves from a preoccupation with skills in characterizing the notion of good teaching and think instead of fostering wisdom in teachers through a program of professional preparation that puts the development of *judgment* at the heart of its efforts. We overlook the importance of cultivating wisdom and judgment in teachers, Biesta argues, when the language we use to characterize education leads us to neglect fundamental questions about the content and purpose of education; and we forget, as a result, that teachers need more than skill to reconcile and balance conflicting educational aims and objectives and to make decisions about what their students need to learn if they are to become truly educated. Biesta's discussion leaves us with many questions to ponder: What qualities and traits do we hope to find in members of the teaching profession? Are there certain virtues that support and sustain our efforts to act wisely? Should teacher education emphasize the formation of teachers who have a sense of judgment? What might teacher education look like if it were oriented around the idea of teachers becoming educationally wise?

Ultimately, these philosophical conceptions of education and teaching must illuminate our own work as teachers and administrators if they are to transform practice, and this means trying to determine how they might contribute to new approaches and objectives in our schools and classrooms. If educators are to see possibilities in general ideas that do not spell out precise directions, they will need to respond to these ideas in an imaginative and exploratory manner. John Dewey (1916/1966) points out the challenge very clearly:

> *Even the most valid aims which can be put in words will, as words, do more harm than good unless one recognizes that they are not aims, but rather suggestions to educators as to how to observe, how to look ahead, and how to choose in liberating and directing the energies of the concrete situations in which they find themselves. (p. 107)*

REFERENCE

Dewey, J. (1966). *Democracy and education.* New York: Macmillan. (Original work published 1916).

25

Literacy for What?

Maxine Greene*

*This chapter was first published as Greene, M. (1982). Literacy for what? *Phi Delta Kappan International, 63*(5), 326–329. Reproduced with permission.

We hear about declining literacy; it has become a fact of life—a drab presence, simply there. We look for scapegoats: teachers, of course; disintegrating families; shiftless children; colleges rotted by relativism and relevance; ubiquitous television. We read William Safire and chortle to ourselves. After all, we reassure our cultivated friends, he speaks for us. We listen to the Underground Grammarian and wag admonishing fingers at our very own colleagues. Naturally, he is not referring to thee and me; his irony and acerbity are meant for "them." And, as we so often do in America, we go in search of the quick fix, a sure way of instilling in students what we have agreed to call "competencies" ("competence" and "capacity" no longer serve), an efficient mode of training in the basic skills. But will intense concentration on the "basics" ensure what William Safire purportedly wants to hear and see? Will "competencies" bring the Grammarian above ground at last and send him on his way? What *do* we mean by literacy? What is it for?

Half a century ago, John Dewey (1954) expressed the need for an articulate public and linked its emergence to a "subtle, delicate, vivid, and responsive art of communication" (p. 164). Only when we have achieved such communication, he said, will democracy come into its own, "for democracy is a name for a life of free and enriching communion. ... It will have its consummation when free social inquiry is indissolubly wedded to the art of full and moving communication" (p. 164). Thirty years later, Hannah Arendt wrote of humans as acting and speaking beings, disclosing themselves as subjects through their acts and words. When they speak directly *to* each other, she said, they create an "inbetween" or a web of relationships (Arendt, 1958, p. 183). Only when such a web is formed is there likely to be what she called a "public space," a space where freedom might finally appear (Arendt, 1958, p. 183). Jurgen Habermas (1976), writing in the last decade, emphasized intersubjectivity and mutual understanding when he described "communicative competence," which contrasts with purely technical talk geared to control (p. 26).

Each of these thinkers has linked communication (surely an expression of literacy) to the existence of a free society. Each has recognized the importance of authentic speaking and writing—the kind of speaking and writing that allows people to reveal themselves to others as they try to make sense of their world. When I read Dewey, Arendt, Habermas, and the many others who have probed the meanings of literacy and thought of new modes of communication and new kinds of literacy, I cannot but ponder existing instances of wordlessness and experiences of powerlessness. I cannot but ponder the *kinds* of speechlessness that occur in these times of proliferating messages and bombarding sounds: the constrained or elliptical talk of so many of the young; the technical talk of so many in the professions (including ours); the hollow kind of public utterance we hear from our nation's capital. And I remember how much language has to do with thinking, how listening to certain kinds of language can stop thinking, how difficult it is to think if one lacks appropriate words. My mind fixes on stock responses, on euphemisms and evasions, on monosyllables, on "Jordache jeans" and "Have a nice day," on the pendulum swings between gobbledygook and the solemn, impenetrable language of what often passes as expertise.

Then, for some reason, I remember Herman Melville's (1967) Billy Budd, who stutters when he is agitated. Billy can find no words to answer the evil Claggart's charge of treason, and so he strikes out at his accuser. Claggart falls to the ground, hits his head, and dies. Billy, you recall, is charged with murder and sentenced to hang from the yardarm (Melville, 1967). Remembering this tale, I am compelled once more to ponder the connections between speechlessness and alienation and violence. Billy was innocent and handsome and illiterate; his shipmates loved him. But the warship, the *Indomitable*, was an exemplar of organized society, in which people were not supposed to listen to their hearts but to words, so Billy, wordless, had to die. I remember, too, another kind of death in Paul Nizan's (1973) novel, *Antoine Bloyé*. It is the existential death of a locomotive engineer in France, a man who spent most of his life as a middle manager on the railroad system:

> *Like many men, he was impelled by demands, ideas, decisions connected with his job. There was no opportunity to think about himself, to meditate, to know himself and know the world. He did no reading; he did not keep himself au courant. Every evening, before going to sleep, he opened his* Life of George Stephenson *and, having read through two pages, which he had got to know by heart, he fell asleep. He glanced at newspapers casually. The events they told of belonged to another planet and did not concern him. The only publications he took a vital interest in were the technical magazines with their descriptions of engines. For a space of fourteen or fifteen years, there was no man less conscious of himself and his own life, less informed on the world than Antoine Bloyé. He was alive, no doubt; who is not alive? To go through the motions of life all you need is a well-fed body. He, Antoine, moved and acted, but the springs of his life, and the drive of his actions were not within himself. (Nizan, 1973, p. 113)*

And the narrator asks, "Will man never be more than a fragment of a man, alienated, mutilated, a stranger to himself?" And I think about naming the world and making sense of it; about the place of literacy in reflective and tonic living, in overcoming automatism, wordlessness, and passivity.

Of course, fundamental skills are needed: knacks, know-how, and *modi operandi*. But I want to see the means of achieving literacy made continuous with the end-in-view, and I would also remind teachers that *literacy ought to be conceived as an opening, a becoming, never a fixed end*. I believe, with Dewey and Gilbert Ryle, that fundamental skills are only the foundation, the first level, and that learning does not actually begin until people begin teaching themselves. Ryle (1967) talks about the importance of advancing beyond low-level skills and employing them in higher-level tasks that cannot be done without thinking. He talks of an ordinary, "unbrilliant, unstupid boy" learning to read:

> He has learned to spell and read monosyllables like 'bat', 'bad', 'at', 'ring', 'sing', etc., and some two-syllable words like 'running', 'dagger', and a few others. We have never taught him, say, the word 'batting'. Yet we find him quite soon reading and spelling unhesistantly the word 'batting'. We ask him who taught him this word and, if he remembers, he says that he had found it out for himself. He has learned from himself how the word 'batting' looks in print, how to write it down on paper and how to spell it out aloud, so in a sense he has taught himself this word — taught it to himself without yet knowing it. (Ryle, 1967, pp. 105–106)

His teacher had taught him how to read monosyllables and some longer words. Thus, the teacher had empowered him to make some independent moves on his own, to make specific applications himself, in the hope that eventually he would transform what he had learned into a personal method of operating by his own "self-criticized practice." Another point is that the boy will learn untaught things if he needs them somewhere, if they respond to questions he is provoked to ask for himself. Ryle says that teaching ought to open gates, not close them; people only begin to learn when they go beyond what they are taught and begin teaching themselves. This is teaching, in my view: creating situations that impel people to reach beyond themselves, to act on their own initiatives. And teaching, too, includes enabling persons to perceive alternative realities, more desirable orders of things. Only when they can see things as if they could be otherwise are they free in any meaningful sense. Only as they can imagine a better condition of life are they able to perceive what is lacking in their present moments and to reach forward, to go beyond.

This view of teaching is very much at odds with the approach taken in many classrooms today, especially in those that concentrate on competencies. Teachers are schooled to think of students as reactive creatures, behaving organisms. Overaffected by the technical ethos, they are likely to focus on measurable or observable performance or to function according to what Ryle (1967) calls a "crude, semi-surgical picture of teaching as the forcible insertion into the pupil's memory of strings of officially approved propositions" (p. 108). When the reward system of a school is geared toward guaranteeing certain predefined performances or the mastery of discrete skills, teachers too often become trainers—drilling, imposing, inserting, testing, and controlling. They are too distanced from their students to talk with them or to them. Instead, they talk *at* them, work *on* them very often, but not *with* them. Teachers who conceive their students as some plastic raw material, or some sort of resistant medium, cannot think of empowering students to learn how to learn, to articulate, to be with one another, or to develop an "in-between."

Teaching for literacy conceives learning as action rather than behaviour. The notion of action involves the reflective taking of initiatives: trying out what has been learned by rote, acting on the so-called competencies. This is in contrast to an unreflective, semi-automatic movement through predefined sequences of what is sometimes optimistically called "mastery." A concern for beginnings, for action rather than behaviour, is different from a preoccupation with end points, with predetermined objectives. Indeed, once teachers approach their students as novices, as newcomers to a learning community extending back through time and ahead into a future, they may well open themselves (as well as their students) to all sorts of untapped experiential possibilities (Arendt, 1961).

The notion of the aesthetic and the importance of the humanities unite in moving people to learn how to learn in this way. "Rooted in language and dependent in particular on writing," writes the Rockefeller Commission on the Humanities (1980), "the humanities are inescapably bound to literacy" (p. 69). And, a few lines later: "In literature and the arts, the imagination gives public expression to private experience" (p. 69). When we work to promote what is called *aesthetic literacy*, an informed awareness of works of art or works in the humanities, we start with the assumption that the more a person can come to know, the more he or she will come to see and hear, certainly where works of art are concerned. We start, too, with the idea that there is no way to realize a work of art, to make it live in a person's experience, if that person is not actively involved with it. It is important to recognize that every encounter with a work of art represents a new beginning, even if the work is moderately familiar and has been encountered before. Every time we become present, say, to a Cezanne painting or an Emily Dickinson poem, we are—whether consciously or not—about to experience something new. Whoever we are, we are at a particular point in our life history; we are different from what we have been, even a day before. (And I want to stress the great importance of feeling oneself to be in process, to be on the way, to be en route to what is not yet.)

It may be that we have learned more, over time, about what it signifies to look at a painting, to attend to its forms, to see its contours emerging, to engage with its thrust of colour or illusions of space. Having thought about it, having questioned it (and ourselves, perhaps), we shall be able to see differently, to see more. And, strangely, we may discover—if we allow ourselves to do so—that every time we come to a Cezanne painting or an Emily Dickinson poem, there is always more to be seen, if we are willing to think about it, to think about our own thinking with respect to it. We can never exhaust it, never use it up. To enter into it imaginatively, to shape the materials of our experience in accord with it, is to find something in our memory, in our consciousness, even in our lived situations that we might never have found were it not for the painting or the poem and our changing awareness of it. It can never be wholly absorbed; it can never be complete. There is always, always more.

I emphasize all this not simply because I believe that the arts should play a central role in schools. It happens that I *do* believe this passionately, knowing as I do that aesthetic experiences are not only affective and intuitive, knowing that they involve persons perceptually and cognitively as much as they do emotionally, knowing that they provoke people to wide-awakeness and to posing questions and pondering their worlds. To be able to attend to the shapes of things and their qualities, to pay heed to sounds, to be in touch with the rhythms of the world: all of this is to be more alive, more open, more resistant to stasis and to all that stands in the way of literacy. But my emphasis on the connections between the arts and literacy also suggests so many things about how teaching in many realms might proceed. I mean the kind of teaching that moves young people to search, to reach out, to think (as Dewey often said) prospectively and as participants. I mean the kind of teaching that enables persons to be observant and imaginative and careful, awake to their own lived worlds and what is deficient about them.

To encounter the arts and other subjects in a mood of discovery and mindfulness and rational passion is to have experiences that exclude inertness. Students experience inertness when they are confronted with information that is solidified, packaged, and in some way dead: pieces of what is incorrectly called knowledge, something students are expected to insert into their minds. Such a barren approach to teaching or to communication can only discourage thinking and mindfulness. (I anticipate with some horror the advent of videodiscs and additional cable networks if we cannot countervail against this.) After all, the value of what we come to know is subordinate to its use in thinking, and inert ideas all too often stop thinking in its tracks (Whitehead, 1957). All of us can recall people (not only children) who say, "I know, I know," meaning that they do not want to think about something. All of us are familiar with the kind of certainty that makes people feel there is no more need to think, and we are familiar with the numbing effect of packaged media messages and categorized "information."

In an encounter with a work of art, the *point* of knowing something about form and colour or imagery and metre is to allow what is being attended to grow in our experience. Simply to store a piece of information about Cezanne's effort to restore structure to the visible world is not to come to know or to learn, nor is it to heighten understanding or to enable oneself to see. The discipline required and the rigour involved are what make freedom in the quest for meanings possible. The point is to nurture the thinking process, the sense-making process—not to move people to say, "I know, I know" and switch the dials or turn off the set.

The notion of literacy of which I am speaking is a notion of process, of restlessness, of quest. I recall Virginia Woolf (1976) writing about how much of her childhood contained what she called "a large proportion of cotton wool," meaning that much of it was not lived consciously. But she also writes about "exceptional moments." She remembers looking at a flower and suddenly seeing the flower as part flower and part earth, and she put away that thought to save. She captured an elusive insight in the net of language. It is the pleasure to be found in making new connections, the insight to be gained in discovering the relations between what is perceived or understood and what follows from it. It is, as Woolf said, the "token of some real thing behind appearances; and I make it real by putting it into words. It is only by putting it into words that I make it whole" (p. 72). It is the significance of discovering an interest, a concern that links one human being to another. All of these cannot but illuminate ongoing experience and expand the spheres of potential meaning.

Surely there are flowers and the equivalents of flowers in the sensed and perceived worlds lived by students: flowers and faces and city streets and burned-out storefronts and other people—phenomena to be attended to as Virginia Woolf attended to what was happening in her world. There are *lived actualities* that raise questions not now answerable, thoughts to be put away in the mind, to be reconceived and re-examined and, later on, explained. Let me emphasize my concern for consciousness and the linking of consciousness to thinking and explaining. To feel passive or powerless is to be open to the despair and horror most of us (including our children) know all too well, perhaps particularly in the cities, but actually across our entire nation.

One of the important contributions to be made to the initiation into articulateness, into literacy, is the overcoming of this sense of powerlessness. Virginia Woolf did this by putting her experiences into words, but I do not think it necessary to be a writer to do so. We must do all we can to enable the young to articulate, to express what they see and hear. They need to be empowered to give voice to what horrifies them, what dulls and deadens them—by telling their stories aloud, writing logs, keeping journals, inventing fictions, creating poetry, editing newsletters, or even rendering what they perceive through paint or gesture or sound. To speak through one of these several languages is not only a way of overcoming passivity; it is a way of being free along with others, because to speak or to express is to give public form to private awareness, to communicate what is known. It is to develop the power Virginia Woolf talks about: the power against nonbeing and loneliness—the "nondescript cotton wool" that obscures so much of life.

Yes, the silence and the powerlessness must somehow be overcome if literacy is to be achieved. The teacher of literacy, to be authentic and effective, must be inquirer, discoverer, critic, sometimes loved one. He or she must be someone who cares, someone who is ready to engage a subject matter or a created form as an always open possibility. The true teacher of literacy is not the kind who comes to class having "done" *Romeo and Juliet* or the history of the Civil War or the science of genetics—with all questions answered and the subject turned into an object ready to be consumed. Rather, he or she must be prepared to think critically, giving good reasons for the claims made and even the demands, encouraging students to look critically upon the performances in which they are asked to engage, participating in discussions with the students, making explicit the norms that govern their being together, keeping the enterprise open, allowing for possibility. Of course, it is a burden for the teacher, but meaningful literacy is most unlikely if teachers do not display, against all odds, the modes of being (and of foresight and integrity) they wish students to choose for themselves.

Our task is to move young people to be able to educate themselves and to create the kinds of classroom situations that stimulate them to do just that. Doing so, they may find themselves in a position to discover and use certain of the concepts that enable literate human beings to impose order and meaning on inchoate experience. Concepts are perspectives of a sort; they are clusters of meaning. They empower persons to organize experience to interpret it, to have some power over it, to see and, yes, to say. To achieve literacy is, in part, to learn how to think conceptually, to structure experience, to look through wider and more diverse perspectives at the lived world.

Obviously, in many schools the public emphasis is on literacy, basic skills, and test results, and there are administrators throughout the US who care mainly about numbers and what is finally quantifiable. And there are abstracted faces in classrooms, young people for whom school is far less important than television or pop music or life on the streets. It is certainly true that, for children who look at television six hours each day, school cannot be interesting or relevant. For one thing, school makes demands that TV does not; it makes people feel inferior, as TV seldom does; it does not seem concerned with "real" things.

It seems evident that, if the school's primary function is to countervail against all of this, the literacy it attempts to make possible must be linked to critical reflectiveness, to wide-awakeness. Indeed, I insist that no other institution or agency in society has that particular responsibility. If we in education do not succeed in accomplishing this mission, we shall (as most of us are quite aware) leave a population passive, stunned, and literally thoughtless in front of television or with miniature speakers in their ears. They will become increasingly fearful in the face of what they see happening in "the world," increasingly confused by the idea of a movie actor playing the president, increasingly numb to terms like "El Salvador" and "budget" and "defence." Horror, despair, passivity, and nondescript cotton wool. We have only to offer the power that comes with the ability to explain, to locate, to conceptualize, to perceive possibilities. That, as I see it, signifies literacy.

Let me conclude with a section from Ntozake Shange's (1977) choreodrama, *For Colored Girls Who Have Considered Suicide When the Rainbow Is Enuf*, because it deals with the theme of this chapter and because it suggests so very much.

> de library waz right down from de trolly tracks
> cross from de laundry-mat
> thru de big shinin floors & granite pillars
> ol st. louis is famous for
> i found toussaint
> but not til after months uv
> cajun katie/ pippi longstockin
> christopher robin/ eddie heyward & a pooh bear
> in the children's room
> only pioneer girls & magic rabbits

& big city white boys
i knew i waznt sposedta
but i ran inta the ADULT READING ROOM
  & came across

  TOUSSAINT

    my first blk man
(i never counted george washington carver
cuz i didnt like peanuts)
    still
TOUSSAINT waz a blk man a negro like my mama say
who refused to be a slave
& he spoke french
& didnt low no white man to tell him nothin
  not napolean
  not maximillien
  not robespierre

TOUSSAINT L'OUVERTURE
waz the beginnin uv reality for me
in the summer contest for
who colored child can read
15 books in three weeks
I won & raved abt TOUSSAINT L'OUVERTURE
at the afternoon ceremony
waz disqualified
  cuz Toussaint
    belonged in the ADULT READING ROOM

(pp. 25–27)

It did not matter. She loved Toussaint. She took him home, and he became her imaginary friend. And she walked with him and explored with him and talked to him, until finally she met a boy named Toussaint Jones who turned out to be not too different from her Toussaint, but this one spoke English and ate apples and was all right with her: "no tellin what all spirits we cd move down by the river." And the section ends, "hey wait."

Would such a person *not* master the basics, with the Adult Reading Room in sight? I ask myself how we can create situations that might release persons to take the kind of leap that girl took—away from the magic rabbits of the children's room to the Adult Reading Room. No one could have predicted that that child would find Toussaint, but I want to believe that there is *always* a Toussaint waiting there ahead, if we dare to think in terms of beginnings, to see from the vantage point of the beginner, the seeker—instead of seeing from the vantage point of the system or the bureaucracy or the framework. What supervisor, principal, test-maker, or other functionary could possibly predict a little girl's making that run into the Adult Reading Room and finding the beginning of her reality that way, making connections, reading 15 books in three weeks? But, from the vantage point of that eight-year-old, why not? And when she says, "hey wait," we know she has that sense of incompleteness that will impel her on, and we know no measurement scale can grasp that either. But think what she will have thought. Think about her gains in literacy.

We owe young people that sort of discontent, as we owe them visions of Adult Reading Rooms. We owe them the sight of open doors and open possibilities. We need to replace the drab presence of declining literacy with images of flowers and new realities. Literacy, after all, ought to be a leap.

REFERENCES

Arendt, H. (1958). *The human condition.* Chicago: University of Chicago Press.

Arendt, H. (1961). *Between past and future.* New York: Viking Press.

Commission on the Humanities. (1980). *The humanities in American life.* Berkeley: University of California Press.

Dewey, J. (1954). *The public and its problems.* Chicago: Swallow Press.

Habermas, J. (1976). *Communication and the evolution of society.* Boston: Beacon Press.

Melville, H. (1967). *Billy Budd, sailor, and other stories.* Baltimore, MD: Penguin Books.

Nizan, P. (1973). *Antoine Bloyé.* New York: Monthly Review Press.

Ryle, G. (1967). Teaching and training. In R.S. Peters (Ed.), *The concept of education* (pp. 105–119). New York: Humanities Press.

Shange, N. (1977). *For colored girls who have considered suicide when the rainbow is enuf: A choreopoem.* New York: Macmillan.

Whitehead, A.N. (1957). *The aims of education.* New York: Macmillan.

Woolf, V. (1976). *Moments of being: Unpublished autobiographical writings* (J. Schulkind, Ed.). New York: Harcourt.

26

Reading the World and Reading the Word

*An Interview with Paulo Freire**

*This chapter was originally published in January 1985 as Reading the world and reading the word: An interview with Paulo Freire. *Language Arts, 62*(1), 15–21, by the National Council of Teachers of English. Reproduced with permission.

Teaching and Educating

Language Arts: Paulo, you are known for your work in what people call liberation education—education to help learners overcome oppression and achieve various kinds of freedom—and the special role which dialogue and literacy play in that process. The teacher's role in this experience is key. Would you describe what being a teacher means to you?

Paulo Freire: I love being a teacher. To me, being a teacher does *not* mean being a missionary or having received a certain command from heaven. Rather a teacher is a professional, one who must constantly seek to improve and to develop certain qualities or virtues, which are not received but must be created. The capacity to renew ourselves every day is very important. It prevents us from falling into what I call "bureaucratization of mind." I am a teacher.

Language Arts: What are some of these virtues or qualities you see as important for the professional teacher?

Paulo Freire: Virtues are qualities which you recreate through action and through practice, qualities which make us consistent and coherent concerning our dreams—a consistency which teachers try to achieve within what they are doing.

Humility is an important virtue for a teacher, the quality of recognizing—without any kind of suffering—our limits of knowledge concerning what we can and cannot do through education. Humility accepts the need we have to learn and relearn again and again, the humility to know *with* those whom we help to know. You must be humble because you don't have any reason not to be humble. But being humble does not mean that you accept being humiliated. Humility implies understanding the pain of others, the feelings of others. We should respect the expectations that students have and the knowledge students have. Our tendency as teachers is to start from the point at which we are and not from the point at which the students are. The teacher has to be *free* to say to students, "You convinced me." Dialogue is not an empty instructional tactic but a natural part of the process of knowing.

Another important virtue for the teacher is patience and its opposite, impatience. We teachers must learn how to make a life together with our students who may be different from us. This kind of learning implies patience and impatience. We must always be impatient about achieving our dream and helping students achieve theirs. Yet, if we and our students push too hard and too fast for our dreams, we may destroy them. Thus, we must be patiently impatient.

Tolerance is another virtue which is very important. It involves both humility and patience. Tolerance means learning how to confront the antagonist. For instance, a classroom of students is not a social class, as such, but is made up of individual students who bring to class with them various social class backgrounds. As a teacher my relationship with them is not a class relationship. My values may be different from the students', but I cannot for that reason take them as my enemies. I must be tolerant.

The story is told about Chairman Mao's niece complaining to him about "Viva Chiang Kai-Shek!" found scrawled on a blackboard at her university. In response to Mao's questions, she told him there were only about two reactionaries among the five thousand students at her university that would have written it. Mao replied that it was too bad there were only two, that it would be better for the Communist side if there were more reactionaries around. He pointed out that people had the right to say what they thought but that the Communist side also had the right to try to convince them they are wrong.

All these virtues connect. For instance, being tolerant implies respect, and being tolerant implies assuming the naivety of the student. A teacher must accept the naivety of the student for practical reasons. You cannot overcome a student's naivety by decree. We must start at the point where the students are. If we start from the point where we are, we must make connections with the position in which the students are. In order for students to go beyond their naivety, it is necessary for them to grasp their naivety into their own hands, and then they will try to make the important leap, but they will leap with you. Assuming the naivety of the students doesn't mean becoming naive or staying at the naive level of the students. To assume the naivety of the student is to understand the naivety and not to refuse it dogmatically, but to say yes to the naivety and mediate to challenge the naive student, so they can go beyond their naive understanding of reality.

The final virtue, if possible, is the ability to love students, in spite of everything. I don't mean a kind of soft or sweet love, but on the contrary a very affirmative love, a love which accepts, a love for students which pushes us to go beyond, which makes us more and more responsible for our task.

Language Arts: You have often used the phrase "teacher learner" in reference to the teacher in the classroom. In a teaching situation how do you see the teacher as a learner?

Paulo Freire: I consider it an important quality or virtue to understand the impossible separation of teaching and learning. Teachers should be conscious every day that they are coming to school to learn and not just to teach. This way we are not just teachers but teacher learners. It is really impossible to teach without learning as well as learning without teaching. We cannot separate one from the other; we create a violence when we try. Over a period of time, we no longer perceive it as violence when we continually separate teaching from learning. Then we conclude that the teacher teaches and the student learns. That unfortunately is when students are convinced that they come to school to be taught and that being taught often means transference of knowledge.

Knowing the concept of an object implies apprehending the object. I first apprehend the object, in apprehending the object I know it, and because I know it, I then memorize it. Apprehending precedes memorization. Learning does not exist without knowing. Teaching for me, then, is challenging the students to know, to apprehend the object.

As teachers, we learn from the process of teaching, and we learn with the students for whom we make possible the conditions to learn. We also learn from the process that the students are also teaching us.

Language Arts: What is your vision of education? What do you hope education would do for the growth of young children?

Paulo Freire: For me education is simultaneously an act of knowing, a political act, and an artistic event. Thus, I no longer speak about a political dimension of education. I no longer speak about a knowing dimension of education. As well, I don't speak about education through art. On the contrary I say education *is* politics, art, and knowing. Education is a certain theory of knowledge put into practice every day, but it is clothed in a certain aesthetic dress. Our very preoccupation with helping kids shape themselves as beings is an artistic aspect of education. While being a teacher demands that we be simultaneously a politician, an epistemologist, and an artist, I recognize that it is not easy to be these three things together.

Thus, to the extent that we are responsible, we must become prepared, competent, capable. We should not frustrate those students who come to us hoping for answers to their expectations, to their doubts, to their desire to know. We must have some knowledge, of course, about our subject, but we must also know how to help them to know. This dimension of *how* is also an artistic one and not just a methodological one.

Many issues and questions arise from this understanding of the act of education. For example, it suggests that we teachers should be constantly asking questions of ourselves and of our students, to create a spirit in which we are certain by not being certain of our certainties. To the extent that we are not quite sure about our certainties, we begin to "walk toward" certainties.

Another example is that education has *politicity*, the quality of being political. As well, politics has *educability*, the quality of being educational. Political events are educational and vice versa. Because education *is* politicity, it is never neutral. When we try to be neutral, like Pilate, we support the dominant ideology. Not being neutral, education must be either liberating or domesticating. (Yet I also recognize that we probably never experience it as purely one or the other but rather a mixture of both.) Thus, we have to recognize ourselves as politicians. It does not mean that we have the right to *impose* on students our political choice. But we do have the duty not to hide our choice. Students have the right to know what our political dream is. They are then free to accept it, reject it, or modify it. Our task is not to impose our dreams on them but to challenge them to have their own dreams, to define their choices, not just to uncritically assume them.

Many teachers unfortunately have been destroyed by the dominant ideology of a society and they tend to impose that way of seeing the world and behaving on kids. They usually view it as "saving" kids, as a missionary would. This tendency stems from a superiority complex. When we fall into this way of thinking, we are touching kids with surgical masks and gloves. The dominant ideology, which serves the interests of the socially powerful, makes the world opaque to us. We often believe the ideological words that are told to us—and which we repeat—rather than believing what we're living. The only way to escape that ideological trap, to unveil reality, is to create a counter-ideology to help us break the dominant ideology. This is accomplished by reflecting critically on our concrete experiences, to consider the raison d'etre of the facts we reflect on. Teachers must be able to play with children, to dream with them. They must wet their bodies in the waters of children's culture first. Then they will see how to teach reading and writing.

Once teachers see the contradiction between their words and their actions, they have two choices. They can become shrewdly clear and aware of their need to be reactionary, or they can accept a critical position to engage in action to transform reality.

I call it "making Easter" every day, to die as the dominator and be born again as the dominated, fighting to overcome oppression.

The Role of Language and Reading

Language Arts: How does language, especially reading, fit in with your vision of education? How can it help develop critical consciousness to know our dreams in order to be free and move toward those dreams?

Paulo Freire: If we think of education as an act of knowing, then reading has to do with knowing. The act of reading cannot be explained as merely reading words since every act of reading words implies a previous reading of the world and a subsequent rereading of the world. There is a permanent movement back and forth between "reading" reality and reading words—the spoken word, too, is our reading of the world. We can go further, however, and say that reading the word is not only preceded by reading the world but also by a certain form of writing it or rewriting it. In other words, of transforming it by means of conscious practical action. For me, this dynamic movement is central to literacy.

Thus, we see how reading is a matter of studying reality that is alive, reality that we are living inside of, reality as history being made and also making us. We can also see how it is impossible to read texts without reading the context of the text, without establishing the relationship between the discourse and the reality which shapes the discourse. This emphasizes, I believe, the responsibility which reading a text implies. We must try to read the context of a text and also relate it to the context in which we are reading the text. And so, reading is not so simple. Reading mediates knowing and is also knowing because language is knowledge and not just mediation of knowledge.

Perhaps I can illustrate by referring to the title of a book written by my daughter, Madalena. She teaches young children in Brazil and helps them learn to read and write, but above all she helps them know the world. Her book describes her work with the children and the nature of their learning. It is entitled *The Passion to Know the World*, not *How to Teach Kids to Read and Write*. No matter the level or the age of the students we teach, from preschool to graduate school, reading critically is absolutely important and fundamental. Reading always involves critical perception, interpretation, and "rewriting" what is read. Its task is to unveil what is hidden in the text. I always say to the students with whom I work, "Reading is not walking on the words; it's grasping the soul of them."

Language Arts: It seems that when children come to school, they already know how to "read" in the sense that they already know how to come to know the world, how to transform it. Yet as we try to work within an uncritical, reproductive education system, it seems that can get in the way and that reading can become "walking on words"—an empty, technical process. How do we prevent that from happening? How is Madalena with the kids; how does she fan the flames of their passion to know the world?

Paulo Freire: Reading words, and writing them, must come from the dynamic movement of reading the world. The question is how to create a fluid continuity between on the one hand reading the world, of speaking about experience, of talking freely with spontaneity, and on the other hand the moment of writing and then learning how to read, so that the words which become the starting point for learning to read and write come from the kids' ideas and not from the teacher's reading book.

In the last analysis, the kids should come full of spontaneity—with their feelings, with their questions, with their creativity, with their risk to create, getting their own words "into their own hands" in order to do beautiful things with them. The basis for critical reading in young children is their curiosity.

Once again, teaching kids to read and write should be an artistic event. Instead, many teachers transform these experiences into a technical event, into something without emotions, without invention, without creativity—but with *repetition*. Many teachers work bureaucratically when they should work artistically. Teaching kids how to read words in the world is something which cannot really be put inside of a program. Normally, kids live imaginatively vis-à-vis reality, but they can feel guilty if they read this way within a technical, bureaucratic, reading program and eventually can give up their imaginative, critical reading for a behaviouristic process.

Reading is more than a technical event for me. It's something that takes my conscious body into action. I must be the subject, with the teacher, of my act of reading and writing and not a mere object of the teaching of how to read and write. I must know! I must get into my hands the process of reading and writing.

Madalena introduces the kids, without any kind of violence, to a serious understanding of the world, of the dimensions of their reality by talking with them, by bringing into the class a text or articles from the newspapers, by reading for them and to them, inviting parents to come and talk about their experiences in life, encouraging the kids to bring in texts, objects, and experiences, constantly putting in print generative words from the kids which express their expectations. The kids begin to reflect on their own language, getting the language "into their hands." Little by little they learn to read and write critically. And this can be done without turning them into arrogant academics.

The teacher must be one with young children— by being curious with them—without being one of them, since children need adults. They need to know that we know more than they do, but also that we are *knowing*. One of Madalena's pupils was shocked one day to learn that Madalena did not know a certain thing but saw in the next few days how she went about learning it. Such an experience has ideological dimensions for schooling and learning. By making the teacher vulnerable, it demystifies her and makes her more lovable. This demystification of adults is the only way for kids to grow up.

The basic question in school is how not to separate reading the word and reading the world, reading the text and reading the context.

Language Arts: It seems that we've come full circle in this conversation. As I look back, I'm afraid I was dichotomizing as I listened to you by focusing at one time on what the teacher does and at another time on what the child does. Actually it seems to be all one question—and one answer. It seems that the kind of reader and writer we want young children to be, we have to be. We have to know it—and teach it—by living it.

Paulo Freire: Yes, that's right!

Language Arts: If teachers have a passion to know the world, if they are curious and wondering, it seems that reading and writing will be treated that way in the classroom, indeed, could be treated in no other way.

Paulo Freire: Yes, I agree. For example, it would have been impossible for Madalena to have done what she did if she had a bureaucratic understanding of reading and education. (I mention Madalena only because we talked about her book. There are many teachers in Brazil who do similar things.) If a teacher has a bureaucratized understanding of education, of reality, of existence, then necessarily that teacher's understanding of reading will also be a bureaucratized one. The challenge for teachers is to re-know for themselves the objects the kids are trying to learn, to find meanings in them hidden to them before. If they don't there is the danger that they may uncritically transmit their knowledge to students. Whether or not a child reads critically depends on whom the child reads with and for.

Let's say that a teacher has me in a course and encounters a new way of thinking—about existence, about education, about reality. If the teacher does not have enough time to reshape his or her understandings, if she or he accepts my ideas just intellectually but not emotionally, not politically, not existentially, what can happen is that she or he returns to working with kids and transforms all the dynamism I suggested for reading the world and reading words into a formula. Once again, the teacher will turn reading into a bureaucracy and maybe will become frustrated because she or he cannot do it the way they thought and will say that Paulo Freire is absolutely mistaken. Rather, the teacher was not able to die as a bureaucratized mind in order to be born again as an open mind, a creative mind.

In knowing as teachers, we must have a humble conviction. When we are too convinced, we often can't accept change. Of course we need to be convinced, but with humility, always waiting to overcome our "convincement." If you are not convinced in a humble way, not only of the principles but also of the concrete experience, you risk transforming these ideas into a bandage and they will not work.

Language Arts: Thank you very much. Is there any final comment you'd like to add?

Paulo Freire: I just want to thank the readers for reading this conversation. I also ask them not just to accept what we said, but to think critically of what we said.

27

Education Writ Large

*Jane Roland Martin**

*This chapter was first published as Martin, J.R. (2008). Education writ large.
In J. Goodlad, R. Soder, & B. McDaniel (Eds.), *Education and the making of a
democratic people* (pp. 47–64). Boulder, CO: Paradigm Publishers. Reproduced
with permission.

When Socrates is asked to track down the nature of justice in Plato's
dialogue *The Republic,* he says that the search requires keen eyesight.
Drawing an analogy to trying to read small letters at a distance and
finding them easier to see when written large, he suggests that he and
his companions look for justice in the city-state before attempting
to observe it in the actions of individuals (Plato, 1974).[1] I propose
that to grasp the nature of education in and for democracy we follow
Socrates's lead: that we look at it first in society as a whole and only
then try to discern it at the level of the individual.

Multiple Educational Agency

In the public mind, education and schooling are nearly synonymous. One opens a newspaper or magazine to its education section expecting to read about schools, colleges, and universities. The government appoints a new commissioner of education and we take it for granted that his or her domain is the nation's school system. A scholar says that educational levels have risen when what he or she really means is that there has been an increase in years of schooling.

Take a hard look at society, however, and one will see education everywhere. Of course, it is discernible in schools. But in the United States, for example, one can also detect it in homes and neighbourhoods; churches, mosques, and synagogues; zoos, parks, and playgrounds; the Boy Scouts, the Girl Scouts, and Little League; museums and libraries; symphony orchestras, ballet companies, and the recording industry; the print and electronic media; stores, banks, businesses, and corporations; the military, governmental agencies, and nonprofit organizations; hospitals, courthouses, and prisons.

The false equation between education and schooling has not gone unnoticed. Philosopher John Dewey (1916) rejected it in the very first pages of *Democracy and Education* (p. 4). In the 1960s, historians Bernard Bailyn (1960) and Lawrence Cremin (1965) showed beyond a shadow of a doubt that, in the past, school was but one of many educational institutions in US society and by no means the most important one. And in his widely read 1972 volume *Deschooling Society*, Ivan Illich (1972) made it evident that the reduction of education to one of its many forms is untenable. Yet despite the whistle-blowers, the assumption that the word "education" means "schooling" is so deeply embedded in most people's consciousness that even those who explicitly acknowledge the mistake are apt to deny the existence of multiple educational agency in their next breaths.

When we examine the big picture, we discover that school is but one element of a vast educational system, and perhaps not the most powerful element at that.[2] He or she will also perceive that education is not always a conscious, voluntary, intentional affair. To be sure, school's express purpose is to foster learning and the designated task of schoolteachers is to figure out how best to do this. But home, church, neighbourhood, the media, and all the rest teach countless lessons, many of which are not consciously intended. Furthermore, school itself produces a whole range of unintended learning outcomes.

Dewey (1963) had traditional schooling in mind when he asked in *Experience and Education*:

> *What avail is it to win prescribed amounts of information about geography and history, to win ability to read and write, if in the process the individual loses his own soul: loses his appreciation of things worth while, of the values to which these things are relative; if he loses desire to apply what he has learned and, above all, loses the ability to extract meaning from his future experiences as they occur? (p. 49)*

Deploring the kind of learning that in 1938 Dewey called "collateral," Illich and other school reformers of the 1960s and 1970s in their turn pinpointed what they labelled the "hidden curriculum" of schooling.

Here again the whistle-blowers have been forgotten and the educational version of the *intentional fallacy* prevails.[3] Nevertheless, whosoever looks unflinchingly at education writ large will find beliefs, attitudes, values, deep-seated feelings, emotions, and even worldviews being passed along by the vast array of educational agents in our midst. Perhaps some of this learning is consciously intended and publicly acknowledged and can therefore be said to belong to a formal, explicit curriculum. But much of it cannot pass this test.[4] Just as medical practices and procedures have unintended and often unanticipated side effects, the practices and procedures of our multiple educational agents produce unintended and often unanticipated learning.

Another feature that commands attention when education is writ large is its broad sweep. How often it is assumed that education is a strictly intellectual affair whose ultimate purpose is the development of mind and whose main business, therefore, is the imparting of knowledge. When one takes into account education's myriad agents and all the unintended learning they produce, one realizes how misleading this cognitive bias is. For one then discovers that education is not a narrowly defined enterprise. On the contrary, it affects all aspects of our lives and our selves.

Finally, when education is written in big letters one is able to see that education can shape our heads, our hands, and our hearts for the better or the worse. Think of the lessons in mendacity and greed that corporations and governmental agencies teach; the unhealthy eating habits that are daily passed down by the food, advertising, and television industries; and the self-indulgent attitudes toward the earth's resources that are inculcated by all of the above. Once the false equation, the intentional fallacy, and the cognitive bias are repudiated, it becomes apparent that education does not necessarily spell improvement. And once the *myth of improvement* is dissipated, it becomes crystal clear that if education in a democracy is to be a moral enterprise, it is up to all of us—to "we the people"—to make it so.

Educative and Miseducative Societies

When he looked at justice writ large, Socrates saw that a state can be just or unjust. Similarly, one who looks at education written in big letters will see that a society can be educative or miseducative. Notice that to call a society educat*ive* is something quite different from saying that it is an educat*ed* or literate society. An *educative* society is one that shapes its members for the better, not the worse. As the case of Nazi Germany demonstrated, a society with a well-schooled, literate populace can be miseducative in the extreme. And so, for that matter, can a society whose every member has a Ph.D.

Another way to understand the educative/miseducative distinction is to think of the knowledge, skills, attitudes, values, worldviews, and so on that the US or Canada or any other nation or group or society passes down to the next generation as constituting that culture's stock. A large portion of this cultural stock can no doubt be counted as cultural wealth, but not all of it. Take, for example, poverty, slavery, terrorism, rape, torture, killing, greed, mendacity, and racism. These and other highly undesirable cultural practices and behaviours fall in the liabilities, rather than the assets, column. An *educative* society is, then, one that tends to transmit cultural assets and not liabilities. A *miseducative* society can, in contrast, be understood as one that tends to transmit cultural liabilities rather than assets (Martin, 2002).

Quite clearly, where educativeness is concerned, good intentions are not enough. A society whose educational agents attempt to transmit assets and block the transmission of liabilities but never actually succeed does not deserve the label "educative." This does not mean that a society's educational agents must only transmit cultural assets to be considered educative, for educativeness is a matter of degree rather than an all-or-nothing affair. Nonetheless, *trying* to be educative is not enough. If a society's educational agents are mainly transmitting cultural liabilities, then even with the best intentions that society must be considered miseducative.

The truth is, however, that most groups and institutions in US society do not even try to pass along cultural assets rather than liabilities. And why would one expect them to when they do not think of themselves as educational agents, and neither does anyone else? To be sure, museums have educational departments, newspapers and magazines have education editors, and television networks have some educational programming. Still, the very fact that an institution allocates one small portion of its resources to education serves as a reminder that it does not consider itself an educator in its own right. After all, schools do not have separate departments whose business is education and school buildings do not have separate education corners. Indeed, it makes no sense for an institution that conceives of itself as an educational agent to have a special educational section or division.

Held captive by the false equation between education and schooling, we do not think to make any educational agent other than school accountable for the miseducation it fosters. In good logic, an unacknowledged educator cannot be charged with contributing to the miseducation of the public.[5] Yet in daily bombarding young people with unwholesome, antisocial models of living and in making these appear fatally attractive, the print and electronic media are nonetheless guilty of doing precisely this. So are manufacturers of computer games when they send messages about the acceptability of violence and the cheapness of life. So are airlines, banks, and hotels when they hand down cultural prejudices toward, for example, people with disabilities. And so are businesses, governmental agencies, and the military when their representatives serve as role models for lying instead of truth-telling and cheating instead of honesty.

Economists and other social analysts in the US have often voiced their misgivings about the financial burdens the older generation is bequeathing to future ones by its military spending, its unwillingness to invest in social welfare, its degradation of the natural environment. The debt created by the miseducative tendencies of many unacknowledged educational agents in our midst is every bit as troubling.[6] Moreover, the problems they create for schooling can scarcely be exaggerated.

Democratic Miseducation

The noted US scholar John Goodlad (1990) has called school "the only institution in our nation specifically charged with enculturating the young into a social and political democracy" (p. 48). In a book subtitled *Educating Citizens for a Democratic Society*, British philosopher of education Patricia White (1996) has said that school is "the obvious site for political education" (p. 23). Even the most cursory inspection of the actions of our myriad educational agents reveals, however, that school is not the only site in which political education occurs.

Contemporary discussions of education for democratic citizenship often draw attention to the knowledge and skills needed for rational deliberation. But important as it is for the members of a democracy to be able to deliberate about the significant political issues of the day, deliberation is not the only aspect of democracy on which education bears. Indeed, the individual's relationship to the law is perhaps an even more basic respect in which democracy differs from authoritarian systems of government. In an *authoritarian* system the individual is supposed to obey laws enacted by others, and that is that. In a *democracy* the individual is both the subject and the author of the law; in other words, we are our own governors: the laws we obey are ones that we or our chosen representatives have written. Furthermore, and very important, in a democracy as opposed to a dictatorship, everyone is subject to the law. No individual or group is above it.

Consider Elaine Mar, whose family immigrated to the US from Hong Kong when she was a young child in the 1970s. In her memoir *Paper Daughter*, she describes being taught authoritarian values by her mother. "A traditional Chinese," writes Mar (1999), her mother "saw herself in relation to family. She was a daughter, sister, and aunt. She spent her life waiting to become a mother" (p. 8). Mar recalls her mother once looking "down in shame" and asking, "How dare I question you?" (p. 23) after challenging something that Elaine's grandmother said. Mar writes about herself, "From birth I was expected to abide by the adults' rules" (p. 9). Her mother told her, "This is what it means to be an adult—you learn to be cautious and follow your elder's lead" (p. 228). On the subject of punishment, Mar says, "I didn't think I had anything to worry about. Didn't everyone always say how clever I was? And didn't 'clever' mean the same as 'obedient'?" (p. 23). Before long, however, Mar's mother was beating her whenever she spoke up or disobeyed.

Elaine Mar's memoir is a poignant reminder that this fundamental principle of democracy cannot be taken for granted. People who are their own legislators are not unthinkingly and unquestioningly supposed to obey laws made by others; they are not supposed to act like sheep. On the contrary, they are expected to speak out when they do not approve of what their representatives are doing.

I do not mean to imply that the hidden curriculum of Mar's home was typical of the United States in the 1970s or that it is so today. On the other hand, it is rash to conclude that her home was unique in passing down undemocratic cultural stock. Consider, for example, this vignette in Frank McCourt's (2005) memoir *Teacher Man*:

Augie was a nuisance in class, talking back, bothering the girls. I called his mother. Next day the door is thrown open and a man in a black T-shirt with the muscles of a weightlifter yells, Hey, Augie, come 'ere.

You can hear Augie gasp.

Talkin' a yeh, Augie. I haveta go in there you wish you was dead. Come 'ere.

Augie yelps, I didn't do nothin'.

The man lumbers into the room, down the aisle to Augie's seat, lifts Augie into the air, carries him over to the wall, bangs him repeatedly, against the wall.

I told you—bang—never—bang—never give your teacher—bang—no trouble—bang. I hear you give your teacher trouble—bang—I'm gonna tear your goddam head off—bang—an' stick it up your ass—bang. You heard me—bang?

… the man drags Augie back to his seat and turns to me. He gives you trouble again, mister, I kick his ass here to New Jersey. He was brought up to give respect. (pp. 91–92).[7]

According to a newsletter of the Child Rights Information network, "As part of their daily lives, children all over Europe are spanked, slapped, hit, smacked, shaken, kicked, pinched, punched, caned, flogged, belted, beaten and battered by adults—mainly by those whom they trust the most (Commissioner for Human Rights, 2006, p. 1)." Even supposing that the US is radically different from Europe in this regard, one must wonder in what percentage of homes the basic tenets of democracy are put into practice.

Let us not forget that homes with young children by their very nature are undemocratic institutions. Children do not choose their parents to be their representatives and the rules parents make are not ones that the parents have to follow. I am not saying that because of the inequality of parents and children, home must inevitably be miseducative where democracy is concerned. An institution can be undemocratic in some very fundamental respects and yet promote democratic learning. But although it is possible to make homes the "breeding grounds" of democratic beliefs and practices and many parents do just this, the unequal relationship can be—and often is—abused.

Home is not, of course, the only educational agent to pass down to the next generation cultural stock that is antithetical to democracy. One who checks the hidden curricula of government, religious institutions, corporations, the military, the Boy Scouts, and neighbourhood gangs will find these and more inculcating belief in the sanctity of hierarchical structures and unquestioning obedience to authority.

Nor is the individual's relationship to the law the only issue. Think for a moment about critical thinking. Although this is by no means universally accepted as a goal of schooling, it appears on many lists of the qualities that the citizens of a democracy must possess. Accordingly, over the years numerous educational theorists and practitioners in the United States have developed critical-thinking programs for their schools and colleges. At the same time, however, some of the most powerful educational agents in the US are the custodians of cultural stock that impedes, and may even prevent, children from acquiring the skills and attitudes associated with critical thinking. Tacitly, but nonetheless systematically, they transmit uncritical modes of thought, unsubstantiated "facts" and theories, worldviews that equate critical thinking with treason or portray it as a sign of the devil, and the belief that it is wrong to question the written or spoken word being passed along to young and old alike.

Lest it be imagined that children are the only ones exposed to daily doses of democratic miseducation, think now of Enron. Here was an energy giant whose stated values were respect, integrity, communication, and excellence but whose culture increasingly fostered and rewarded greed, selfishness, arrogance, hypocrisy, deception, self-indulgence, ruthlessness, and disdain for the greater good (McLean & Elkind, 2003). To be sure, no single item in Enron's hidden curriculum, except possibly disdain for the greater good, can be considered undemocratic in and of itself. Still, the hidden curriculum of the Enron culture as a whole appears to have been inconsistent with the requirements of democracy.[8]

Think also about the more than 30 million full-time workers in the US who have been laid off since the early 1980s. In *The Disposable American*, Louis Uchitelle (2006) refers repeatedly to the loss of self-esteem these men and women have suffered. "Everything you think is important and do for your life's work, isn't. To have someone senior in the company say that so bluntly in public is terrible," says one executive (p. 101). Unfortunately, self-esteem happens to be a quality that looms as large as critical thinking on lists of the traits a democratic citizen must possess. Writes political theorist Michael Sandel, "In political debate in the public arena people have to have a certain economic security, otherwise they are likely to feel adrift, anxious and victims of circumstances beyond their control" (as cited in Uchitelle, 2006, p. 34).

It would require volumes to document all the sources and the full content of the political education and miseducation occurring in the United States today. For now it suffices to note that with young children being exposed to political miseducation at home and in the community, and with mature men and women developing traits at work that run counter to democracy, education for democratic citizenship is best thought of as a lifelong process.

Lifelong does not necessarily mean linear. An individual's self-esteem can go up and down, the skills of critical thinking can be turned on and off, democratic virtues can atrophy over time, and undemocratic attitudes and values can take root. Furthermore, the democratic miseducation of one group can rub off on another. Telling Uchitelle (2006) that layoffs are a trauma to the entire family, a psychiatrist who treated several patients for "laid-off related ailments" said:

> All of a sudden the parent sits at home and can't find a job and is depressed. And suddenly the child's role model sort of crumbles. Instead of feeling admiration for the parent, the child eventually begins to feel disrespect. Because the children identify with the parents, they begin to doubt that they can accomplish anything. They feel they won't be successful in life and their self-esteem plummets. (pp. 187–188)

School's Place in the Educational Firmament

The fact that education for democratic citizenship begins before children go to school, continues after they leave school, and occurs outside school's walls while they attend school does not release school from its duties as an educator in and for democracy. Rather, it means that school needs to keep education writ large in mind even as it concentrates on education writ small: which is to say that it needs to take multiple educational agency into account in decisions about the education of schoolchildren. Simple as this advice may sound, it requires a radical rethinking of school's place in the educational firmament.

In the United States and elsewhere, the question of what schools should teach is hotly contested. The often radically different proposals have one thing in common, however: they tend to treat school as if it exists in an educational vacuum. Thus, subject matter is selected, objectives are set, learning activities are chosen, and methods of teaching are decided upon as if school were the only educational agent in children's lives.[9]

The aims of schooling are also contested, and once again the false equation and the intentional fallacy hold sway. Literacy, individual autonomy, appreciation of the arts, good health, responsible sexual behaviour, or something else entirely: whatever the goal may be, the idea that other educational agents might be transmitting cultural stock that interferes with the achievement of school's aims is seldom entertained.

Discussions of education for democratic citizenship exemplify the tendency to think and act as if school is the one and only significant educator in children's lives. Political thinkers have distinguished many different forms of democracy[10] and, on the basis of these, different lists have been compiled of the traits or dispositions that democratic citizens must possess. Yet despite the very real disputes regarding the items on the lists and the weight given them, the various proposals are alike in paying scant attention to multiple educational agency. Not only is there agreement that it is school's job to educate citizens. Even those who acknowledge the existence of educational agents other than school stop short of asking if the lessons they transmit conflict with school's mission.[11]

Taking its cue from an old established theory of society, the resistance to acknowledging the educational role of home and family is particularly strong. "We don't want to deal with inequality in the private realm, because the only way you can deal with inequality in the private realm is to encroach on the private realm, order and regulate relations there in a totalitarian fashion, and create egalitarianism," says political theorist Benjamin Barber (1997, p. 113) when discussing education for democracy. "Families are appropriately protected from political regulation by rights of privacy," affirm political theorists Amy Gutmann and Dennis Thompson (2004) after stating, "If schools do not equip children to deliberate, other institutions are not likely to do so" (p. 36).

In Western thought it has long been standard practice to divide society into two separate "spheres" or "realms"—the public and the private—and to place home and family in the private sector and work, politics, and the professions in the public.[12] In this two-sphere ideology, education—which the false equation translates into schooling— is assigned the task of preparing children who grow up in the private world for membership in the public world. Now, in view of school's designated function, one might expect that it would be represented as having a foothold in both worlds. But the two-sphere ideology posits a wall of separation between public and private that does not allow for this eventuality. And so it positions school squarely within the public world.[13] In consequence, the ideology tacitly regards the children who arrive in school as homeless individuals.[14]

In reality there is no wall between home and family on the one hand and work, politics, and the professions on the other. Schoolchildren leave home each morning and return home each afternoon and so do adults. Where rules and regulations are concerned, the interaction between the two supposedly separate spheres is also continuous. Thus, for example, marriages are subject to civil law, births are publicly recorded, polygamy is outlawed, and abused children are removed from home and family by governmental agencies. In sum, the wall of separation posited by the two-sphere theory is not a historical necessity or a brute fact of nature. It is an ideological construct whose value must be demonstrated.

One mark against the wall-of-separation concept is its disconnect with political and social realities. Another is that in treating children as blank political slates on which home and community have never written, schoolteachers are forced to deny their own experience. And a third is that acceptance of the wall of separation makes it that much harder for school to fulfill its duty of creating democratic citizens.

"A popular Government without popular information or the means of acquiring it, is but a Prologue to a Farce or a Tragedy or perhaps both," said James Madison after the US Constitution was adopted. One might say the same of an educational agent that is assigned the task of creating democratic citizens yet denied knowledge, or the means of acquiring it, about democratic miseducation. "People who mean to be their own Governors, must arm themselves with the power knowledge gives," he added (as cited in Nichols & McChesney, 2005, p. 1). So, too, schools that mean to turn children into their own governors must arm themselves with the power that knowledge can give.

It goes without saying that education for democratic citizenship should not proceed in a totalitarian fashion or violate people's rights. Fortunately, schools do not have to make a forced choice between two evils: either act in a totalitarian manner or ignore the reality of multiple educational agency. There is nothing undemocratic about acknowledging that children experience one or another degree of democratic miseducation before they ever arrive at school and continue to do so throughout their years of schooling and beyond. There is nothing sinister about admitting that if school is to teach democratic citizenship successfully, it will have to counteract whatever democratic miseducation children are receiving at home. There is no risk of totalitarianism in school recognizing that home is also an educator of our young and that the education for democracy it provides can, as in school's case, be for the better or the worse.

I have singled out home for special discussion here because so many educational thinkers place it out of bounds. But for better or worse, church, mosque, synagogue, government, business, the media, and the myriad other institutions in a democratic society also contribute to the making—and in many instances the unmaking—of democratic citizens. If we the people do not take seriously the fact that school is but one of the many significant educational agents in the firmament, and if school itself does not acknowledge this and act on the belief as it focuses on education writ small, how can school possibly live up to its reputation as the preferred site of education for democracy?

Making Democratic Citizens

"A democracy is more than a form of government; it is primarily a mode of associated living," said Dewey (1916, p. 87) in *Democracy and Education*. Echoing this thesis, John Goodlad, Corinne Mantle-Bromley, and Stephen John Goodlad (2004) wrote in *Education for Everyone*, "Democracy, first and foremost, is a shared way of life" (p. 82). Consider what these statements mean: a "mode of living," a "way of life" is how anthropologists and sociologists define culture.

If we proceed on the assumption that democracy is a particular type of culture—and I firmly believe that we must—we need to keep in mind that one becomes a member of a culture by being immersed in it. Two-day-old Henri does not learn to be a Frenchman by studying the history, geography, and governmental structure of France. He becomes French by breathing in the culture of France with the air.

Think what a simple matter the education of democratic citizens would be if children in the US breathed democracy in with the air from Day 1: if their homes inducted them into a democratic mode of associated living and if the other educational agents in their lives did so as well. In that event, there would be no reason to single out school as the obvious or most appropriate site of citizenship education. Our educative society would do the bulk of the work and school would only have to add the finishing touches. Because democratic miseducation is rife in the early 21st century, both at home and in society at large, the claim that education for democracy is school's job takes on new meaning. Indeed, it all but entails that school become a site of democratic culture. For, then, children will be able to breathe in democracy with at least some degree of regularity.[15]

I speak of school *becoming* a site of democratic culture because the culture of many schools is at present undemocratic: governing structures are often hierarchical; rules are not always applied equally to children of different races, classes, genders, etc.; and many classroom practices deny children such fundamental democratic rights as freedom of speech and association. One does not have to agree with the sentiment that schools today "may conduct themselves as the least democratic institutions" (Darling-Hammond, 1997, p. 111) to believe that the culture of many schools would have to undergo significant change for them to make the grade.

The proposal that school's culture become democratic is also a tall order because it requires a ringing denunciation of the cognitive bias. When democracy is understood to be a way of life, education must be of the whole person: it must necessarily engage head, hands, and heart. You can teach Augie the 3Rs; all the history, literature, science, and political philosophy you wish; and also the skills of critical thinking and political deliberation. But if in school he does not breathe in democracy's "middle way" between unquestioning submission to authority and rampant disobedience of the law; if he does not learn to respect both majority rule and minority rights; if he does not begin to act as if no one—not Augie and not Augie's father— is above the law; and if he does not also become disposed to protect his own rights and those of others, and to speak out when he sees democracy being subverted, he will not have learned to be a democratic citizen.[16]

Yet although it may not be easy to make school a site of democratic culture, it can be done. Because there is a fundamental inequality at the heart of schooling resembling the one that characterizes home— namely that children do not stand in an equal relationship to their teachers—no school can be perfectly democratic. But perfection is not required. Being a democratic culture is a matter of degree and to provide apprenticeships in democracy, the culture of schools need only approximate the ideal. Furthermore, one has only to read the historical record to know that where there has been the will to overcome the cognitive bias, there has been the way.[17]

When, overcoming all obstacles, school becomes a site of democratic culture, two long-neglected aspects of education for democratic citizenship writ small will make themselves felt. One is that this education is not a mere matter of addition. Discussions of citizenship education often leave the impression that school only has to give children a bit of knowledge about democracy, a few democratic skills, and some new democratic behavioural patterns. Add these up and, voila, democracy will have new citizens! To the extent, however, that Augie, Elaine Mar, and their peers have absorbed the lessons of democratic miseducation, their education for democratic citizenship will have to involve addition, subtraction, and transformation. Yes, they will need to acquire some portion of the culture's democratic stock. But they will also have to let go of the undemocratic beliefs, attitudes, values, and patterns of behaviour they have already made their own. And in so doing they will, in effect, become brand new people.

A second neglected aspect of citizenship education writ small that will cry out for attention is that those children who have become accustomed to living under authoritarian rule will be making a culture crossing. Just as other kinds of culture crossings—for instance, Elaine Mar's from a Chinese child to an American schoolgirl—are apt to give rise to anger, guilt, alienation, and feelings of betrayal, so is this one.[18] Thus, for instance, home, religious institution, or neighbourhood gang may object strenuously to the fact that school is teaching children to question the dictates of authority and to make up their own minds about significant issues of the day; the children may feel guilty about casting off the teachings of one or another educational agent; those who live in especially undemocratic homes and communities may find it increasingly difficult to switch back and forth each day between two opposite cultures and may end up feeling alienated from both.

Like it or not, when democracy is understood to be a form of culture and it is agreed that one of school's main functions is to create democratic citizens, the issue of school's relationship to the other educational agents in children's lives cannot be avoided. Goodlad, Mantle-Bromley, and Goodlad (2004) have truly said that schools "cannot counteract the influence of parents, peers, media, and all that constitutes the social surround" (p. 86). But this does not mean that those who care about education for democracy can in good conscience act as if these influences do not exist or that school can afford to ignore them.

Once it is understood that culture crossing can occasion pain and suffering, the question naturally arises of whether it is morally acceptable to establish school as a site of democratic culture while disregarding the repercussions in the "social surround." In view of the Enron case and Uchitelle's study, the question also arises of whether school's democratic lessons are for naught; if, in other words, whatever democratic cultural stock children do acquire in school is likely to disappear once they graduate. Given the degree and scope of the democratic miseducation that fills the "social surround," it is also necessary to ask if it is possible for school to become a site of democratic culture—or, assuming that it can become one, how long school can survive as one.

Interestingly enough, Socrates's definition of justice is relevant here. Making justice a matter of internal cooperation and overall health rather than the fair distribution of rewards and punishments, he argued that a just state is one in which the several parts of society work together for the good of the whole. By analogy he then determined that a just person is one in whom each part of the soul makes its own contribution to the well-being of the individual.

We have already seen that when education for democracy is writ small, it requires something akin to what Socrates envisioned in regard to justice, namely the full cooperation of head, hands, and heart. Writ large, education for democratic citizenship requires the cooperation of school, home, neighbourhood, religious institutions, the media, government, and all the other significant educational agents in children's lives.[19] For to the extent that the nonschool educational agents undermine school's designated task of educating for citizenship, that society's health or well-being is surely in jeopardy.

Cooperation must not be confused with the suppression of disagreement or conformity of belief. A democratic society's educational agents can work together to foster democratic citizenship while disagreeing about matters large and small. Indeed, since freedom of thought is a basic tenet of democracy, it is imperative that differences of opinion are encouraged rather than stifled, whether they be about public policy issues or the nature of democracy itself. Thus, this plea for cooperation can be considered to be, among other things, a call for open-mindedness across the whole wide range of educational agents.

Conclusion

What can we the people do to make education in and for democracy a moral enterprise? How can we create the kind of culture in which all our children breathe democracy in with the air?

Above all, we need to persuade the wide range of educational agents other than school in our midst to acknowledge their status as educators; and to agree that, like school, they therefore have an obligation to contribute to the making and maintaining of a democratic citizenry. But this is a long-term project. In the interim we need to figure out how to counteract the democratic miseducation that is being purveyed here and now and we also must remember that not a single one of us stands outside the educational process. Those myriad educational agents are not abstract philosophical entities. They are made up of flesh-and-blood human beings, and we are those people. Thus, in our everyday capacities as family members, churchgoers, breadwinners, sports fans, and all the rest, each of us needs to be eternally vigilant that we ourselves and the educational agencies to which we belong are not undermining but making positive contributions to democratic living.

REFERENCES

Bailyn, B. (1960). *Education in the forming of American society.* New York: Vintage.

Barber, B. (1997). Public schooling: Education for democracy. In J.I. Goodlad & T.J. McMannon (Eds.), *The public purpose of education and schooling* (pp. 21–32). San Francisco: Jossey-Bass.

Commissioner for Human Rights. (2006). Children and corporal punishment: "The right not to be hit, also a children's right." Council of Europe: Child's Rights Information Network. Retrieved from https://wcd.coe.int/ViewDoc.jsp?id=1237635&Site=CM

Cremin, L. (1965). *The genius of American education.* New York: Vintage.

Darling-Hammond, L. (1997). Education, equity, and the right to learn. In J.I. Goodlad & T.J. McMannon (Eds.), *The public purpose of education and schooling.* San Francisco: Jossey-Bass.

Dewey, J. (1916). *Democracy and education.* New York: Macmillan.

Dewey, J. (1963). *Experience and education.* New York: Macmillan.

Dykstra, S.W. (1996). The artist's intentions and the intentional fallacy in fine arts conservation. *Journal of the American Institute for Conservation, 35*(3), 197–218.

Goodlad, J.I. (1990). *Teachers for our nation's schools.* San Francisco: Jossey-Bass.

Goodlad, J.I., Mantle-Bromley, C., & Goodlad, S.J. (2004). *Education for everyone.* San Francisco: Jossey-Bass.

Gutmann, A., & Thompson, D. (2004). *Why deliberative democracy?* Princeton, NJ: Princeton University Press.

Hernandez, L. (2000). *Families and schools together: Building organizational capacity for family-school partnerships.* Cambridge, MA: Harvard Family Research Project.

Illich, I. (1972). *Deschooling society.* New York: Harrow Books.

Ladson-Billings, G. (2006). From the achievement gap to the education debt: Understanding achievement in US schools. *Educational Researcher, 35*(7), 3–12. doi:10.3102/0013189X035007003

Mar, M.E. (1999). *Paper daughter.* New York: Harper Collins.

Martin, J.R. (1994). *Changing the educational landscape: Philosophy, women, and curriculum.* New York: Routledge.

Martin, J.R. (2002). *Cultural miseducation.* New York: Teachers College Press.

Martin, J.R. (2007). *Educational metamorphoses.* Lanham, MD: Rowman & Littlefield.

McCourt, F. (2005). *Teacher man.* New York: Scribner.

McLean, B., & Elkind, P. (2003). *The smartest guys in the room.* New York: Penguin Group.

Nichols, J., & McChesney, R.W. (2005). *Tragedy & farce.* New York: The New Press.

Plato. (1974). *The republic* (G.M.A. Grube, Trans.). Indianapolis: Hackett Publishing Co.

Robbins, A. (2006). *The overachievers.* New York: Hyperion.

Shapiro, I. (2003). *The state of democratic theory.* Princeton, NJ: Princeton University Press.

Uchitelle, L. (2006). *The disposable American: Layoffs and their consequences.* New York: Alfred A. Knopf.

Weiss, H.B., Caspe, M., & Lopez, M.E. (2006, Spring). *Family involvement in early childhood education* (Family Involvement Makes a Difference No. 1). Cambridge, MA: Harvard Family Research Project.

White, P. (1996). *Civic virtues and public schooling: Educating citizens for a democratic society.* New York: Teachers College Press.

Wimsatt, W.K., & Beardsley, M.C. (1946). The intentional fallacy. *Sewanee Review, 54,* 468–488.

Wimsatt, W.K., & Beardsley, M.C. (1954). *The verbal icon: Studies in the meaning of poetry.* Lexington: University of Kentucky Press.

NOTES

1 I thank Ann Diller, Susan Franzosa, John Goodlad, Barbara Houston, Michael Martin, Jennifer Radden, and Janet Farrell Smith for helpful comments on an earlier draft of this chapter.

2 For more on the false equation and the concept of multiple educational agency, see Martin (2002).

3 The *intentional fallacy* is generally associated with the field of literary criticism and, more particularly, the New Critics and is, roughly, the belief that disputes regarding the meaning of a text are decided by appeal to the author's intentions. The concept is usually attributed to Wimsatt and Beardsley (1946; cf. Wimsatt & Beardsley, 1954).

4 For an extended analysis of the concept of hidden curriculum, see Martin (1994, Ch. 8).

5 To be sure, the media are often criticized—for example, for showing too much sex and violence. My point is that if the critics are accusing the media of being miseducative, they are implicitly attributing to the media the status of educational agent. I suspect, however, that many of those concerned about the effects of sex and violence on the audience do not take the further step of conceptualizing what is occurring in educational terms.

6 For an interesting discussion of educational debt, see Ladson-Billings (2006).

7 Compare the home life of "AP Frank" in Robbins (2006).

8 This is not to say that a single individual who possesses the Enron package of traits poses a threat to democracy. My point is simply that from the standpoint of democracy, Enron's culture was seriously miseducative.

9 Schools do, of course, reach out and incorporate aspects of the environment into their planning. But for a school to bring, for example, television or computers into the classroom as an aid to teaching and learning is quite different from acknowledging that a TV network or the computer industry is an educational agent in its own right.

10 To identify the different types and determine how they are related to one another is a huge task that fortunately need not be undertaken here. For a discussion of a number of types, see, for example, Shapiro (2003).

11 See, for example, the discussion of television in Gutmann and Thompson (2004, p. 36).

12 It should be noted that, in the past, gender played a vital role in this ideology in that the world of the private home and family was considered to be women's domain and the world of work, politics, and the professions, men's domain. Although the ways in which the gendered aspect of the two-sphere ideology has changed as more and more women have entered the workplace is an extremely important question, it is not one that has to be addressed here.

13 Home-schooling can be construed as an attempt to keep inside the wall that part of children's education that historically came to be located in school.

14 This is not to say that everyone views schoolchildren in this way. See, for example, the work of the Harvard Family Research Project, particularly Weiss, Caspe, and Lopez (2006), and Hernandez (2000).

15 That is, children would be able to breathe in democracy unless their parents opt for a kind of home-schooling that does not foster democratic living or for schools that perpetuate democratic miseducation.

16 I am not ruling out here that some children may have learned all this at home or in their communities.

17 Consider the schools established by Johann Heinrich Pestalozzi and Maria Montessori, those modelled on the thought of John Dewey, A.S. Neill's Summerhill,

and the open classrooms of the 1960s and 1970s. These are but a few instances of the education of head, hand, and heart.

18 For more on this subject, see Martin (2007).

19 This does not mean that every single educational agent must cooperate. In a democracy there will always be room for some institutions that intentionally or unintentionally promote democratic miseducation. When, however, democratic miseducation becomes an obstacle to the achievement of education for democratic citizenship, it is time to be concerned.

28

Teacher Education for Educational Wisdom

*Gert Biesta**

*This is a shortened and slightly edited version of a paper originally published as Biesta, G. (2012). The future of teacher education: Evidence, competence or wisdom? *Research on Steiner Education, 3*(1), 8–21. Reproduced with permission.

Introduction

In recent years policy makers and politicians have become increasingly interested in teacher education. In the UK the government has recently published a new policy framework for school education in England—a paper called "The Importance of Teaching"[1]—which not only sets out the parameters for a significant transformation of state-funded school education but also contains specific proposals for the education of teachers. In Scotland the government recently commissioned a review of Scottish teacher education. The report, with the title "Teaching Scotland's Future,"[2] also makes very specific recommendations about teacher education and the further professional development of teachers. In many countries discussions about teacher education are being influenced by developments at a European level, particularly in the context of the Lisbon Strategy, which, in 2000, set the aim of making the European Union into "the most competitive and dynamic knowledge-based economy in the world,"[3] and the Bologna Process, aimed at the creation of a European Higher Education Area. In the wake of the 2005 Organisation for Economic Co-operation and Development (OECD) report on the state of teacher education—a report called "Teachers Matter: Attracting, Developing and Retaining Effective Teachers"[4]—the European Commission produced a document in 2007 called "Improving the Quality of Teacher Education,"[5] which proposed "shared reflection about actions that can be taken at Member State level and how the European Union might support these." As part of this process the European Commission also produced a set of "Common European Principles for Teacher Competences and Qualifications."[6] While none of these documents have any legal power in themselves, they do tend to exert a strong influence on policy development within the member states of the European Union—a point to which I will return below.

One could see the attention from policy makers and politicians for teacher education as the expression of a real concern for the quality of education at all levels and as recognition of the fact that the quality of teacher education is an important element in the overall picture. But one could also read it more negatively by observing that now that governments in many countries have established a strong grip on schools through a combination of curriculum prescription, testing, inspection, measurement, and league tables, they are turning their attention to teacher education to establish total control over the educational system. Much, of course, depends on how, in concrete situations, discourse and policy will unfold or have unfolded already. In this regard it is interesting that whereas in the English situation teaching is being depicted as a *skill* that can be picked up in practice (with the implication that teacher education can be shifted from universities to so-called "training schools"), the Scottish discussion positions teaching as a *profession* that requires proper teacher education and further professional development.

While there are, therefore, still important differences on the ground, we are, at the very same time, seeing an increasing *convergence* in discourse and policy with regard to teaching that, in turn, is leading to a convergence in discourse and policy with regard to teacher education. The main concept that is emerging is the notion of "competence" (see, for example, Deakin Crick, 2008; Mulder, Weigel & Collins, 2007). The notion of competence is interesting for at least two reasons. First, it has a certain rhetorical appeal—who, after all, would want to argue that teachers should *not* be competent? Second, competence focuses the discussion on the question of what teachers should be able to *do* rather than only on what teachers need to *know*. One could say, therefore, that the idea of *competence* is more practical and, in a sense, also more holistic in that it seems to encompass knowledge, skills, and action as an integrated whole, rather than to see action as the application of knowledge or the implementation of skills. Whether this is indeed so also depends on the particular approach to and conception of competence one favours. Mulder, Weigel, and Collins (2007) show, for example, that within the literature there are three distinctive traditions—the behaviourist, the generic, and the cognitive—which put different emphases on the "mix" between action, cognition, and values. While some definitions of competence are very brief and succinct—such as Eraut's (2003) definition of *competence* as "(t)he ability to perform the tasks and roles required to the expected standards" (p. 117, as cited in Mulder, Weigel & Collins, 2007)—others, such as Deakin Crick's (2008) definition of *competence* as "a complex combination of knowledge, skills, understanding, values, attitudes and desire which lead to effective, embodied human action in the world, in a particular domain" (p. 313), are so broad that it may be difficult to see what is *not* included in it.

What is worrying, however, is not so much the notion of competence itself but first and foremost the fact that the idea of competence is beginning to monopolize the discourse about teaching and teacher education. After all, if there is no alternative discourse, if a particular idea is simply seen as "common sense," then there is a risk that it stops people from thinking at all. While European documents about teaching and teacher education have no *legal* power—decisions about education remain located at the level of the member states— they do have important *symbolic* and *rhetorical* power in that they often become a reference point many want to orient themselves toward, perhaps on the assumption that if they don't adjust, they run the risk of being left behind. We can see a similar logic at work in the problematic impact that OECD's Programme for International Student Assessment (PISA) has had on education throughout Europe. What I have in mind here is not the fact that PISA is only interested in particular "outcomes"—although there are important questions to be asked about that as well—but first of all the fact that PISA and similar systems create the illusion that a wide range of different educational practices *is* comparable and that, by implication, these practices therefore *ought to* be comparable. Out of a fear of being left behind, out of a fear of ending up at the bottom end of the league table, we can see schools and school systems transforming themselves into a definition of education that "counts" in systems like PISA, the result of it being that more and more schools and school systems begin to become the same.

It is, however, not only the tendency toward uniformity that is problematic. It is also that through the discourse about competence that a very particular view about education is being repeated, promoted, and *multiplied*. This is often not how ideas about the competences that teachers need are being presented. Such competences are often presented as general, as relatively open to different views about education, as relatively neutral with regard to such views, and also as relatively uncontested. They are, in other words, presented as "common sense." One thing that is important, therefore, is to open up this common sense by showing that it is possible to think *differently* about education and about what teachers should be able to do, at least to move away from an unreflected and unreflective common sense about education. But I also wish to argue that the particular common sense about education that is being multiplied is problematic in itself, because it has a tendency to promote what I would see as a rather un-educational way of thinking about education. And this is the deeper problem that needs to be addressed to have a better starting point for our discussion about the future of teacher education.

The "Learnification" of Education

I invite you to have a brief look at the key competences enlisted in the document from the Directorate-General for Education and Culture of the European Commission, called "Common European Principles for Teacher Competences and Qualifications."

Making it work: the key competences

Teaching and education add to the economic and cultural aspects of the knowledge society and should therefore be seen in their societal context. Teachers should be able to:

Work with others: *they work in a profession which should be based on the values of social inclusion and nurturing the potential of every learner. They need to have knowledge of human growth and development and demonstrate self-confidence when engaging with others. They need to be able to work with learners as individuals* *and support them to develop into fully participating and active members of society. They should also be able to work in ways which increase the collective intelligence of learners and co-operate and collaborate with colleagues to enhance their own learning and teaching.*

Work with knowledge, technology and information: *they need to be able to work with a variety of types of knowledge. Their education and professional development should equip them to access, analyse, validate, reflect on and transmit knowledge, making effective use of technology where this is appropriate. Their pedagogic skills should allow them to build and manage learning environments and retain the intellectual freedom to make choices over the delivery of education. Their confidence in the use of ICT should allow them to integrate it effectively into learning and teaching. They should be able to guide and support learners in the networks in which information can be found and built. They should have a good understanding of subject knowledge and view learning as a lifelong journey. Their practical and theoretical skills should also allow them to learn from their own experiences and match a wide range of teaching and learning strategies to the needs of learners.*

Work with and in society: *they contribute to preparing learners to be globally responsible in their role as EU citizens. Teachers should be able to promote mobility and co-operation in Europe, and encourage intercultural respect and understanding. They should have an understanding of the balance between respecting and being aware of the diversity of learners' cultures and identifying common values. They also need to understand the factors that create social cohesion and exclusion in society and be aware of the ethical dimensions of the knowledge society. They should be able to work effectively with the local community, and with partners and stakeholders in education—parents, teacher education institutions, and representative groups. Their experience and expertise should also enable them to contribute to systems of quality assurance. Teachers' work in all these areas should be embedded in a professional continuum of lifelong learning which includes initial teacher education, induction and continuing professional development, as they cannot be expected to possess all the necessary competences on completing their initial teacher education.*[7]

I would like to make two observations. The first is that in this text school education is very much positioned as an instrument that needs to deliver all kinds of societal goods. Education needs to produce such things as social cohesion, social inclusion, a knowledge society, lifelong learning, a knowledge economy, EU citizens, intercultural respect and understanding, a sense of common values, and so on. This is a very functionalist view of education and a very functionalist view of what is core to what teachers need to be able to do. It paints a picture where society—and there is, of course, always the question of who "society" actually "is"—sets the agenda, and where education is seen as an instrument for the delivery of this agenda. In this text the only "intellectual freedom" granted to teachers is about *how* to "deliver" this agenda, not about what it is that is supposed to be "delivered." (I put "delivery" in quotation marks to highlight that it is a very unfortunate and unhelpful metaphor to talk about education in the first place.) This functionalist or instrumentalist view of education does not seem to consider the idea that education may have other interests—perhaps its own interests (I return to this below)—but predominantly thinks of the school as the institution that needs to solve "other people's problems."

My second observation concerns the fact that in this text education is predominantly described in terms of *learning*. We read that teachers are supposed to nurture the potential of every learner, that they need to be able to work with learners as individuals, that they should aim at increasing the collective intelligence of learners, that they should be able to build and manage learning environments, integrate ICT effectively into learning and teaching, provide guidance and support to learners in information networks, and view learning as a lifelong journey. For me this document is another example of what elsewhere (see particularly Biesta 2004; 2006) I have referred to as the rise of a "new language of learning" in education. This rise is manifest in several "translations" that have taken place in the language used in educational practice, policy, and research. We can see it in the tendency to refer to students, pupils, children, and even adults as "learners." We can see it in the tendency to refer to teaching as the facilitation of learning or the creation and management of learning environments. We can see it in the tendency to refer to schools as places for learning or as learning environments. And we can see it in the tendency no longer to speak about adult education but rather to talk about lifelong learning.

Now, one could argue that there is no problem with this. Isn't it, after all, the purpose of education that children and students learn? Isn't it therefore reasonable to think of the task of teachers as that of supporting such learning? And doesn't that mean that schools are and should be understood as learning environments or places of learning? Perhaps the quickest way to make my point is to say that for me the point of education is *not* that students learn but that they learn *something*, that they learn this for particular *purposes*, and that they learn this from *someone*.[8] A main problem with the language of learning is that it is a language of *process* but not a language of content and purpose. Yet education is never just about any learning but always about the learning of something for particular purposes. In addition, education is always about learning from someone. Whereas the language of learning is an *individualistic* language—learning is, after all, something you can do on your own—the language of education is a *relational* language, where there is always the idea of someone educating somebody else. The problem with the rise of the language of learning in education is therefore threefold: it is a language that makes it more difficult to ask questions about content; it is a language that makes it more difficult to ask questions of purpose; and it is a language that makes it more difficult to ask questions about the specific role and responsibility of the teacher in the educational relationship.

All this is not to say that learning is a meaningless idea, or that learning has no place in education. But it is to highlight the fact that the language of learning is not an *educational* language, so that when discussions about education become entirely framed in terms of learning, some of the most central educational questions and issues—about purpose, content, and relationships—begin to disappear from the conversation and, subsequently, run the risk of beginning to disappear from the practice of education, too. In my own work I have referred to this development as the "learnification" of education (Biesta, 2010a). I have deliberately constructed an ugly word for this because, from the standpoint of education, I think that this is a very worrying trend. This means that if we wish to say anything *educational* about teacher education—if, in other words, we wish to move beyond the language of learning—we need to engage with a way of speaking and thinking that is more properly educational. Once we do this we may find—and this is what I will be arguing below—that the idea of competences becomes less attractive and less appropriate to think about teacher education and its future. Let me move, then, to the next step in my argument, which has to do with the nature of educational practices.

What Is Education For?

I have suggested that the language of learning is unhelpful as an educational language because if we just say that students should learn—or that teachers should support or promote students' learning—but do not specify what the learning is supposed to achieve or result in, we are actually saying nothing at all. This shows something particular about educational practices, namely that they are *teleological* practices—the Greek word *telos* meaning aim or purpose—that is, practices that are *constituted* by certain aims, which means, that if you take the orientation toward aims away, you take the very thing that makes a practice into an educational practice away. In my work—particularly the book *Good Education in an Age of Measurement* (Biesta, 2010a)—I have therefore argued that if we want to move back from "learning" to "education," we need to engage explicitly with the question of purpose in education. I have referred to this as the question of *good* education to highlight that when we engage with the question of purpose in education we are always involved in value judgments, that is, in judgments about what is educationally desirable.[9]

By arguing that there is a need to engage with the question of educational purpose, I am not trying to define what the purpose of education should be. But I do wish to make two points about how I think we should engage with the question of purpose. The first point is that educational practices always serve more than one purpose—and do so at the very same time. The *multi-dimensionality of educational purpose* is precisely what makes education interesting. It is also, second, why a particular kind of judgment is needed in education. By saying that that question of educational purpose is multi-dimensional, I am trying to say that education "functions" or "works" in several different dimensions and that in each of these dimensions the question of purpose needs to be raised. In my own work I have suggested that we can distinguish three dimensions in which the question of purpose needs to be raised—or to put it in more simple language: I have suggested that educational processes and practices tend to function in three different domains. I have referred to these domains as *qualification, socialization,* and *subjectification* (see Biesta, 2010a [for a Swedish version Biesta, 2011]; see also Biesta, 2009). *Qualification* has to do with the ways in which education qualifies people for doing things—in the broad sense of the word—by equipping them with knowledge, skills, and dispositions. Education is however not only about knowledge, skills, and dispositions but also has to do with the ways in which, through education, we become part of existing social, cultural, and political practices and traditions. This is the *socialization* dimension of education. While some take a very strict and narrow view of education and would argue that the only task of schools is to be concerned about knowledge and skills and dispositions, we can see that over the past decades the socialization function has become an explicit dimension of discussions about what schools are for. We can see this specifically in the range of societal "agendas" that have been added to the school curriculum, such as environmental education, citizenship education, social and moral education, sex education, and so on. The idea here is that education not only exerts a socialising force on children and students, but that it is actually desirable that education should do this.

While some would argue that these are the only two proper and legitimate dimensions that school education should be concerned about, I wish to argue that there is a third dimension in relation to which education operates and should operate. This has to do with the way in which education impacts on the person as a subject of action and responsibility. This is the *subjectification* dimension of education. It is important to see that subjectification and socialization are not the same—and one of the important challenges for contemporary education is how we can actually articulate the distinction between the two (for more on this see Biesta, 2006). Socialization has to do with how we become part of existing orders, how we identify with such orders and thus obtain an identity; subjectification, on the other hand, is always about how we can exist "outside" of such orders. With a relatively "old" but still crucially important concept, we can say that subjectification has to do with the question of human freedom— which, of course, then raises further questions about how we should understand human freedom (for my ideas on this see, again, Biesta, 2006; and also Chapter 4 in Biesta, 2010a).

To engage with the question of purpose in education requires that we engage with this question in relation to all three domains. The reason why engagement with the question of purpose requires that we "cover" all three domains lies in the fact that anything we do in education potentially has "impact" in any of these three domains. It is important to acknowledge that the three domains are *not separate*, which is why they can be depicted as a Venn-diagram of three overlapping areas.

The overlap is important because on the one hand this indicates opportunities for *synergy*, whereas on the other hand it can also help us to see potential *conflict* between the different dimensions.

Given the possibility of synergy and of conflict, and given the fact that our educational activities almost always "work" in the three domains at the very same time, looking at education through these dimensions begins to make visible something that in my view is absolutely central about the work of teachers, which is the need for making situated judgments about what is educationally desirable in relation to these three dimensions. What is central to the work of teachers is not simply that they set aims and implement them. Teachers *constantly* need to make judgments about how to balance the different dimensions; they need to set priorities and they need to be able to

Figure 1: The three domains of educational purpose

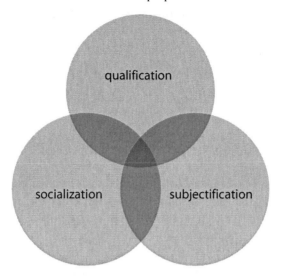

handle tensions, conflicts, and "trade-offs"—as gains in relation to one dimension often imply losses in relation to another.

What is beginning to emerge from this line of thinking is that because education is a teleological practice and because the question of the *telos* of education is a multi-dimensional question, judgment about what is educationally desirable is an absolutely crucial element of what teachers do.

Judgment and Wisdom in Education

If I try to bring the lines of my argument so far together, the point that is emerging is that the question is not so much whether teachers should be competent to do things—one could say that, of course, they should be competent—but that competence, the ability to do things, is in itself *never enough*. To put it bluntly: a teacher who possesses all the competences teachers need but who is unable to judge which competence needs to be deployed when, is a useless teacher. Judgments about what needs to be done always need to be made with reference to the purposes of education, which is why the language of learning is unhelpful as it is not a language in which the question of purpose can easily be raised, articulated, and addressed. And since the question of the purpose of education is a multi-dimensional question, judgment needs to be *multi-dimensional*, taking into consideration that a gain with regard to one dimension may be a loss with regard to another dimension—so that there is a need to make judgment about the right *balance* and the right *trade-off* between gains and losses, so to speak. Exerting such judgments is not something that is done at the level of school policy documents but lies at the very heart of what goes on in the classroom and in the relationships between teachers and students—and this goes on again, and again, and again.

The idea that education cannot do without judgment about what is educationally desirable stands in sharp contrast to another recent trend in discussions about teaching and teacher education, which is the suggestion that teaching should become an "evidence-based" profession totally driven by scientific knowledge about "what works." This idea is problematic for several reasons, a discussion of which partly lies beyond the scope of this paper (for more on this see Biesta, 2007, 2010b [in German, Biesta, 2010c]), albeit the main problem here is not dissimilar from what I have said about the idea of competences, which is that while insights from research may give us an indication of what might be *possible* (albeit the extent to which research can say anything about this is far more limited than the proponents of evidence-based education tend to assume), whether what is possible is educationally desirable remains a question that such research cannot answer but that requires the judgment of teachers and others involved in the educational process.

Discussions about the role of scientific evidence in teaching do relate to a much older question in the educational discussion, which is the question of whether teaching should be understood as an art or a science. One person who has very concisely and very convincingly argued against the idea of teaching as a science is the American psychologist William James (1842–1910). James (1899) writes:

> *Psychology is a science, and teaching is an art; and sciences never generate arts directly out of themselves. An intermediary inventive mind must make the application, by using its originality.*
>
> *The most such sciences can do is to help us to catch ourselves up and check ourselves, if we start to reason or to behave wrongly; and to criticise ourselves more articulately after we have made mistakes.*
>
> *To know psychology, therefore, is absolutely no guarantee that we shall be good teachers. To advance to that result, we must have an additional endowment altogether, a happy tact and ingenuity to tell us what definite things to say and do when the pupil is before us. That ingenuity in meeting and pursuing the pupil, that tact for the concrete situation, though they are the alpha and omega of the teacher's art, are things to which psychology cannot help us in the least. (pp. 14–15)*

While James provides a convincing argument why teaching should not and cannot be understood as a science—and actually needs tact, ingenuity, and, so I wish to add, judgment—James has less to say about the positive side of the argument, that is, the idea that education should therefore be understood as an art. A thinker who I think has something very helpful and important to say with regard to this question is Aristotle (384–322 BC), and the interesting question he allows us to ask is not *whether* teaching is an art or not, but *what kind of art* teaching is (see Aristotle, 1980).

Aristotle's argument starts from the distinction between the theoretical life and the practical life. While the theoretical life has to do with "the necessary and the eternal" (Aristotle, 1980, p.140) and thus with a kind of knowledge to which Aristotle refers as science (*episteme*), the practical life has to do with what is "variable" (p. 142), that is with the world of change. This is the world in which we act and in which our actions make a difference. With regard to our engagement with the world of change, Aristotle makes a distinction between two modes of acting, *poiesis* and *praxis* or, in Carr's (1987) translation, "making action" and "doing action." Both "modes" of action require judgment, but the kind of judgment (and hence the kind of knowledge needed to make such judgments) is different. *Poiesis* is about the production or fabrication of things—such as, for example, a saddle or a ship. It is, as Aristotle (1980) puts it, about "how something may come into being which is capable of either being or not being" and about things "whose origin is in the maker and not in the thing made" (which distinguishes *poiesis* from biological phenomena such as growth and development) (p. 141). *Poiesis* is, in short, about the creation of something that did not exist before. The kind of knowledge we need for *poiesis* is *techne* (usually translated as "art"). It is, in more contemporary vocabulary, technological or instrumental knowledge, "knowledge of how to make things" (Aristotle, 1980, p. 141). Aristotle comments that the end of *poiesis* is *external* to the means, which means that *techne*, the knowledge of how to make things, is about finding the means that will produce the thing one wants to make. *Techne*, therefore, encompasses knowledge about the materials we work with and about the techniques we can apply to work with those materials. But making a saddle is never about simply following a recipe. It involves making judgments about the application of our general knowledge to *this* piece of leather, for *this* horse, and for *this* person riding the horse.

But the domain of the variable is not confined to the world of things but also includes the social world: the world of human action and interaction. This is the domain of *praxis.* The orientation here is not toward the production of things but toward bringing about "goodness" or human flourishing (*eudamonia*). *Praxis* is "about what sort of things conduce to the good life in general" (Aristotle, 1980, p. 142). It is about good action, but good action is not seen as a means for the achievement of something else. "(G)ood action itself is its end" (Aristotle, 1980, p. 143). The kind of judgment we need here is "about *what is to be done*" (Aristotle, 1980, p. 143, emphasis added). Aristotle refers to this kind of judgment as *phronesis,* which is usually translated as practical wisdom.

Two points follow from this. The first has to do with the nature of education. Here I would argue, with Aristotle, that we should never think of education *only* as a process of production, that is, of *poiesis.* While education is clearly located in the domain of the variable, it is concerned with the interaction between human beings, not the interaction between human beings and the material world. Education, in other words, is a social art and the aesthetics of the social is in important ways different from the aesthetics of the material (which is not to say that they are entirely separate). This does not mean that we should exclude the idea of *poiesis* from our educational thinking. After all, we do want our teaching and our curricula to have effect and be effective; we do want our students to become good citizens, skilful professionals, knowledgeable human beings; and for that we do need to think about educational processes in terms of *poiesis,* that is, in terms of bringing about some*thing.* But that should never be the be all and end all of education. Education is always more than just production, and ultimately education is precisely what production/*poiesis* is not because at the end of the day we, as educators, cannot claim that we produce our students; instead we educate them, and we educate them *in* freedom and *for* freedom. That is why what matters in education lies in the domain of *praxis.*

The second point is that the idea of "practical wisdom" captures quite well what I have been saying about educational judgment. Educational judgments are, after all, judgments about what needs to be done, not with the aim to produce something in the technical sense but with the aim to bring about what is considered to be educationally desirable (in the three—overlapping—domains I have identified). Such judgments are, therefore, not "technical" judgments but value judgments—and perhaps we can even call them moral judgments. What Aristotle adds to the picture—and this is important for developing these views about education into views about teacher education—is that practical wisdom is not to be understood as a set of skills or dispositions or competencies, but denotes a certain quality or excellence of the person. The Greek term here is ἀρετή (*arete*) and the English translation of ἀρετή is virtue. The ability to make wise educational judgments should therefore not be seen as some kind of "add on," that is, something that does not affect us as a person, but rather denotes what we might call a holistic quality, something that permeates and characterizes the whole person—and we can take "characterize" here quite literally, as virtue is often also translated as "character."

The question for teacher education is therefore not: how can we learn *phronesis?* The question rather is: how we can become a *phronimos;* how can we become a practically wise *person?* And more specifically the question is: how can we become *educationally wise?* This is the question of teacher education, and in the final step I will present some suggestions for what all this might mean for the future of teacher education.

Virtuosity: Becoming Educationally Wise

The main idea emerging from the discussion so far is that teachers need to develop the "ability" to make wise educational judgments. This "ability" should not be seen as a skill or competence (which is why I put it in quotation marks) but should be understood as a quality of the person. This means that the overarching orientation of teacher education should be the question of how teachers can become educationally wise. But how can we become educationally wise?

One interesting observation Aristotle (1980) makes in relation to this is "that a young man of practical wisdom cannot be found" (p.148). This suggests that practical wisdom is something that comes with age—or perhaps it's better to say that wisdom comes with *experience.* This is one important point for teacher education, to which I will return below. The second point that is relevant here is that when Aristotle comes to points in his writing where one would expect a definition of what a practically wise person looks like, he doesn't come with a description of certain traits or qualities but actually comes with *examples*—and one main example in Aristotle's writings is Pericles. Pericles appears in the argument as someone who *exemplifies phronesis:* he exemplifies what a practically wise person looks like. It is as if Aristotle is saying: if you want to know what practical wisdom is, if you want to know what a practically wise person looks like, look at him, look at her, because they are excellent examples.

If this makes sense, it suggests three things for the education of teachers, and we could see this as three "parameters" for our thinking about the future of teacher education.

It first of all means that teacher education is about the *formation of the person* (not, so I wish to emphasize, as a private individual but as a professional). It starts, to use the terms I introduced earlier, in the domain of subjectification. Teacher education is not about the acquisition of knowledge, skills, and dispositions per se (qualification) nor about just doing as other teachers do (socialization) but starts from the formation and transformation of the person-as-educational-professional, and it is only from there that questions about knowledge, skills, and dispositions, about values and traditions, about competence and evidence come in, so to speak—*never the other way around*. What we are after in the formation of the person is educational wisdom, the "ability" to make wise educational judgments. Following Aristotle, we can call this a virtue-based approach to teacher education. While we could say that what we are after here is for teacher students to become virtuous professionals, I prefer to play differently with the idea of "virtue" and would like to suggest that what we should be after in teacher education is a kind of *virtuosity* in making wise educational judgments. The idea of virtuosity might help us to appreciate the other two "parameters" of my thinking about teacher education, because if we ask how we can develop virtuosity—and here we can think, for example, about how musicians develop virtuosity—we do it through *practice*, that is, by doing the very thing we are supposed to be doing (after all, it is impossible to gain virtuosity in piano playing by studying the flute), and we do it through careful study of the virtuosity of others. And these are precisely the two other "parameters" of the approach to teacher education I wish to propose.

The second component, therefore, is the idea that we can develop our virtuosity for wise educational judgment only by practicing judgment, that is, by being engaged in making such judgments in the widest range of educational situations possible. It is not, in other words, that we can become good at making judgments by reading books about it; we have to do it, and we have to learn from doing it. At one level one may argue that this is not a very original idea, i.e., that we can only really learn the art of teaching by doing it. But I do think that there is an important difference between, say, learning on the job (the picking-skills-up-on-the-job-approach the English government seems to be returning to), or reflective practice, or even problem-based learning, and what I am after here. What I am after is what we might call judgment-based professional learning, or judgment-focused professional learning. It is not just about any kind of experiential or practical learning, but one that constantly takes the "ability" for making wise educational judgments as its reference point and centre (which means that student teachers should be engaging with the question as to what is educationally desirable from day one).

The third component has to do with learning from examples. While on the one hand we can only develop virtuosity through practicing judgment ourselves, I think that we can also learn important things from studying the virtuosity of others, particularly those who we deem to have reached a certain level of virtuosity.[10] This is not to be understood as a process of collaborative learning or peer-learning. The whole idea of learning from studying the virtuosity of others is that you learn from those who exemplify the very thing you aspire to, so to speak. The process is, in other words, asymmetrical rather than symmetrical. The study of the virtuosity of other teachers can take many different forms. It is something that can be done in the classroom through observation of the ways in which teachers make embodied and situated wise educational judgments—or at least try to do so. We have to bear in mind, though, that such judgments are not always "visible"—also because they partly belong to the domain of what is known as tacit knowledge—so there is also need for conversation, for talking to teachers to find out why they did what they did. This can be done on a small scale—teacher students interviewing teachers about their judgments and their educational virtuosity—but it can also be done on a bigger scale, for example through life-history work with experienced teachers, so that we not only get a sense of their virtuosity but perhaps also of the trajectory through which they have developed their educational virtuosity. (We also should bear in mind that, as with musicianship, to keep up your virtuosity you need to continue practicing it.) And we can also go outside of educational practices and study images of teachers in literature, in film, in popular culture, and the like. We will, of course, encounter both success and failure, and we can, of course, learn important things about the virtuosity of educational wisdom from both.

Conclusion

These, then, are three reference points or parameters for thinking about the future of teacher education: a focus on the formation and transformation of the person toward educational wisdom; a focus on learning through the practicing of educational judgments; and a focus on the study of the educational virtuosity of others. It is what follows when we approach the task of teacher education in an educational way rather than with reference to a language of learning, and if we take the role of the teacher seriously rather than letting this be replaced by evidence and competence—also to grasp that wise educational judgment is never the repetition of what was in the past but is always a creative process that is open toward the future for the very reason that each educational situation—each moment in the practice of education in which judgment is called for is in some respect radically new and radically unique. If we recognize this as being at the very heart of educational processes and practices then, so I wish to conclude, we need teacher education that is neither oriented toward evidence, nor toward competence, but toward the promotion of educational wisdom.

REFERENCES

Aristotle. (1980). *The Nicomachean ethics*. Oxford: Oxford University Press.

Biesta, G.J.J. (2004). Against learning. Reclaiming a language for education in an age of learning. *Nordisk Pedagogik, 23*(1), 70–82.

Biesta, G.J.J. (2006). *Beyond learning: Democratic education for a human future*. Boulder, CO: Paradigm Publishers.

Biesta, G.J.J. (2007). Why 'what works' won't work. Evidence-based practice and the democratic deficit of educational research. *Educational Theory, 57*(1), 1–22. doi:10.1111/j.1741-5446.2006.00241.x

Biesta, G.J.J. (2009). Good education in an age of measurement: On the need to reconnect with the question of purpose in education. *Educational Assessment, Evaluation and Accountability, 21*(1), 33–46. doi:10.1007/s11092-008-9064-9

Biesta, G.J.J. (2010a). *Good education in an age of measurement: Ethics, politics, democracy*. Boulder, CO: Paradigm Publishers.

Biesta, G.J.J. (2010b). Why 'what works' still won't work. From evidence-based education to value-based education. *Studies in Philosophy and Education, 29*(5), 491–503. doi:10.1007/s11217-010-9191-x

Biesta, G.J.J. (2010c). Evidenz und Werte in Erziehung und Bildung. Drei weitere Defizite evidenzbasierter Praxis. In H.-U. Otto, A. Polutta & H. Ziegler (Hrsg.) *What Works - Welches Wissen braucht die Soziale Arbeit?* (pp. 99–115). Opladen: Barbara Burdich.

Biesta, G.J.J. (2011). *God utbildning i mätningens tidevarv*. Stockholm: Liber.

Biesta, G.J.J. (2013). Receiving the gift of teaching: From 'learning from' to 'being taught by.' *Studies in Philosophy and Education, 32*, 449–461.

Carr, W. (1987). What is an educational practice? *Journal of Philosophy of Education, 21*(2), 163–175. doi:10.1111/j.1467-9752.1987.tb00155.x

Deakin Crick, R. (2008). Key competencies for education in a European context. *European Educational Research Journal, 7*(3), 311–318. doi:10.2304/eerj.2008.7.3.311

Eraut, M. (2003). National vocational qualifications in England: Description and analysis of an alternative qualification system. In G.A. Straka (Ed.), *Zertifizierung non-formell und informell erworbener beruflicher Kompetenzen* [The certification of

vocational competences that have been obtained non-formally or informally]
(pp. 117–126). Münster, New York, München, and Berlin: Waxmann.

James, W. (1899). *Talks to teachers on psychology: And to students on some of life's ideals.*
New York: Henry Holt and Company. doi:10.1037/10814-000

Mulder, M., Weigel, T., & Collins, K. (2007). The concept of competence in the development of vocational education and training in selected EU member states. A critical analysis. *Journal of Vocational Education and Training, 59*(1), 67–85. doi:10.1080/13636820601145630

NOTES

1 Retrieved February 27, 2011, from http://www.education.gov.uk/b0068570/the-importance-of-teaching/

2 Retrieved February 27, 2011, from http://www.reviewofteachereducationinscotland.org.uk/teachingscotlandsfuture/index.asp

3 Retrieved February 27, 2011, from http://www.consilium.europa.eu/uedocs/cms_data/docs/pressdata/en/ec/00100-r1.en0.htm

4 Retrieved Februrary 27, 2011, from www.oecd/edu/teacherpolicy

5 Retrieved February 27, 2011, from http://ec.europa.eu/education/com392_en.pdf

6 Retrieved February 27, 2011, from http://ec.europa.eu/education/policies/2010/doc/principles_en.pdf

7 Retrieved February 27, 2011, from http://ec.europa.eu/education/policies/2010/doc/principles_en.pdf

8 This is a rather "quick" way of putting it. Elsewhere I have argued for the importance of the distinction between "learning from" and "being taught by," suggesting that it is the latter notion that really allows us to engage with what is distinctive about education (see Biesta, 2013).

9 The idea of "good education" is also meant to provide an alternative for the idea of "effective education" and the idea of "excellent education," which both, in my view, are highly problematic notions.

10 An interesting question here is whether we should only focus on those who exemplify educational virtuosity or we can also learn from studying those who do not exemplify this virtuosity. The more general question here is whether we can learn most from good examples or bad examples. With regard to educational virtuosity, I am inclined to argue that it is only when we have developed a sense of what virtuosity looks like that we can begin to learn from those cases where such virtuosity is absent.

Contributors

Wayne Au is Associate Professor of Education, University of Washington, Bothell, Washington.

Heesoon Bai is Professor, Faculty of Education, Simon Fraser University, Burnaby, British Columbia.

Robin Barrow is Professor of Philosophy of Education and former Dean of Education, Simon Fraser University, British Columbia. He was previously Reader in Philosophy of Education at the University of Leicester, UK.

Gert Biesta is Professor of Educational Theory and Policy, Faculty of Language and Literature, Humanities, Arts and Education, University of Luxembourg.

Dwight Boyd is Professor Emeritus, Department of Humanities, Social Sciences and Social Justice Education, Ontario Institute for Studies in Education, University of Toronto, Ontario.

Paul T. Clarke is Professor, Faculty of Education, University of Regina, Saskatchewan.

Trudy Conway is Professor of Philosophy, Mount Saint Mary's University, Emmitsburg, Maryland.

Andrea R. English is Assistant Professor, Faculty of Education, Mount Saint Vincent University, Halifax, Nova Scotia.

Harold Entwistle is Professor Emeritus of Education, Concordia University, Montreal.

Michelle Forrest is Associate Professor, Faculty of Education, Mount Saint Vincent University, Halifax, Nova Scotia.

The late Paulo Freire was formerly Professor of Philosophy and Education, University of Recife, Brazil; Consultant for the World Council of Churches in Geneva; and Secretary of Education for São Paulo.

Dianne Gereluk is Associate Professor and Chair, Leadership and Policy Studies, Faculty of Education, University of Calgary, Alberta.

Maxine Greene is William F. Russell Professor Emerita of the Foundations of Education, Teachers College, Columbia University, New York.

David T. Hansen is the Weinberg Professor in the Historical and Philosophical Foundations of Education, and Director of the Program in Philosophy and Education, Teachers College, Columbia University, New York.

William Hare is Professor Emeritus, Faculty of Education, Mount Saint Vincent University, Halifax, Nova Scotia.

William J. Hull, Jr., is a New Mexico State Public Defender.

Emery J. Hyslop-Margison is Professor and Chair, Department of Curriculum, Culture and Educational Inquiry, Florida Atlantic University, Florida.

Kathy Hytten is Professor, Department of Educational Leadership and Cultural Foundations, University of North Carolina at Greensboro, North Carolina.

Frances M. Kroeker is a school principal with Edmonton Public Schools, Alberta.

Samuel LeBlanc is an Instructor, Université de Moncton, and a Ph.D. student in Educational Studies, University of New Brunswick, Fredericton, New Brunswick.

Bruce MacDougall is Professor of Law, University of British Columbia, Vancouver, British Columbia.

Jane Roland Martin is Professor Emerita of Philosophy, University of Massachusetts, Boston.

Francine Menashy is Assistant Professor, Department of Leadership in Education, College of Education and Human Development, University of Massachusetts, Boston.

Nel Noddings is Lee Jacks Professor of Education, Emerita, Stanford University, Stanford, California.

Stephen P. Norris is Professor and Canada Research Chair in Scientific Literacy, Department of Educational Policy Studies, University of Alberta, Edmonton, Alberta.

Trevor Norris is Assistant Professor, Faculty of Education, Brock University, St. Catharines, Ontario.

Laura Elizabeth Pinto is Assistant Professor, College of Education, Niagara University, New York.

John P. Portelli is Professor, Department of Humanities, Social Sciences, and Social Justice Education, Ontario Institute for Studies in Education, University of Toronto, Ontario.

Claudia W. Ruitenberg is Associate Professor, Philosophy of Education, Department of Educational Studies, University of British Columbia, Vancouver, British Columbia.

Eugenie C. Scott is Executive Director, National Center for Science Education, Inc., Oakland, California.

Harvey Siegel is Professor of Philosophy, University of Miami, Coral Gables, Florida.

Douglas J. Simpson is Associated Professor, Texas Christian University, Fort Worth, Texas, and Adjunct Professor, Mount Saint Vincent University, Halifax, Nova Scotia.

Ann B. Vibert is Professor and Director, School of Education, Acadia University, Wolfville, Nova Scotia.

About the Editors

William Hare is Professor Emeritus of Education at Mount Saint Vincent University, Halifax, Nova Scotia. His books include *Open-mindedness and Education* (1979), *In Defence of Open-mindedness* (1985), *Attitudes in Teaching and Education* (1993), and *What Makes A Good Teacher* (1993). He co-edited *Key Questions for Educators* (2007 with John P. Portelli).

John P. Portelli is Professor of Education, Department of Humanities, Social Sciences, and Social Justice Education, and Co-Director of the Centre for Leadership and Diversity at OISE, University of Toronto. His books include *Student Engagement in Urban Schools: Beyond Neoliberal Discourses* (2012 with Brenda McMahon), *Leading for Equity* (2009 with Rosemary Campbell-Stephens), and *Key Questions for Educators* (2007, with William Hare).